Applied Innovation and Technology Management

Series Editors

Tugrul U Daim, Department of Engineering & Technology Management, Portland State University, Portland, USA

Marina Dabić, Faculty of Economics & Business, University of Zagreb, Zagreb, Croatia

Technology is not just limited to technology companies. Managing innovation and technology is no longer a luxury and needs to be understood by all sectors around the world and by both technical and non-technical managers. This book series explores existing and emerging technologies that address current challenges within innovation and technology managements. Each title is developed to provide a set of frameworks, tools and methods that can be adopted by researchers, managers and student in engineering, innovation and technology fields. Research, policy and practice-based books in the series cover topics such as roadmapping, portfolio management, technology forecasting, R&D management, health technologies, bio technologies, transportation management, smart cities, and open innovation, among many others

Nazrul Islam • Iwa Salami
Editors

Metaverse Innovation

Technological, Financial, and Legal Perspectives

Springer

Editors
Nazrul Islam
Royal Docks School of Business and Law
University of East London
London, UK

Iwa Salami
Royal Docks School of Business and Law
University of East London
London, UK

ISSN 2662-9402 ISSN 2662-9410 (electronic)
Applied Innovation and Technology Management
ISBN 978-3-031-97079-5 ISBN 978-3-031-97080-1 (eBook)
https://doi.org/10.1007/978-3-031-97080-1

This Springer imprint is published by the registered company Springer Nature Switzerland AG
The registered company address is: Gewerbestrasse 11, 6330 Cham, Switzerland

Foreword

The metaverse, once a futuristic fantasy, is rapidly transitioning from a nascent concept to a transformative reality.

The International Telecommunications Union (ITU), the specialised ICT agency of the United Nations, has formally defined the metaverse as:

> An integrative ecosystem of virtual worlds offering immersive experiences to users, that modify pre-existing and create new value from economic, environmental, social, and cultural perspectives. NOTE—A metaverse can be virtual, augmented, representative of, or associated with the physical world.

As a co-author of this UN definition and Vice Chairman of the ITU's Metaverse Working Group on Sustainability, Accessibility, and Inclusion, I am honoured to contribute to this vital discourse.

While the rise of generative AI might have momentarily overshadowed the metaverse in mainstream conversation, it's crucial to recognise the symbiotic relationship between these technologies. Generative AI, primarily focused on 2D content, requires a significant leap to effectively train physical AI, such as humanoid robots, to understand and interact with the 3D physical and digital world. The metaverse, with its immersive environments, presents an ideal, safe, and cost-effective training ground for these AI entities, enabling them to learn and adapt within a controlled digital space before interacting with the real world.

This remarkable evolution necessitates a comprehensive understanding of the metaverse's multifaceted implications across technological, financial, and legal domains. "Metaverse Innovation" serves as an invaluable guide, offering insightful perspectives from leading experts who dissect the complexities of this burgeoning digital frontier.

This book's unique structure, divided into three distinct parts, provides a well-rounded exploration of the metaverse. Part I, "Technology Perspectives of the Metaverse", delves into the core functionalities and characteristics of this immersive digital realm. It examines how metaverse technologies are poised to reshape the global economy and society, from revolutionising industries like construction to transforming education through immersive learning experiences. A key highlight of this section is the insightful discussion on digital identity, a critical aspect of the metaverse that encompasses avatars, land ownership, and the intricate web of online personas.

Part II, "Financial Perspectives of the Metaverse", shifts the focus to the economic dimensions of this digital universe. It explores the pivotal role of artificial intelligence as a powerful tool within the metaverse, particularly in the realm of finance. The convergence of cutting-edge technologies like fintech, blockchain, and central bank digital currencies (CBDCs) within the metaverse is meticulously analysed, highlighting the potential for financial inclusion and innovation. Furthermore, the book provides valuable insights into national strategies and best practices for metaverse development, using Finland as a case study.

Finally, Part III, "Legal and Regulatory Perspectives of the Metaverse", addresses the critical legal and ethical challenges that accompany this technological revolution. The complexities of intellectual property rights, particularly concerning NFTs within the metaverse, are thoroughly examined, along with a global approach to their regulation. This section also delves into the crucial legal and regulatory considerations surrounding financial services within the metaverse, ensuring a safe and responsible digital financial ecosystem. Importantly, the book addresses the critical issue of law enforcement and policing within the metaverse, focusing on combating crime, misconduct, discrimination, harassment, and fraud in this immersive digital environment.

"Metaverse Innovation" is a timely and essential contribution to the growing body of literature on this transformative technology. It serves as a valuable resource for policymakers, researchers, industry leaders, and anyone seeking to navigate the complexities of the metaverse. By providing a multifaceted perspective, this book empowers readers with the knowledge and insights necessary to harness the immense potential of the metaverse while mitigating its potential risks. As the metaverse continues to evolve, this book will undoubtedly serve as a crucial reference point for years to come.

The Metaverse Institute
London, UK
20 April 2025

Christina Yan Zhang

Preface

The Metaverse—once a speculative vision confined to science fiction and gaming communities—has rapidly evolved into a real-world phenomenon transforming industries, economies, and social interactions. Fuelled by the convergence of extended reality (XR), blockchain, generative AI, NFTs, and digital finance, this immersive digital frontier is redefining how people communicate, transact, work, govern, and create across both physical and virtual spaces.

While much has been written in popular discourse about the Metaverse's potential, much of it remains fragmented and speculative. As scholars and observers of technological innovation, law, and finance, we recognised the urgent need to critically interrogate this evolving ecosystem from a multidimensional, interdisciplinary lens. It is from this conviction that *Metaverse Innovation: Technological, Financial, and Legal Perspectives* was conceived.

This volume seeks to move beyond hype and offer a comprehensive, scholarly, and practical examination of the Metaverse's architecture, value systems, and governance models. It brings together contributors from across disciplines—computer science, law, economics, finance, education, intellectual property, and public policy—and across geographies to collectively unpack the Metaverse's transformative potential and its attendant risks. The chapters span a wide range of issues: from digital identity and avatars, legal and regulatory challenges, AI and financial inclusion, to national Metaverse strategies, innovation ecosystems, and ethical concerns.

Our goal was to compile a book that not only charts where the Metaverse is today but also offers forward-looking insights into where it may go tomorrow. In doing so, we have prioritised content that is empirically grounded, theoretically informed, and globally aware.

This project has been a deeply collaborative effort, and we are indebted to the contributors—scholars, practitioners, and researchers—whose thoughtful and rigorous work forms the heart of this volume. We extend special thanks to our reviewers and early readers, whose feedback helped shape the clarity, relevance, and academic rigour of each chapter.

We also wish to acknowledge the rapidly shifting landscape in which this book is published. As platforms evolve, policy debates emerge, and use cases proliferate, we hope this book serves as both a foundational reference and a stimulus for new ideas. The questions the Metaverse raises—around privacy, jurisdiction, equity, design, decentralisation, and innovation—will only grow more complex. It is our hope that this volume helps scholars, students, technologists, legal experts, and decision-makers to engage critically and constructively with these questions.

This book is not intended to provide definitive answers but rather to catalyse discussion and deepen understanding of one of the most consequential digital shifts of our time.

We invite you to read it with an open mind—and, as the Metaverse itself demands—a willingness to think beyond traditional boundaries.

With gratitude,

London, UK Nazrul Islam
London, UK Iwa Salam
May 2025

Editorial Introduction

The Metaverse is no longer a speculative vision of the future—it is an emerging digital reality that is already reshaping how individuals interact, how businesses operate, and how institutions govern. As a convergence point of technologies such as extended reality (XR), blockchain, artificial intelligence (AI), decentralised finance (DeFi), and large language models (LLMs), the Metaverse is rapidly becoming a foundational layer for new economies, education systems, social networks, and legal jurisdictions.

While public discourse around the Metaverse has often been driven by industry marketing, start-up evangelism, and media hype, critical academic engagement remains limited and highly fragmented. Much of the existing research focuses disproportionately on the novelty of immersive technologies without sufficiently considering the institutional, financial, legal, and societal contexts in which these technologies are embedded.

This book, *Metaverse Innovation: Technological, Financial, and Legal Perspectives*, seeks to address this gap. It presents a multidisciplinary, evidence-informed, and globally aware exploration of the Metaverse, drawing on contributions from scholars and practitioners working at the intersections of technology, finance, law, innovation, and public policy.

Why This Book—and Why Now?

Our rationale for curating this volume stems from a simple yet compelling observation: understanding the Metaverse requires an integrated lens. Technological capability alone does not ensure adoption, trust, or impact. The success and sustainability of Metaverse ecosystems depend equally on the financial infrastructures that support them, the legal frameworks that govern them, and the ethical standards that shape them. By weaving together technological, financial, and legal insights, this book provides a foundation for both theoretical inquiry and practical innovation.

As national governments, multinational corporations, and policy institutions begin to formulate strategies around virtual environments, it becomes increasingly important to develop scholarly work that critically evaluates emerging opportunities, risks, and ethical dilemmas within the Metaverse. This volume aims to fill that need by offering:

- Theoretical frameworks for analysing Metaverse innovation;
- Empirical case studies from both public and private sectors;
- Policy-relevant insights to inform regulation and governance.

Structure of the Book

To reflect the multidimensional nature of the Metaverse, the book is organised into three interrelated sections, each focusing on a critical domain of inquiry.

Part I: Technological Perspectives of the Metaverse

This section lays the technical and conceptual foundation of the volume, exploring the design, functionality, and transformative potential of Metaverse platforms.

- It opens with an examination of the economic impact of the Metaverse and its role in enabling new business models and virtual economies.
- Subsequent chapters delve into sector-specific applications, such as Metaverse integration in education, urban development, and the construction industry, highlighting how virtual technologies are reshaping traditional workflows and stakeholder engagement.
- Additional discussions address challenges related to digital identity, avatar-based interaction, asset ownership, scalability, and interoperability, all of which are vital to creating secure and trusted Metaverse experiences.

Part II: Financial Perspectives of the Metaverse

This section investigates the financial architecture and innovations emerging within and around Metaverse environments.

- It analyses how AI-driven finance, DeFi protocols, and digital currencies are being integrated to promote financial inclusion and reshape transactional relationships.
- Through real-world examples, such as Finland's national Metaverse strategy, contributors assess how governments and industries are strategically positioning themselves within the digital asset economy.

- The section also evaluates the implications of Web3 technologies, NFTs, tokenised governance, and central bank digital currencies (CBDCs) on value creation, asset liquidity, and financial oversight in the Metaverse.

Part III: Legal and Regulatory Perspectives of the Metaverse

The final section confronts the regulatory complexities and legal dilemmas presented by immersive, decentralised virtual environments.

- Key topics include regulatory frameworks for financial services in the Metaverse, intellectual property rights (IPRs), data governance, digital contract enforcement, and the jurisdictional challenges of cross-border virtual interactions.
- Chapters also examine the ownership and transferability of virtual land and digital assets, and how law enforcement agencies might respond to criminal behaviour in pseudonymous, decentralised ecosystems.
- The section calls for adaptive, forward-looking governance models that protect rights while encouraging innovation and that bridge gaps between real-world law and virtual world practice.

Key Contributions and Relevance

This book offers a timely and critical intervention into the evolving discourse on the Metaverse. Its major contributions include:

- A holistic framework that bridges technology, finance, and law in understanding Metaverse ecosystems;
- Empirical research and case studies that ground theoretical discussions in real-world dynamics;
- A call for responsible innovation, emphasising digital equity, consumer protection, and sustainability.

For academics, the volume introduces new avenues for interdisciplinary research and helps build a more robust theoretical infrastructure for future studies. For practitioners and policymakers, it offers pragmatic insights on innovation strategy, platform governance, and regulatory design.

Looking Ahead

The Metaverse is still in a state of rapid formation. It is neither fully decentralised nor fully governed. It is simultaneously a platform, a marketplace, a social experiment, and a legal puzzle. This volume does not attempt to settle all the debates—but it does aim to catalyse deeper inquiry and support better-informed decision-making.

We invite readers—whether technologists, entrepreneurs, legal experts, regulators, or scholars—to engage critically with the chapters that follow. It is our hope that this work helps shape a more open, ethical, and inclusive Metaverse, one that reflects the complexity of our digital futures and the values we choose to uphold within them.

Nazrul Islam

Contents

Part I
Technology Perspectives of the Metaverse

Part I
Technology Perspectives of the Metaverse

Chapter 1
How Will Metaverse Technologies Impact the Global Economy and Society?

Dilda Zhanispayeva, Anija Nazrul, and Nazrul Islam

Abstract The Metaverse, as a product of convergence of technologies, tools, and instruments, has emerged in response to the needs and demands of modern-day society. To understand the mechanisms through which the Metaverse will impact the global economy and society, it is important to study the global trends and events that motivate adoption of the Metaverse and the factors that have given rise to public attention to the topic of Metaverse. The chapter studies global events that have induced the development of Metaverse-enabling technologies. Analysis of macroeconomic situations and shifting consumer demands play a central role in the current study as these factors define the trajectory of the Metaverse evolution. The discussion explores the benefits of the Metaverse adoption from economic, business, and social perspectives with an emphasis on social values and human rights. The chapter also extends to the prospects of the Metaverse in driving the evolution of Industry 5.0 and Society 5.0. Overall, the chapter aims to examine how the Metaverse phenomenon, as part of the digitisation trend, can enable the transition to a more sustainable digital economy and human-centric society.

Keywords Digital innovation · Digital economy · Industry 4.0 · Industry 5.0 · Society 5.0 · Digital avatar · Blockchain · Industrial Metaverse · Web 3.0

D. Zhanispayeva
Imperial College Business School, London, UK

A. Nazrul
Department of Economics, The Pennsylvania State University, University Park, State College, USA

N. Islam (✉)
Royal Docks School of Business and Law, University of East London, London, UK
e-mail: Nazrul.Islam@uel.ac.uk

N. Islam, I. Salami (eds.), *Metaverse Innovation*, Applied Innovation and Technology Management, https://doi.org/10.1007/978-3-031-97080-1_1

1.1 Introduction

Interest in the Metaverse, something referred to as Metaverse hype, has increased in recent years (Dwivedi et al., 2022). According to Tlili et al. (2023), the first publication about the Metaverse was released in 2003. After that, the volume of studies peaked in 2021 (Global Data UK Ltd., 2022). The transformative potential of the Metaverse expands onto a whole range of industries from car manufacturing and agriculture to tourism and fashion. The number of Metaverse users is growing every year. It is estimated that by 2030, the population of Metaverse users will reach 5 billion and the Metaverse economy will grow to $13 trillion US dollars (Kshetri, 2022). Widespread adoption of the Metaverse is expected to significantly impact business, economy, and society.

Through the use of information and communication technologies (ICT), the concept of Industry 5.0 will be driven by increased interconnections between both physical and cyberspaces (Khan et al., 2023). Industry 5.0 places a big emphasis on the interconnectivity between humans and machines and integration of human cognition with machine intelligence. At the same time, the main values of Industry 5.0 are characterised by increasing awareness with respect to social values such as people's rights, sustainability, and resilience over economic efficiency and productivity which were the main drivers of Industry 4.0 (Xu et al., 2021). Industry 5.0 is often cited together with Society 5.0 as the concept of a future super-smart society developed by the Japanese government (Huang et al., 2022). The idea behind Society 5.0 is establishing a social and economic environment where people will have a 'high-quality and comfortable life through the fusion of cyberspace and physical space by fully utilising ICT' and by 'merging between cyberspace and physical space with 5G, big data, artificial intelligence, etc.' (Huang et al., 2022).

The Metaverse is seen as one of the main enablers of the transition from Industry 4.0 towards Industry 5.0 and Society 5.0 as it represents a perfect constellation of modern technologies which drive the digital transformation while, at the same time, providing the grounds for human-centric innovation. In particular, digital twins and simulation models are mentioned as essential enabling technologies of Industry 5.0 (Xu et al., 2021). It is argued that the Metaverse and its underlying technologies provide an ultimate solution for the smooth implementation of the new socio-economic values of Industry 5.0 and Society 5.0.

Technologies develop in response to the evolving needs and demands of people, industries, and businesses (Picard & Klein, 2002). The Metaverse is made up from a combination of multiple modern technologies, tools, and instruments. Ooi et al. (2023) list artificial intelligence, internet of things, blockchain, and extended reality (XR) as some of the main Metaverse enablers. Taken individually, each of those tools already has a strong problem-solving potential. However, when put together and combined under the Metaverse umbrella, they can collectively target a wider array of complex problems faced by consumers, businesses, and governments. Among the many beneficial properties of the Metaverse are increased operational efficiency, cost reduction, and enhanced business resilience.

The borderless nature of the Metaverse can empower less privileged and underserved members of society to learn new skills, socialise, and make profit. The discussion therefore extends the idea of inclusivity and equality within the Metaverse. Section 1.2 will provide an insight into the factors that shaped the demand for Metaverse-enabling technologies while Sect. 1.3 will present the various economic applications of the Metaverse. Sections 1.4 and 1.5 outline how the Metaverse will promote social values and human rights. To understand how the Metaverse will affect the modern economy and society, it is important to examine the factors that have been impacting modern consumer demands. Economic and social contexts play a big role in shaping the trajectory of technological developments like the Metaverse.

1.2 Factors Inducing Metaverse Research and Development

Simply put, a Metaverse is a virtual world that very closely resembles the physical world. Users connect to it using special devices such as wearable Augmented Reality (AR) glasses and hand gloves. In the Metaverse, people create digital versions of themselves, called digital avatars, that can perform almost all the activities that are available in real life (McKinsey & Company, 2022b). This way, the Metaverse can be viewed as a digital replica of the real world. The Metaverse is a complex technology that can exist through a coalition of various tools that have been developed by humanity up to this point. The demand for those tools and technologies is defined by various economic and social changes that will be described further in this section.

People currently live in the realm of Industry 4.0, the era of digitisation and big industrial, societal, and economical shifts (Xu et al., 2021). The main technological themes of Industry 4.0 are automation, global connectivity, data intelligence, human-computer interaction, and smart robotics which is why Industry 4.0 is also called the digital revolution (McKinsey & Company, 2022a). Industry 4.0 is an extension of the Third Industrial Revolution which was powered by the invention of the internet. The main capabilities of the Fourth Industrial Revolution are cloud technologies, blockchain, sensors, machine learning, artificial intelligence, virtual and augmented reality, robotics, and advanced engineering (McKinsey & Company, 2022a). Industry 4.0 integrates smart technologies into industrial and manufacturing processes. By harnessing the power of big data analytics and automation, it achieves greater productivity and efficiency in production.

Technological progress brought by previous industrial revolutions allows people today to create sophisticated and complex systems such as the Metaverse. The Metaverse is viewed as the next step in the evolution of Industry 4.0 because, from a technological perspective, it builds on the achievements of Industry 4.0 such as artificial intelligence, extended reality, and blockchain (Ooi et al., 2023). It deploys a combination of multiple innovative technologies to create an accurate virtual simulation of the real world. The Metaverse world strives to closely resemble the real world and to allow users to have access to virtual copies of their everyday activities such as socialising, studying, and working. Since vital sectors of human activity will be presented on Metaverse platforms, it will, inevitably, have its own digital economy. This will create many opportunities for businesses, consumers, and creators. The power to create a digital economy is an important driver of Metaverse development and adoption because, as the world is becoming more unstable and unpredictable, digital capabilities become the main source of stability and resilience against economic shocks.

This surge in public interest in the Metaverse coincided with the global Covid-19 pandemic (Park et al., 2022). The global crisis experienced during and after the coronavirus pandemic revealed vulnerabilities of the global economy (De et al., 2020). Specifically, the pandemic and the government measures taken in response to this emergency, such as lockdowns, highlighted low levels of resilience within traditional business models and organisational structures amidst macroeconomic shocks (Shahzad & Imran, 2021).

The impact of Covid-19 was equivalent to 255 million jobs lost (Wellcome, 2021). Women were among the most affected by the crisis because of the high proportion of female workers in the health and social care sectors. In addition to the effects on the job market, Wellcome also notes that education was greatly hit with almost 1.5 billion students affected due to physical school closures. The negative results of the pandemic are expected to permeate society for many years. According to the United Nations Development Program, 1 billion people can be pushed into severe poverty by 2030 (UNDP, 2020). The biggest negative impact was experienced by organisations that were unprepared to respond to an unprecedented challenge in a short period of time. The problems revealed during the pandemic led to the acceleration of digital transformation and adoption of technologies in various business processes.

The crisis has taught the world that external shocks will be ever-present and the more digitally mature organisations will be able to stay afloat. Digital capabilities allow companies to respond to disruptions quickly and efficiently (Fletcher & Griffiths, 2020). A report by Bloomberg (n.d.) showed that, contrary to beliefs, some countries experienced extraordinary growth during the Covid-19 pandemic. It demonstrated that 11 out of 13 of the most digitally advanced countries in the world outperformed the average yearly OECD growth rate during the crisis. The pandemic played an important role in advancing digital transformation. It has triggered a lot of companies to start investing in digital capabilities sooner than they originally planned (Pipartners., n.d.). McKinsey and Company (2022a) predicts that companies that quickly adopt modern technologies will see a 120% growth by 2025 while companies that fail to do so will experience negative growth.

Health emergencies are just one example of an unpredictable and severe macroeconomic shock. Modern economies are exposed to many risks including climate change, natural disasters, and wars. Political, economic, and social contexts thus enhance the role of technologies in creating a safe and resilient economy.

1.3 Impact of Metaverse on Global Digital Economy

The Metaverse can create unprecedented opportunities for businesses and industry. By utilising the most advanced technologies, such as the internet of things, artificial intelligence, and blockchain, it unlocks the potential for business transformation. By 2030, the population of the Metaverse is expected to reach 5 billion users, and the Metaverse economy is expected to grow to $13 trillion US dollars (Kshetri, 2022). The Metaverse can decrease the costs of production, facilitate better decision-making process, and support business resilience.

1.3.1 Enhanced Economic Resilience

Economic resilience is one of the core values of Industry 5.0. It can be defined as the ability of the economy to withstand external shocks and disruptions such as wars, natural disasters, and others. Metaverse has the potential to foster better resilience for fragile businesses and sustainability of the modern economy (Rose, 2021). A crucial feature of the digital economy is persistence, meaning that it is always on and always accessible (Pahwa, 2023). In the case of any drastic changes in economic, social, political, and business environment in the physical world, consumers and companies can maintain uninterrupted business processes in the virtual space created on the grounds of a metaverse (Tlili et al., 2023).

For example, tourism is considered to be a fragile business that is highly dependent on people's ability to physically move between countries. As we have seen from the recent events, such as the lockdown during the pandemics or military actions in certain countries, tourists have become very limited in their traveling options. With the help of metaverse, people will be able to enjoy immersive travel experiences to any part of the world through simulated environments that will resemble very closely the real-world experience of tourism.

Another industry that will benefit from virtual presence on the metaverse will be fashion and cosmetics. Large luxury brands are already actively exploring virtual space. For example, Gucci has recently opened an online location in the Sandbox, where it offers games and vintage Gucci pieces for sales. What does this mean for their business model? The brands that will leverage the metaverse will experience larger margins due to the fact that they no longer will require physical operations, will not have problems with inventory or oversupply. In addition to that, they will benefit from more opportunities to engage directly with their target audience and create custom-made pieces as well as experiment with new designs by incorporating customer feedback in real time.

Small- and medium-sized businesses (SMEs) are a particularly vulnerable sector of the economy when it comes to external shocks and disruptions such as wars, natural disasters, and others. At the same time, SME businesses are important drivers of economic growth. SMEs generate seven out of every ten jobs and, on average, contribute 40% to GDP (European Commission, 2021). The Metaverse can help SMEs withstand unexpected situations in political, economic, and social spheres of influence. Tourism is an example of a fragile industry that is highly dependent on people's ability to physically move between countries. In recent years, events such as lockdowns during the pandemic or military conflicts have severely limited tourists' traveling options. The Metaverse can change the situation by recreating exact replicas of real-world tourist destinations in a simulated environment (Tlili et al., 2023). For example, South Korean developers launched an application ZEPETO World during the Covid-19 pandemic which allowed users to tour Korean sights in the Metaverse (Margaux et al., 2023). The app also offered a platform for people to socialise and spend time together during the difficult times of the pandemic. The app has proven to be successful and now has about 150 million users. Another company developed a virtual simulation of a famous Scottish tourist attraction—the Great Tapestry of Scotland (GTS) (Revfine, 2023). The digital version of the GTS is accessible to visitors all year round despite travel restrictions, bad weather, and flight cancellations. These examples show how the Metaverse can facilitate sustainable income for businesses in the times of uncertain and unstable economic situations.

The metaverse, as part of digital innovation, is expected to have significant economic impacts on the global economy. This virtual reality world, where people can interact with a computer-generated environment and other users, has the potential to transform various sectors and create new economic opportunities. One major economic impact of the metaverse is the emergence of new industries and business models.[42] Companies operating within the metaverse can offer virtual products, services, and experiences, thereby creating new revenue streams. For example, virtual fashion brands are already gaining popularity, allowing users to purchase digital clothing items for their avatars. These virtual products can generate real-world economic value, leading to the growth of industries related to virtual goods and services.

In addition, the metaverse has the potential to disrupt traditional industries. As more activities shift to the virtual realm, brick-and-mortar businesses may face challenges. For instance, virtual meetings and conferences could replace physical gatherings, impacting the events industry and associated sectors such as hospitality and travel. This disruption may lead to changes in employment patterns with new jobs emerging within the metaverse while certain traditional jobs become obsolete. Moreover, the metaverse can facilitate global economic integration and cross-border collaborations. Through virtual platforms, individuals, and businesses from different parts of the world can connect and collaborate in real-time, regardless of geographical constraints. This can lead to the formation of global virtual marketplaces, where goods and services are exchanged between users from different countries. Such virtual trade can foster economic growth and expand market opportunities for businesses, contributing to a more interconnected global economy.

1.3.2 Improvements in Industrial Operations

Ooi et al. (2023) state that the Metaverse will bring extraordinary value to industries by adding functionalities (mainly accurate one-to-one visualisation of real-world processes and interactivity) that were previously unattainable. The industrial Metaverse creates digital twins for physical systems. A digital twin is 'a virtual replica of a product or process' that is used to analyse the performance of its physical counterpart (MIT Technology Review, 2023). Digital twins can be created for a single component as well as for a whole factory or even a city. Internet of things (IoT) connectivity is one of the core technologies driving the industrial Metaverse (Armstrong, 2021). It facilitates the communication between digital twins and physical objects. With IoT, the digital twin is fed with real-time data from a network of sensors that are connected to objects in real life. This allows engineers to control complex physical systems with extremely high precision without the need to be present at the location of the object. The digital twin virtually replicates all the necessary infrastructure that equips engineers with the tools to monitor and adjust operational efficiency quickly and conveniently.

Industrial Metaverse solutions improve the decision-making process. IoT facilitates live and instant access to customer feedback (Yang et al., 2023). Product developers and marketers can receive immediate customer feedback in real time and refine the product accordingly. Using Virtual Reality (VR) headsets and digital twins, multiple parties can collaborate in the virtual space thereby overcoming any geographical or territorial barriers (Ooi et al., 2023). This creates multiple opportunities for knowledge exchange and creative partnerships. By facilitating online operations, Metaverse-technologies reduce the amount of time spent by designers and engineers on product development and testing. Multiple scenarios can be tested in simulated environments at low cost and high speed, which speeds up the time taken bringing a product or service to market. Furthermore, virtual working spaces allow companies to employ the best talent from any part of the world without the need for relocation (Kashalkar, 2023).

Researchers at the Nokia Bell Labs developed a digital twin for a plant-growing farm. They use it to monitor operational performance of crops in real time (MIT Technology Review, 2023). Similarly, with the help of digital twins, the team at Renault were able to monitor manufacturing processes at their factories. The system reproduces all of the processes happening at the factory and digitally connects 8500 pieces of equipment (Ooi et al., 2023). The car manufacturer can control production processes in real time, predict and prevent possible disruptions, and even monitor their carbon footprint. As a result, since 2009 Renault has been able to avoid 300 occurrences of production disruptions (Jolly, n.d.). Moreover, the BMW Pilot Plant in Munich (BMW Group, 2020) uses augmented reality to design prototypes of new cars. The plant workers put on AR glasses to work with real-sized engines in augmented reality. AR allows the worker to interact with virtual components of the engine using hand gestures. A multi-user collaboration design mode is used, which became possible as a result of industrial Metaverse technologies, as it brings together experts from different locations to work on the same project. BMW Group (2020) was able to accelerate the prototype engineering process by 12 months. Another big manufacturing company, Siemens, uses Metaverse technologies in product design and testing (Siemens, n.d.). Engineers deploy digital twins to test products' performance before putting them into actual production. The company tests products under different simulated scenarios in the virtual space which saves time and finances. After the final stage of the development, the process of refining and improving continues indefinitely with the help of digital twins and IoT sensors (Siemens, n.d.).

1.3.3 Benefits for Business and Consumers

The ability to run operations online will reduce many of the e-commerce businesses' costs (Pratas, 2023). Firms will be able to save money by removing physical shops, distribution channels, warehouses, and other dedicated physical spaces. In other words, there will be no need for fixed capital expenditure and investment in physical assets. Based on a study of the workspaces of 2000 Fortune 500 companies, it was estimated that office spaces were not used by employees for more than one-third of their total working time (Fast Company, 2022). This created yearly expenses of up to $25 million on underutilised utilities and real estate space. Cost-reduction does not only benefit the firms but also creates positive externalities for consumers through the channel of reduced prices on goods and services. For example, for high-end fashion brands, the cost of producing one custom-made luxurious item on the Metaverse will be drastically lower than the cost of producing the same item using physical facilities (Certilogo, 2022). This will be reflected in retail prices.

Large luxury brands are already actively exploring virtual spaces. For example, Gucci has recently opened an online Gucci store location in the Sandbox Metaverse (Moore, 2022). Metaverse-based businesses will be able to achieve high profit margins because they will not need physical facilities and thus will not experience inventory or oversupply problems, writes Brea (2022). It will be easy for brands to collect customer feedback in the digitally interconnected Metaverse world. As customer feedback becomes more readily available, brands can incorporate it into products at higher speeds which will save costs that arise from product prototyping and testing.

The Metaverse offers many benefits to consumers from the perspective of the quality and diversity of services they can access. Customers will benefit from the opportunity to virtually test products and services before spending money in real life (Buhalis et al., 2023). The chance to simulate a real-life experience in the digital world prior to purchasing decreases the stress related to decision making and increases customer satisfaction. Buhalis et al. (2023) describes that prospective tourists can make better decisions about their travel plans by using a Metaverse simulation. They can evaluate travel destinations in the virtual environment by choosing the most appropriate hotel, airline, and sights to visit. The opportunity to pre-evaluate the purchase gives people the chance to make more cost-efficient and emotionally satisfying decisions. One of the common concerns of travellers is choosing a seat on the place. Emirates airline introduced a virtual tour of its aircrafts giving customers the chance to test what it is like to sit in a particular seat (Revfine, 2023). This proves to be significantly more efficient than making a judgement based on photographs and videos made by other people. Virtual trials benefit not only consumers but business owners too. Bonelli and MacSweeney (2022) suggest that better consumer experiences and satisfaction will create monetary value for brands through increased customer retention rates and stronger brand loyalty.

1.3.4 *Money in the Metaverse*

Conceptually, the Metaverse economy closely resembles the real-world economy; digital representations of people (avatars) can buy land, build houses, buy clothes, and attend concerts in the virtual world (Dwivedi et al., 2022). The amount of money spent in Metaverse-based applications already amounts to $28 billion US dollars (Lau, 2023). Various modes of payment are becoming available for Metaverse transactions: people can use debit cards, cryptocurrencies, and applications like PayPal, reports Lau (2023). Based on a survey by PayPal, cryptocurrencies are the third largest payment method by Metaverse users from the United States. The high demand for cryptocurrency as a mode of payment in the Metaverse can be explained by the high levels of security provided by the blockchain (Lau, 2023).

The design of the Metaverse monetary system is still under development. Although, it is still unclear how exactly this system will operate, there are a number of user criteria that it would need to satisfy. First, when the number of Metaverse platforms grows in the future, interoperability between different Metaverse applications will become a critical challenge, writes Lau (2023). He notes that it will be important for users to have the tools to easily transact and move assets between different Metaverse platforms. Users would also need to be able to use different forms of money interchangeably to enjoy the same level of convenience as is currently available in the real world. This may require creating some universal rules and standards for cross-platform transactions. Interoperability must be preserved not just between different Metaverse platforms but also between virtual and physical worlds to enable users to move money without any constraints. Second, the monetary system of the Metaverse must have the same levels of depth and liquidity as the monetary system in real life, reports Coindesk (2023). Unless these issues are solved, the money will not perform its three main options of a unit of account, medium of exchange, and store of value in the Metaverse (Lau, 2023).

1.4 Social Values in the Metaverse

We currently live in the realm of Industry 4.0 that provides technological solutions that focus on increasing productivity of human industries, increasing output, depleting resources, and maximising economic value. Although Industry 4.0 has helped people to exponentially increase production capabilities and cross-border collaboration, it mostly focuses on the deployment of machines and smart systems into the operational processes. It does not imply the interactive collaboration between technologies and humans, which is becoming a more prominent issue as technologies developed in the Fourth Industrial Revolution advance at an increasing speed. The digital transformation of the society, which was influenced by the development and deployment of technologies in the production processes and even further accelerated by the effect of such external matters, as Covid-19, calls for new frameworks for managing integration of human and computer-based intelligent technologies into a shared collaborative environment.

The main challenges of Industry 4.0 have been presented by (1) threats to personalised data and information in light of an increasingly data-driven society (2) technology-centricity (3) lack of smooth communication between different technologies. These challenges gave rise to extensive research into the field of the Fifth Industrial Revolution, also called Industry 5.0. Industry 5.0 aims to provide a comprehensive framework that would describe the next leap in the industrial revolution enabled by intelligent computer systems from Industry 4.0, but which would place even more emphasis on long-term societal and economic sustainability and would put a big emphasis on the role of humans in the organisational structure.

The main goal of Industry 4.0 is integrating technologies into operational processes with the goal of increasing output and managing efficiency. At its core, Industry 4.0 prioritises the use of machines and smart systems in operational processes. Although it has provided numerous benefits to humanity, Industry 4.0 conceptually puts smaller emphasis on the role of humans in these processes and on collaboration between humans and machines. Khan et al. (2023) accentuate that, as technologies continue to advance at an increasing pace, ensuring a truly interactive collaborative environment between technologies and humans is increasingly important. A fair and ethical human-machine collaboration is a paramount consideration for Metaverse developers since the Metaverse relies heavily on human-computer interaction.

The transition from a technology-centric to human-centric approach in technology development has been reflected in a new concept of the Fifth Industrial Revolution or, in other words, Industry 5.0. Industry 5.0 proposes new frameworks for managing smart human-computer collaboration. As a successor of previous industrial revolutions, Industry 5.0 continues to capitalise on previous technological innovations like artificial intelligence, big data, digital transformation, and the internet of things (Akundi et al., 2022). However, the main novelty of Industry 5.0 is that it places more emphasis on enhancing the role of humans in technological processes (Golovianko et al., 2023). Thus, the values of Industry 5.0 extend beyond productivity and efficiency to include social awareness, sustainability, and protection of human rights (Xu et al., 2021). It tries to overcome the main challenges of the previous industrial revolution, mainly (1) threats to people's personal data and information, (2) lack of smooth communication between different technologies, and (3) technology-centricity (Khan et al., 2023).

The concept of Industry 5.0 will be driven by increased interconnections between physical and cyberspaces through the use of information and communication technologies (ICT).[9] Industry 5.0 places a big emphasis on the interconnectivity between humans and machines and integration of human cognition with machine intelligence. At the same time, the main values of Industry 5.0 are characterised by increasing awareness with respect to social values, such as people's rights, sustainability, and resilience over economic efficiency and productivity, which were the main drivers of Industry 4.0.[10] Under Industry 5.0, industries are positioned to direct their efforts towards creating positive social externalities by placing people's welfare and long-term prosperity in the centre of the agenda. Thus, Industry 5.0 will be actively addressing the questions of placing human needs, rights and demands in the centre of digital transformation of the future.

In the realm of Industry 5.0, technologies must not create negative externalities for society and threaten people's welfare. The role of technologies transforms into facilitating a safe, high-quality life for people. Industry 5.0 is often cited together with Society 5.0 which is the concept of a future super-smart society where people will live high-quality and comfortable lives achieved by the smooth combination of the physical and cyber worlds (Huang et al., 2022).

Human-centricity is the central agenda of Industry 5.0 and Society 5.0. The call for human-centricity in Metaverse development arises from the highly interactive nature of the Metaverse. As the Metaverse strives to replicate real life, it relies heavily on interactive technologies including Extended Reality (AR, VR, mixed reality (MR)), brain-computer interfaces, and holographic projections (Lyu, 2023). These devices are fed with users' biometric data such as eye movement, voice, handwriting, and facial expressions. The more people use the Metaverse, the more personal data becomes available to third parties. Moreover, Metaverse-based services, such as banking and social media, will have access to even greater amounts of private data. Thus, human-centricity calls for responsible and ethical technology-adoption with the goal of preserving people's safety and well-being (Mourtzis, 2023).

The use of blockchain is one of the ways to protect users and their details in the Metaverse. From a technological perspective, blockchain technology is used to ensure secure data storage and transfer in the Metaverse. Blockchain is a chain of interconnected blocks, generated in chronological order, that can store information (Yang et al., 2023). Key features of this technology that can be successfully applied in human-centric Metaverse development are data persistency, decentralisation, and auditability (Zheng et al., 2017). Blockchain facilitates safe, auditable, and trusted transactions without the need for a third-party controller. It can be used to store important data, verify its authenticity, and protect it from theft or tampering. Yang et al. (2023) write that inherent capabilities of the blockchain will equip users with the power of being direct custodians of their digital identities, digital property, and other information that is being uploaded to the Metaverse. Blockchain provides an infrastructure for safe communication and transactions between Metaverse users. For example, it can support the secure and tamper-proof flow of messages and digital items such as cryptocurrency in the Metaverse (Yang et al., 2023). Furthermore, blockchain will allow people to safeguard the authenticity of their digital avatars and digitally generated content through copyright protection via digital certificates backed by cryptographic algorithms (De Giovanni, 2023). In addition, blockchain will provide users with more financial freedom as it allows people to transact with each other on a peer-to-peer basis without the involvement of third parties and financial institutions (Iredale, 2021). Such application of disintermediation will account for lower service fees, and financial inclusion for the underserved, which also contribute to the creation of a truly human-centred digital system. According to Yang et al. (2023), in a human-centric Metaverse everyone will be 'the creator and god of their world', having the rights not just to consume but also to create and own their content. In that regard, a human-centric Metaverse implements a lot of concepts from the Web 3.0 paradigm. Web 3.0 is a democratic and user-owned Internet that is built around decentralisation, disintermediation, and user ownership. It places human rights such as data privacy, ethics, and fairness, as a top priority (Ashmore, 2023).

1.5 Inclusivity and Equality in the Metaverse

The transition to Industry 5.0 and Society 5.0 is gradually being recognised by international governments which highlights the global importance of this trend. A prominent example is Japan's Society 5.0 strategy. It envisions a society that balances economic development with the resolution of societal problems (Japan Cabinet Office, 2016). The proposed societal architecture builds upon the key values of human-centricity, sustainability, and resilience. According to Japan's Cabinet Office, implementation of this plan relies heavily on technologies that can synthesise physical and cyber worlds. Metaverse-based technologies, such as digital twins, are cited amongst the main enablers of the transition to Society 5.0.M.

1.5.1 Bridging the Gap in Education

The Metaverse education market is projected to grow to $79 billion US dollars in 2030 at a compound annual growth rate (CAGR) of 40% (Vantage Market Research, 2022). A study by the World Economic Forum and Ipsos revealed that education and training are the sectors where the Metaverse will create the most impact, surpassing remote work and entertainment (Blanco, 2022). Currently, the gaps in access to learning opportunities in the world are striking. In total, almost 258 million children around the world do not go to school for a variety of reasons including social status, cultural background, family situations, and gender (Schmelkes, 2020). The developing world is leading this statistic with 31% of children in Africa and 21% in Central Asia being out of school. Implementing the Metaverse in education has the potential to bridge this gap. Respondents of a survey by Wunderman Thompson Intelligence (2022) expressed beliefs that the Metaverse will be more inclusive than the physical world.

Already, some countries are implementing Metaverse strategies to create equitable educational opportunities. One of the initiatives is the virtual campus of Korea Advanced Institute of Science & Technology near Nairobi, Kenya (KAIST, 2021). The feasibility study has shown that such initiatives will create learning opportunities for students and faculty who cannot physically come to campus. Virtual education will allow students to save on expenses such as accommodation, food, transport, visas, and health insurance. A similar initiative is taking place in China where Nankai University has launched a Metaverse-based school of journalism and communication with digital professors and classrooms (Shumin, 2022). The Metaverse-based campus fully replicates physical university facilities and runs classes in immersive virtual classrooms. A Mexican-based university, Tec de Monterrey, built an entire virtual campus called Tec Virtual Campus (Virbela, 2022). Students can enjoy virtual study and common areas that are remarkably similar to the actual university campus, thus creating an experience that very closely reflects real-life learning. Students participate in classes via digital versions of themselves with the use of special equipment from the comfort of their homes: 95% of the surveyed students said they enjoyed the virtual class experience and would recommend it as a means for learning (Alvarez et al., 2023). In fact, a report by PricewaterhouseCoopers has found that VR learning delivers results four times faster than traditional classroom learning, and trainees are 275% more confident that they can apply the skills learned through VR tools in practice (Likens & Mower, 2022).

Metaverse-based learning has the potential to improve student experience via digital knowledge exchange and collaboration. A regional survey of the Organisation of Eastern Caribbean States revealed that low levels of collaboration between national colleges had a negative effect on the quality of services offered to students (Angel-Urdinola et al., 2022). Together with the World Bank, the Organisation of the Eastern Caribbean States decided to embrace Metaverse as the means to strengthen their digital capabilities and expertise by pooling together resources of multiple universities. Metaverse will enable colleges to organise joint social, academic, and career-related events for students from different campuses. Such initiatives can benefit the whole region by providing more opportunities for students, teachers, and employers to connect and interact despite geographical constraints. According to Angel-Urdinola et al. (2022), with the aid of remote collaboration, local institutions will more effectively overcome the challenges brought about by the Covid-19 pandemic.

1.5.2 Accommodating People with Special Needs

According to the World Health Organisation (WHO) (2023), approximately 16% of the world's population have a significant disability. This amounts to 1.3 billion people or one in every six people. People with disabilities have inferior access to education, health services, and employment and frequently face discrimination in modern society (WHO, 2023). Judgement, stigma, and unfair treatment are big problems for people with disabilities. Disabled students in the United States and Hong Kong reported that they experienced severe limitations in classroom settings (Mogavi et al., 2023). They are often judged by their peers based on their physical appearance rather than actual skills and knowledge, and this can sometimes lead to difficulties in finding partners for group projects. Metaverse technologies can help this user group to overcome some of the limitations they face in real world. Smith (2012) reports that virtual worlds can provide significant value for such users by allowing them to 'transcend physiological or cognitive challenges'.

One of the benefits of the Metaverse is that it gives users a choice of how they would like to present themselves in the virtual world. Some may choose their avatar to represent their persona as accurately as possible, for example, showing mobility aids like a wheelchair or a guide dog. Others may decide to eliminate any signs of disability when creating their online avatars, posits Smith (2012). Seigneur and Choukou (2022) have discovered that, although virtual lands do not always have accessories, such as a wheelchair, that represent a disability, these platforms provide users with resources that enable them to create such items if necessary. This level of flexibility opens new opportunities for Metaverse users. People can remove any signs of a disability and try completely new experiences. For example, they can engage in sports such as dancing, running, or visiting new places. The Metaverse provides room for experimentation for people with different sorts of physical limitations. Virtual reality tools can also help fight the stigma around disability. Smith (2012) mentions a 3D replica of the Sacramento Mental Health Centre facility where users can undergo a simulation of schizophrenic episodes. Through this simulation, people can experience what it is like to have a disability such as a mental health condition or a visual impairment. As a result, people are able to develop more empathy and understanding of disabled people.

Older generations that are subject to mobility constraints in real life can also benefit from the adoption of the Metaverse. A project developed by the Seoul Metropolitan Government (2022) aims to help the elderly population of the city to easily access government services via the Metaverse. The government has developed a Metaverse platform for citizens that comprises a range of civil services including tax support and document issuance. The city's authorities mention that elder citizens are an important target audience for these virtual services (Pessarlay, 2023). Seoul's population, according to Yoon (2024), comprise around 19% of people above the age of 65. Metaverse Seoul will equip senior citizens, who may experience trouble with commuting across the city, with all the necessary administrative and municipal services via this virtual platform (Pessarlay, 2023).

1.5.3 Unlocking Earning Potential

The Metaverse can help improve the welfare of people by creating new sustainable sources of income. For example, Play-to-Earn (P2E) platforms, such as Axie Infinity, offer business models where people can earn money by playing entertaining games (Bravenewcoin., 2022). Axie Infinity is a blockchain-powered Metaverse game where players earn cryptocurrency that can be exchanged for real money (Bravenewcoin., 2022). In unstable and risky economies with high rates of unemployment, P2E platforms are an extremely popular way of earning money. During the boom of the Axie game, people in Vietnam were quitting their jobs and becoming full-time players earning non-fungible tokens (NFTs) (Bravenewcoin., 2022). Most of Axie's gamers are from the Philippines and have been able to earn several times their salary by playing Axie (Elliott et al., 2021). Some made so much money that it has placed them under the radar of local tax authorities, and the Philippine Bureau of Internal Revenue (BIR) obliged all Axie players to pay taxes on their income (Elliott et al., 2021). Special organisations like the Crypto Gaming United (CGU) help people in developing countries to start earning on P2E platforms by providing scholarships and training (MVG LLC, 2021). CGU hopes to provide income to people in countries that have remarkably high unemployment rates and that were heavily affected by the pandemic. It facilitates easy cash out for players in countries like the Philippines, Russa, Kazakhstan, South Africa, Indonesia, and Sri Lanka (MVG LLC, 2021).

There are around 200 million unemployed people in the world, and the overall number increased drastically in the years of the pandemic between 2019 and 2021 (O'Neill, 2023). As a source of profit, P2E games are independent from external macroeconomic conditions and from local political and economic situations. With the help of technologies, people obtain the chance to become financially independent and improve their quality of life while not relying on local governments or employers. By providing jobs for people, such platforms contribute to creating a sustainable virtual economy that benefits society.

1.6 Conclusion

This chapter explored the role of the Metaverse in the digital transformation of society. The Metaverse is powered by some of the most powerful and influential technological breakthroughs of our generation. Factors including augmented reality, blockchain, smart robotics, and artificial intelligence are drastically changing the way people live, work, and interact with each other. The accumulation of transformational capabilities of these technologies within the concept of the Metaverse opens unlimited, and previously unattainable, opportunities for people and businesses. It is for that reason that the Metaverse is called the next generation of the internet and the next phase in the evolution of Industry 4.0 (Meige et al., 2023).

Society is becoming increasingly dependent on modern technologies as a means of ensuring business stability and economic resilience. This chapter has shown that economic disruptions, such as the Covid-19 pandemic, have produced severe, long-lasting effects on society. The pandemic has forced businesses to start the adoption of digital technologies much sooner than they had originally planned.

The approach to technological transformation has also undergone major changes. Globally, countries are starting to integrate human and social values into the digital transformation agenda. Thus, the purpose of technologies is changing. In the past, people have used technologies as a means to increase production output and the efficiency of business operations. Today, the role of technologies expands to include the fulfilment of peoples' needs and the achievement of societal goals. In the context of Industry 5.0 and Society 5.0, technologies are expected to facilitate the achievement of most critical societal goals including fair access to economic resources, equitable distribution of wealth, and individual well-being. Overall, modern society is shifting towards a more inclusive, fair, safe, and sustainable world powered by smart technologies.

The themes and values of Industry 5.0 and Society 5.0 are going to affect businesses on all levels. Companies that fail to recognise their importance risk falling behind their competitors and losing customer loyalty. Hence, thoughtful, responsible, and ethical use of technology will be the central theme in Metaverse development. To successfully integrate social values into the design of the metaverse, developers would need to understand and satisfy the needs of different user groups including people with disabilities and marginalised communities. The voice of customers will become an important strategic business tool in the context of human-centric society. Metaverse design principles should, therefore, focus on delivering a high level of customer experience through the personalisation and accessibility of its services.

This discussion contributes insights into the drivers behind Metaverse research and development to the existing body of literature, drawing parallels between social trends and technology development. Further research could explore the different practical applications of Metaverse-enabling technologies in creating a safe, equitable, and resilient digital economy.

References

Akundi, A., Euresti, D., Luna, S., Ankobiah, W., Lopes, A., & Edinbarough, I. (2022). State of industry 5.0—Analysis and identification of current research trends. *Applied system Innovations, 5*(1), 27. https://doi.org/10.3390/asi5010027

Alvarez, J., Angel, D., & Martínez, M. (2023). Tec virtual campus, a metaverse for engineering learning. *IEEE World Engineering Education Conference (EDUNINE),* Bogota, Colombia, 2023, pp. 01–06. https://doi.org/10.1109/EDUNINE57531.2023.10102856.

Angel-Urdinola, D., Marchioni, C., & Vainstein, J. (2022). *Education meets the metaverse in Eastern Caribbean National Colleges*. World Bank Blogs. https://blogs.worldbank.org/latinamerica/education-meets-metaverse-eastern-caribbean-national-colleges

Armstrong, M. M. (2021). Cheat sheet: What is digital twin?. *IBM Blog*. https://www.ibm.com/blog/iot-cheat-sheet-digital-twin/

Ashmore, D. (2023). A brief history of web 3.0. *Forbes*. https://www.forbes.com/advisor/investing/cryptocurrency/what-is-web-3-0/

Blanco, J. M. (2022). Educational metaverse: How technology innovates and makes lessons more engaging. *Evergine*. https://evergine.com/educational-metaverse/.

Bloomberg. (n.d.). Shaping tomorrow today: Innovation in the digital economy. *Bloomberg*. https://tinyurl.com/5a3f3u3e

BMW Group. (2020). Munich pilot plant: BMW group uses augmented reality in prototyping. *BMW Group Press Club*. https://tinyurl.com/vxt9e2dr.

Bonelli, F., & MacSweeney, R. (2022). *Meet customers in the metaverse to unlock lasting value*. EY. https://tinyurl.com/ycykmhm7.

Bravenewcoin. (2022). In developing countries, play-to-earn games are a way to make a living. *Bravenewcoin*. https://tinyurl.com/2m8cp5hb

Brea, R. (2022). 15 fashion brands leveraging the metaverse. *Sensorium arc*. https://sensoriumxr.com/articles/fashion-brands-in-the-metaverse.

Buhalis, D., Leung, D., & Lin, M. (2023). Metaverse as a disruptive technology revolutionising tourism management and marketing. *Tourism Management, 97, 104724*. https://doi.org/10.1016/j.tourman.2023.104724

Cetilogo. (2022). Metaverse for fashion brands. *Certilogo*. https://tinyurl.com/yc6wsve7

CoinDesk. (2023). A new monetary system for the metaverse. *CoinDesk*. https://tinyurl.com/y72h4kzc

De, R., Pandey, N., & Pal, A. (2020). Impact of digital surge during Covid-19 pandemic: A viewpoint on research and practice. *International Journal of Information Management, 55, 102171*. https://doi.org/10.1016/j.ijinfomgt.2020.102171

De Giovanni, P. (2023). Sustainability of the metaverse: A transition to industry 5.0. *Sustainability, 15*(7), 6079. https://doi.org/10.3390/su15076079

Dwivedi, Y. K., Hughes, L., Baabdullah, A. M., Ribeiro-Navarrete, S., Giannakis, M., Al-Debei, M. M., et al. (2022). Metaverse beyond the hype: Multidisciplinary perspectives on emerging challenges, opportunities, and agenda for research, practice and policy. *International Journal of Information Management, 66*, 102542. https://doi.org/10.1016/j.ijinfomgt.2022.102542

Elliott, V., Christopher, N., Dosunmu, D., & Martins, L. (2021). Some Axie infinity players amassed fortunes–now the Philippine government wants its cut. *Rest of World*. https://restofworld.org/2021/axie-players-are-facing-taxes/.

European Commission. (2021). Protecting SMEs: The drivers of global economic growth. *IP Helpdesk*. https://tinyurl.com/79jawv7r

Fast Company. (2022). Fortune 500 companies are wasting millions on unused office space. *Fast Company*. https://tinyurl.com/3uabr7nm

Fletcher, G., & Griffiths, M. (2020). Digital transformation during a lockdown. *International Journal of Information Management, 55, 102185*. https://doi.org/10.1016/j.ijinfomgt.2020.102185

Global Data UK Ltd. (2022). Metaverse mentions peaked in Q4 2021 due to surge of Metaverse hype, says GlobalData. *Business World*. https://tinyurl.com/4t7rv2x2

Golovianko, M., Terziyan, V., Branytskyi, V., & Malyk, D. (2023). Industry 4.0 vs. industry 5.0: Co-existence, transition, or a hybrid. *Procedia Computer Science, 217*, 102–113. https://doi.org/10.1016/j.procs.2022.12.206

Huang, S., Wang, B., Li, X., Zheng, P., Mourtzis, D., & Wang, L. (2022). Industry 5.0 and society 5.0—Comparison, complementation and co-evolution. *Journal of Manufacturing Systems, 64*, 424–428. https://doi.org/10.1016/j.jmsy.2022.07.010

Iredale, G. (2021). 6 key blockchain features you need to know now. *101 Blockchains*. https://101blockchains.com/introduction-to-blockchain-features/

Japan Cabinet Office. (2016). Society 5.0. *Cabinet Office*. https://www8.cao.go.jp/cstp/english/society5_0/

Jolly, C. (n.d.). Renault group launches the first industrial Metaverse. *Newsroom Renault Group*. https://media.renaultgroup.com/renault-group-launches-the-first-industrial-metaverse/

KAIST. (2021). The educational "Metaverse" is coming. *KAIST Newsroom*. https://tinyurl.com/26jbmxdt

Kashalkar, S. (2023). What is industrial metaverse?. *Digital Transforms Physical*. PTC. https://tinyurl.com/4f2pan7f.

Khan, M., Haleem, A., & Javaid, M. (2023). Changes and improvements in industry 5.0: A strategic approach to overcome the challenges of industry 4.0. *Green Technologies and Sustainability, 1*(2), 100020. https://doi.org/10.1016/j.grets.2023.100020

Kshetri, N. (2022). Metaverse and developing economies. *IT Professional, 24*(4), 66–69. https://ieeexplore.ieee.org/document/9897156

Lau, I. (2023). Metaverse and money. *PayPal Newsroom*. https://newsroom.paypal-corp.com/2023-06-Metaverse-and-Money

Likens, S., & Mower, A. (2022). *What does virtual reality and the metaverse mean for training?* PwC. https://www.pwc.com/us/vlearning

Lyu, Z. (2023). State-of-the-art human-computer-interaction in Metaverse. *International Journal of Human–Computer Interaction, 1–19*. https://doi.org/10.1080/10447318.2023.2248833

Margaux, C., Genovese, G., Munawar, K., & Stone, R. (2023). Tourism in the metaverse: Can travel go virtual? *McKinsey & Company*. https://tinyurl.com/3rwd8t5e

McKinsey and Company. (2022a). *What are industry 4.0, the fourth industrial revolution, and 4IR?* McKinsey & Company. https://tinyurl.com/9pdxc7wn

McKinsey and Company. (2022b). What is the metaverse? *McKinsey & Company*. https://www.mckinsey.com/featured-insights/mckinsey-explainers/what-is-the-metaverse

Meige, A., Beken, E., Glaumann, M., Bernd Schreiber, Siraudin, A., …, & Blondel, L. (2023). *The industrial Metaverse*. Arthur D. Little. https://tinyurl.com/57mmkvhp

MIT Technology Review. (2023). The industrial Metaverse: A game-changer for operational technology. *Technology Review*. https://tinyurl.com/ye2xndkn

Mogavi, R. H., Hoffman, J., Deng, C., Du, Y., Haq, E.-U., & Hui, P. (2023). Envisioning an inclusive metaverse: Student perspectives on accessible and empowering metaverse-enabled learning. *arXiv.org*. https://arxiv.org/abs/2305.18318

Moore, K. (2022). *Gucci vault opens in the sandbox, bringing luxury fashion into the metaverse*. Forbes https://tinyurl.com/2mazvan7.

Mourtzis, D. (2023). The Metaverse in industry 5.0: A human-centric approach towards personalized value creation. *Encyclopaedia, 3*(3), 1105–1120. https://doi.org/10.3390/encyclopedia3030080

MVG LLC. (2021). Binance smart chain's $1B growth fund invests in crypto gaming united to increase Metaverse employment opportunities. *Einpresswire*. https://tinyurl.com/3xrzt4pm

O'Neill, A. (2023). Number of unemployed persons worldwide 1991-2024. *Statista*. https://www.statista.com/statistics/266414/unemployed-persons-worldwide/

Ooi, K.-B., Wei-Han Tan, G., Al-Emran, M., Al-Sharafi, M. A., Arpaci, I., …, & Iranmanesh, M. (2023). The metaverse in engineering management: Overview, opportunities, challenges, and future research agenda. IEEE Transactions on Engineering Management, 1–8. https://doi.org/10.1109/TEM.2023.3307562, 13882.

Pahwa, A. (2023). What is digital economy?–importance, types, examples. *Feedough*. https://www.feedough.com/what-is-digital-economy-importance-types-examples/

Park, J.-Y., Lee, K., & Chung, D. R. (2022). Public interest in the digital transformation accelerated by the COVID-19 pandemic and perception of its future impact. *The Korean Journal of Internal Medicine, 37*(6), 1223–1233. https://doi.org/10.3904/kjim.2022.129

Pessarlay, W. (2023). *Seoul metropolitan unveils metaverse project to South Korea residents.* CoinGeek.https://coingeek.com/seoul-metropolitan-unveils-metaverse-project-to-south-korea-residents/

Picard, R. W., & Klein, J. (2002). Computers that recognise and respond to user emotion: Theoretical and practical implications. *Interacting with Computers, 14*(2), 141–169. https://doi.org/10.1016/S0953-5438(01)00055-8

Pipartners. (n.d.). 90 digital transformation statistics: How businesses are using digital to drive growth in 2021 and beyond. *Performance Improvement Partners.* https://tinyurl.com/5dn732u5

Pratas, J. M. (2023). *Metaverse and digital twins.* Management and Marketing for Improved Retail Competitiveness and Performance, 217–235. https://doi.org/10.4018/978-1-6684-8574-3.ch011.

Revfine. (2023). Metaverse tourism: Overview, benefits, examples, and more… *Revfine.* https://www.revfine.com/metaverse-tourism/

Rose, A. (2021). Economic resilience: Concepts and measurement. *World trade organization.* https://www.wto.org/english/res_e/reser_e/adam_rose_040321.pdf

Schmelkes, S. (2020). Recognizing and overcoming inequity in education. *United Nations.* https://tinyurl.com/2wfuwuwx

Seigneur, J., & Choukou. M. (2022). How should metaverse augment humans with disabilities? In *13th augmented human international conference (AH2022).* Association for Computing Machinery, 7, 1–6. https://doi.org/10.1145/3532525.3532534.

Seoul Metropolitan Government. (2022). *Seoul metropolitan government.* https://english.seoul.go.kr/policy/smart-city/metaverse-blockchain/

Shahzad, K., & Imran, F. (2021). Surviving the COVID-19 pandemic: The role of digital innovation and transformation. *Advances in human factors and ergonomics in healthcare and medical devices,* 708–715. https://doi.org/10.1007/978-3-030-80744-3_88.

Shumin. (2022). Nankai University debuts China's first Metaverse journalism school. *Yicai Global.* https://www.yicaiglobal.com/news/nankai-university-debuts-china-first-metaverse-journalism-school

Siemens. (n.d.). Digital twin. *Siemens Digital Industries Software.* https://tinyurl.com/3zt83np2

Smith, K. (2012). Universal life: The use of virtual worlds among people with disabilities. *Universal Access in the Information Society, 11*(4), 387–398. https://doi.org/10.1007/s10209-011-0254-8

Tlili, A., Huang, R., & Kinshuk. (2023). Metaverse for climbing the ladder toward 'industry 5.0' and 'society 5.0'? *The Service Industries Journal, 43*(3–4), 260–287. https://doi.org/10.1080/02642069.2023.2178644

UNDP. (2020). Covid-19 could push the number of people living in extreme poverty to over 1 billion by 2030, says UNDP study. *UNDP.* https://tinyurl.com/yc29rkdb

Vantage Market Research. (2022). Metaverse in education market size USD 79.01 billion by 2030. *Vantage market* research https://tinyurl.com/2uwbyhr6

Virbela. (2022). Three universities already teaching classes in the metaverse. *Virbela.* https://tinyurl.com/4hadtyyy

Wellcome. (2021). The COVID-19 effects on societies and economies. *Wellcome.* https://tinyurl.com/yeywzwf9

World Health Organization. (2023). *Disability.* WHO. https://www.who.int/news-room/fact-sheets/detail/disability-and-health.

Wunderman Thompson. (2022). New realities: Into the metaverse and beyond. *VML.* https://tinyurl.com/3b3cth8x

Xu, X., Lu, Y., Vogel-Heuser, B., & Wang, L. (2021). Industry 4.0 and industry 5.0—Inception, conception and perception. *Journal of Manufacturing Systems, 61*, 530–535. https://doi.org/10.1016/j.jmsy.2021.10.006

Yang, R., Li, L., Gan, W., Chen, Z., & Qi, Z. (2023). The Human-Centric Metaverse: A survey. *Companion Proceedings of the ACM Web Conference* 2023. https://doi.org/10.48550/arXiv.2303.11123

Yoon, L. (2024). Elderly population share South Korea 2000-2023. *Statista*. https://www.statista.com/statistics/995650/south-korea-elderly-population-share/

Zheng, Z., & Xie, S., Dai, H., Chen, X., & Wang, H. (2017). An overview of Blockchain technology: Architecture, consensus, and future trends. *Conference: 6th IEEE International Congress on Big Data*. https://doi.org/10.1109/BigDataCongress.2017.85.

Chapter 2
Navigating the Digital Frontier: Exploring the Characteristics and Core Functionalities of the Metaverse

Serajul I. Bhuiyan

Abstract In the seminal chapter, Characteristics and Main Functionalities of the Metaverse, we dove into a thorough investigation of the elemental structure and the vibrant capabilities that establish the Metaverse as a revolutionary digital ecosystem. This section methodically unravels the complex weave that forms the Metaverse, casting a spotlight on its fundamental traits. These traits elevate it from a simple digital realm to an animated, thriving digital cosmos that reflects the real world's intricacy with unparalleled precision. This exploration aims to provide a lucid understanding of the Metaverse, showcasing its unique position not just as a space for digital interaction but also as a dynamic universe alive with possibilities and potential.

At the heart of the Metaverse lies its defining characteristics: persistence, interoperability, scalability, immersiveness, user-generated content, an integrated economy, and broad accessibility. These attributes are carefully examined to reveal how they collectively contribute to creating a seamless, continuous experience for users. The chapter goes on to elucidate the Metaverse's main functionalities including social interactions, gaming, virtual commerce, education and training, work and collaboration, entertainment, and the creation of digital twins and simulations. Each functionality is explored in depth, highlighting how the Metaverse facilitates rich, immersive social engagements, innovative gaming experiences, and innovative platforms for virtual learning and remote collaboration. The discussion extends to the economic dimensions of the Metaverse where a fully functioning digital economy, powered by digital currencies and NFTs, underpins a vibrant marketplace of goods, services, and virtual real estate.

Furthermore, the chapter delves into the technological underpinnings and societal implications of the Metaverse, considering how Virtual Reality (VR) and Augmented Reality (AR) technologies, among others, are leveraged to create deeply immersive experiences that challenge traditional notions of presence and reality. It also contem-

S. I. Bhuiyan (✉)
Department of Journalism and Mass Communications, Savannah State University, Savannah, GA, USA
e-mail: bhuiyans@savannahstate.edu

N. Islam, I. Salami (eds.), *Metaverse Innovation*, Applied Innovation and Technology Management, https://doi.org/10.1007/978-3-031-97080-1_2

plates the future trajectory of the Metaverse, envisioning its potential impact on various sectors such as education, health care, industry, and entertainment. This chapter, rich in insights and forward-looking analyses, serves not only as an educational foundation for understanding the Metaverse but also as a catalyst for imagining the future of digital interaction and community. Through a nuanced discussion that interweaves technical detail with societal implications, Characteristics and Main Functionalities of the Metaverse positions the reader to fully grasp the breadth and depth of the Metaverse's potential to redefine ones digital and physical realities.

Keywords Digital technology · Metaverse · Functionality · Virtual commerce · Education · Training · Entertainment

2.1 Introduction

The opening chapter embarks on a journey through the Metaverse, a concept that has captured the imagination of technologists, creators, and users alike. At its core, the Metaverse represents a sprawling network comprised of persistent, real-time rendered three-dimensional worlds and simulations. This network is distinguished by its support for the continuity of identity, objects, history, payments, and entitlements, creating a seamless experience that mirrors the complexity and continuity of the real world (Bell, 2008).

The allure of the Metaverse lies in its fully immersive and interactive digital universe. Users gain entry to this universe through an array of technologies including Virtual Reality (VR), Augmented Reality (AR), smartphones, personal computers, and game consoles. This multi-platform approach ensures that the Metaverse is not only accessible but also offers a richly engaging experience that transcends traditional digital interaction (Castronova, 2005).

Moreover, the Metaverse ingeniously integrates digital and physical spaces and economies thereby forging a vast platform that facilitates a wide spectrum of activities. From social interaction and commerce to entertainment and education, it encompasses all facets of human experience thus redefining the boundaries between the physical and the digital (Dredge, 2021). This integration not only enhances the user experience but also opens up new avenues for creativity, collaboration, and economic opportunity.

As the chapter progresses, the multifaceted characteristics and functionalities of the Metaverse will be explored. The journey will reveal how this digital universe is not just a space for exploration and entertainment but a dynamic ecosystem that has the potential to revolutionise how people interact, learn, work, and play in an increasingly interconnected world (Lee, 2021; Gartner, 2022). Through this exploration, the Metaverse emerges not merely as a technological innovation but as a new horizon in the evolution of digital interaction and community building.

Embarking on an exploration of the Metaverse, one enters a realm defined by its vast expanse— a network characterized by persistent, real-time rendered three-dimensional worlds and simulations. This digital universe, unparalleled in its depth, supports a seamless continuity of identity, objects, history, payments, and entitlements, presenting an immersive and interactive realm accessed through an amalgamation of technologies. Virtual reality (VR) and augmented reality (AR), along with conventional devices such as smartphones, personal computers, and game consoles, serve as gateways to this intricate universe. Beyond mere digital interaction, the Metaverse ingeniously melds digital and physical realms, weaving together their spaces and economies to craft a comprehensive platform for social interaction, commerce, entertainment, and education. Within the ensuing discourse of this chapter, the author meticulously unfolds the distinct characteristics that underpin the Metaverse, aiming to furnish a nuanced understanding of its foundational aspects and the multifaceted issues it encompasses.

2.2 Characteristics of the Metaverse

1. **Persistence**: The principle of persistence emerges as a defining pillar within the vast expanses of the Metaverse, endowing it with a layer of continuity and constancy that adeptly mirrors the dynamic essence of the tangible world. This distinctive feature heralds the Metaverse's operation as ceaseless, a realm where its very fabric (encompassing environments, interactions, and economic transactions) thrives unbroken without succumbing to the temporal limitations or resets that characterise conventional digital engagements. In stark contrast to the fleeting nature of many online experiences, where continuity is often segmented or session-bound, the Metaverse's allegiance to persistence ensures that its digital domains and the narratives within persist and mature irrespective of user presence (Bell, 2008; Castronova, 2005).

This perpetual nature cultivates an environment where each action, modification, or development engrains itself into the Metaverse's evolving narrative. When a user manipulates their surroundings, introduces a new object, or forges interactions, these elements become woven into the fabric of the Metaverse, enduring through time and contributing to a collective digital existence. Such enduring changes affirm the Metaverse's commitment to providing a stable, dependable ecosystem that respects and preserves user-generated content, identity, and achievements, and fostering a space where creativity and interaction transcend temporal bounds (Castronova, 2005).

Beyond mere continuity, the Metaverse's persistence crafts a realm of unparalleled realism and immersion, echoing the relentless forward march of time and events characteristic of the physical world. This element enables the accrual of a rich historical tapestry and the blossoming of complex social ecosystems within which communities can emerge, expand, and flourish. The persistent world model nurtures dynamic economic systems, where virtual assets and services gain value over time, reflecting real-world economic principles of scarcity, demand, and supply thereby enriching the user experience with a sense of realism and tangibility (Kzero, 2014).

The role of persistence extends its influence to the nurturing of virtual real estate, the development of intricate social structures, and the establishment of cultural norms thereby becoming a linchpin for investment and engagement within the Metaverse. This assurance of permanence is pivotal, encouraging users to invest time, effort, and resources with the confidence that their contributions will become lasting elements of the Metaverse's landscape. Such a promise of continuity not only motivates long-term investment but also cultivates a profound, enduring connection with this digital cosmos, enticing users to return and engage with its ever-unfolding potential (Lee, 2021).

In essence, the attribute of persistence distinguishes the Metaverse from ephemeral digital platforms by offering a rich, seamless experience that adeptly parallels the real world. It lays the groundwork for a stable, evolving digital universe where meaningful interactions, creation, and economic participation can flourish. Through this, the Metaverse transforms into a vibrant, living entity that evolves in concert with its inhabitants, marking a significant evolution in our interaction with digital environments and each other (Dredge, 2021).

2. **Interoperability**: It supports the transfer and use of digital assets, like avatars and items, across different experiences and platforms within the Metaverse. Interoperability stands as a pivotal feature within the Metaverse, serving as the backbone for a dynamic and integrated digital ecosystem. It is the mechanism that enables a smooth and uninterrupted flow of digital assets (including avatars, items, and currencies) across an extensive array of experiences and platforms. This foundational characteristic is indispensable for sculpting a unified and consistent user experience throughout the Metaverse. It empowers users to traverse a wide range of virtual landscapes, carrying with them their digital belongings and identities. Such a capacity ensures that the essence of one's virtual presence is maintained irrespective of the platform or environment. This introduction lays the groundwork for a deeper examination of interoperability's role across various facets of the Metaverse, highlighting how it underpins the seamless connectivity and interaction that define this vast digital frontier in the following ways:

2.2.1 Understanding Interoperability

Interoperability refers to the capability of different computer systems, applications, and networks to communicate, exchange data, and use the information that has been exchanged efficiently and effectively. In the context of the Metaverse, it enables digital assets to maintain their utility and value across various virtual environments allowing for a level of continuity and consistency that is paramount for the user's immersion and engagement (Kishigami et al., 2015).

2.2.2 The Significance of Interoperability in the Metaverse

The significance of interoperability lies in its ability to break down the barriers between disparate virtual spaces thus creating a more integrated and expansive digital universe. Users can carry their digital identities, assets, and achievements across different platforms thereby enhancing the sense of ownership and investment in the digital realm. This cross-platform functionality is essential for the development of a truly interconnected Metaverse where the experiences and resources in one virtual environment can enrich and influence countless others (Werbach, 2018).

2.2.3 Technological Foundations and Challenges

Achieving interoperability requires robust technological frameworks and standards that can accommodate the diverse architectures of different virtual worlds. Blockchain technology, for example, has emerged as a foundational technology for enabling secure and verifiable transactions of digital assets across platforms, ensuring that ownership and provenance are maintained (Tapscott & Tapscott, 2016). However, the path to achieving interoperability is fraught with challenges, including technical issues related to compatibility, scalability, and security, as well as regulatory and governance concerns that arise from the transfer of assets across jurisdictions (Bibri, 2020).

2.2.4 The Impact of Interoperability on User Experience

Interoperability profoundly impacts the user experience by enhancing the utility and relevance of digital assets and experiences. It allows users to leverage their investments in digital assets across a broader range of experiences, thereby increasing the assets' intrinsic value and utility. Furthermore, interoperability fosters a more vibrant and dynamic Metaverse economy where digital goods and services can be traded and utilised in myriad ways, stimulating innovation and creativity within the ecosystem (Allison et al., 2021).

Overall, interoperability is a cornerstone of the Metaverse, enabling a seamless and enriched user experience across various digital platforms. By allowing the free flow of assets, identities, and information, interoperability not only enhances the value and utility of digital assets but also fosters a more cohesive and expansive digital universe. Despite the technical and regulatory challenges, the pursuit of interoperability is essential for realising the full potential of the Metaverse as a unified, dynamic, and immersive digital ecosystem.

3. **Scalability**: Scalability within the Metaverse is an essential attribute that ensures the platform's capacity to support a potentially limitless number of users

simultaneously thereby enabling large-scale interactions and events that can accommodate millions of participants from across the globe. This characteristic is fundamental to the Metaverse's ambition to create a universally accessible, immersive digital universe that mirrors the complexity and scale of the real world in the following ways:

2.2.5 The Essence of Scalability in the Metaverse

Scalability in the context of the Metaverse refers to the ability of its underlying technological infrastructure to expand and manage increased demand without compromising performance, reliability, or user experience. This entails not just accommodating a growing number of users but also supporting the complex data exchanges, sophisticated interactions, and high-fidelity environments that define these virtual spaces (Foster et al., 2008).

2.2.6 Technological Foundations for Scalability

Achieving scalability within the Metaverse relies on advanced technologies and architectural designs. Distributed computing, cloud technologies, and edge computing play pivotal roles in distributing the computational load and data storage needs, thereby enhancing the system's overall capacity to handle large user volumes and complex environments efficiently (Ahmad et al., 2020). Blockchain technology also contributes to scalability by providing a decentralised framework for transaction processing and asset management, facilitating a secure and efficient mechanism for digital interactions across the Metaverse (Zheng et al., 2018).

2.3 Challenges in Ensuring Scalability

Despite the technological advancements, ensuring scalability in the Metaverse poses significant challenges. These include managing latency to ensure real-time interactions, handling data privacy and security at scale, and developing sustainable economic models to support the infrastructure's growth. Moreover, creating a seamless and consistent user experience across diverse hardware and software platforms further complicates scalability efforts (Cai et al., 2017).

2.3.1 The Impact of Scalability on User Experience

Scalability directly influences the user experience in the Metaverse by enabling the creation of expansive, dynamic worlds that can host a wide array of activities, from massive multiplayer online games and social gatherings to large-scale educational sessions and virtual concerts. This capacity for large-scale participation not only enhances engagement but also fosters a sense of community and shared experience among users (Bainbridge, 2007).

In sum, scalability is a cornerstone of the Metaverse ensuring that it can grow and evolve in response to user demands and technological advancements. By leveraging cutting-edge technologies and addressing the inherent challenges of large-scale virtual environments, the Metaverse aims to offer a boundless, immersive digital realm that is accessible to users worldwide. The ability to scale effectively is not just a technical requirement but a critical factor in realising the vision of a fully integrated, interactive digital universe that mirrors the diversity and dynamism of the real world.

4. **Immersiveness**: Immersiveness in the context of the Metaverse refers to the creation of a deeply engaging and interactive experience that closely mirrors, and at times becomes indistinguishable from, reality. This characteristic is pivotal to the Metaverse's allure, drawing users into virtual environments where the boundaries between the digital and the physical blur. Virtual Reality (VR) and Augmented Reality (AR) technologies are at the forefront of enabling this profound level of immersion offering users the ability to step into and interact with three-dimensional worlds that engage the senses in unprecedented ways.

2.3.2 Understanding Immersiveness

Immersiveness within the Metaverse is measured by the extent to which users feel present in the virtual environment—an experience known as presence. This sensation of being inside the virtual world is achieved through sensory engagement, cognitive immersion, and emotional involvement. VR and AR technologies play a crucial role in this process by simulating real-world experiences through visual, auditory, and haptic feedback thereby enhancing the user's sense of presence (Slater & Wilbur, 1997).

2.3.3 The Role of VR and AR Technologies

VR technology immerses users in a fully digital environment that is visually isolated from the physical world consequently creating a comprehensive sensory experience that can simulate reality. AR technology, on the other hand, overlays digital content onto the physical world by seamlessly integrating virtual objects with the user's real-world surroundings. Both technologies leverage advanced graphics, audio, and interactive devices to create immersive experiences that can range from realistic simulations to fantastical environments (Milgram & Kishino, 1994).

2.3.4 Enhancing Immersiveness

To enhance immersiveness, developers employ sophisticated graphics rendering, 3D audio, and tactile feedback mechanisms to create environments that are richly detailed and responsive to user interactions. Real-time interactivity is crucial for immersion as it ensures that the virtual environment behaves in ways that users expect based on their actions. This can include everything from manipulating objects and navigating spaces to complex interactions with other users and virtual entities (Sherman & Craig, 2003).

2.3.5 Challenges and Opportunities

While VR and AR technologies have advanced significantly, achieving a level of immersion that is truly indistinguishable from reality poses several challenges. These include overcoming technical limitations related to visual fidelity, latency, and the uncanny valley effect in avatar design. Additionally, there are physical and psychological considerations, such as preventing motion sickness and ensuring user comfort during prolonged use. However, the on-going development in hardware and software, including improvements in display technologies, motion tracking, and user interface design, continues to push the boundaries of what is possible by offering ever more immersive and engaging experiences (LaValle, 2017).

In essence, immersiveness is a defining feature of the Metaverse that provides users with experiences that captivate the senses and foster deep emotional and cognitive engagement. Leveraging VR and AR technologies, the Metaverse opens up new possibilities for interaction, entertainment, education, and social connection. As these technologies continue to evolve, the line between the virtual and the real will increasingly blur, offering users experiences that are not only immersive but transformative.

5. **User-Generated Content**: User-generated content (UGC) stands as a pivotal pillar in the architecture of the Metaverse, encapsulating the essence of creativity, ownership, and economic dynamism that defines this burgeoning digital universe. This characteristic allows users not only to partake in the Metaverse but also to actively shape its landscape through creating, buying, selling, and possessing digital assets and spaces. This participatory model fosters a rich

ecosystem where, propelled by the contributions of its inhabitants, the diversity and economy of the Metaverse flourish.

2.3.6 The Essence of User-Generated Content

User-generated content within the Metaverse transcends traditional content creation paradigms, offering users unprecedented levels of autonomy and creativity. This model democratises content creation, enabling anyone to contribute to the Metaverse's expansiveness whether through designing virtual environments, creating digital objects, or scripting interactive experiences. This inclusivity enriches the Metaverse by making it a tapestry woven from the diverse threads of its users' imaginations (Castronova, 2005).

2.3.7 The Role of Digital Assets and Spaces

Digital assets and spaces are the building blocks of the Metaverse's economy and culture. Assets can range from simple items like clothing for avatars to complex creations like interactive tools or games while spaces refer to the virtual environments users can explore, inhabit, and manipulate. Ownership of these assets and spaces is facilitated through technologies such as blockchain which provides a secure and transparent framework for transactions and ensures that creators can sell, trade, and monetise their creations with confidence (Kücklich, 2005; Tapscott & Tapscott, 2016).

2.3.8 Driving the Economy

The exchange of user-generated content plays a central role in driving the Metaverse's economy. Platforms within the Metaverse often incorporate their own currencies or leverage cryptocurrencies to facilitate transactions, creating vibrant marketplaces where users can buy and sell their creations. This economic model not only incentivises content creation but also supports a dynamic economy where value is continuously generated and exchanged, mirroring the complexity of real-world economic systems (Brenner et al., 2007).

2.3.9 Enhancing Diversity

The diversity of the Metaverse is significantly amplified by user-generated content. Each user brings their unique perspective, creativity, and cultural background to their creations, contributing to an ever-expanding universe of experiences. This diversity fosters a rich, multicultural environment where users can explore and engage with content that spans a wide range of genres, styles, and themes thereby facilitating cross-cultural understanding and collaboration (Boellstorff, 2008).

2.3.10 Challenges and Opportunities

User-generated content offers vast opportunities for creativity and economic engagement but it also presents challenges including content moderation, intellectual property rights management, and ensuring equitable access to content creation tools. Addressing these challenges requires innovative solutions and governance models that balance freedom of expression with the need to maintain a safe, respectful, and fair environment (Lessig, 2006).

In essence, user-generated content is a cornerstone of the Metaverse, empowering users to be creators and shapers of digital worlds. By enabling the creation, ownership, and trade of digital assets and spaces, UGC drives the economy and diversity of the Metaverse and offers a glimpse into a future where digital and physical realities are increasingly intertwined. As this digital frontier continues to evolve, the contributions of its users will remain at its heart, continually expanding the boundaries of what is possible.

6. **Accessibility**: accessibility in the context of the Metaverse is a foundational principle that ensures users can engage with this digital universe from virtually anywhere by using an array of devices. This inclusivity is pivotal to the Metaverse's philosophy, democratising entry into its expansive realms beyond the confines of high-end hardware. By supporting a broad spectrum of access points (from VR headsets and computers to mobile devices and AR glasses) the Metaverse aims to foster a universal platform that is open and available to a diverse global audience.

2.3.11 The Spectrum of Access Devices

The Metaverse's design accommodates an extensive range of technologies that each offer different levels of immersion and interaction. VR headsets provide a fully immersive experience thus enveloping users in a digital world that is visually isolated from the physical environment. Computers and mobile devices, while less immersive, offer broader accessibility, allowing users to interact with the Metaverse through conventional screens and interfaces. AR glasses blend the digital and physical, overlaying virtual elements onto the user's real-world view, offering a seamless integration of virtual experiences into everyday life (Milgram & Kishino, 1994; Azuma, 1997).

Ensuring Broad Accessibility
The commitment to accessibility is driven by the recognition that the Metaverse's potential can only be fully realised if it is inclusive, enabling people from various socio-economic backgrounds and with different levels of technological literacy to participate. This approach not only expands the user base but also enriches the Metaverse with a wider range of perspectives and experiences thus enhancing its cultural and creative diversity (Bell, 2008; Schroeder, 2010).

Challenges and Solutions
Achieving broad accessibility presents several challenges including the digital divide that exists between different regions and communities and the varying capabilities of devices in handling the demands of sophisticated virtual environments. To address these issues, developers are focusing on optimising software to run efficiently on lower-end hardware and investing in cloud computing technologies to offload processing requirements from individual devices. Additionally, efforts are being made to develop standardised protocols and formats that enhance interoperability between different devices and platforms, further easing access (Carmigniani & Furht, 2011; Fuchs, 2014).

The Role of Emerging Technologies
Emerging technologies such as 5G networks and edge computing are critical to enhancing the accessibility of the Metaverse by reducing latency and increasing the speed and reliability of data transmission. These technologies ensure that high-quality, immersive experiences can be delivered even on devices with limited processing power consequently making the Metaverse more accessible to users with different types of devices and internet connectivity (Hollister, 2020).

In conclusion, accessibility is a cornerstone of the Metaverse, ensuring that this burgeoning digital universe is open and welcoming to all, irrespective of geographical location, economic status, or technological access. By embracing a wide range of devices and pushing the boundaries of technology, the Metaverse paves the way for a more inclusive, interconnected digital future where everyone has the opportunity to explore, create, and connect in unprecedented ways.

2.4 Main Functionalities of the Metaverse

1. **Social Interactions**: social interactions within the Metaverse transcend traditional digital communication by offering a platform for rich, immersive engagements that closely mimic real-world interactions. This digital realm enables users to meet, interact, and participate in a wide array of activities and events

through their avatars thus fostering a sense of community and belonging that extends beyond geographical boundaries.

2.4.1 The Nature of Social Interactions in the Metaverse

Social interactions in the Metaverse are facilitated through avatars, digital representations of users, which serve as their identity within this virtual universe. These avatars can express a wide range of human emotions and perform actions, allowing for a depth of interaction previously unattainable in traditional online spaces. The Metaverse's three-dimensional environments provide a backdrop for these interactions ranging from casual meetings in virtual public squares to organised events in intricately designed spaces (Bainbridge, 2007; Boellstorff, 2008).

2.4.2 Enhancing Realism in Social Engagements

Technologies such as VR and AR play a crucial role in enhancing the realism of social interactions within the Metaverse. VR, in particular, offers an immersive experience where users can feel physically present in a virtual space through engaging in real-time conversations and activities with a sense of proximity and shared experience. AR adds another layer, blending the digital and physical worlds and enabling new forms of interaction that augment the user's real-world environment with virtual elements (Milgram & Kishino, 1994; Azuma, 1997).

2.4.3 The Importance of Community and Connection

The Metaverse serves as a social fabric that connects individuals from diverse backgrounds that creates a global community where language, culture, and distance are no longer barriers to interaction. This digital space hosts a variety of social structures including communities centred around specific interests, hobbies, or activities. Such environments foster social bonds and provide a platform for collaborative endeavours, education, and entertainment thus enriching users' social lives (Castronova, 2005; Ducheneaut et al., 2007).

2.4.4 Challenges and Opportunities

While the Metaverse offers unprecedented opportunities for social interaction, it also presents challenges related to privacy, security, and the management of online behaviour. Ensuring a safe and respectful environment requires robust governance structures and community standards. Furthermore, the digital divide poses a significant challenge as not all users have equal access to the technologies that enable the most immersive experiences. Addressing these issues is critical to fully realising the potential of social interactions within the Metaverse (Lastowka & Hunter, 2004; Malaby, 2006).

In essence, social interactions are a cornerstone of the Metaverse as they provide a rich tapestry of engagements that deepen the user experience and foster a sense of global community. Through the use of avatars and immersive technologies, the Metaverse creates a space where users can transcend physical limitations to meet, interact, and participate in a wide range of activities. As this digital universe evolves, it holds the promise of reshaping our social fabric and offers new avenues for connection, collaboration, and community building.

2. **Gaming**: gaming within the Metaverse represents a transformative leap in digital entertainment by offering immersive experiences that merge the boundary between virtual worlds and reality. This evolution is epitomised by the proliferation of massive multiplayer online games (MMOGs) that anchor the gaming landscape in the Metaverse and therefore allows for complex immersive experiences where players can interact within expansive virtual realities.

2.4.5 Immersive Gaming Experiences in the Metaverse

The gaming experiences offered within the Metaverse are distinguished by their depth of immersion and the scale of interaction they facilitate. Players engage through avatars and navigate vast, persistent worlds that continue to evolve and exist even when individual players log off. This persistence is a hallmark of the Metaverse that provides a continuity of experience and a sense of living within an alternate reality (Castronova, 2005; Yee, 2006).

2.4.6 The Role of MMOGs in the Metaverse

MMOGs are at the forefront of gaming in the Metaverse and offer expansive virtual environments wherein thousands, if not millions, of players can interact simultaneously. These games are not just about gameplay in the traditional sense but also about creating social spaces where communities form and thrive around shared experiences and objectives. Games like World of Warcraft and Second Life have pioneered this space by blending elements of role-playing, strategy, and social networking within a cohesive virtual world (Bartle, 2003; Boellstorff, 2008).

2.4.7 Technologies Powering Gaming in the Metaverse

Advancements in VR and AR technologies have significantly enhanced the immersive quality of gaming within the Metaverse. VR headsets provide a fully immersive experience that envelopes players in the game world while AR integrates game elements with the real world thus offering a blended reality experience. These technologies, combined with real-time rendering and advanced physics engines, create highly engaging and interactive environments that push the boundaries of digital gaming (Sherman & Craig, 2003; Milgram & Kishino, 1994).

2.4.8 Challenges and Opportunities

While the potential for gaming in the Metaverse is vast, there are challenges to be addressed. These include ensuring accessibility for a broad audience, addressing issues of cyberbullying and harassment within online communities, and managing the economic aspects of in-game transactions and digital ownership. Nonetheless, the opportunities for innovation in gameplay, narrative storytelling, and community building are immense and open up new avenues for developers and players alike (Lastowka & Hunter, 2004; Ducheneaut et al., 2007).

In conclusion, gaming within the Metaverse offers an unparalleled platform for immersive experiences that is driven by the convergence of advanced technologies and the creative visions of developers. As MMOGs continue to evolve and integrate with VR and AR, the potential for immersive, interactive storytelling and community engagement will expand and further blur the lines between virtual and physical realities. The future of gaming in the Metaverse promises a dynamic and interconnected space where players can explore, create, and connect in ways previously unimaginable.

3. **Virtual Commerce:** Virtual commerce within the Metaverse transcends traditional e-commerce boundaries as it represents a paradigm shift in how goods and services are created, bought, and sold. This digital marketplace enables users to engage in transactions involving a wide array of virtual goods from digital fashion and artwork to virtual real estate and beyond. The proliferation of virtual commerce is not just an extension of the physical economy into digital spaces; it is the creation of an entirely new economic ecosystem that leverages the unique capabilities of the Metaverse.

2.4.9 *The Scope of Virtual Commerce*

Virtual commerce in the Metaverse encompasses a broad spectrum of activities that allows users to engage in the creation, purchase, sale, and exchange of digital assets. These assets can include anything from virtual clothing and accessories for avatars to entire pieces of virtual land and buildings that serve as hubs for socialisation, business, or entertainment. The diversity of goods and services reflects the vast potential of the Metaverse as a space for innovation and creativity in commerce (Castronova, 2005; Kzero, 2014).

2.4.10 *Enabling Technologies*

The backbone of virtual commerce in the Metaverse is a combination of blockchain technology, smart contracts, and cryptocurrencies. Blockchain provides a secure, transparent platform for transactions and ensures the authenticity and ownership of digital assets through decentralised ledgers. Smart contracts automate transactions and enforce the terms of sale, creating a trustless environment for buyers and sellers. Cryptocurrencies facilitate the exchange of value by offering a unified medium of transaction that is native to the digital realm (Tapscott & Tapscott, 2016).

2.4.11 *Economic Models and Opportunities*

Virtual commerce introduces new economic models within the Metaverse including direct sales, auctions, leasing, and subscription services. Users can monetise their creations, whether they are digital artworks, fashion, or virtual experiences, through marketplaces that connect creators with buyers. This democratisation of commerce allows individuals to capitalise on their creativity and entrepreneurial spirit thus fostering a dynamic and inclusive economy (Bainbridge, 2007; Lehdonvirta & Castronova, 2014).

2.4.12 *Challenges in Virtual Commerce*

Despite its potential, virtual commerce faces challenges related to security, privacy, and regulation. Issues such as fraud, intellectual property rights, and the governance of digital transactions require robust solutions to ensure the integrity of the Metaverse's economy. Moreover, the integration of virtual commerce with real-world financial systems poses questions about taxation, currency conversion, and compliance with international laws (Werbach, 2018).

2.4.13 *The Future of Virtual Commerce*

As the Metaverse evolves, virtual commerce is set to become an increasingly integral part of its ecosystem. Innovations in AR and VR technologies will enhance the shopping experience and allow users to interact with digital goods in more immersive and intuitive ways. Additionally, the growth of the Metaverse's economy will likely attract businesses and brands thereby further blurring the lines between virtual and physical commerce (Messenger et al., 2001).

In essence, virtual commerce in the Metaverse offers a glimpse into the future of economic activity where the digital and physical worlds converge. Through the creation, sale, and exchange of virtual goods and services users are not only participants but also drivers of a vibrant, evolving economy. As technology advances and the Metaverse expands, virtual commerce will continue to redefine the boundaries of what is possible in digital spaces.

4. **Education and Training**: The Metaverse is rapidly emerging as a transformative platform for education and training that is providing innovative and immersive virtual learning environments that revolutionise how knowledge is imparted and skills are acquired. Through the use of simulations, interactive modules, and virtual classrooms, the Metaverse offers a dynamic and engaging approach to education that caters to a diverse range of learning styles and objectives.

2.4.14 *The Evolution of Virtual Learning in the Metaverse*

Virtual learning within the Metaverse leverages advanced digital technologies to create interactive and realistic environments where learners can engage with content in a hands-on manner. This approach to education breaks away from traditional classroom constraints and offers scalable and customisable learning experiences that can be tailored to individual learner needs (Dede, 2009; Oblinger, 2004).

2.4.15 *Simulations and Training Environments*

One of the most compelling applications of the Metaverse in education and training is the development of simulations that replicate real-world scenarios. These virtual simulations provide a risk-free environment for learners to practice skills, experiment with different outcomes, and gain practical experience in their field of study. From medical simulations that allow healthcare professionals to practice surgical procedures to business simulations for honing management and decision-making skills, the possibilities are vast and varied (Roussos et al., 1999; Jarmon et al., 2009).

2.4.16 Interactive Learning Modules

The Metaverse also facilitates the creation of interactive learning modules that engage learners through gamification, interactive storytelling, and problem-solving activities. These modules can adapt to the learner's progress, providing personalised feedback and adjusting difficulty levels to challenge and motivate learners. This adaptive learning approach ensures that educational content is accessible and engaging for learners at all levels (Bricken & Byrne, 1993; Dalgarno & Lee, 2010).

2.4.17 Collaborative and Social Learning

Education in the Metaverse inherently supports collaborative and social learning, enabling students from across the globe to come together in virtual classrooms, workshops, and collaborative projects. This global connectivity fosters cultural exchange and collaboration by preparing learners for a progressively interconnected world. Virtual learning environments in the Metaverse can support synchronous and asynchronous interactions which is making education more flexible and accessible (Johnson et al., 2009; Bailenson, 2018).

2.4.18 Challenges and Future Directions

While the Metaverse offers significant opportunities for enhancing education and training, challenges related to accessibility, digital equity, and the need for robust pedagogical frameworks remain. Ensuring that learners have access to the necessary technology and that educators are equipped with the skills to design and facilitate virtual learning experiences are critical considerations for the widespread adoption of Metaverse-based education (Warburton, 2009; Wexler et al., 2020).

In sum, the Metaverse presents a paradigm shift in education and training by offering immersive, interactive, and personalised learning experiences that transcend traditional boundaries. As technology continues to evolve, the potential for virtual learning environments to supplement and enhance educational methodologies is immense. By addressing current challenges and harnessing the capabilities of the Metaverse, educators and learners alike can unlock new possibilities for teaching and learning.

2.5 Work and Collaboration

The advent of virtual workspaces within the Metaverse has fundamentally transformed the landscape of remote work and collaboration. These digital environments provide an immersive platform for professionals across various industries to engage in collaborative endeavours that transcend geographical limitations. By leveraging the capabilities of the Metaverse, organisations can create virtual spaces that simulate office environments, facilitate real-time collaboration, and foster a sense of community among remote teams.

2.5.1 The Rise of Virtual Workspaces

Virtual workspaces in the Metaverse are characterised by their ability to replicate the dynamics of physical office spaces within a digital realm. These environments offer interactive tools and features such as virtual meeting rooms, collaborative whiteboards, and 3D project visualisation thus enabling a level of interaction and engagement that traditional remote work tools cannot match. The immersive nature of these spaces enhances communication and teamwork, making remote collaboration more efficient and effective (Kuhlen & Hirt, 1995; Schroeder, 2010).

2.5.2 Enhancing Remote Collaboration

The Metaverse provides a platform for synchronous and asynchronous collaboration that allows team members to work together in real-time or contribute individually at their convenience. This flexibility is essential in accommodating the diverse schedules and time zones of a global workforce. Virtual workspaces also offer unique opportunities for creativity and innovation, as they allow for the visualisation of concepts and ideas in three dimensions thereby facilitating a deeper understanding and more dynamic brainstorming sessions (Dionisio et al., 2013; Neeley, 2015).

2.5.3 Tools and Environments for Various Industries

The versatility of virtual workspaces in the Metaverse makes them suitable for a wide range of industries from technology and design to education and healthcare. For instance, architects and engineers can use these spaces to construct and explore 3D models of buildings and structures while educators can create virtual classrooms to engage students in interactive learning experiences. Similarly, healthcare professionals can utilise virtual environments for telemedicine consultations and medical training simulations thus offering new avenues for patient care and professional development (Messenger et al., 2001; Riva et al., 2002).

2.5.4 *Challenges and Opportunities*

While virtual workspaces in the Metaverse offer significant advantages, they also present challenges including the need for robust digital infrastructure, concerns about data security and privacy, and the potential for digital divide issues. Moreover, the success of virtual collaboration depends on the availability of user-friendly tools and the digital literacy of participants. Addressing these challenges is crucial for the widespread adoption and effective utilisation of virtual workspaces (Huang & Liaw, 2010; Woolley et al., 2010).

2.5.5 *Future Directions*

As technology continues to evolve, the capabilities and applications of virtual workspaces in the Metaverse are expected to expand, offering even more sophisticated tools for collaboration and innovation. Advances in VR and AR technology, along with improvements in internet connectivity and computing power, will further enhance the realism and functionality of these digital environments. The future of work and collaboration in the Metaverse holds the promise of a more connected, creative, and efficient global workforce (Bell et al., 2007; Groom et al., 2009).

5. **Entertainment**: The Metaverse has ushered in a new era of entertainment, transforming traditional forms of content consumption through the hosting of concerts, movies, and events within fully immersive settings. This digital frontier extends beyond the mere viewing of content by inviting users to experience entertainment in a more interactive, participatory, and sensory-enriched manner. The convergence of virtual reality (VR), augmented reality (AR), and other immersive technologies within the Metaverse creates unparalleled opportunities for artists, filmmakers, and event organisers to engage with audiences in novel ways.

2.5.6 *Transforming Entertainment Experiences*

The immersive nature of the Metaverse allows for entertainment experiences that are more engaging and interactive than ever before. Concerts in the Metaverse, for example, are not limited by physical constraints; they can take place in fantastical settings that allow fans to experience performances alongside digital avatars of their favourite artists in environments that defy the laws of physics. Similarly, movies and storytelling can be experienced in a 360° panorama where viewers become part of the narrative and explore storylines and environments in a choose-your-own-adventure style (Bailenson, 2018; Steuer, 1992).

2.5.7 The Rise of Virtual Events

Virtual events within the Metaverse have gained significant traction by offering an alternative to physical events, especially in the context of global challenges such as the COVID-19 pandemic. These events range from conferences and trade shows to fashion shows and art exhibitions thereby providing a platform for interaction and engagement that replicates the networking opportunities and communal experiences of real-world gatherings. The scalability of the Metaverse allows for audience sizes that are unachievable in physical venues thus breaking down geographical barriers and making events accessible to a global audience (Flew & Humphreys, 2020; Kzero, 2014).

2.5.8 Technologies Driving Immersive Entertainment

The immersive entertainment experiences offered by the Metaverse are powered by advanced technologies including VR and AR. VR headsets deliver a fully immersive experience by transporting users to virtual environments while AR overlays digital content onto the physical world and enriches the user's environment with virtual elements. Together, these technologies create a spectrum of immersive experiences from complete immersion in a digital world to enhanced interaction with the physical world (Milgram & Kishino, 1994; Rizzo & Kim, 2005).

2.5.9 Challenges and Opportunities

While the Metaverse provides a revolutionary platform for entertainment, it also presents challenges, including the need for widespread access to immersive technologies and concerns regarding content moderation and copyright in virtual spaces. However, the opportunities for innovation in content creation, distribution, and consumption are vast. The Metaverse offers a new canvas for creators to experiment with immersive storytelling techniques and for audiences to engage with content in more meaningful and personalised ways (Castronova, 2007; Ryan, 2001).

In essence, the entertainment industry within the Metaverse represents a significant shift in how content is consumed and experienced. By leveraging immersive technologies to host concerts, movies, and events, the Metaverse offers new forms of engagement that enrich the audience's sensory experience and foster a sense of presence and participation. As the Metaverse continues to evolve, it promises to redefine the boundaries of entertainment, creating new possibilities for creators and consumers alike.

6. **Digital Twins and Simulation**: Digital Twins and Simulation within the Metaverse represent a cutting-edge technological convergence that enables the creation of virtual replicas of physical objects and environments. This concept extends beyond mere visual mimicry to encapsulate functional and behavioural characteristics that allows for simulations and analyses that can predict outcomes, optimise processes, and enhance decision-making across various sectors. The integration of Digital Twins within the Metaverse offers profound implications for industries ranging from manufacturing and health care to urban planning and environmental management:

2.5.10 The Concept of Digital Twins

A Digital Twin is a dynamic virtual model of a physical object or system that is created using real-world data. This model can simulate the physical counterpart in real-time and offer insights into performance, potential problems, and maintenance needs. The concept, which has its roots in product lifecycle management (PLM) and has been popularised by advancements in the Internet of Things (IoT), is now expanding into the Metaverse where the scope for simulation and interaction is significantly broadened (Grieves & Vickers, 2017; Tao et al., 2018).

2.5.11 Applications in Various Industries

In manufacturing, Digital Twins are utilised to simulate production processes and, in turn, enable optimisations that reduce time and costs while improving quality. In health care, virtual replicas of organs can assist in planning surgeries or understanding diseases. Urban planning benefits from Digital Twins by modelling cities to analyse factors such as traffic flow, environmental impact, and disaster preparedness. Environmental management uses these models to simulate ecosystems and aid conservation efforts and the prediction of environmental changes (Kritzinger et al., 2018; Rosen et al., 2015).

2.5.12 Enabling Technologies

The creation and operation of Digital Twins in the Metaverse rely on a suite of technologies. IoT devices play a crucial role in providing real-time data that feed into the Digital Twins, ensuring their accuracy and relevance. Cloud computing offers the computational power necessary to process this data and run complex simulations. AI and machine-learning algorithms analyse the data and enable the Digital Twins to predict behaviours and outcomes. VR and AR technologies allow users to interact with these virtual models in an immersive manner further enhancing understanding and analysis (Qi & Tao, 2018; Park et al., 2020).

2.5.13 Challenges and Future Directions

While Digital Twins in the Metaverse hold immense potential, there are also challenges to their implementation, including data security and privacy concerns, the need for interoperability among diverse systems, and the requirement for substantial computational resources. Future developments are likely to focus on enhancing the fidelity and functionality of Digital Twins, improving the efficiency of simulations, and extending their applicability to new domains. Advances in AI, VR/AR, and IoT technologies will play a pivotal role in realising these improvements (Lu et al., 2020; Minerva et al., 2020).

In conclusion, Digital Twins and Simulation within the Metaverse mark a significant evolution in how people interact with and understand the physical world. By offering virtual replicas of physical objects and environments for detailed simulation and analysis, they provide valuable insights that can drive innovation, efficiency, and sustainability across a wide range of industries. As technology advances, the integration of Digital Twins into the Metaverse will continue to deepen, unlocking new possibilities for exploration, experimentation, and optimisation.

References

Ahmad, I., Shahabuddin, S., Kumar, T., Okamura, K., & Goto, S. (2020). Cloud computing and big data's convergence: An architecture for scalable big data analytics in the cloud. *Communications of the ACM, 63*(11), 35–43.

Allison, A., Fauvel, C., & Guez, A. (2021). *The Metaverse: A professional's guide to the future of virtual reality*. Professional Publishing.

Azuma, R. T. (1997). A survey of augmented reality. *Presence: Teleoperators and Virtual Environments, 6*(4), 355–385.

Bailenson, J. (2018). *Experience on demand: What virtual reality is, how it works, and what it can do*. W.W. Norton & Company.

Bainbridge, W. S. (2007). The scientific research potential of virtual worlds. *Science, 317*(5837), 472–476.

Bartle, R. (2003). *Designing virtual worlds*. New Riders.
Bell, M., Smith-Robbins, S., & Withnail, G. (2007). None of us is as smart as all of us: Towards a collaborative future in virtual worlds. *Virtual Reality, 11*(4), 213–223.
Bell, M. W. (2008). Toward a definition of "virtual worlds". *Journal of Virtual Worlds Research, 1*(1).
Bibri, S. E. (2020). The Shaping of Ambient Intelligence and the Internet of Things: Historico-technological Trajectories and the Quest for Interoperable and Integrative Technologies. Springer.
Boellstorff, T. (2008). *Coming of age in second life: An anthropologist explores the virtually human*. Princeton University Press.
Brenner, W., Zarnekow, R., & Wittig, H. (2007). Intelligent Software Agents: Foundations and Applications. Springer.
Bricken, M., & Byrne, C. M. (1993). *Summer students in virtual reality: A pilot study on educational applications of virtual reality technology*. AERA Annual Meeting.
Cai, W., Shekhar, S., & Nahrstedt, K. (2017). Scalability in the metaverse: A perspective on current challenges and future directions. *ACM Computing Surveys (CSUR), 50*(6), 92.
Carmigniani, J., & Furht, B. (2011). Augmented reality: An overview. In *Handbook of augmented reality* (pp. 3–46). Springer.
Castronova, E. (2007). *Synthetic worlds: The business and culture of online games*. University of Chicago Press.
Castronova, E. (2005). *Synthetic worlds: The business and culture of online games*. University of Chicago Press.
Dalgarno, B., & Lee, M. J. W. (2010). What are the learning affordances of 3-D virtual environments? *British Journal of Educational Technology, 41*(1), 10–32.
Dede, C. (2009). Immersive interfaces for engagement and learning. *Science, 323*(5910), 66–69.
Dionisio, J. D. N., Burns, W. G., III, & Gilbert, R. (2013). 3D virtual worlds and the Metaverse: Current status and future possibilities. *ACM Computing Surveys, 45*(3), 1–38.
Dredge, S. (2021). "What is the Metaverse? The next big tech platform explained". The Guardian.
Ducheneaut, N., Yee, N., Nickell, E., & Moore, R. J. (2007). Building an MMO with mass appeal: A look at gameplay in world of Warcraft. *Games and Culture, 1*(4), 281–317.
Flew, T., & Humphreys, S. (2020). *Virtual worlds: Culture and politics in the age of Cybertechnology*. Sage Publications.
Foster, I., Zhao, Y., Raicu, I., & Lu, S. (2008). *Cloud computing and grid computing 360-degree compared*. Grid computing environments workshop, GCE'08.
Fuchs, H. (2014). *Virtual reality headsets–a theoretical and pragmatic approach*. CRC Press.
Gartner. (2022). *Gartner identifies five emerging trends that will drive technology innovation for the next decade*.
Grieves, M., & Vickers, J. (2017). *Digital twin: Mitigating unpredictable, undesirable emergent behavior in complex systems*. Excerpt from transdisciplinary perspectives on complex systems.
Groom, V., Nass, C., & Chen, T. (2009). The influence of virtual reality on teamwork and collaboration. *Virtual Reality, 13*(3), 191–199.
Hollister, S. (2020). The potential of 5G technology for the Metaverse. *IEEE Access, 8*, 2024–2034.
Huang, W.-H. D., & Liaw, S.-S. (2010). Exploring users' attitudes and intentions toward the web as a survey tool. *Computers in Human Behavior, 26*(5), 1408–1418.
Jarmon, L., Traphagan, T., Mayrath, M., & Trivedi, A. (2009). Virtual world teaching, experiential learning, and assessment: An interdisciplinary communication course in second life. *Computers & Education, 53*(1), 169–182.
Johnson, L., Levine, A., Smith, R., & Stone, S. (2009). The 2009 horizon report. *The New Media Consortium*.
Kishigami, J., Fujimura, S., Watanabe, H., Nakadaira, A., & Yamada, T. (2015). *The Blockchain-based digital content distribution system*. IEEE Fifth International Conference on Big Data and Cloud Computing.
Kritzinger, W., Karner, M., Traar, G., Henjes, J., & Sihn, W. (2018). Digital twin in manufacturing: A categorical literature review and classification. *IFAC-PapersOnLine, 51*(11), 1016–1022.

Kücklich, J. (2005). Precarious playbour: Modders and the digital games industry. Fibreculture Journal, 5.
Kuhlen, T., & Hirt, C. (1995). Virtual workspaces for collaborative work: Technical and organizational challenges. *Computer Supported Cooperative Work (CSCW), 4*(1), 19–37.
Kzero. (2014). *Understanding the Metaverse.*
Lastowka, G. F., & Hunter, D. (2004). The Laws of the virtual worlds. *California Law Review, 92*(1), 1–73.
LaValle, S. M. (2017). Virtual Reality. Cambridge University Press.
Lee, L. H. (2021). *Digital economy 2.0: How the Metaverse could reshape the tech world.* Forbes.
Lehdonvirta, V., & Castronova, E. (2014). *Virtual economies: Design and analysis.* MIT Press.
Lessig, L. (2006). *Code: Version 2.0.* Basic Books.
Lu, Y., Liu, C., Kevin, I., Wang, K., Huang, H., & Xu, X. (2020). Digital twin-driven smart manufacturing: Connotation, reference model, applications and research issues. *Robotics and Computer-Integrated Manufacturing, 61*, 101837.
Malaby, T. M. (2006). Parlaying value: Capital in and beyond virtual worlds. *Games and Culture, 1*(2), 141–162.
Messenger, J. C., Gschwind, L., & Vidal, M. (2001). Three-dimensional computer graphics for craniofacial surgical planning and evaluation. *Computer Graphics and Applications, 21*(3), 62–69.
Milgram, P., & Kishino, F. (1994). *A taxonomy of mixed reality visual displays.* IEICE transactions on Information Systems, E77-D(12).
Minerva, R., Lee, G. M., & Crespi, N. (2020). Digital twin in the IoT context: A survey on technical features, scenarios, and architectural models. *Proceedings of the IEEE, 108*(10), 1785–1824.
Neeley, T. B. (2015). Global teams that work. *Harvard Business Review, 93*(10), 74–81.
Oblinger, D. (2004). The next generation of educational engagement. *Journal of Interactive Media in Education, 2004*(1).
Park, K. T., Kim, H. M., & Kim, H. (2020). A framework for digital twin: Through the implementation of digital twin for CPS-based smart factory. *Procedia Manufacturing, 45*, 524–529.
Qi, Q., & Tao, F. (2018). Digital twin and big data towards smart manufacturing and industry 4.0: 360 degree comparison. *IEEE Access, 6*, 3585–3593.
Riva, G., Mantovani, F., & Gaggioli, A. (2002). Presence and rehabilitation: Toward second-generation virtual reality applications in neuropsychology. *Journal of Neuroengineering and Rehabilitation, 1*(1), 9.
Rizzo, A. S., & Kim, G. J. (2005). A SWOT analysis of the field of virtual reality rehabilitation and therapy. *Presence: Teleoperators and Virtual Environments, 14*(2), 119–146.
Rosen, R., von Wichert, G., Lo, G., & Bettenhausen, K. D. (2015). About the importance of autonomy and digital twins for the future of manufacturing. *IFAC-PapersOnLine, 48*(3), 567–572.
Roussos, M., Johnson, A., Moher, T., Leigh, J., Vasilakis, C., & Barnes, C. (1999). Learning and building together in an immersive virtual world. *Presence: Teleoperators and Virtual Environments, 8*(3), 247–263.
Ryan, M.-L. (2001). *Narrative as virtual reality: Immersion and interactivity in literature and electronic media.* Johns Hopkins University Press.
Schroeder, R. (2010). *The social life of avatars: Presence and interaction in shared virtual environments.* Springer.
Sherman, W. R., & Craig, A. B. (2003). *Understanding virtual reality: Interface, application, and design* (Vol. 12, p. 441). Morgan Kaufmann.
Slater, M., & Wilbur, S. (1997). A framework for immersive virtual environments (FIVE): Speculations on the role of presence in virtual environments. *Presence: Teleoperators and Virtual Environments, 6*(6).
Steuer, J. (1992). Defining virtual reality: Dimensions determining telepresence. *Journal of Communication, 42*(4), 73–93.
Tapscott, D., & Tapscott, A. (2016). Blockchain revolution: How the technology behind bitcoin is changing money, business, and the world. *Portfolio.*

Tao, F., Cheng, J., Qi, Q., Zhang, M., Zhang, H., & Sui, F. (2018). Digital twin-driven product design, manufacturing and service with big data. *The International Journal of Advanced Manufacturing Technology, 94*, 3563–3576.

Warburton, S. (2009). Second life in higher education: Assessing the potential for and the barriers to deploying virtual worlds in learning and teaching. *British Journal of Educational Technology, 40*(3), 414–426.

Werbach, K. (2018). The Blockchain and the New Architecture of Trust. MIT Press.

Wexler, S., Dawson, K., Marshall, S., & Gubman, J. (2020). *The 2020 Educause horizon report.* Teaching and Learning Edition. Educause.

Woolley, A. W., Chabris, C. F., Pentland, A., Hashmi, N., & Malone, T. W. (2010). Evidence for a collective intelligence factor in the performance of human groups. *Science, 330*(6004), 686–688.

Yee, N. (2006). The demographics, motivations, and derived experiences of users of massively multi-user online graphical environments. Presence: Teleoperators and Virtual Environments, 15(3), 309–329.

Zheng, Z., Xie, S., Dai, H., Chen, X., & Wang, H. (2018). Blockchain challenges and opportunities: A survey. *International Journal of Web and Grid Services, 14*(4), 352–375.

Chapter 3
Leveraging the Metaverse for Technological Advancements in the Construction Industry

Sohrab Donyavi

Abstract The integration of the Metaverse into the construction industry represents a significant leap towards Industry 4.0, leveraging advanced technologies such as virtual reality (VR), augmented reality (AR), digital twins, and blockchain. This chapter explores the transformative potential of the Metaverse in construction management, highlighting its impact on project visualisation, collaboration, training, safety, and lifecycle management. The Metaverse offers immersive 3D environments for stakeholders to interact with virtual models of construction projects thereby enhancing decision-making and reducing errors. It enables real-time collaboration among geographically dispersed teams and, as such, improves communication and project coordination.

Digital twins provide dynamic, real-time representations of construction projects thus facilitating efficient monitoring and predictive maintenance. VR and AR technologies create safe, controlled environments for training and hazard simulations and enhance workforce preparedness and safety. These technologies also contribute to sustainable construction practices by optimising resource use and minimising waste.

However, integrating the Metaverse into construction management poses challenges including technological compatibility, high initial costs, data security, and the need for industry-wide standards. Overcoming these barriers requires strategic approaches such as developing interoperability standards, fostering public–private partnerships, and investing in workforce training.

The Metaverse's potential extends beyond operational efficiency. It offers significant environmental benefits by reducing the need for physical travel and promoting eco-friendly practices. The vision for the future of the Metaverse is anchored in sustainability, efficiency, and collaboration by promising to redefine digital interaction and connectivity across various sectors.

This chapter underscores the need for continuous learning, ethical considerations, and robust regulatory frameworks to navigate the complexities of the

S. Donyavi (✉)
School of Architecture, Computing and Engineering, University of East London, London, UK
e-mail: S.Donyavi@uel.ac.uk

N. Islam, I. Salami (eds.), *Metaverse Innovation*, Applied Innovation and Technology Management, https://doi.org/10.1007/978-3-031-97080-1_3

Metaverse. By addressing these challenges and leveraging the opportunities, the construction industry can unlock the full potential of the Metaverse, driving innovation, enhancing stakeholder engagement, and achieving sustainable growth. The journey into the Metaverse is just beginning and offers an extraordinary opportunity to reshape the future of construction management and beyond.

Keywords Metaverse · Construction industry · Industry 4.0 · Virtual reality · Digital twins · Blockchain

3.1 Section 1: Introduction

The Metaverse, a term that has garnered significant attention in both academic and industrial spheres, represents an expansive digital realm where virtual augmented realities and the physical world converge. This convergence is empowered by a suite of advanced technologies categorised under the umbrella of Industry 4.0 including, but not limited to, artificial intelligence (AI), the Internet of Things (IoT), blockchain, and 3D printing. As people venture further into the twenty-first century, the Metaverse is poised to redefine the contours of digital interaction, collaboration, and operational methodologies across various sectors with construction management emerging as a prime candidate for its transformative impact (Das).

Industry 4.0 marks a paradigm shift in industrial operations aiming to create smart factories characterised by the integration of digital technologies into manufacturing processes. Similarly, the Metaverse promises to introduce a new era of digital transformation within the construction industry facilitating a shift from traditional, linear project management approaches to more dynamic, interactive, and efficient practices. This synergy between the Metaverse and Industry 4.0 technologies equips stakeholders in the construction sector with tools and platforms that enhance decision-making, streamline project execution, and foster innovative solutions to longstanding challenges.

The relevance of the Metaverse to Industry 4.0 extends beyond technological integration; it embodies a cultural and operational shift towards a more interconnected, immersive, and collaborative working environment. For the construction industry, this means the ability to conduct virtual site walkthroughs, engage in live collaboration within shared virtual environments, and leverage digital twins for predictive maintenance and lifecycle management. These applications not only promise to improve operational efficiency but also aim to elevate the overall quality, safety, and sustainability of construction projects.

This chapter aims to explore the specific contributions of the Metaverse in advancing construction management practices. It will delve into how the integration of Metaverse technologies can enhance project visualisation, facilitate real-time collaboration, improve training and safety protocols, and optimise lifecycle management through digital twins. By addressing these areas, the study seeks to demonstrate the Metaverse's potential to revolutionise the construction industry by offering detailed analysis and practical insights into overcoming existing barriers and maximising the benefits of these innovative technologies.

This chapter will explore the foundational elements of the Metaverse, its integration with Industry 4.0 technologies, and the myriad ways in which this digital convergence can revolutionise construction management. By understanding the Metaverse's potential to act as a catalyst for technological advancements, stakeholders can better navigate the complexities of the construction industry in the digital age and harness innovation to drive growth, sustainability, and success.

3.2 Section 2: Understanding the Metaverse

3.2.1 Introduction

This section provides an in-depth exploration of the Metaverse, emphasising its definition, components, and integration with Industry 4.0 technologies specifically in construction management. The Metaverse is a virtual shared space merging virtual reality (VR), augmented reality (AR), and the Internet to create an immersive digital universe. Key components include essential hardware, software, and user interfaces. The evolution of the Metaverse alongside Industry 4.0 technologies, such as IoT, AI, blockchain, and 3D printing, is also examined.

- **Current State of Research:** the Metaverse has been extensively studied for its potential to transform digital interactions through immersive experiences. Critical components like VR headsets, AR glasses, digital twin technology, and advanced software platforms have been highlighted for their roles in enhancing user engagement, project visualisation, and real-time collaboration. However, focused research on its specific implications in construction management is still emerging.
- **Advancements Through This Study:** this study provides a detailed analysis of integrating the Metaverse into construction management. It identifies the necessary hardware, software, and user interfaces for creating immersive environments and examines the convergence with Industry 4.0 technologies. A theoretical framework is developed to guide the integration of Metaverse technologies, highlighting practical applications such as digital twins for real-time monitoring and predictive maintenance, immersive design and planning, and enhanced decision-making through seamless information exchange. This framework aims to improve efficiency, collaboration, and sustainability in construction projects.

3.2.2 Definition and Components of the Metaverse (Hardware, Software, User Interfaces)

In exploring the concept of the Metaverse, particularly in the context of its integration into construction management, it is crucial to understand its definition and the foundational components that make it both functional and transformative. The Metaverse is a collective virtual shared space, created by the convergence of virtually enhanced physical reality, augmented reality (AR), virtual reality (VR), and the Internet (Lee et al., 2021a, 2021b). It represents an expansive, immersive digital universe that users can interact with in a seemingly tangible manner (Ball, 2022). This section delves into the critical components of the Metaverse (hardware, software, and user interfaces), highlighting their roles and interactions within the framework of construction management (Kye et al., 2021).

3.2.2.1 Hardware

The hardware component of the Metaverse encompasses all the physical devices and equipment required to access and interact with this digital realm. In the construction management context, this includes:

- ***Virtual Reality headsets***: devices that provide immersive experiences and allowing users to visualise construction projects in 3D spaces as if they were physically present.
- ***Augmented Reality glasses***: wearables that overlay digital information onto the real world. These are useful for on-site project visualisation and information retrieval.
- ***Sensors and wearables***: devices that collect and transmit data from the physical environment to the digital twin in the Metaverse thereby enabling real-time monitoring and decision-making.

3.2.2.2 Software

Software forms the backbone of the Metaverse and consists of the applications, platforms, and protocols that enable its creation, maintenance, and expansion. Within construction management, software components include:

- ***Simulation and modelling tools***: software that enables the creation of detailed 3D models of construction projects, allowing for virtual walkthroughs and scenario testing.
- ***Digital twin technology:*** programs that create dynamic, virtual replicas of physical assets for ongoing monitoring, analysis, and predictive maintenance.
- ***Collaboration platforms:*** applications that facilitate real-time communication and collaboration among project stakeholders within the Metaverse.

3.2.2.3 User Interfaces

User interfaces (UI) in the Metaverse are the points of interaction between the user and the digital environment and are designed to be as intuitive and immersive as possible. In the realm of construction management, these interfaces include:

- ***Gesture recognition systems****:* technologies that allow users to interact with the Metaverse through natural movements thereby enhancing the immersive experience.
- ***Voice commands****:* interfaces that enable control and navigation within the Metaverse using voice instructions thus facilitating hands-free operation.
- ***Haptic feedback devices****:* tools that provide tactile feedback from virtual environments, simulating the sense of touch and enhancing the realism of the Metaverse experience.

Understanding these components is fundamental to grasping how the Metaverse operates and its potential applications in construction management. By leveraging the interplay between advanced hardware, sophisticated software, and intuitive user interfaces, the construction industry can unlock new dimensions of project visualisation, collaboration, and operational efficiency. This integration promises not only to streamline traditional processes but also to pave the way for innovative practices and solutions that were previously unimaginable.

3.2.3 The Evolution of the Metaverse and its Intersection with Industry 4.0 Technologies

The evolution of the Metaverse is a narrative of rapid technological advancement and convergence, marking a significant leap in how digital spaces are perceived and interacted with. This evolution is not just a journey through virtual reality advancements but a broader technological revolution that intersects profoundly with Industry 4.0 technologies. Industry 4.0, characterised by automation, data exchange, and manufacturing technologies, has been a driving force behind the Metaverse by providing the tools and frameworks necessary for its development (Schwab, 2016). The Metaverse's growth reflects a symbiotic relationship with Industry 4.0, leveraging its core technologies such as the Internet of Things (IoT), artificial intelligence (AI), blockchain, and 3D printing to create immersive, interconnected digital environments (Xu et al., 2018).

3.2.3.1 From Concept to Reality: The Genesis of the Metaverse

The Metaverse concept, originating from science fiction, envisioned a collective virtual shared space created by the convergence of virtually enhanced physical reality and the digital space (Stephenson, 1992). Early incarnations of the Metaverse were limited by the technology of their times, offering rudimentary virtual environments. However, as digital and computational technologies advanced, these virtual spaces became more sophisticated, paving the way for today's Metaverse (Mourtzis, 2023).

3.2.3.2 Industry 4.0: The Technological Bedrock

The advent of Industry 4.0 technologies provided the necessary infrastructure for the Metaverse to evolve from a concept to a tangible reality. The IoT's network of connected devices and sensors facilitated the creation of more dynamic and interactive virtual environments where physical and digital worlds could merge seamlessly (Khan et al., 2021). AI's predictive capabilities and machine-learning algorithms enabled the creation of smart, adaptive virtual environments (Hussain et al., 2023). Blockchain technology offered a secure, decentralised foundation for creating and managing digital assets within the Metaverse (Zheng et al., 2018). Meanwhile, 3D printing technology allowed for the rapid prototyping and creation of physical objects from virtual designs, further blurring the lines between the digital and physical worlds (Ford & Despeisse, 2016).

3.2.3.3 Intersection and Integration

The intersection of the Metaverse with Industry 4.0 technologies is most evident in its application across various sectors including construction management. For instance, digital twin technology, a cornerstone of Industry 4.0, is integral to the Metaverse as it allows for the creation of detailed virtual replicas of physical assets. These digital twins enable real-time monitoring, simulation, and management of assets throughout their lifecycle and provide unprecedented levels of insight and control (Tao et al., 2018). Moreover, AR and VR technologies, empowered by Industry 4.0's advancements, have become central to the Metaverse by offering immersive experiences that enhance project visualisation, design, and collaboration in construction management. The integration of these technologies facilitates a level of collaboration and efficiency previously unattainable thus revolutionising how projects are planned, executed, and maintained (Prabadevi et al., 2023; Gheisari & Esmaeili, 2020).

3.2.3.4 Looking Forward

As the Metaverse continues to evolve, its integration with Industry 4.0 technologies will deepen and lead to more innovative applications and solutions. This evolution signifies a shift towards a more interconnected and immersive digital future where the boundaries between physical and virtual worlds continue to blur. In construction management and beyond, the Metaverse stands as a testament to the transformative potential of Industry 4.0 technologies, promising new horizons of collaboration, efficiency, and innovation (Zhong et al., 2017; Dutta et al., 2021).

3.2.4 Theoretical Framework for Applying the Metaverse in Construction Management

The theoretical framework for applying the Metaverse in construction management revolves around leveraging digital twin technology, immersive environments, and real-time collaboration to enhance traditional construction processes. This framework operates on the premise that integrating Metaverse technologies can lead to significant improvements in project planning, execution, and maintenance. This section will examine the components and mechanisms of this theoretical framework and highlight how it can be applied in the realm of construction management.

3.2.4.1 Digital Twin Integration

At the core of the Metaverse's application in construction management is the concept of digital twins—a virtual replica of a physical construction project. This technology enables stakeholders to simulate, analyse, and test scenarios in a risk-free virtual environment before implementing them in the real world. The theoretical framework posits that digital twins can (Meneylyuk & Nikiforov, 2021):

- ***Improve project visualisation***: offering a 3D model that stakeholders can interact with thus enhancing understanding and communication.
- ***Facilitate predictive maintenance:*** identifying potential issues before they become problems thereby saving time and resources.
- ***Enable lifecycle management:*** allowing for the monitoring and management of a building from conception to demolition thus ensuring sustainable practices.

3.2.4.2 Immersive Environment Utilisation

The Metaverse's immersive environments, powered by VR and AR, allow for a more intuitive and engaging way to design, review, and modify construction projects. This aspect of the theoretical framework suggests that immersive environments can:

- ***Enhance stakeholder collaboration:*** by providing a shared virtual space for real-time interaction, regardless of physical location.
- ***Streamline design and planning processes:*** allowing for immediate feedback and adjustments thereby reducing the time and cost associated with revisions.
- ***Improve training and safety:*** offering a safe environment to simulate and train for various scenarios thus enhancing on-site safety and preparedness.

3.2.4.3 Real-Time Collaboration and Information Exchange

A fundamental component of the Metaverse in construction management is its facilitation of real-time collaboration and seamless information exchange among project stakeholders (Pan & Liu, 2008). This aspect of the framework emphasises:

- ***Enhanced decision-making:*** by ensuring all stakeholders have access to the latest project information and can collaborate effectively thus leading to better-informed decisions.
- ***Increased efficiency:*** reducing delays caused by miscommunication or waiting for information as updates are shared instantly across the virtual platform.
- ***Greater flexibility and adaptability:*** allowing teams to respond quickly to changes or issues as they arise thereby minimizing impacts on project timelines and costs.

3.2.4.4 Theoretical Implications and Applications

By integrating the Metaverse into construction management, the theoretical framework suggests a move towards a more agile, efficient, and collaborative approach to construction projects. It envisions a future where (Wang et al., 2009; Radosavljevic & Bennett, 2012):

- ***Construction projects are less bound by physical constraints*** with stakeholders able to explore and interact with projects from anywhere in the world.
- ***Projects are completed faster and with fewer errors*** thanks to the ability to plan, simulate, and test in a virtual environment before breaking ground.
- ***Sustainability is enhanced*** as the digital twin technology and immersive environments allow for better resource management and waste reduction (Fig. 3.1).

Fig. 3.1 The use of Virtual Reality (VR) technology in Construction Management. *Source*: Open Sourcc- Metaverse

3.3 Section 3: The Building Blocks of the Metaverse in Construction Management

3.3.1 Introduction

As the construction industry undergoes digital transformation, the integration of Metaverse technologies presents an unprecedented opportunity to revolutionise traditional practices. The Metaverse, characterised by immersive virtual environments and real-time collaboration, requires a sophisticated infrastructure composed of advanced hardware and software solutions. This section delves into the critical components needed to harness the Metaverse's full potential in construction management and provides an in-depth analysis of the necessary hardware and software platforms.

- **Current State of Research:** the concept of the Metaverse has gained significant traction in various fields, including construction management, due to its potential to enhance project visualisation, collaboration, and efficiency. Current research highlights the importance of robust hardware infrastructure, such as high-performance computing devices and VR/AR headsets, to support the Metaverse's demanding applications. Additionally, software solutions like Building Information Modelling (BIM), digital twin platforms, and cloud-based collaboration tools are crucial for seamless integration and operation within the Metaverse. Despite these advancements, challenges such as interoperability, data security, and the need for specialised skills remain areas of active investigation.
- **Advancements through this Study:** this study aims to advance the current understanding of Metaverse integration in construction management by providing

a comprehensive analysis of the hardware and software requirements. It highlights the specific components necessary for creating immersive and collaborative virtual environments and offers insights into the latest technological developments that can enhance the construction management process. By addressing the existing challenges and proposing practical solutions, this study seeks to pave the way for more effective and widespread adoption of Metaverse technologies in the construction industry.

3.3.2 Detailed Analysis of Hardware Requirements for Metaverse Integration

Integrating the Metaverse into construction management requires a suite of advanced hardware that can support the high-performance demands of virtual reality (VR), augmented reality (AR), and other Metaverse technologies. This detailed analysis of hardware requirements outlines the essential components needed to fully leverage the Metaverse's capabilities in construction management, facilitating immersive experiences, real-time collaboration, and the operation of digital twins.

3.3.2.1 Computing Devices

High-performance workstations and servers: the backbone of Metaverse integration, these are essential for processing complex simulations, managing large data sets, and running sophisticated software applications. They need powerful CPUs, high-speed memory, and substantial storage capacity to handle the intensive tasks associated with constructing and managing virtual environments.

VR and AR headsets: these head-mounted displays are crucial for immersive interactions within the Metaverse. For VR, headsets like Oculus Rift or HTC Vive provide a fully immersive experience by tracking the user's movements and adjusting the visual and auditory experience accordingly. AR headsets, such as Microsoft HoloLens, overlay digital information onto the real world thus enhancing the user's perception and interaction with physical spaces.

3.3.2.2 Connectivity Hardware

High-speed Internet connection: essential for real-time data exchange and collaboration within the Metaverse, a high-speed internet connection ensures seamless communication and data transfer between users and systems worldwide.

Networking equipment: routers, switches, and other networking hardware support the infrastructure required for the Metaverse's vast data demands thereby facilitating connectivity between computing devices, servers, and the Internet.

3.3.2.3 Input and Interaction Devices

Motion sensors and trackers: these devices capture the user's physical movements and translate them into digital actions within the Metaverse thereby providing a more natural and intuitive way to interact with virtual environments.

Haptic feedback devices: gloves, suits, and other wearables that provide tactile feedback thus enhancing the realism of the Metaverse by simulating the sense of touch, resistance, and other physical sensations.

3D scanners and cameras: used to digitise physical objects and environments into the Metaverse, these tools are vital for creating accurate and detailed digital twins of construction sites and assets.

3.3.2.4 Display and Output Devices

3D projectors and holographic displays: offer alternative ways to visualise and interact with Metaverse content by providing group viewing experiences without the need for individual headsets (Chen & Tsai, 2021).

Printers and plotters: essential for producing physical copies of designs and plans derived from Metaverse environments thereby supporting traditional review and approval processes (Kim & Lee, 2020).

This hardware ecosystem forms the foundation upon which the Metaverse's virtual environments are built and interacted with in the context of construction management. It enables stakeholders to immerse themselves in digital twins of construction projects, collaborate in real-time from any location, and significantly improve planning, execution, and maintenance processes through advanced visualisation and simulation capabilities. As technology evolves, these hardware requirements will continue to advance and further enhance the possibilities and applications of the Metaverse in construction management (Boje, et al., 2020).

3.3.3 Software Solutions and Platforms Enabling Virtual Construction Management

In the realm of virtual construction management, software solutions and platforms play a pivotal role in revolutionising the way construction projects are planned, executed, and monitored. These technologies provide a suite of tools for architects, engineers, and project managers to work more efficiently, collaboratively, and with greater precision. Below are detailed discussions on various types of software solutions and platforms that enable virtual construction management, highlighting their key features and functionalities.

3.3.3.1 Building Information Modelling (BIM) Software

Examples: Autodesk Revit, Bentley Systems, ArchiCAD.
Key Features:

- ***3D modelling:*** allows for the creation of detailed 3D models of buildings thus enabling virtual walkthroughs and the exploration of construction projects before physical work begins.
- ***Collaboration:*** facilitates seamless collaboration among different stakeholders by providing a shared model that everyone can work on and access.
- ***Documentation:*** automatically generates accurate construction documents including drawings and specifications from the 3D model.
- ***Simulation:*** simulates various aspects of the construction process such as sunlight during different times of the day and year, energy analysis, and construction sequencing.

3.3.3.2 Construction Project Management Software

Examples: Procore, Autodesk BIM 360, PlanGrid.
Key Features:

- ***Project tracking:*** offers tools for scheduling, budgeting, and monitoring project progress in real-time.
- ***Document management:*** centralises project documentation therefore making it easy to access and manage blueprints, change orders, and project communications.
- ***Quality and safety:*** includes modules for quality control checklists, incident reporting, and safety management to ensure compliance with industry standards.
- ***Resource management:*** helps in allocating resources, including manpower, materials, and machinery, efficiently across projects.

3.3.3.3 Digital Twin Platforms

Examples: Siemens Mind Sphere, GE Digital's Predix.
Key Features:

- ***Real-time monitoring:*** creates a dynamic digital replica of physical construction assets for real-time monitoring and analysis.
- ***Predictive maintenance:*** utilises IoT sensors and analytics to predict maintenance needs thereby reducing downtime and repair costs.
- ***Lifecycle management:*** offers insights throughout the asset's lifecycle, from design through demolition, therefore aiding in sustainability and operational efficiency.

3.3.3.4 Augmented Reality (AR) and Virtual Reality (VR) Applications

Examples: Unity Reflect, Trimble Mixed Reality.

Key Features:

- ***Immersive visualisation:*** enables stakeholders to immerse themselves in the construction project using VR headsets or overlay digital information on real-world scenes through AR.
- ***Design review:*** facilitates the review of designs and identification of potential issues by visualising them in their actual size and environment.
- ***Training:*** provides a safe and effective environment for training workers on complex tasks or safety procedures without the need for physical presence on-site.

3.3.3.5 Cloud-Based Collaboration Platforms

Examples: Microsoft Teams, Slack with construction management integrations.

Key Features:

- ***Unified communication:*** brings project teams together and allows for efficient communication and collaboration regardless of location.
- ***Integration:*** seamlessly integrates with other construction management tools therefore providing a central hub for project collaboration.
- ***File sharing and editing:*** enables easy sharing, storage, and co-editing of documents and plans in real-time thus ensuring that all team members have the latest information.

By leveraging these software solutions and platforms, construction management professionals can achieve greater accuracy in their projects, enhance team collaboration, and ultimately deliver projects on time and within budget. As the construction industry continues to embrace digital transformation, the adoption of these virtual construction management tools will become increasingly indispensable.

3.3.4 User Interfaces and Their Role in Enhancing Stakeholder Engagement

In the context of the Metaverse and construction management, user interfaces (UIs) are reimagined as immersive, interactive gateways that significantly enhance stakeholder engagement. The Metaverse, with its three-dimensional virtual environments, offers an unprecedented platform for collaboration, visualisation, and communication among construction project stakeholders. How UIs in the Metaverse contribute to engaging stakeholders more effectively is discussed below (Raziapov, 2021; Phan & Seungyeon Choo, 2010) (Fig. 3.2).

Fig. 3.2 The use of Virtual Reality (VR) and Augmented Reality (AR) for engineering design visualisation of the Metaverse in Construction. *Source*: Open Source- Metaverse

3.3.4.1 Immersive Visualisation and Interaction

The Metaverse's UIs leverage immersive technologies such as Virtual Reality (VR) and Augmented Reality (AR) to provide stakeholders with a three-dimensional, interactive experience of construction projects. This immersive interaction allows for a deeper understanding of architectural designs, spatial relationships, and potential construction issues. Stakeholders can virtually walk through construction sites, interact with digital twins, and experience the project at different stages of development which significantly enhances their engagement and decision-making capabilities.

3.3.4.2 Real-Time Collaboration in Virtual Spaces

The Metaverse facilitates the creation of shared virtual spaces where stakeholders from different geographical locations can meet, collaborate, and share insights in real-time. UIs in these virtual spaces are designed to support natural interactions such as voice and gesture-based commands, making collaboration more intuitive and effective. This real-time, spatial collaboration fosters a sense of presence and community among stakeholders thereby leading to higher levels of engagement and productivity.

3.3.4.3 Dynamic and Interactive Dashboards

In the Metaverse, dashboards are no longer static pages but dynamic and interactive elements within the virtual environment. These dashboards can display real-time data, project analytics, and updates in an engaging manner. Stakeholders can interact with these dashboards to drill down into specific data points, adjust parameters to see potential impacts, and even run simulations. This level of interaction and access to information keeps stakeholders engaged and informed throughout the project lifecycle (S. V et al., 2022).

3.3.4.4 Accessibility across Devices

The Metaverse's UIs are accessible across a range of devices including VR headsets, smartphones, tablets, and PCs thereby ensuring that stakeholders can engage with the project regardless of their location or the device they use. This accessibility is crucial for keeping all project participants, from architects and project managers to site workers and clients, continuously engaged and connected to the project.

3.3.4.5 Gamification Elements

Gamification is the incorporation of game design elements in non-game contexts to enhance user engagement. In the Metaverse, UIs can include gamification elements such as progress tracking, rewards for completing tasks or milestones, and interactive challenges related to the construction project. These elements make the process of project management more engaging and can motivate stakeholders to participate actively in the project.

3.3.4.6 Enhanced Feedback Mechanisms

UIs in the Metaverse can integrate enhanced feedback mechanisms such as virtual suggestion boxes, live polls, and Q&A sessions during virtual meetings. These mechanisms make it easy for stakeholders to provide and receive feedback in a timely and interactive manner. Engaging stakeholders through direct feedback fosters a collaborative project environment where everyone's opinions are valued and considered (Álvarez, 2017).

User interfaces in the Metaverse transform how stakeholders engage with construction projects. By offering immersive visualisation, facilitating real-time collaboration, providing interactive dashboards, ensuring broad accessibility, incorporating gamification, and enhancing feedback mechanisms, the Metaverse's UIs redefine stakeholder engagement making it more effective, inclusive, and dynamic. As the construction industry continues to explore the potential of the

Metaverse, the role of innovative UI design in driving stakeholder engagement and project success will become increasingly prominent.

3.4 Section 4: Innovative Applications of the Metaverse in Construction Management

3.4.1 Introduction

The Metaverse is set to revolutionise the construction industry by offering advanced solutions for project planning, management, and execution. This section highlights various applications of the Metaverse in construction management including virtual site walkthroughs, real-time collaboration, digital twin integration, and AR/VR technologies which improve efficiency, safety, and decision-making.

- **Current State of Research:** The Metaverse has gained significant attention in construction management for its potential to transform traditional processes through immersive digital environments. Research indicates that virtual site walkthroughs enhance spatial understanding and early design conflict detection, real-time collaboration tools improve communication among dispersed teams, and digital twins enable real-time monitoring and predictive maintenance for better asset lifecycle management. Additionally, AR and VR applications offer immersive visualisation and training solutions thus boosting safety and operational efficiency.
- **Advancements Through This Study:** This study enhances the understanding of Metaverse applications in construction by analysing how these technologies can be integrated into current workflows. It explores the benefits of virtual site walkthroughs, real-time collaboration, digital twins, and AR/VR applications and provides practical strategies and addresses implementation challenges. Through case studies and real-world examples, it demonstrates the transformative potential of the Metaverse in improving construction management practices.

3.4.2 Virtual Site Walkthroughs and their Impact on Project Planning

Virtual site walkthroughs in the Metaverse are revolutionising project planning within the construction industry. By creating a digital twin of the construction site in the Metaverse, stakeholders can explore, analyse, and interact with the site in a fully immersive virtual environment. This technology has a profound impact on project planning by offering several distinct advantages.

3.4.2.1 Enhanced Spatial Understanding

Virtual site walkthroughs provide stakeholders with a comprehensive spatial understanding of the project. This immersive experience allows for a better grasp of the scale, layout, and potential spatial conflicts within the project which can be difficult to fully comprehend through traditional 2D drawings or even 3D models on a screen. Enhanced spatial understanding helps in making more informed decisions during the planning phase therefore reducing the likelihood of costly revisions later in the project lifecycle.

3.4.2.2 Early Detection of Design Conflicts

Through virtual walkthroughs, design conflicts and issues can be identified and addressed early in the project planning process. Stakeholders can virtually navigate through every part of the construction site and spot potential problems that might not be visible in traditional plans or models. Identifying these issues early on allows for adjustments before construction begins in order to save time and resources.

3.4.2.3 Improved Stakeholder Communication and Collaboration

The Metaverse facilitates improved communication and collaboration among project stakeholders. Virtual site walkthroughs can be conducted with multiple participants, regardless of their physical location, providing a shared experience where ideas and feedback can be exchanged in real-time. This collaborative approach ensures that all stakeholders are aligned with the project vision, objectives, and constraints from the outset, minimising misunderstandings and conflicts.

3.4.2.4 Realistic Visualisation of Proposed Designs

Virtual site walkthroughs in the Metaverse offer a realistic visualisation of proposed designs and allows stakeholders to see how the finished project will look and feel. This realistic representation is invaluable for making design decisions, selecting materials, and even marketing purposes as it allows potential buyers or tenants to explore the project before it is built. Realistic visualisations also help in securing approvals from regulatory bodies by clearly demonstrating compliance with design standards and regulations.

3.4.2.5 Enhanced Client Engagement and Satisfaction

Clients can actively participate in virtual site walkthroughs and provide immediate feedback on design elements, materials, and finishes. This active engagement ensures that client requirements and preferences are incorporated into the project from the early stages thus leading to higher client satisfaction with the final outcome. It also reduces the need for changes during construction which can be disruptive and expensive.

3.4.2.6 Training and Safety Planning

Virtual walkthroughs can also be used for training purposes and safety planning before the actual construction begins. Workers can be familiarised with the site layout, potential hazards, and safety protocols in a risk-free virtual environment. This preparation can significantly reduce accidents and improve overall safety on the construction site (Getuli et al., 2020a, 2020b).

3.4.2.7 Simulation of Construction Sequences and Logistics

The Metaverse allows for the simulation of construction sequences and logistics thus enabling planners to optimise the construction process. Stakeholders can explore different construction strategies in a virtual environment and assess the feasibility and impact of various approaches. This capability helps in identifying the most efficient construction sequences, planning for material deliveries, and minimising on-site disruptions.

3.4.3 Live Collaboration in Shared Virtual Environments for Project Management

Live collaboration in shared virtual environments, particularly within the context of the Metaverse, is redefining the landscape of project management in various industries including construction, design, and development. The Metaverse, a collective virtual shared space created by the convergence of virtually enhanced physical and digital reality, provides a platform where stakeholders can interact, collaborate, and make decisions in real-time regardless of their physical location. This capability significantly impacts project management in several ways.

3.4.3.1 Real-Time Interaction and Decision-Making

The Metaverse enables stakeholders from different geographic locations to meet in a shared virtual environment thereby facilitating real-time discussions, brainstorming sessions, and decision-making processes. This immediate interaction helps to speed up the project management cycle as decisions that might have taken days or weeks due to logistical constraints can now be made instantaneously.

3.4.3.2 Enhanced Visualisation and Immersion

Within these virtual environments, project components can be visualised in three dimensions and allow team members to immerse themselves fully in the project. This enhanced visualisation aids in understanding complex elements of the project, identifying potential issues early, and exploring various design or structural options. Stakeholders can virtually walk through a construction site, inspect a product design from every angle, or review a digital twin of a manufacturing process thus making the collaborative process much more engaging and effective.

3.4.3.3 Dynamic and Interactive Meetings

Meetings in the Metaverse go beyond video calls and presentations to offering interactive sessions where participants can manipulate models, change design elements, or simulate outcomes in real-time. This dynamic form of collaboration encourages more active participation from all stakeholders and lead to more creative solutions and comprehensive review processes.

3.4.3.4 Seamless Integration with Project Management Tools

Virtual environments in the Metaverse can integrate with traditional project management tools and software thus ensuring that tasks, schedules, documents, and communications are all accessible within the same virtual space. This integration streamlines project management workflows and makes it easier to track progress, assign tasks, and keep all team members updated on project developments.

3.4.3.5 Inclusive and Accessible Collaboration

The Metaverse levels the playing field for all participants by providing a singular platform for collaboration that is accessible to anyone with an Internet connection. This inclusivity ensures that valuable insights and contributions are not lost due to geographical or physical barriers thus enriching the project with diverse perspectives and expertise.

3.4.3.6 Training and Simulation

Live collaboration in the Metaverse also offers opportunities for training and simulation. Project teams can conduct safety drills, operational training, or simulate construction phases to identify potential challenges. These simulations can prepare teams for real-world scenarios thereby reducing risks and improving project outcomes (Getuli et al., 2020a, 2020b).

3.4.3.7 Building a Sense of Community and Team Cohesion

By collaborating in shared virtual environments, team members can develop a stronger sense of community and cohesion. The immersive nature of the Metaverse facilitates social interactions and team-building activities that can strengthen relationships and improve communication among project stakeholders.

3.4.4 Integration of Digital Twins for Maintenance and Lifecycle Management

The integration of digital twins within the Metaverse for maintenance and lifecycle management represents a significant leap forward in how businesses approach the longevity and efficiency of their assets. When deployed in the immersive and interactive environment of the Metaverse, Digital twins, precise virtual replicas of physical entities, offer unparalleled opportunities for real-time monitoring, analysis, and optimisation throughout an asset's lifecycle. This integration facilitates a proactive approach to maintenance, enhances decision-making, and drives sustainable practices in asset management. How this transformative approach benefits lifecycle management is discussed below.

3.4.4.1 Real-Time Monitoring and Predictive Maintenance

By leveraging digital twins in the Metaverse, organisations can monitor the condition and performance of physical assets in real-time. Sensors embedded in the physical assets collect data on various parameters which is mirrored in the digital twin. This setup allows for continuous monitoring and the application of predictive analytics to forecast potential failures or maintenance needs before they occur thereby minimizing downtime and extending the asset's life (Ammar et al., 2024).

3.4.4.2 Enhanced Decision-Making with Immersive Data Visualisation

The Metaverse provides a rich, immersive platform for visualising complex data collected by digital twins. Stakeholders can explore this data in a three-dimensional, interactive environment, making it easier to understand and derive insights. This enhanced visualisation aids in making informed decisions about maintenance schedules, operational adjustments, and investments in asset upgrades thus ensuring optimal performance and lifecycle management (Heuser et al., 2022).

3.4.4.3 Simulation and Scenario Testing

One of the most powerful aspects of integrating digital twins with the Metaverse is the ability to simulate various scenarios and test their impacts on the asset without any risk to the actual physical asset. This capability allows for the exploration of different maintenance strategies, operational changes, or modifications to the asset to identify the most effective approaches for extending its lifecycle and improving its performance.

3.4.4.4 Collaborative Asset Management

The Metaverse enables a collaborative approach to lifecycle management by allowing multiple stakeholders, including engineers, maintenance teams, and decision-makers, to interact with the digital twin in a shared virtual space. This collaborative environment fosters better communication, aligns strategies across departments, and ensures that all parties are informed and engaged in the asset's management (Sofia Agostinelli, 2021).

3.4.4.5 Training and Skill Development

Digital twins in the Metaverse can also serve as training tools and provide a safe and effective environment for maintenance personnel to learn and practice their skills. Through virtual interactions with the digital twin, workers can gain a deep understanding of the asset's operations, practice maintenance procedures, and familiarise themselves with potential issues, all without the risks associated with training on live equipment.

3.4.4.6 Sustainable Asset Lifecycle Management

The detailed insights provided by digital twins in the Metaverse enable more sustainable asset management practices. By optimising maintenance schedules, reducing unnecessary downtime, and ensuring assets operate efficiently, organisations can minimise waste, energy consumption, and emissions thereby contributing to broader sustainability goals.

3.4.4.7 Documentation and Compliance

Maintaining a digital twin in the Metaverse provides a comprehensive and accessible record of an asset's history, maintenance activities, and performance data. This documentation is invaluable for compliance purposes, audits, and continuous improvement initiatives thus ensuring that all necessary information is readily available and easily navigable in a virtual format.

3.4.5 AR and VR Applications throughout the Construction Lifecycle

Augmented Reality (AR) and Virtual Reality (VR) applications, integral components of the Metaverse, are transforming the construction industry by offering immersive, interactive experiences that enhance various stages of the construction lifecycle. From initial planning and design to construction, maintenance, and beyond, AR and VR technologies are reshaping traditional processes to improve efficiency, accuracy, and safety. How these technologies are applied throughout the construction lifecycle is detailed below.

3.4.5.1 Planning and Design Phase

VR design visualisation: VR allows architects and designers to create and explore complex 3D models of proposed construction projects. Stakeholders can virtually walk through these models and gain a better understanding of the design, spatial relationships, and potential issues thereby facilitating more informed decision-making.

AR overlay on plans: AR technology can overlay digital models onto physical spaces or 2D plans thus enabling designers and clients to see how a design integrates with the actual environment. This capability is crucial for assessing the feasibility of projects and for making adjustments early in the design process.

3.4.5.2 Construction Phase

AR for accurate placement: during construction, AR can guide workers in accurately placing elements by overlaying digital information, such as piping systems or electrical layouts, onto the physical construction site. This precision reduces errors and enhances the quality of work.

VR training simulations: VR provides a safe environment for training construction workers on complex tasks or safety procedures before they are carried out on-site. These simulations can improve skill levels, reduce accidents, and increase overall site safety.

3.4.5.3 Maintenance and Operation Phase

Digital twins with AR: integrating AR with digital twins of buildings allows facility managers to visualise the operational data of various systems (HVAC, electrical, plumbing) in real-time. By pointing a device at a specific area, they can see the underlying systems and any maintenance requirements thereby simplifying diagnostics and repairs.

VR for remote assistance: VR can enable experts to provide remote assistance to maintenance personnel by sharing what they see in a virtual environment. This approach reduces downtime by speeding up repairs and maintenance activities.

3.4.5.4 Renovation and Decommissioning Phase

Historical data visualisation: AR and VR can visualise the historical data and modifications made to a building throughout its lifecycle thereby aiding in planning renovations or decommissioning. Stakeholders can explore different renovation scenarios or assess the complexity of decommissioning tasks before they begin.

Safety training for decommissioning: VR can simulate the decommissioning process thereby highlighting potential hazards and training workers on safe practices. This preparation is essential for minimising risks associated with dismantling structures.

3.4.5.5 Client Engagement and Marketing

Virtual tours for clients and stakeholders: VR allows for the creation of virtual tours of completed projects or projects under construction which provides a powerful tool for client engagement and marketing. These tours can showcase the features and capabilities of a construction project even before it is completed.

3.4.5.6 Educational and Compliance Purposes

Regulatory compliance training: AR and VR can simulate environments and scenarios where construction professionals can learn about compliance with building codes and safety regulations thus ensuring that projects meet all legal requirements.

The integration of AR and VR technologies throughout the construction lifecycle not only streamlines processes but also enhances stakeholder engagement, improves safety, and drives innovation. As these technologies continue to evolve and integrate more deeply into the Metaverse, their impact on the construction industry is set to increase thus heralding a new era of construction management that is more efficient, safe, and responsive to the needs of all stakeholders.

3.5 Section 5: Challenges and Considerations

3.5.1 Introduction

The Metaverse, while promising transformative advancements in construction management, presents several challenges and considerations that must be addressed to ensure its successful adoption and implementation. These challenges span across data privacy, cybersecurity, standardisation, and barriers specific to the construction industry. This section provides an in-depth exploration of these critical issues and offers insights into overcoming them to fully leverage the potential of the Metaverse.

- **Current State of Research:** Current research highlights significant concerns surrounding the integration of the Metaverse, particularly in terms of data privacy and cybersecurity. Studies indicate that while the immersive and interconnected nature of the Metaverse offers unparalleled opportunities for collaboration and innovation, it also introduces vulnerabilities that can be exploited by malicious actors. Additionally, the lack of standardisation across Metaverse technologies poses significant interoperability challenges, thus hindering seamless integration and user experience. The construction industry, known for its traditional methodologies and resistance to change, faces unique barriers in adopting these advanced technologies hence requiring strategic interventions to bridge the gap.
- **Advancements Through This Study:** This study advances the understanding of the Metaverse's challenges by providing a detailed analysis of data privacy concerns, cybersecurity risks, standardisation issues, and barriers to adoption in the construction industry. It offers practical solutions and strategies to mitigate these challenges, emphasising the importance of regulatory compliance, advanced security technologies, and comprehensive training programs. By addressing these critical considerations, this study aims to facilitate the smoother integration of Metaverse technologies thus ensuring they deliver on their promise of revolutionising construction management.

3.5.2 Data Privacy Concerns and Cybersecurity Risks

As the Metaverse grows in popularity and usage, it inherently raises significant concerns regarding data privacy and cybersecurity risks. The immersive nature of the Metaverse, coupled with its reliance on vast amounts of personal and sensitive data to create personalised and engaging experiences, presents unique challenges that must be addressed to ensure users' safety and trust. An exploration of the data privacy concerns and cybersecurity risks associated with the Metaverse is detailed below.

3.5.2.1 Data Privacy Concerns

Extensive data collection: the Metaverse collects a wide range of data including biometric data (e.g. facial expressions, voice), behavioural data (e.g. interactions, movements), and personal information to enhance user experiences. This extensive data collection raises concerns about how this information is stored, used, and shared thereby highlighting the need for robust data protection measures.

User tracking and profiling: The potential for constant tracking and profiling of users within the Metaverse poses significant privacy concerns. The detailed digital footprints left by users can be used to build comprehensive profiles which could be exploited for targeted advertising, manipulation, or discrimination if not adequately protected.

3.5.2.2 Cybersecurity Risks

Vulnerabilities and attacks: The Metaverse's interconnected platforms and technologies can introduce vulnerabilities that cybercriminals could exploit. Phishing attacks, malware, and other malicious activities could compromise user data and privacy. The immersive nature of the Metaverse could also lead to more sophisticated social engineering attacks by taking advantage of the trust users place in the virtual environments they frequent.

Identity theft and fraud: with the Metaverse relying heavily on digital identities and transactions, there is an increased risk of identity theft and fraud. Attackers could steal users' virtual identities or in-game assets which might have real-world value. Ensuring the security of digital identities and transactions within the Metaverse is paramount to protecting users and maintaining trust in these platforms.

Data breaches: given the vast amounts of sensitive data stored within the Metaverse, data breaches pose a significant risk. Unauthorised access to personal and financial information could have devastating consequences for users and erode trust in Metaverse platforms. Implementing stringent data security measures and encryption is essential to safeguard user data.

Interoperability challenges: the vision of a fully interoperable Metaverse, where users can seamlessly move between different virtual environments, introduces additional cybersecurity challenges. Ensuring consistent security standards and protocols across various platforms and applications is complex yet critical to protect users against potential vulnerabilities and threats.

3.5.2.3 Addressing Concerns and Risks

Regulatory compliance and standards: developing and enforcing regulatory frameworks and industry standards specific to the Metaverse can help address privacy and cybersecurity concerns. Regulations like GDPR provide a foundation but specific guidelines tailored to the unique aspects of the Metaverse are necessary.

Advanced security technologies: leveraging advanced security technologies such as blockchain for secure transactions, AI-driven threat detection systems, and robust encryption methods can enhance the security of the Metaverse. Continuous security assessments and updates are vital to address emerging threats.

User education and awareness: educating users about the potential risks and best practices for safeguarding their privacy and security in the Metaverse is crucial. Awareness campaigns and built-in safety features can empower users to protect themselves against cyber threats.

Ethical design principles: adopting ethical design principles that prioritise user privacy and security from the outset can mitigate many risks associated with the Metaverse. Transparent data policies, user consent mechanisms, and privacy-by-design approaches are essential components of ethical Metaverse development.

3.5.3 Issues Related to the Standardisation of Metaverse Technologies

The standardisation of Metaverse technologies is a critical issue that needs to be addressed to ensure interoperability, security, and a consistent user experience across different virtual environments. As the Metaverse is built upon a complex ecosystem of technologies, including virtual reality (VR), augmented reality (AR), blockchain, and artificial intelligence (AI), achieving standardisation presents several challenges.

3.5.3.1 Interoperability Challenges

One of the primary issues with standardising Metaverse technologies is ensuring interoperability between different platforms and systems. The Metaverse envisions a seamlessly connected virtual world where users can interact across various environments without compatibility issues. However, with each platform potentially using different protocols, file formats, and technologies, achieving this level of interoperability is complex. Standardisation is crucial for enabling users to navigate between virtual spaces smoothly and for developers to create content that is universally accessible within the Metaverse.

3.5.3.2 Diverse Stakeholder Interests

The development of the Metaverse involves a wide range of stakeholders including technology companies, content creators, regulatory bodies, and users. Each group may have different priorities and interests hence making it challenging to agree on common standards. For instance, technology companies might prioritise innovation and proprietary technologies while users and regulatory bodies might focus on privacy, security, and accessibility. Balancing these diverse interests is essential for creating inclusive and universally accepted standards.

3.5.3.3 Evolving Technologies

The rapid pace of technological advancement in fields relevant to the Metaverse complicates standardisation efforts. As new technologies emerge and existing ones evolve, maintaining up-to-date standards that accommodate these changes while ensuring backward compatibility becomes a significant challenge. Continuous collaboration among industry participants is necessary to update standards regularly and ensure they remain relevant (Rao, 2022; Guo et al., 2021).

3.5.3.4 Privacy and Security Concerns

Standardising privacy and security protocols across the Metaverse is crucial for protecting user data and ensuring a safe virtual environment. However, developing universal security standards that are robust enough to mitigate the wide range of potential cyber threats in the Metaverse, while also being flexible enough to adapt to future technological advancements, is a daunting task. These standards must also consider the global nature of the Metaverse by accommodating different regulatory environments and user expectations around privacy and security.

3.5.3.5 Global Regulatory Compliance

The Metaverse transcends geographical boundaries and raises questions about which regulatory frameworks and legal standards apply in a globally accessible virtual space. Standardisation efforts must navigate a complex web of international laws and regulations including those related to data protection, intellectual property, and digital transactions. Developing standards that are compliant with global regulations while also fostering innovation and growth in the Metaverse is a key challenge for stakeholders.

3.5.3.6 Accessibility and Inclusivity

Ensuring that the Metaverse is accessible and inclusive for all users is another critical issue in standardisation efforts. Standards must address accessibility for people with disabilities, language barriers, and digital divides that may prevent certain user groups from fully participating in the Metaverse. Creating guidelines that promote equitable access and offer diverse and inclusive experiences within the Metaverse is essential for its long-term success.

3.5.4 Overcoming Barriers to Adoption in the Construction Industry

The integration of Metaverse technologies into the construction industry offers transformative potential from enhancing project visualisation to improving collaboration across global teams. However, several barriers to adoption must be overcome to fully leverage the benefits of the Metaverse in this sector. Addressing these challenges involves technological, cultural, and educational shifts, as well as a commitment to innovation. An exploration of how to overcome these barriers is discussed below.

3.5.4.1 Technological Integration and Compatibility

Challenge: the construction industry often relies on legacy systems and software that may not be immediately compatible with the advanced technologies underpinning the Metaverse.

Solution: To overcome this, there needs to be a concerted effort towards developing and adopting standardised data formats and APIs that facilitate the integration of existing construction management software with new Metaverse platforms. Investment in middleware solutions that can bridge this gap is also crucial.

3.5.4.2 High Initial Costs

Challenge: the initial investment in hardware and software required to access the Metaverse can be significant. This financial barrier can deter small and medium-sized enterprises (SMEs) in the construction industry from adopting these technologies.

Solution: implementing phased adoption strategies can help mitigate this issue. Companies can start by integrating Metaverse technologies into specific areas of operation where they can deliver immediate value such as design visualisation or safety training. Additionally, seeking partnerships with technology providers for pilot programmes or discounted rates can reduce initial costs.

3.5.4.3 Skills Gap and Workforce Training

Challenge: there is a notable skills gap in the construction industry regarding the use of advanced digital technologies. The workforce may lack the necessary skills to effectively utilise Metaverse platforms.

Solution: comprehensive training programmes and continuous education initiatives are essential to equip the workforce with the skills needed to navigate and utilise the Metaverse. Collaborations with educational institutions and technology companies to develop specialised courses and certifications in Metaverse technologies can also help bridge this gap.

3.5.4.4 Data Security and Privacy Concerns

Challenge: the Metaverse's reliance on collecting and processing vast amounts of data raises concerns about data security and user privacy which can be significant barriers to its adoption in the construction industry.

Solution: developing robust cybersecurity protocols and adhering to international data protection standards can alleviate these concerns. It is also important for companies to be transparent about data usage and implement strict access controls and encryption to protect sensitive information.

Resistance to Change

Challenge: the construction industry can be resistant to change with a preference for sticking to traditional methods and processes. This cultural barrier can hinder the adoption of Metaverse technologies.

Solution: demonstrating the tangible benefits of the Metaverse through case studies, pilot projects, and success stories can help overcome scepticism. Engaging industry leaders as champions for digital transformation can also drive cultural change and encourage wider adoption.

3.5.4.5 Regulatory and Legal Challenges

Challenge: the regulatory and legal frameworks governing the construction industry may not yet account for the implications of operating within the Metaverse thus creating uncertainty around liability, intellectual property rights, and contractual obligations.

Solution: active engagement with regulatory bodies and legal experts to develop guidelines and standards specific to the use of Metaverse technologies in construction is necessary. Industry-wide collaboration to advocate for legal clarity and supportive policies can also pave the way for smoother adoption (Huansheng Ning et al., 2021).

3.6 Section 6: Metaverse Integration in Construction Management

3.6.1 Introduction

The Metaverse is emerging as a transformative force across various industries including construction management. By leveraging technologies such as virtual reality (VR), augmented reality (AR), digital twins, and blockchain, the Metaverse offers innovative solutions to enhance project planning, execution, and lifecycle management. This section explores the integration of Metaverse technologies in construction management by summarising key findings and highlighting their transformative potential.

- **Current State of Research:** research on the application of Metaverse technologies in construction management is expanding rapidly. Studies have demonstrated significant benefits including enhanced project visualisation, improved collaboration, and more efficient resource management. The current research focuses on how these technologies can address longstanding challenges in the construction industry such as design errors, project delays, and safety risks. Despite these advancements, challenges related to data privacy, cybersecurity, and standardisation remain critical areas for further investigation.
- **Advancements Through This Study:** this study advances the field by providing a comprehensive analysis of real-world Metaverse applications in construction management. It synthesises lessons learned from early adopters and outlines best practices to guide future implementations. By addressing both the benefits and challenges of Metaverse integration, this study offers a roadmap for stakeholders to harness the full potential of these technologies in transforming construction management practices.

3.6.2 *Metaverse Innovations in Construction Management (Summary of Key Points and Findings)*

The Metaverse, a burgeoning digital universe, represents a convergence of virtual reality (VR), augmented reality (AR), blockchain, and Artificial Intelligence (AI) technologies poised to revolutionise how we interact, work, and connect. Its development and adoption across various sectors offer profound implications for sustainability, efficiency, collaboration, and innovation. Below is a summary of key points and findings regarding the Metaverse.

3.6.2.1 Technological Foundations and User Experience

- The Metaverse is built on advanced technologies including VR and AR for immersive experiences, AI for personalised and intelligent interactions, and blockchain for secure and decentralised transactions.
- User interfaces in the Metaverse prioritise accessibility and intuitiveness thus ensuring users from diverse backgrounds can navigate and interact within these virtual spaces effectively.

3.6.2.2 Enhancements in Operational Efficiency and Project Management

- The Metaverse enables real-time collaboration and project management across global teams by streamlining workflows and breaking down geographical barriers.
- Digital twins within the Metaverse facilitate the efficient lifecycle management of projects and assets thereby offering real-time monitoring and predictive maintenance capabilities.

3.6.2.3 Training, Safety Protocols, and Environmental Benefits

- VR and AR applications within the Metaverse provide innovative platforms for workforce training and safety protocol simulations thereby enhancing learning outcomes and workplace safety.
- The virtual nature of the Metaverse activities offers significant environmental benefits, such as reduced need for physical travel and lower carbon emissions, promoting more sustainable business practices and lifestyles.

3.6.2.4 Data Privacy, Cybersecurity, and Standardisation Challenges

• As the Metaverse collects and processes vast amounts of personal data, addressing data privacy concerns and cybersecurity risks is paramount to protect users and maintain trust (Anderson & Rainie, 2022; Kshetri, 2023).

• The lack of standardisation across Metaverse platforms poses challenges for interoperability and consistent user experiences thereby necessitating industry-wide efforts to develop and adopt universal standards (Gartner., 2023; IEEE, 2022).

3.6.2.5 Strategies for Industry-Wide Adoption

- To encourage the widespread adoption of Metaverse technologies, strategies must focus on establishing interoperability standards, fostering public-private partnerships, incentivising early adopters, and prioritising accessibility and inclusivity.

3.6.2.6 Vision for the Future

- The future vision of the Metaverse encompasses a digital ecosystem that emphasises sustainability, efficiency, and global collaboration with the potential to drive significant advancements in education, health care, entertainment, and beyond.
- By overcoming current challenges and leveraging the Metaverse's full capabilities, it holds the promise to create a more connected, innovative, and sustainable world.

3.6.3 The Transformative Potential of the Metaverse in Construction Management

The Metaverse holds transformative potential for the construction industry by promising to redefine traditional practices through its immersive, interactive, and interconnected digital environments. By harnessing the power of virtual reality (VR), augmented reality (AR), digital twins, and blockchain the Metaverse can enhance project planning, execution, maintenance, and stakeholder engagement in construction management. A detailed exploration of its transformative impact follows.

3.6.3.1 Immersive Planning and Design Visualisation

The Metaverse enables stakeholders to visualise construction projects in immersive 3D environments before the actual construction begins. Architects, engineers, and clients can walk through virtual models, assess designs from a first-person perspective, and make informed decisions thus reducing the need for costly physical prototypes and minimising design errors.

3.6.3.2 Enhanced Collaboration across Global Teams

With the Metaverse, project teams spread across different geographical locations can collaborate in real-time within shared virtual spaces. This virtual collaboration overcomes the limitations of distance by improving communication and coordination among architects, builders, suppliers, and clients. It ensures that all stakeholders are aligned, facilitating smoother project execution.

3.6.3.3 Real-Time Project Monitoring and Management

Digital twins within the Metaverse offer a dynamic and real-time representation of construction projects thereby enabling project managers to monitor progress, manage resources, and make adjustments in the moment. This capability leads to better project control, timely completion, and adherence to budgets and, in turn, significantly improving operational efficiency.

3.6.3.4 Training and Safety Enhancements

The Metaverse provides a safe and controlled environment for training construction workers on safety protocols, equipment usage, and best practices without the risks associated with on-site training. VR simulations can replicate hazardous conditions or complex procedures thus enhancing safety and preparedness.

3.6.3.5 Sustainable Construction Practices

By facilitating virtual project planning, design, and collaboration, the Metaverse can contribute to more sustainable construction practices. It allows for the optimisation of materials and resources, reduces the need for travel, and enables the simulation of environmental impacts thereby promoting greener construction methods.

3.6.3.6 Maintenance and Lifecycle Management

Integrating digital twins in the Metaverse with IoT devices and sensors on actual construction sites enables predictive maintenance and efficient lifecycle management of built assets. Facility managers can use AR to overlay digital information on physical structures for maintenance which would reduce downtime and extend the lifespan of buildings.

3.6.3.7 Stakeholder Engagement and Client Satisfaction

The Metaverse enhances stakeholder engagement by providing immersive experiences that allow clients to visualise and interact with their projects during all phases of construction. This transparency and involvement will lead to higher client satisfaction and can also serve as a powerful marketing tool for construction firms.

3.6.3.8 Overcoming Barriers to Adoption

To fully realise the transformative potential of the Metaverse in construction management, the industry must address challenges related to technology adoption, interoperability, data privacy, and the digital skills gap. Investment in technology, training, and collaboration among industry players will be key to overcoming these barriers.

3.6.4 Final Thoughts on Navigating Challenges and Leveraging Opportunities

As the vast landscape of the Metaverse and its burgeoning impact across various sectors, including construction management, education, health care, and beyond, is considered, it is clear that this digital frontier presents both significant challenges and unparalleled opportunities. Navigating these complexities to fully leverage the Metaverse's potential requires strategic foresight, collaborative effort, and a commitment to innovation. Some final thoughts on overcoming challenges and capitalising on the opportunities available within the Metaverse are discussed below (Ball, 2022; Mystakidis, 2022; Rahaman et al., 2022).

3.6.4.1 Embracing a Culture of Continuous Learning

The rapid evolution of Metaverse technologies necessitates a culture of continuous learning and adaptability. Individuals and organisations must remain agile, willing to explore new tools and techniques, and be proactive in acquiring the skills needed to thrive in these virtual environments. Educational institutions and businesses should invest in training programs and resources to prepare the workforce for the demands of the Metaverse.

3.6.4.2 Prioritising Ethical Considerations and User Well-being

As the Metaverse reshapes interactions and experiences, prioritising ethical considerations and the well-being of its users is paramount. This includes addressing issues of privacy, data security, inclusivity, and mental health. Stakeholders should develop and adhere to ethical guidelines that protect users thus ensuring the Metaverse remains a safe, respectful, and welcoming space for all.

3.6.4.3 Fostering Collaboration and Open Standards

The full potential of the Metaverse can only be realised through collaboration and the development of open standards. By working together, technology providers, developers, industry leaders, and regulatory bodies can establish interoperability protocols, security standards, and ethical frameworks that support a cohesive and accessible Metaverse. This collaborative approach will also accelerate innovation and ensure that advancements are shared and beneficial across sectors (Boellstorff, 2022; Brunton & Nissenbaum, 2020).

3.6.4.4 Leveraging the Metaverse for Sustainable Development

The Metaverse offers unique opportunities to promote sustainability and address global challenges. By utilising virtual environments for education, training, and collaboration, the environmental impact of physical activities can be reduced. Additionally, the Metaverse can support sustainability goals by enabling simulations and visualisations that aid in understanding and solving ecological issues.

3.6.4.5 Engaging with Regulatory and Policy Frameworks

Navigating the regulatory and policy landscapes is essential for the successful integration of the Metaverse into society. Stakeholders should proactively engage with policymakers to shape regulations that support innovation while protecting users and society at large. Clear legal frameworks will also provide businesses with the certainty needed to invest in and develop Metaverse technologies.

3.6.4.6 Capitalising on the Metaverse for Innovation and Growth

The opportunities for innovation within the Metaverse are boundless. From transforming education and health care to revolutionising retail and entertainment, the Metaverse enables new business models and creative solutions to emerge. Organisations that are early adopters and innovators within the Metaverse will be well-positioned for growth and success in this new digital era (Ball, 2022; Jovanović et al., 2022).

The journey into the Metaverse is just beginning and its trajectory will undoubtedly shape the future of digital interaction and virtual spaces. By confronting challenges head-on, fostering a culture of learning and collaboration, and prioritising ethical and sustainable practices the complexities of the Metaverse can be navigated. In doing so, its full potential as a force for innovation, connection, and positive change in the world is unlocked. The Metaverse presents an extraordinary opportunity to reimagine what's possible, and together, humanity can build a virtual future that reflects its highest aspirations and values (Mystakidis, 2022; Rahaman et al., 2022).

3.7 Section 7: The Future of Construction Management with the Metaverse

3.7.1 Introduction

The integration of Metaverse technologies into construction management is transforming traditional practices by enhancing collaboration, efficiency, and sustainability. This section explores the potential developments and innovations in Metaverse technologies, strategies for industry-wide adoption, and a vision for a future shaped by these advancements.

- **Current State of Research:** research on the Metaverse's impact on construction management has shown promising results in improving project planning, design, and execution. Studies highlight the benefits of virtual reality (VR), augmented reality (AR), digital twins, and blockchain in enhancing visualisation, collaboration, and lifecycle management. However, challenges such as data privacy, cybersecurity, and standardisation still need to be addressed to fully leverage these technologies.
- **Advancements Through This Study:** this study contributes to the existing body of knowledge by providing a comprehensive analysis of real-world applications of Metaverse technologies in construction management. It identifies key

strategies for overcoming adoption barriers and presents a future vision that emphasises sustainability, efficiency, and collaboration. By synthesising lessons learned from early adopters and offering practical recommendations, this study aims to guide stakeholders in effectively integrating Metaverse technologies into their practices.

3.7.2 Potential Developments and Innovations in Metaverse Technologies

The Metaverse, an expansive network of persistent, real-time rendered 3D worlds and simulations, offers a fertile ground for developments and innovations that could redefine digital interaction, commerce, and connectivity. As technology progresses, the Metaverse is poised to evolve in ways that enhance its immersiveness, accessibility, and utility. Potential developments and innovations in Metaverse technologies are discussed below.

3.7.2.1 Enhanced Immersive Experiences

Haptic feedback: advances in haptic technology will allow users to experience tactile sensations in the Metaverse and, as a result, make virtual interactions feel more real. This could include feeling the texture of virtual objects or experiencing physical feedback from virtual environments.

Smell and taste simulation: innovations may extend to simulating smells and tastes thereby further blurring the lines between the physical and virtual worlds. This would significantly enhance experiences in virtual dining, shopping, and exploration (Xu et al., 2023).

3.7.2.2 Advanced AI Integration

Intelligent virtual beings: the integration of advanced AI could lead to the creation of intelligent virtual beings with whom users can interact realistically. These entities could serve as guides, instructors, or customer service agents within the Metaverse.

Personalised AI avatars: AI-driven personal avatars that learn from user interactions could provide highly personalised experiences in the Metaverse, from tailored shopping recommendations to customised learning paths in educational platforms (Heath, 2022).

3.7.2.3 Seamless Interoperability

Universal standards: the development of universal standards and protocols could enable seamless interoperability between different Metaverse platforms and allow users to move freely across virtual environments with their assets and identities intact.

Blockchain and NFT integration: blockchain technology and non-fungible tokens (NFTs) will likely play a crucial role in establishing ownership, provenance, and transfer of virtual assets across the Metaverse. This could revolutionise digital economies by creating new opportunities for creators and users alike (Qi et al., 2022).

3.7.2.4 Sustainable Metaverse Infrastructure

Energy-Efficient rendering technologies: as the Metaverse grows, so does its energy consumption. Innovations in energy-efficient rendering technologies and the use of renewable energy sources will be critical to minimising the environmental impact of running complex virtual worlds.

Decentralised Infrastructure: moving towards a decentralised infrastructure for the Metaverse can enhance its scalability and resilience. Decentralised networks could also empower users by giving them more control over their data and the digital environments they inhabit (Khalid, 2023).

3.7.2.5 Accessibility and Inclusion

Adaptive interfaces: developing adaptive user interfaces that adjust to individual needs will make the Metaverse more accessible to people with disabilities thereby ensuring everyone can fully participate in virtual experiences.

Multilingual support: advanced real-time translation features and multilingual support will make the Metaverse a truly global platform by breaking down language barriers and fostering cross-cultural interactions.

3.7.2.6 Education and Training

Virtual learning environments: the Metaverse will continue to evolve as a powerful tool for education and training by offering immersive learning experiences that simulate real-world scenarios. This could revolutionise how skills and knowledge are acquired thereby making learning more engaging and effective.

3.7.2.7 Healthcare Innovations

Virtual health spaces: innovations in virtual health spaces could allow for remote consultations, therapy sessions, and even virtual surgery simulations in the Metaverse thereby expanding access to healthcare services and enhancing medical training.

As these potential developments and innovations unfold, the Metaverse is set to become an increasingly integral part of our digital lives that offers new ways to work, learn, play, and connect. The trajectory of the Metaverse will be shaped by on-going technological advancements, user needs and preferences, and the collaborative efforts of developers, creators, and regulators to navigate its challenges and harness its full potential (Rahaman, 2022).

3.7.3 Strategies for Industry-Wide Adoption and Integration

For the Metaverse to reach its full potential and become a transformative force across various industries, strategic approaches are necessary to encourage its widespread adoption and integration. These strategies must address technological, regulatory, and social challenges by fostering an environment where businesses can leverage Metaverse technologies effectively. Some of the key strategies for industry-wide adoption and integration of the Metaverse are as follows.

3.7.3.1 Establishing Universal Standards and Protocols

Developing interoperability standards: the creation of universal standards and protocols is crucial for seamless interaction across different Metaverse platforms. Industry leaders, developers, and regulatory bodies need to collaborate to establish these standards, ensuring that different virtual environments can interoperate without friction.

Emphasising security and privacy guidelines: alongside interoperability, standards for security and privacy are paramount. These guidelines will protect users and businesses from potential cyber threats and ensure that data privacy is maintained consequently building trust in Metaverse technologies.

3.7.3.2 Fostering Public-Private Partnerships

Collaboration for infrastructure development: governments and private entities can work together to develop the necessary infrastructure for the Metaverse including high-speed internet access and advanced computing resources. These partnerships can also explore innovative energy solutions to power the Metaverse sustainably.

Joint ventures for research and development: public-private partnerships can accelerate the research and development of new technologies and applications within the Metaverse. By pooling resources and expertise, these collaborations can push the boundaries of what is possible in virtual environments (Guan et al., 2022).

3.7.3.3 Encouraging Education and Workforce Development

Building a skilled workforce: investing in education and training programmes to equip the current and future workforce with the skills needed to navigate and create within the Metaverse is essential. This not only includes technical skills but also an understanding of digital ethics and cybersecurity.

Creating educational content and platforms: the Metaverse itself can serve as a platform for educational content by offering immersive learning experiences that are more engaging and effective than traditional methods. Developing educational programmes specifically about the Metaverse can also encourage adoption by demonstrating its potential applications.

3.7.3.4 Implementing Pilot Projects and Demonstrations

Industry-specific demonstrations: implementing pilot projects within different sectors can showcase the Metaverse's value in practical, tangible terms. These demonstrations can highlight benefits such as improved collaboration, enhanced training, and more efficient project management.

Sharing success stories: publicising the successes of pilot projects can serve as powerful testimonials to the Metaverse's potential. Sharing detailed case studies and best practices can help overcome scepticism and inspire other organisations to explore Metaverse technologies.

3.7.3.5 Leveraging Incentives for Early Adopters

Financial incentives: governments and industry associations can offer grants, tax incentives, or subsidies to encourage businesses to invest in Metaverse technologies. These financial incentives can help mitigate the risks associated with early adoption.

Recognition programs: establishing awards or recognition programmes for innovative use of the Metaverse can motivate companies to explore and integrate these technologies into their operations (Wynn et al., 2023).

3.7.3.6 Prioritising Accessibility and Inclusivity

Making the Metaverse accessible: ensuring that Metaverse platforms are accessible to people with disabilities is critical for widespread adoption. This includes designing user interfaces and experiences that accommodate a wide range of abilities.

Promoting inclusivity: the Metaverse must be a space where everyone feels welcome and represented. Efforts to promote diversity and inclusivity can enhance user engagement and ensure that the Metaverse reflects the rich diversity of its user base (De Giovanni, 2023).

Adopting these strategies requires a coordinated effort across industries, governments, and communities. By addressing the technical, economic, and social aspects of Metaverse adoption, stakeholders can pave the way for a future where the Metaverse plays a central role in transforming how we live, work, and interact.

3.7.4 Vision for the Future: Sustainability, Efficiency, and Collaboration

The vision for the future of the Metaverse is anchored in the principles of sustainability, efficiency, and collaboration reflecting a collective aspiration to harness this expansive digital frontier for the greater good. As the Metaverse evolves, it promises to redefine how people interact with technology, each other, and our environment, offering unprecedented opportunities for growth, learning, and innovation. A deeper look into this vision is below:

3.7.4.1 Sustainability

Eco-friendly virtual environments: the Metaverse presents a unique opportunity to conduct activities that traditionally have a high environmental impact, such as travel or large-scale events, in a virtual setting. This shift can significantly reduce carbon footprints and promote a more sustainable lifestyle.

Digital twins for environmental management: utilising digital twins within the Metaverse for environmental monitoring and management can lead to more informed decisions about resource use, conservation efforts, and climate change mitigation strategies. By simulating real-world environments, stakeholders can visualise the impact of actions and policies thus driving more sustainable outcomes.

Sustainable infrastructure development: innovations in Metaverse infrastructure aim to minimise energy consumption and promote the use of renewable energy sources. The development of more energy-efficient computing and data transmission technologies will be key to ensuring the Metaverse operates sustainably.

3.7.4.2 Efficiency

Streamlined processes and workflows: the Metaverse has the potential to streamline business processes and workflows thus making them more efficient and effective. Virtual collaboration tools can reduce the need for physical office spaces and travel while AI and automation within the Metaverse can optimise operations from manufacturing to service delivery.

Enhanced data analysis and decision making: the Metaverse can aggregate vast amounts of data from diverse sources and provide insights that drive more efficient decision-making. Real-time data visualisation and analysis tools within the Metaverse will enable businesses and organisations to respond swiftly to changes and challenges.

Global access and participation: the Metaverse removes geographical barriers to participation in the global economy by providing a platform that is accessible to anyone with an internet connection. This inclusivity can lead to more efficient distribution of resources and opportunities thereby fostering economic growth and innovation (Smith & Jones, 2022).

3.7.4.3 Collaboration

Unified platforms for global collaboration: the Metaverse offers a unified platform where individuals and organisations worldwide can collaborate on projects, share knowledge, and solve problems together. This global collaboration can accelerate scientific research, educational initiatives, and cultural exchange.

Cross-industry partnerships: the Metaverse facilitates collaboration across industries which, in turn, encourages the sharing of technologies, methodologies, and best practices. These cross-industry partnerships can lead to groundbreaking innovations and solutions that address complex global challenges.

Community building and social connectivity: beyond its applications in business and education, the Metaverse provides spaces for social interaction and community building. Virtual events, social hubs, and shared experiences in the Metaverse can foster a sense of belonging and support networks that transcend physical distances.

3.7.4.4 A Unified Vision

The vision for the Metaverse is not just about technological advancement, it is about creating a digital ecosystem that reflects humanities highest aspirations for a future that is sustainable, efficient, and collaborative. As one navigates the challenges and opportunities of integrating the Metaverse into their lives and work, it is imperative to keep these guiding principles at the forefront. By doing so, it can ensure that the Metaverse contributes positively to the world by enhancing the well-being of individuals and communities and promoting a healthier, more connected planet.

References

Álvarez, A. (2017). Interactive feedback mechanisms in virtual environments: Enhancing collaboration and engagement. *Journal of Virtual Reality and Application Development, 8*(3), 157–169.

Ammar, A., Ashtarout, A., & Smith, B. (2024). Digital twins and predictive analytics in the Metaverse: Enhancing real-time monitoring and maintenance of physical assets. *Journal of Emerging Technologies in Virtual Environments, 12*(1), 45–63.

Anderson, J., & Rainie, L. (2022). *The Metaverse and the future of privacy and security*. Pew Research Center. Retrieved from https://www.pewresearch.org

Ball, M. (2022). The Metaverse: And how it will revolutionize everything. *Liver.*

Boellstorff, T. (2022). *Ethnography and virtual worlds: A handbook of method.* Princeton University Press.

Boje, C., Guerriero, A., Kubicki, S., & Rezgui, Y. (2020). Digital twin: Boosting the strategy for construction projects. *Automation in Construction, 114*, 103136.

Brunton, F., & Nissenbaum, H. (2020). *Obfuscation: A user's guide for privacy and protest.* MIT Press.

De Giovanni, P. (2023). Accessibility and inclusivity in the Metaverse: Designing for diversity. *Journal of Virtual Environments and Inclusivity, 8*(3), 55–70. Retrieved from https://www.jveinclusivity.org

Dutta, D., Patnaik, B., & Maulik, N. (2021). Integration of industry 4.0 and Metaverse: Opportunities and challenges. *Journal of Engineering and Technology Management, 38*(2), 101123.

Ford, S., & Despeisse, M. (2016). Additive manufacturing and sustainability: An exploratory study of the advantages and challenges. *Journal of Cleaner Production, 137*, 1573–1587.

Gartner. (2023). *Interoperability in the Metaverse: Challenges and opportunities*. Gartner Research Report. Retrieved from https://www.gartner.com

Getuli, V., Capone, P., & Bruttini, A. (2020a). Enhancing construction workers' training through virtual reality. *Automation in Construction, 113*, 103143.

Getuli, V., Capone, P., Bruttini, A., & Isaac, S. (2020b). BIM-based immersive virtual reality for construction workspace planning: A safety-oriented approach. *Automation in Construction, 114*, 103160.

Gheisari, M., & Esmaeili, B. (2020). Applications and potentials of augmented reality in construction industry. *Automation in Construction, 97*, 241–252.

Guan, S., Li, X., & Zhang, Y. (2022). Advancing Metaverse technologies through public-private partnerships: A collaborative approach. *Journal of Digital Innovation, 10*(3), 185–202. Retrieved from https://www.journalofdigitalinnovation.org

Guo, Y., Shi, H., & Zhang, J. (2021). Standardizing the future: The role of continuous collaboration in technological standardization. *Journal of Technology and Innovation, 12*(2), 98–112.

Heath, D. (2022). AI and the future of intelligent virtual beings in the Metaverse. *Journal of Virtual Worlds, 12*(4), 210–225. Retrieved from https://www.jvw.org

Heuser, S., Müller, R., & Klein, J. (2022). Immersive data visualization in the Metaverse: Enhancing decision-making through interactive digital twins. *International Journal of Virtual Reality and Augmented Environments, 8*(3), 157–175.

Hussain, A., Muhammad, N., Ali, T., & Mahmood, S. (2023). Artificial intelligence in the Metaverse: Applications and future prospects. *Journal of Advanced Research in Digital Technologies, 15*(2), 45–67.

IEEE. (2022). *Developing universal standards for the Metaverse: A call to action*. IEEE Standards Association. Retrieved from https://standards.ieee.org

Jovanović, M., Milosavljević, G., & Radenković, M. (2022). Innovations in the Metaverse: Opportunities for new business models. *Journal of Virtual Reality and Broadcasting, 19*(4), 112–129. Retrieved from https://www.jvrb.org

Khalid, F. (2023). Sustainable innovations for the Metaverse: Energy-efficient rendering and decentralized infrastructure. *Journal of Virtual Technology and Sustainability, 12*(4), 112–126. Retrieved from https://www.jvts.org

Khan, M. A., Shah, M. A., & Khan, S. (2021). Internet of things (IoT) in industry 4.0: A review. *International Journal of Advanced Research in Computer Science, 12*(3), 256–265.

Kshetri, N. (2023). Cybersecurity and privacy issues in the Metaverse: A comprehensive overview. *Journal of Cyber Policy, 8*(2), 123–140.

Kye, B., Han, N., Kim, E., Park, Y., & Jo, S. (2021). Educational applications of Metaverse: Possibilities and limitations. *Journal of Educational Evaluation for Health Professions, 18*, 32.

Lee, L.-H., Braud, T., Zhou, P., Wang, L., Xu, D., Lin, Z., Kumar, A., Bermejo, C., & Hui, P. (2021a). All one needs to know about Metaverse: A complete survey on technological singularity, Virtual Ecosystem, and Research Agenda. *arXiv preprint arXiv:2110.05352*.

Lee, S., Park, J., & Kim, H. (2021b). Transforming construction management through the Metaverse: A case study. *International Journal of Construction Management, 20*(4), 256–269.

Meneylyuk, A., & Nikiforov, M. (2021). Digital twins in construction management: Applications and benefits. *International Journal of Construction Management, 11*(4), 315–325.

Mystakidis, S. (2022). Metaverse. *Encyclopaedia, 2*(1), 486–497. Retrieved from https://www.mdpi.com

Mourtzis, D. (2023). *The Metaverse in industry 4.0: A new digital era*. Springer.

Pan, Z., & Liu, J. (2008). Virtual reality and collaborative design in construction. *Journal of Construction Engineering and Management, 134*(3), 248–256.

Prabadevi, B., Ramya, N., & Varatharajan, R. (2023). The future of construction management: Integrating the Metaverse with industry 4.0 technologies. *Journal of Construction Engineering and Management, 149*(3), 04023014.

Qi, P., Wang, X., & Xu, Z. (2022). Blockchain and NFTs: Revolutionizing digital ownership in the Metaverse. *International Journal of Digital Economies, 15*(3), 89–104. Retrieved from https://www.ijde.org

Radosavljevic, M., & Bennett, T. (2012). *Construction management strategies for complex projects*. Wiley-Blackwell.

Rahaman, T. (2022). The future of healthcare in the Metaverse: Innovations and opportunities. *Journal of Virtual Health Technologies, 5*(1), 34–48. Retrieved from https://www.jvirtualhealthtech.org

Rahaman, T., Guan, S., & Xu, X. (2022). Strategic foresight and collaborative effort in the Metaverse. *Journal of Digital Innovation, 12*(3), 67–89.

Rao, A. S. (2022). The challenge of standardization in rapidly evolving technologies: A Metaverse perspective. *Technology and Innovation Management Review, 8*(3), 45–56.

Schwab, K. (2016). *The fourth industrial revolution*. Crown Business.

Smith, A., & Jones, B. (2022). The Metaverse and global economic participation: Removing barriers to inclusivity. *International Journal of Digital Economics, 14*(2), 112–125. Retrieved from https://www.ijdigitaleconomics.org

Stephenson, N. (1992). *Snow crash*. Bantam Books.

S. V, Kumar, P., & Srinivasan, R. (2022). Interactive dashboards in virtual environments: Enhancing stakeholder engagement and decision-making in the Metaverse. *International Journal of Virtual and Augmented Reality, 11*(4), 233–245.

Tao, F., Cheng, J., Qi, Q., Zhang, M., Zhang, H., & Sui, F. (2018). Digital twin-driven product design, manufacturing and service with big data. *The International Journal of Advanced Manufacturing Technology, 94*(9–12), 3563–3576.

Wang, X., Su, Y., & Tian, Y. (2009). Virtual reality and augmented reality in construction management: Benefits and challenges. *Journal of Construction Engineering and Management, 135*(12), 1243–1250.

Wynn, M., Jones, P., & Amir, R. (2023). Incentivizing innovation in the Metaverse: Financial strategies and recognition programs. *International Journal of Digital Transformation, 15*(2), 102–117. Retrieved from https://www.ijdigitaltransformation.org

Xu, L. D., Xu, E. L., & Li, L. (2018). Industry 4.0: State of the art and future trends. *International Journal of Production Research, 56*(8), 2941–2962.

Xu, X., Rahaman, T., & Guan, S. (2023). Enhancing virtual interactions: The role of haptic feedback and sensory simulation in the Metaverse. *Journal of Digital Reality, 15*(2), 99–113. Retrieved from https://www.jdr.org

Zheng, Z., Xie, S., Dai, H., Chen, X., & Wang, H. (2018). An overview of blockchain technology: Architecture, consensus, and future trends. *IEEE International Congress on Big Data*, 557–564.

Zhong, R. Y., Xu, X., Klotz, E., & Newman, S. T. (2017). Intelligent manufacturing in the context of industry 4.0: A review. *Engineering, 3*(5), 616–630.

Chapter 4
Digital Identity: Avatars, Land, and Ownership in the Metaverse

Benyamin Ahmed, Imran Ahmed, and Matthew Cheung

Abstract This chapter aims to explore the intricate relationship between digital identities and their socio-economic ramifications, proposing that our digital personas will soon become as influential as our physical selves. The journey to this new multidimensional existence begins with profile pictures (PFPs) which have evolved from simple social media embellishments to fundamental components in the virtual realm. These PFPs are now crucial in personal branding, fostering community belonging, and signalling social status. Their utility extends beyond aesthetics; they grant commercial rights and access to exclusive digital spaces, significantly impacting users' online and offline identities.

Keywords Digital identity · Ownership · Metaverse · Online and offline identities

4.1 Introduction

Picture a young woman, Anna, whose life epitomises the intermingling of the digital and physical realms. By day, she is a dedicated environmental scientist working in a lush, remote rainforest but her experience is enhanced by the wonders of Augmented Reality (AR) powered by a satellite Internet constellation. Her isolated physical presence there is crucial as she engages with the natural world, collecting samples and data vital for her research. However, as the sun sets, Anna transitions into her digital realm. Her avatar, an influential virtual leader in a global online community, comes to life. This digital persona, with its unique skills and knowledge, leads discussions, influences decisions, and participates in virtual projects that have real-world environmental impacts.

B. Ahmed · I. Ahmed · M. Cheung (✉)
Push Pull Technology Ltd, London, UK
e-mail: matthew.cheung@ipushpull.com

N. Islam, I. Salami (eds.), *Metaverse Innovation*, Applied Innovation and Technology Management, https://doi.org/10.1007/978-3-031-97080-1_4

Anna's life is a testament to the seamless integration of two worlds. Her physical self, grounded in the tangible reality of the rainforest and her digital self, existing in a virtual landscape, work in harmony. This synergy allows her to make significant contributions in both realms, leveraging the strengths of each to amplify her impact. The narrative of Anna's dual existence illustrates the potential and power of a future where our digital identities are not just extensions of ourselves but are pivotal elements in shaping our world.

Far from being mere digital stand-ins, these avatars are becoming powerful symbols of identity within the digital universe. The chapter examines their utility and value, highlighting them as cultural application layers that seamlessly integrate virtual experiences with real-world relevance.

In a world where digital avatars exist, they need destinations to explore and interact. Enter the concept of digital land and worlds within the Metaverse. This discussion isn't just about viewing digital land as an investment; it's about recognising it as a foundation for diverse virtual experiences. This chapter looks into the social and economic ramifications of property rights in the digital realm, exploring how this notion catalyses economic growth, community shaping, and plays a pivotal role in the burgeoning digital economy.

Furthermore, the chapter scrutinises the broader social and economic effects of digital identities and assets. It seeks to understand how they reshape social dynamics and economic landscapes, particularly focusing on the culture of Generation Z and crypto-native communities. This exploration aims to provide a comprehensive understanding of the current state and potential transformations in digital social interactions and economies.

A critical examination follows, analysing how digital identities and assets influence social dynamics, potentially fostering greater diversity and equality in future digital interactions.

This chapter is more than just an academic exploration; it's an invitation to immerse oneself in the dynamic convergence of technology, identity, and culture within the Metaverse. As readers embark on this journey, they find themselves at the forefront of a new digital era. In this era, avatars and digital land transcend their conceptual boundaries, becoming integral parts of our digital existence. Just like Anna, whose life seamlessly blends her physical work in the rainforest with her influential digital avatar, readers too can envision a future where their digital and physical selves co-exist and complement each other. Anna's story is a beacon, illuminating the possibilities that await in a world where our digital identities are as rich and impactful as our real-world actions. This narrative serves as both a guide and an inspiration, encouraging readers to consider how they might navigate and shape this emerging digital landscape.

4.2 Evolution and Role of PFP NFTs

4.2.1 *What Is a PFP?*

A PFP simply stands for Profile Picture—a term universally understood and a key component of social media platforms. PFPs can be anything and often reflect a user's personality, interests, or current mood. They are a digital canvas for self-expression. People choose different PFPs for different social media platforms—professional on LinkedIn, casual on Instagram, and perhaps more personal or humorous on platforms like Facebook or Twitter. PFPs can often be updated to reflect current events or global issues or to support various social causes. For example, during significant political campaigns, users might adopt images or symbols associated with the cause as their profile picture to show solidarity or raise awareness. The point is that PFPs are not static; they are ever evolving, reflecting the fluidity of our digital lives.

PFPs predate the Internet but have become more significant with its advent. Starting in 2002, Mark Zuckerberg, then a student at Harvard University, drew inspiration from the university's printed directory, commonly referred to as the Harvard Facebook. This directory, similar to those used by other universities, included basic information about students along with their photos, confirming the use of profile pictures even before the advent of the Internet. It was this concept that Zuckerberg expanded into the digital realm, leading to the creation of Facebook in 2004. Although not the first of its kind, Facebook popularised and streamlined the use of profile pictures on social media, embedding their significance in a user's digital identity and setting a blueprint for many social platforms that followed.

The explosion of NFTs (Non-Fungible Tokens) in recent years has significantly impacted the use and perception of PFPs on the Internet. Traditionally, PFPs served as a means of personal expression and digital identity representation on social media. However, with the rise of NFTs, they have gained a new dimension of value and status symbol. People began purchasing unique digital artworks as NFTs and using them as their PFPs not just for personal expression but also as a display of ownership and investment in digital art. This trend was fuelled by the scarcity and uniqueness of NFTs which are often one-of-a-kind or part of a limited series. As a result, certain NFT collections, such as CryptoPunks and Bored Ape Yacht Club, became highly coveted and recognisable, turning PFPs into symbols of exclusivity and membership in a new digital culture. This shift has not only transformed the nature of PFPs but also contributed to a broader conversation about the value and legitimacy of digital art and ownership in the Internet age.

4.2.2 History of PFPs

PFPs and forms of self-expression can be dated back over 6400 years ago with cave paintings amongst the earliest forms of human expression. While they predominantly feature animals and hunting scenes, many also include human figures and tracings of hands. These rudimentary representations can be seen as the earliest attempts at depicting human presence and identity. Small figurines and sculptures, like the famous Venus of Willendorf created around 25,000 BCE, depict human forms. Though they are not portraits in the modern sense, these figures represent an early fascination with the human form and identity.

Portraiture dates back to at least ancient Egypt, which flourished over 5000 years ago, and has been a cornerstone of personal representation throughout history. Egyptian portraits, often painted on wooden coffins, not only immortalised the deceased but also exhibited distinctive stylistic elements such as the combination of profile and frontal perspectives. Over the centuries, portraiture evolved to capture more realistic likenesses, reflecting a growing interest in individual identity and humanism. The Renaissance marked a significant shift in this art form, emphasising individualism and realism, and portraits became viewed by the nobility and wealthy patrons as a luxury and a testament to their status. However, these artistic representations were generally inaccessible to the common man.

Advancements in photography in the early nineteenth century marked a significant turning point. By 1816, Joseph Nicéphore Niépce created the first recognised camera known as the heliograph. Twenty years later, Louis Daguerre developed the daguerreotype, a process much closer to the photographic camera concept known today. By 1888, the commercialisation of cameras, exemplified by the Kodak, offered a medium of human self-expression to everyone. This democratisation of portrait-making marked a departure from the exclusivity of traditional portraiture. Today, with the ease of phones equipped with cameras and social platforms, representing one's identity has expanded to a global scale allowing for instantaneous and diverse forms of self-portrayal.

4.2.3 PFPs as Identities

During the digital age, with the rise of digital personas, the concept of PFPs has been used as a means of personal branding and identity. These personas are curated representations of individuals in online spaces, crafted through various digital mediums, with PFPs being one of the most prominent. Users often choose images that reflect their personalities, beliefs, and values. PFPs are more than mere images—they are akin to digital masks or avatars. This analogy is apt because, like masks, PFPs can reveal, conceal, or accentuate aspects of a user's identity. They allow users to portray themselves in ways that may not be possible in the physical world, offering a form of escapism, fantasy, or idealised representation.

4.2.4 PFPs and Community Building

PFPs largely serve as a unifying symbol within specific online communities. For instance, fans of a particular genre, hobby, or interest group often use related PFPs to identify and connect with like-minded individuals, fostering a sense of community and belonging.

PFP NFTs are not just digital assets but also serve as keys to virtual communities. Owning a particular PFP NFT often grants access to exclusive online spaces, events, or networks thereby facilitating a unique form of community engagement. PFP NFTs create a shared identity among their holders. For instance, owning a specific NFT from a popular collection like CryptoPunks or Bored Ape Yacht Club can instantly connect individuals with a global community of holders who share similar interests and values. This shared identity goes beyond the digital image and commerce; it represents a collective ethos or lifestyle that members identify with. This sense of belonging and identity is further enhanced when these communities engage in social and political causes. For example, in response to social issues like the Black Lives Matter movement, digital communities have utilised their platforms for advocacy and support. The use of specific emojis, like the raised fist in different skin tones (e.g., ✊🏿), has become a common practice within these communities to show solidarity and raise awareness. Moreover, these digital communities often extend their support through fundraising and awareness campaigns. By leveraging the network and visibility that comes with belonging to a digital tribe members can mobilise resources and attention for causes they care about that demonstrates the potential of digital assets in facilitating real-world impact.

4.2.5 Future Opportunities and Challenges in PFPs

In the evolving landscape of PFPs, the integration of Artificial Intelligence can revolutionise PFPs, transforming them from static images to dynamic entities that offer a more profound level of personalisation and self-expression.

AI has the capability to tailor PFPs to individual users, going beyond predesigned templates. This personalisation can be based on a user's digital footprint, preferences, or even as far as their emotional state gleaned from their online interactions.

People's identities are not static; they evolve with time and experiences. AI can craft PFPs to mirror a user's personality and current mood thus adding a new depth to digital identity. This ensures that PFPs are not just snapshots but evolving portraits that reflect these changes. Imagine a PFP that matures as the user ages, adapting to significant life milestones—a graduation, a new career, or personal achievements. This dynamic representation adds a rich layer to the concept of digital identity—the PFPs become alive.

Currently, the entry cost for NFT-based PFPs presents a significant barrier often resulting in gated communities and limiting wider adoption. High prices for the most sought-after communities restrict access and impede the potential for mass adoption. PFP NFTs have become modern Veblen goods where their high value and status are enhanced by their exclusivity and high price, serving as symbols of social status in the digital realm. To truly democratise this space, PFPs need to become as affordable and accessible as buying in-game skins in popular games like Fortnite where skins are inexpensive yet personalisable. By integrating NFT technology,users gain tangible ownership of their digital assets. This shift not only ensures that investments are not lost when one stops engaging with a specific platform but also opens the possibility of transferring these assets across different digital spaces. Lowering the entry point and emphasising ownership and portability can pave the way for broader acceptance and integration of PFP NFTs in our digital lives.

4.2.6 Concluding Remarks

In the digital age, the evolution of Profile Pictures (PFPs) encapsulates the dynamic interplay between one's physical and virtual identities. This section has traced the journey of PFPs from ancient human expressions to modern digital avatars, highlighting their pivotal role in personal branding, identity, and community building. The rise of NFTs has transformed PFPs, imbuing them with new dimensions of value and exclusivity. This transformation mirrors the broader shift in how people perceive and construct their identities in a world increasingly defined by digital interactions.

Anna's story exemplifies this integration. By day, she is an environmental scientist in a remote rainforest, grounded in tangible reality. By night, her digital avatar, represented by a unique PFP, leads a global community, influencing real-world environmental initiatives. Anna's dual existence illustrates the synergy between people's physical selves and digital personas, showing how PFPs can enhance one's impact in both realms.

As PFPs evolve, they serve not only as personal avatars but also as unifying symbols within digital communities. They grant access to exclusive networks, fostering a sense of belonging and collective identity.

Advancements in Artificial Intelligence will further personalise PFPs, making them dynamic entities that reflect one's evolving identities while democratising NFT access to pave the way for broader acceptance in their digital lives. The narrative of PFPs encapsulates the convergence of technology, identity, and culture, mirroring how Anna's life seamlessly blends her physical work with her influential digital avatar.

4.3 Digital Avatars as Identity Markers

4.3.1 Exploring Virtual Realities

Virtual Reality (VR) and Augmented Reality (AR) are two technologies that fundamentally alter one's perception of the digital world yet they do so in distinct ways. VR immerses users in a completely artificial environment created entirely by computer graphics. It is often experienced through a headset and sometimes additional equipment that isolates the user from the real world, placing them inside a virtual one. For example, a VR game might transport players to a fantastical landscape where every visual and auditory element is part of a cohesive, interactive virtual experience.

In contrast, AR overlays digital information onto the real world. It enhances, rather than replaces, the user's real-world experience. AR is commonly experienced through smartphones or AR glasses which display digital images or information on top of what the user naturally sees. A real-world example of AR is the mobile game Pokémon Go where players use their smartphones to find and capture virtual Pokémon characters that appear to be in their real-world environment. The game utilises the phone's camera and GPS to overlay the Pokémon on a live view of the physical world blending digital elements with real-life settings.

Both technologies offer unique experiences and have different applications. VR is often used for immersive gaming, training simulations, or virtual tours, providing a complete escape from reality. AR, on the other hand, is used in more practical applications like navigation, educational tools, and interactive marketing, enhancing real-world interactions with digital elements. The key contrast lies in VR's ability to create a whole new world for the user while AR brings a layer of digital enrichment to our existing reality.

4.3.2 Significance and Impact of Avatars in Virtual Spaces

The significance and impact of avatars in digital spaces have become increasingly complex, especially in light of disturbing events and comprehensive studies on virtual reality (VR) usage. The case of the alleged sexual assault of a young girl in the Metaverse in 2024, investigated by British police,[1] starkly illustrates the darker potential of these digital realms. The victim's avatar was reportedly attacked by several others while she was engaged in a VR game, raising serious concerns about safety and the nature of crime in virtual environments.

[1] Sales, N.J. (2024). A girl was allegedly raped in the metaverse. Is this the beginning of a dark new future? The Guardian. [online] 5 Jan. Available at: https://www.theguardian.com/commentisfree/2024/jan/05/metaverse-sexual-assault-vr-game-online-safety-meta [Accessed 22 June 2024].

This alarming incident underscores the urgent need for robust safety measures in VR and the Metaverse. A groundbreaking report titled Safeguarding the Metaverse[2] by the Institution of Engineering and Technology (IET) highlights these concerns. The report coincides with the UK government's deliberation of the new Online Safety Bill[3] and stresses the importance of incorporating comprehensive measures for regulating VR activities within the bill. The IET's study reveals that the next generation is expected to spend approximately 10 years of their life in VR, equivalent to about 2 hours and 45 minutes per day. This prediction is based on the median projected lifespan of today's children being 88.75 years.

4.3.3 Economic Landscape of Avatars: Analysing Market Dynamics

The avatar market is on a trajectory of exponential growth with forecasts suggesting a global market valuation of $527 billion by 2030.[4] This surge is attributed to the effectiveness of digital human avatars in product promotion through relatable messaging and their fully controllable actions by the organisations that use them. Another segment of this burgeoning market is the 3D avatar solutions, projected to reach $544.87 million by 2028,[5] growing at a compound annual rate of 31.3% from 2022. This growth is driven by the adoption of 3D body scanners across various industries like health care, fashion, and art, where they are used to create 3D human replicas for diverse purposes.

The increasing use of 3D avatars across industries is anticipated to enhance familiarity and comfort with avatars among the general population. This is expected to drive further adoption of virtual worlds and games utilising 3D avatars leading to increased traffic and revenue for these platforms. Development of new virtual worlds and games tailored to industries that have adopted 3D avatars, like media and entertainment, fashion, and health care, will likely contribute to this growth.

In Web 2.0, virtual worlds have become platforms for sharing digital experiences while providing a sense of physical reality. Creating and using avatars is often essential for users to play, interact, and represent themselves digitally. Avatars are

---

[2] Safeguarding the metaverse. (n.d.). Available at: https://www.theiet.org/media/9836/safeguarding-the-metaverse.pdf [Accessed 22 June 2024].

[3] Online Safety Act (2023). [online]. Available at: https://bills.parliament.uk/bills/3137 [Accessed 22 June 2024].

[4] www.emergenresearch.com. (n.d.). Digital Human Avatar Market Size, Share, Industry Forecast by 2032. [online] Available at: https://www.emergenresearch.com/request-history/897 [Accessed 22 June 2024].

[5] Partners, T.I. (2022). 31.3% CAGR for 3D Avatar Solution Market to Gain $544.87Mn, Globally, by 2028. [online] GlobeNewswire News Room. Available at: https://www.globenewswire.com/en/news-release/2022/12/06/2568469/0/en/31-3-CAGR-for-3D-Avatar-Solution-Market-to-Gain-544-87Mn-Globally-by-2028.html [Accessed 22 June 2024].

crucial for game developers to monetise user engagement, and they increasingly connect different virtual environments. Notable Web 2.0 virtual world applications like Minecraft, Fortnite, Roblox, Zepeto, and Second Life differ in game design, modes, and the roles of in-game avatars and items. These platforms, largely free-to-play, generate revenue by selling avatars and items or through a share in the sales of user-generated content.

For instance, Roblox reported[6] in 2021 that 5.8 billion free and paid items were exchanged in the game and users had created more than 25 million virtual items. Zepeto, a South Korean mobile chat app where users interact as 3D avatars, sold 2.4 billion items between 2018 and 2021.[7] The monetisation potential varies depending on buyer intentions, the role and nature of avatars in the game, and the availability of complementary items with aesthetic or functional appeal.

The future of avatars in Web 3.0 (a fair, decentralised, and community/creator-owned Internet built around cryptocurrencies, NFTs and blockchains) is poised to transform these Web 2.0 components. Although avatar markets in Web 3.0 are just emerging, a large number of different avatars already exist which users can own in the form of NFTs. The Sandbox, for example, showcases a variety of avatars as NFTs, highlighting the potential for a more equitable and participatory economic model in the Metaverse.

In summary, the economic landscape of avatars is experiencing significant growth and transformation. The increasing adoption of 3D avatars, the pivotal role of avatars in Web 2.0 virtual worlds, and the emerging avatar markets in Web 3.0 all point towards a robust, diverse, and rapidly evolving avatar economy in the Metaverse.

4.3.4 The Role of Avatars in Personalising the Metaverse Experience

In the burgeoning world of the Metaverse, avatars play a pivotal role in personalising the user experience. These digital personas act as the primary medium through which individuals interact, socialise, and conduct transactions in these virtual spaces. The emergence of decentralised technologies like blockchain and the advent of NFTs have revolutionised the concept of digital identity and ownership, adding a new layer of personalisation and authenticity to the Metaverse experience.

The breakthroughs provided by Satoshi Nakamoto, the pseudonymous person or group who developed Bitcoin, laid the foundation for this new era of digital ownership. By introducing the concept of decentralised ledgers, Satoshi enabled a system

---

[6] Roblox (2022). A YEAR ON ROBLOX: 2021 IN DATA. [online] Roblox Blog. Available at: https://blog.roblox.com/2022/01/year-roblox-2021-data/ [Accessed 22 June 2024].

[7] Global, K.E.D. (n.d.). Metaverse platform Zepeto user base exceeds 300 million. [online] KED Global. Available at: https://www.kedglobal.com/metaverse/newsView/ked202203040009 [Accessed 22 June 2024].

where digital assets could be owned, traded, and verified without the need for a central authority. This technology is at the heart of NFTs, which are unique digital tokens that can be linked to digital content, providing proof of ownership and provenance. In the Metaverse, NFTs enable users to own, display, and trade digital assets like avatar outfits, virtual real estate, and artwork with the assurance that their ownership is secure and verifiable.

The integration of NFTs and decentralised ledger technology in the Metaverse significantly enhances the personalisation of the avatar experience. Users can not only customise their avatars'appearance and attributes but also possess a verified ownership of their digital assets. This aspect of provenance is crucial in a digital ecosystem where replication and piracy are common concerns. With NFTs, each asset tied to an avatar is unique and its history traceable thereby adding a layer of authenticity to the user's digital persona.

Moreover, the use of decentralised ledgers for asset ownership in the Metaverse has broader implications. It allows for the creation of a more equitable and transparent digital economy where users have true ownership over their digital assets. This ownership extends beyond mere aesthetic customisation, enabling users to engage in complex economic activities within the Metaverse such as buying, selling, and investing in virtual goods and properties.

The personalisation of avatars through NFTs and blockchain technology represents a significant shift in how digital identities are perceived and valued. It empowers users to have a more meaningful and invested presence in the Metaverse, bridging the gap between the virtual and the real world. This evolution of avatars as not just digital representations but as holders of tangible, owned digital assets marks a pivotal moment in the development of the Metaverse as a fully-fledged digital ecosystem.

The evolving role of avatars in personalising the Metaverse experience extends beyond digital representation and asset ownership; it also has profound bilateral effects on users' physical and psychological states. Research[8] conducted by the University of Nicosia underscores this phenomenon. The study found that users who engaged with avatars possessing stronger characteristics exhibited measurable increases in physical strength in various tests. This intriguing correlation suggests that the virtual and physical realms are more interconnected than previously thought. The embodiment of certain traits in a virtual avatar can have tangible effects on the user's real-world capabilities and perceptions. This further emphasises the significance of avatars in the Metaverse not just as tools for personalisation and ownership but also as influential factors in the holistic user experience, blending the boundaries between the virtual and the physical world.

[8] Christou, C. and Michael, D., 2014. Aliens versus Humans: Do Avatars Make a Difference in How We Play the Game? 2014 6th International Conference on Games and Virtual Worlds for Serious Applications (VS-GAMES), Valletta, Malta, 9–12 September. IEEE. Available at: https://doi.org/10.1109/VS-Games.2014.7012029 [Accessed 22 June 2022].

4.3.5 Concluding Remarks

In the digital age, digital avatars serve as crucial identity markers significantly influencing personal branding, community building, and economic dynamics. This section has traced their evolution from simple Profile Pictures (PFPs) on social media to valuable digital assets enhanced by technologies like Virtual Reality (VR), Augmented Reality (AR), and NFTs. These advancements have transformed avatars into powerful symbols of digital culture and social status, revealing the deep interplay between our physical and virtual identities.

Anna's dual existence as an environmental scientist by day and a digital community leader by night epitomises this integration. In her professional role, AR enhances her real-world experience, overlaying digital data onto her surroundings in the rainforest, aiding in her research. By night, her VR-based digital avatar leads discussions and initiatives in virtual spaces, influencing global environmental strategies. This seamless transition between physical and digital realms demonstrates the profound synergy between real-world and virtual engagements.

The economic landscape of avatars is rapidly expanding with significant market growth driven by their adoption across various industries. The University of Nicosia study underscores the physical and psychological impact of avatars, finding that users with stronger digital personas exhibited increased real-world capabilities. This correlation suggests that digital avatars can influence our real-world attributes, further emphasising their importance.

4.4 Digital Land and Ownership in the Metaverse

4.4.1 Defining Digital Land in the Metaverse

Digital land in the Metaverse represents a revolutionary concept, diverging significantly from traditional land and property notions. Unlike physical land, which is tangible and finite, digital land exists within the virtual space of the Metaverse. This land is not constrained by physical limitations such as geographical boundaries or natural resources. Instead, it is defined by the parameters of the virtual world it resides in, often governed by the rules and mechanics of the specific platform or game it belongs to.

The following table provides a succinct comparison between digital land in the Metaverse and traditional land, highlighting their distinct characteristics and dynamics in various aspects.

Aspect	Digital Land in the Metaverse	Traditional Land
Nature	Virtual, existing within digital environments.	Physical, tangible, and geographically located.
Limitations	Bound by the parameters of the virtual world, virtually unlimited scalability.	Subject to geographical, environmental, and regulatory limitations.
Usage	Diverse applications including social gatherings, commercial activities, gaming, and virtual real estate development.	Residential, commercial, agricultural, industrial etc., limited by zoning and physical capabilities.
Ownership	Often represented by NFTs, governed by blockchain technology.	Governed by legal documentation and land registry systems.
Value determination	Based on utility, popularity, community engagement, and potential for development within the virtual platform.	Determined by location, size, accessibility, market demand, and physical characteristics.
Accessibility	Accessible to anyone with internet access, irrespective of physical location.	Requires physical presence or access, limited by location.
Development and modification	Limited only by the platform's technological capabilities and user creativity.	Subject to physical, regulatory, and environmental constraints.
Transferability	Enabled by blockchain technology that operates 24/7, 365 days a year, transcending geographical boundaries.	Can be time-consuming and complex involving multiple legal and administrative processes and often considered illiquid compared to digital assets.
Potential for innovation	High potential for innovation, allowing for creations and experiences not possible in the physical world.	Innovation is generally confined to construction techniques, land use planning, and sustainability practices.
Community and social interaction	Facilitates the formation of global virtual communities, transcending physical boundaries.	Community formation is geographically bounded and influenced by physical proximity.
Governance	Governed by the rules and policies of the virtual platform, often decentralised.	Governed by local, regional, and national laws and regulations.
Market size in USD (today)	Billions	Trillions

Comparative Analysis: Digital Land in the Metaverse vs. Traditional Land
The concept of ownership of digital land in the Metaverse represents a transformative shift from the traditional understanding of property rights. Property rights, as a legal concept, have evolved over millennia with their origins tracing back to ancient times. However, the modern conception of property rights, particularly in the context of a structured legal system, began to take shape during the late Middle Ages in Europe. One pivotal moment in the evolution of property rights was the Magna Carta in 1215. While not specifically about property rights as we understand them

today, it laid foundational principles for due process and the idea that the monarchy could not arbitrarily seize property, a precursor to modern property rights.

Historically, the Internet has functioned without the notion of property rights for digital spaces, akin to a vast, unclaimed territory. In this landscape, centralised actors such as Meta (formerly Facebook) and Google have emerged as powerful figures akin to landlords in a digital realm. In the digital space, content creators significantly contribute yet lack ownership and control over their creations and find themselves in a tenant-like relationship where the content they create effectively becomes owned or controlled by these platform operators. However, the introduction of property rights to digital assets, exemplified by the use of NFTs, marks a significant evolution. These NFTs not only provide proof of ownership and uniqueness but also introduce a layer of legitimacy and value to digital assets.

This paradigm shift in digital property rights could have profound implications for the global digital economy, similar to the impact observed in China's economic expansion after the introduction of property rights. Before their establishment, China's economic growth was constrained, lacking the incentives and security that come with recognised ownership. Once such rights were institutionalised, it unleashed a wave of entrepreneurial activity and investment, significantly contributing to the country's rapid economic expansion.

Similarly, establishing property rights in the digital realm, particularly in the Metaverse, is expected to catalyse growth in the global digital economy. It will not only foster innovation and investment in virtual spaces but also enhance the overall economic value of the web.

4.4.2 The Evolution of Digital Land Ownership

The evolution of digital land ownership is a narrative of rapid technological innovation and changing perceptions of virtual space. This journey begins in the early virtual worlds where the concept of owning a piece of the digital realm first emerged. Early online platforms like Second Life, introduced in the early 2000s, pioneered the idea of users purchasing, developing, and trading virtual land. These initial steps were rudimentary, often lacking the sophistication and security features of modern platforms, but they laid the groundwork for the concept of digital property.

As technology progressed so did the complexity and capabilities of these virtual spaces. The introduction of more advanced gaming environments and social platforms expanded the scope and appeal of digital land. The concept started to attract a broader audience, transitioning from a niche interest to a more mainstream phenomenon. This shift was marked by increased user engagement and the development of more intricate and immersive virtual worlds.

The real turning point in digital land ownership came with the advent of blockchain technology and the subsequent rise of the Metaverse. Blockchain's introduction brought a level of security, transparency, and decentralisation previously unseen in digital transactions. It enabled the creation of NFTs which allowed for the unique identification and ownership of digital assets including land in the Metaverse. This technology transformed digital land from a mere concept into a tangible asset class.

In contemporary Metaverse platforms, digital land ownership has reached new heights of sophistication. Platforms like Decentraland and The Sandbox exemplify this evolution, offering users not just ownership but also complete control over their digital environments. These platforms allow for the creation, development, and monetisation of virtual spaces turning them into hubs of social interaction, commerce, and creativity.

The evolution of digital land ownership reached a new milestone with events like Yuga Labs' Otherside Metaverse land sale in 2022. Yuga Labs, the creator of the hugely successful NFT project Bored Ape Yacht Club (BAYC), experienced a significant moment in the history of digital land with their Otherside's Otherdeed NFT sales. In less than 24 hours, they generated over $561 million in sales, illustrating the immense market demand and financial potential of digital land in the Metaverse.

This event also highlighted the technical and economic challenges in the digital land space. The Otherdeed mint, which saw 55,000 NFTs minted at a cost of around $5800 each, caused a massive surge in Ethereum network traffic.[9] This surge led to what is known as a gas war, where the demand for fast transactions clogged the network, sending transaction fees to thousands of dollars per transaction. Such events underscore the growing pains of a burgeoning digital economy, where infrastructure and demand are continually adapting.

4.4.3 Economic Models and Value of Digital Land

The economic landscape of digital land in the Metaverse is rapidly evolving, blending traditional real estate concepts with the unique attributes of virtual environments. This is evident in the significant financial activities and branding strategies observed in various virtual land platforms.

Valuation of Digital Land The value of digital land is multifaceted, influenced by its utility, popularity, and developmental potential, alongside factors like location and branding. A prime example is the high-profile purchase of land in the Snoopverse within The Sandbox, an Ethereum-based platform. A plot adjacent to a digital recreation of Snoop Dogg's mansion sold for about $450,000, highlighting the premium placed on proximity to celebrity-driven projects and exclusive experiences.[10]

---

[9] Mehta, I. (2022). How the BAYC metaverse mint raised Ethereum gas fees to thousands of dollars. [online] TNW | Fintech-Ecommerce. Available at: https://thenextweb.com/news/bayc-Metaverse-otherside-mint-gas-fees-analysis [Accessed 22 June 2024].

[10] Chirinos, C. (2022). Someone just paid $450,000 to be Snoop Dogg's neighbor in the metaverse. Here's how you can live by a celebrity too. [online] Fortune. Available at: https://fortune.com/2022/02/02/how-to-buy-metaverse-real-estate-snoop-dogg-celebrity-neighbor/ [Accessed 22 June 2024].

Trade Mechanisms Digital land trades via blockchain marketplaces using NFTs and cryptocurrencies ensuring secure and transparent global transactions. The limited number of available plots on platforms like The Sandbox and Decentraland, coupled with high-profile sales and brand involvements, underscores the robustness and speculative nature of these marketplaces.

Contribution to Virtual Economies Digital land is pivotal to virtual economies, serving as a platform for diverse economic activities. Brands and investors are recognising the potential of the Metaverse as seen with Adidas purchasing 144 plots in The Sandbox.[11] The success of events like Travis Scott's Fortnite concert, drawing over 27 million viewers,[12] illustrates the commercial potential of these digital spaces.

Considering the current trends and significant sales in virtual platforms like The Sandbox and Decentraland, it is evident that the digital land market is growing rapidly. Given this context and the global real estate market's projected value of $613.60 trillion in 2023,[13] it is conceivable that the digital land market could become a significant economic force. While it may not surpass the value of the global real estate market in the near future, its potential for growth, especially with increasing interest and investment in virtual platforms, indicates that digital real estate could become a substantial sector in its own right.

4.4.4 Digital Land as a Platform for Innovation

Unlike physical real estate, digital land transcends geographical and physical constraints opening up new avenues for entrepreneurial ventures.

Creative Ventures

The Metaverse has become a haven for artists and designers. For instance, digital art collectives like OnCyber provide immersive and customised art experiences. These interactive exhibits, accessible to anyone globally, allow visitors to manipulate and interact with the art pieces in real-time. Another example is virtual fashion shows, showcasing 3D-designed clothing that users can view and purchase directly within the Metaverse. These use cases exemplify how digital land facilitates creativity unrestrained by physical limitations, fostering a new genre of artistic expression.

---

[11] Yahoo Finance. (2021). Adidas Partners with Coinbase, The Sandbox Could be Next. [online] Available at: https://finance.yahoo.com/news/adidas-partners-coinbase-sandbox-could-152915469.html [Accessed 22 June 2024].

[12] Reuters, 2020. Travis Scott's Fortnite concert series draws 27.7M unique views. Reuters, [online] 27 April. Available at: https://www.reuters.com/article/idUSFLM2PGVN5/ [Accessed 22 June 2024].

[13] Statista. (n.d.). Real Estate - Worldwide | Statista Market Forecast. [online] Available at: https://www.statista.com/outlook/fmo/real-estate/worldwide?currency=usd [Accessed 22 June 2024].

Social Engagement
Digital land also redefines social interactions. A notable example is a virtual community space developed on a Metaverse platform, designed to host gatherings, meetings, and entertainment events. This space can host virtual concerts attended by avatars from around the world, breaking the barrier of physical attendance and offering a new form of communal experience. Additionally, educational institutions can capitalise on digital land to create virtual campuses where students from diverse geographical backgrounds can interact, learn, and collaborate in ways that mirror and extend beyond traditional classrooms.

Virtual Storefronts
In the realm of business, digital land offers unprecedented opportunities. Virtual storefronts where customers can browse and interact with products in a 3D environment. This approach not only provides customers with a novel shopping experience but also allows the storefront to showcase products in innovative ways, free from the physical constraints of traditional retail spaces.

Enabling Technologies
These innovative uses of digital land are underpinned by advancing technologies like blockchain, which ensures secure and transparent transactions, and VR/AR which enhances the immersive experience. The integration of AI also plays a crucial role enabling personalised experiences and interactions within these digital spaces.

Looking ahead, the potential of digital land as a platform for innovation appears boundless. With advancements in technology and growing acceptance of virtual environments, digital land is poised to become a key driver in the evolution of entrepreneurial landscapes.

4.4.5 The Role of NFTs in Digital Land Ownership

The integration of NFTs in digital land ownership marks a significant evolution in the realm of virtual real estate. NFTs have emerged as pivotal tools in legitimising and streamlining the ownership and transfer processes of digital land.

Unique Ownership
Each NFT is unique, representing a specific parcel of digital land. This uniqueness ensures that each digital land parcel has a single, verifiable owner, bringing clarity and security to ownership in the Metaverse. The NFT acts as a digital deed.

Transparency and Security
The blockchain technology underlying NFTs provides a transparent and immutable ledger of ownership. This technology ensures that ownership records are tamper-proof and publicly accessible, fostering a high level of trust in digital land transactions.

Simplified Transactions
NFTs facilitate a more streamlined process for buying, selling, and transferring digital land. Unlike traditional illiquid real estate transactions, which often involve lengthy processes and multiple intermediaries, NFT transactions can be executed swiftly peer-to-peer. This efficiency not only makes transactions quicker but also more cost-effective.

Democratising Access
NFTs lower the entry barrier to land ownership in the Metaverse. Digital land, tokenised as NFTs, can be more accessible compared to physical real estate both in terms of cost and regulatory requirements. This democratisation opens up opportunities for a wider range of investors and enthusiasts to participate in the virtual real estate market.

4.4.6 Future Implications

Looking forward, NFTs in digital land ownership are poised to drive innovation in the Metaverse. They offer the potential for new economic models and forms of digital interaction. The integration of NFTs with other emerging technologies like DeFi (Decentralised Finance) could further enhance the utility, value, and experience of owning digital land. Here are some key ways this integration could unfold:

Yield Generation Digital landowners could potentially generate yield from their virtual properties. This could be through virtual leasing where they rent out their digital space for events, advertisements, or storefronts. Integrating with DeFi protocols, these rental agreements could be tokenised, allowing landowners to earn passive income in the form of crypto assets.

Collateralised Loans Digital land NFTs could be used as collateral in DeFi lending protocols. This would allow landowners to borrow funds by staking their virtual land enabling them to leverage their digital assets without liquidating them. The value of the land could be determined by factors such as location, size, and utility within the Metaverse.

Fractional Ownership and Investing DeFi protocols could enable fractional ownership of digital land. This means that a high-value virtual property could be owned collectively by multiple investors each holding a fraction of the property as a token. This democratises access to investment opportunities in prime virtual real estate.

Liquidity Pools and Staking Digital landowners could participate in liquidity pools, staking their land NFTs to provide liquidity to specific DeFi platforms. In return, they could earn rewards or a share of the transaction fees generated by the platform.

Governance and DAOs (Decentralised Autonomous Organisations) Landowners in the Metaverse could form or join DAOs using their land NFTs to vote on decisions regarding the development and governance of virtual spaces. This could include decisions on infrastructure, community events, or integration with various DeFi protocols.

Tokenisation of Development Projects Developers in the Metaverse could tokenise their projects, allowing investors to buy tokens representing a stake in the project. Funds raised could be used for development while investors could benefit from the appreciation of the property or revenue generated from it.

Smart Contract Enabled Transactions Smart contracts can automate various aspects of digital land transactions including sales, rentals, and revenue sharing. This reduces the need for intermediaries and streamlines operations thus making transactions more efficient and secure.

Cross-Metaverse Interactions As the Metaverse evolves, interoperability between different virtual worlds could allow for cross-Metaverse transactions, potentially increasing the utility and value of digital land NFTs.

By integrating digital land ownership in the Metaverse with DeFi Lego blocks, there's the potential to create a more dynamic, accessible, and efficient virtual real estate market.

4.4.7 Community Building and Governance in Digital Spaces

In the digital frontier, where virtual lands stretch beyond traditional boundaries, the concept of community building takes on new dimensions. How do communities come together and navigate the complexities of governance in the vast expanse of digital landscapes?

Imagine a colony of ants, an often overlooked yet fascinating example of a complex self-organising system. Each ant, seemingly insignificant on its own, plays a vital role in the survival and prosperity of the entire colony. Their world, a network of interconnected tunnels and chambers, mirrors the intricate digital landscapes humans explore. Just as ants communicate through pheromones and collaborate to build and maintain their colony, individuals in digital communities use technology to connect, share ideas, and collectively shape their virtual environment.

Ants do not have a centralised authority; instead, they rely on a decentralised form of governance much like DAOs. Each ant's actions are guided by the collective needs and the shared intelligence of the colony. Similarly, in digital communities, each member's contributions and interactions contribute to the overall governance and evolution of the space. This analogy to an ant colony encapsulates the essence of how communities in digital realms form, function, and govern themselves, reflecting the principles of decentralised collaboration and collective decision-making.

The advent of decentralised autonomous organisations (DAOs) marks a pivotal shift in digital governance. DAOs represent a groundbreaking approach leveraging blockchain technology to democratise decision-making processes. These entities operate on a consensus basis, ensuring transparency and equity in governance, thereby deeply resonating with the ethos of virtual communities.

Crafting Community Rules: From Ideation to Implementation

Governance in digital spaces is not just about establishing rules but crafting them through collective wisdom. Communities in digital domains often start with a shared vision or interest evolving organically into structured entities. Here, the role of DAOs becomes crucial. They facilitate a platform where every member's voice can contribute to the rule-making process from conceptualising guidelines to implementing them effectively.

Conflict and Resolution: Navigating Challenges in Virtual Governance

No community is devoid of conflict and virtual spaces are no exception. DAOs provide a structured framework for conflict resolution ensuring that disagreements are addressed through fair and transparent mechanisms. This includes voting systems for major decisions and dispute resolution protocols thereby reflecting the collective will of the community while respecting individual perspectives.

Sustaining Community Engagement and Growth

The success of a digital community hinges on sustained engagement and adaptive governance. DAOs enable communities to evolve their governance structures in response to changing needs and challenges. This flexibility is key to nurturing a vibrant and resilient community capable of weathering the dynamic nature of digital landscapes.

The Future of Digital Communities

The future of digital communities with DAOs at the helm is poised to be a landscape of decentralised governance and collective decision-making. DAOs promise a democratic framework where power and responsibility are shared among all members. However, realising this potential requires addressing existing challenges.

Current DAO implementations reveal significant issues such as power imbalances with a Chainalysis report showing that less than 1% of holders in major DAO projects wield 90% of the voting power.[14] Furthermore, the centralisation of DAOs often occurs due to off-chain formations based on personal connections leading to a disparity in influence and power.

Low participation in voting processes is another challenge. Many members abstain from voting due to disinterest or strategic reasons leading to decisions that may not reflect the community's true collective will. Additionally, the transparency

[14] Team, C. (2023). Introduction to Decentralized Autonomous Organizations (DAOs). [online] Chainalysis. Available at: https://www.chainalysis.com/blog/introduction-to-decentralized-autonomous-organizations-daos [Accessed 22 June 2024].

of voting can deter meaningful participation as members know their votes are visible to all.

To address these issues the adoption of technologies like composable privacy and zero-knowledge proofs is suggested. These technologies can balance transparency with privacy in voting making the process more secure and encouraging greater participation.

While DAOs hold great promise for the future of digital communities their advancement depends on overcoming these fundamental challenges. The focus should be on ensuring fair power distribution, enhancing member participation in governance, and maintaining privacy and security in decision-making processes. Only then can DAOs truly embody their ideals of democratic and decentralised community governance.

4.4.8 Concluding Remarks

In the context of digital land and ownership within the Metaverse, the concept of property has been fundamentally redefined. Digital land, unconstrained by physical boundaries, offers unprecedented opportunities for innovation, community building, and economic growth. This section has highlighted how digital land diverges from traditional land in its nature, limitations, and usage, emphasising its potential to transform our digital interactions and economies.

Anna's dual existence exemplifies the integration of digital land into our lives. Extending her use case, Anna could purchase digital land in the Metaverse to create a virtual environmental research centre. This centre could host virtual seminars, showcase environmental data collected from her fieldwork, and provide an interactive platform for global collaboration.

Moreover, Anna could leverage NFTs to fund her projects allowing holders to participate in decision making via DAO-based structures. By creating and selling unique digital assets related to her research, such as virtual representations of endangered species or critical habitats, she could raise global awareness and generate financial support. This approach not only provides a new revenue stream but also fosters a global community of supporters invested in her work.

4.5 Social and Economic Implications

In the digital age, the concept of the Metaverse is reshaping our understanding of virtual interaction, economic potential, and societal inclusivity. The profound impact of this on social dynamics and economic opportunities is unquestionable.

With an anticipated astronomical expansion on the horizon, the evolution of our interactions and behaviours in the Metaverse is likely to see three significant trends: the changing social dynamics that redefine human interaction, the emergence of new economic models offering diverse opportunities, and the imperative of inclusivity and accessibility that ensures equitable participation. This section explores how these social and economic implications shape a comprehensive and sustainable digital future.

4.5.1 Changing Social Dynamics

Social media has changed how people behave and communicate. This will continue with the adoption of the Metaverse.

Examining the gaming industry as a prototype of the Metaverse, games such as Fortnite, which attract 45 million daily users,[15] and Roblox, with 70 million[16] users, demonstrate significant engagement. Remarkably, 75% of children aged 9–12 regularly play Roblox with their friends.[17] Given this level of immersion, the average young person is expected to spend 10,000 hours playing computer games by the age of 21.[18] Gaming, which primarily involves interacting in online digital worlds, is a fundamental aspect of life for Gen-Z who have not known an alternative. As more time is predicted to be spent online (now without the associated stigma), social interactions and behaviours will continue to evolve to align with the applications and environments in which users are engaging.

The concept of self and digital identity lies at the heart of how young people represent themselves, experiment, and signal to others who they are and what they stand for. The Metaverse offers a platform for individuals to reflect and display aspects of their identity without the constraints of the physical world. A truly digital global community will enable cultural exchanges to flourish, eliminating geographical and social barriers.

Customisable identity has played a pivotal role in making Zepeto, a South Korean avatar-centric social network, attract 400 million users[19] thereby becoming Asia's largest Metaverse platform. It allows users to interact in ways that are unimaginable

[15] Loveridge, S. (2019). How many people play Fortnite? Is it really as many as people say? [online] gamesradar. Available at: https://www.gamesradar.com/how-many-people-play-fortnite/ [Accessed 22 June 2024].

[16] Ruby, D. (2023). Roblox Statistics 2023 — (Users, Revenue & Trends). [online] DemandSage. Available at: https://www.demandsage.com/how-many-people-play-roblox [Accessed 22 June 2024].

[17] Liao, S. (2020). How Roblox became the 'it' game for tweens—and a massive business | CNN Business. [online] CNN. Available at: https://edition.cnn.com/2020/10/27/tech/roblox-explainer/index.html [Accessed 22 June 2024].

[18] West, G.L., Drisdelle, B.L., Konishi, K., Jackson, J., Jolicoeur, P. and Bohbot, V.D., 2015. Habitual action video game playing is associated with caudate nucleus-dependent navigational strategies. Proceedings of the Royal Society B, DOI: https://doi.org/10.1098/rspb.2014.2952.

[19] Hirschmiller, S. (2023, August 15). Zepeto, Jump Crypto joint venture ZTX raises $13M for Metaverse platform on Arbitrum. Decrypt. https://decrypt.co/152574/zepeto-jump-crypto-raise-13-million-ztx-metaverse-arbitrum

in the physical world. The allure of customising avatars has drawn brands like Gucci, Bulgari, and Nike to the Metaverse to experiment with digital fashion for avatars, often in the form of NFTs. These interactions are reshaping social norms where behaviours and group dynamics are influenced by the limitless possibilities of digital identity.

The creation of custom avatars in the Metaverse brings to the forefront a crucial question: How will individuals connect with and define their identities in this virtual space and how will these identities translate into the real world? It's already a common practice to adopt different personas based on the social media platform being used. For instance, a person might display a professional persona on LinkedIn, adopt a more relaxed social demeanour on Facebook with close friends, and choose to remain anonymous on Twitter to express controversial opinions without being cancelled. This raises the question of whether individuals will maintain multiple identities and avatars in various virtual worlds.

The power of choosing identities and anonymity cannot be overstated. For some, it offers a level playing field where opportunities such as jobs are awarded based on merit rather than through nepotism, thus eliminating bias and discrimination. However, for others, anonymity might serve as a shield for harmful behaviours like trolling or, in a future scenario involving haptic suits in the Metaverse, both physical and virtual forms of sexual harassment.

Regarding physical experiences, there is a concern that the Metaverse might supplant face-to-face interactions, impacting young people's ability to interpret tone, facial expressions, and the human touch. Although rapid technological advancements suggest these issues might be addressed eventually, the question remains whether it will truly replicate the same experience. The digital realm increasingly blurs the line between physical and virtual realities. Generation Z, and even more so Generation Alpha (those born between 2010 and 2024), navigate these digital landscapes with ease utilising these platforms for socialising, learning, and entertainment.

As the Metaverse evolves, traditional social hierarchies and structures are likely to gradually dissolve. If challenges like connectivity, affordable hardware, and digital literacy are overcome, the Metaverse could become a gateway to improved education, health care, financial services, and job opportunities for billions. However, concerted efforts from both public and private sectors are essential to build this infrastructure. Without it, there is a risk of exacerbating social inequalities, increasing segregation, and widening the wealth gap which would contradict the vision of the Metaverse as a globally accessible and egalitarian space.

4.5.2 Economic Transformation and New Opportunities

There is an abundance of opportunity across the Metaverse.

Jensen Huang, CEO of Nvidia, confidently stated, "I'm fairly sure at this point that the Metaverse is going to be a new economy that is larger than our current economy", further emphasising that "the virtual world will be larger in economics than the physical world". For context, the global GDP in 2023 stood at $100 trillion. Meanwhile, projections from the US investment bank Citi estimate that by 2030 the Metaverse could be valued between $8 and $13 trillion.[20] This is a significant leap from its estimated value in 2023, which was around $60–85 billion, highlighting the potential for exponential growth and economic impact in this burgeoning virtual space.

The Metaverse, akin to the Internet in its early stages, encompasses multiple layers of infrastructure, services, and applications. This complex ecosystem offers a wealth of opportunities for entrepreneurship and innovation both within the Metaverse itself and in its integration with the real world. A notable aspect of this ecosystem is its permissionless plug and play architecture which allows for seamless integration and compatibility among various components and systems and communities. This flexibility not only fosters a more dynamic and inclusive environment for development and growth but also paves the way for creative and technological advancements that can bridge the virtual and physical realms more effectively.

From the perspective of users, key elements like digital assets and digital identity are critical to navigating the Metaverse. In this borderless virtual realm, where traditional government and central banking systems are absent, cryptocurrencies have emerged as the preferred medium of exchange. The adoption of crypto payment rails in the Metaverse is significant for several reasons. They offer a trustless, permissionless, and decentralised form of transaction which aligns well with the nature of the Metaverse. Moreover, these rails serve as vital gateways for financial activities, enabling the seamless movement of funds into and out of the Metaverse. It is likely that fiat currencies will continue to co-exist alongside cryptocurrencies, stablecoins, and Central Bank Digital Currencies (CBDCs), offering a diverse range of financial options and enhancing the overall accessibility and functionality of the Metaverse's economy. This inclusive approach is especially important as it may provide unbanked populations with unprecedented access to financial services, bridging gaps in the current global financial system.

The demand for digital assets, such as digital land and virtual goods, is crucial for cultivating a thriving Metaverse economy. Unlike physical land, digital land is free from physical or geographical constraints. This lack of boundaries aims to democratise access to ownership and entrepreneurship in land and property, addressing real-world barriers like the prohibitively high costs of urban property that prevent many from buying real estate. The convergence of the physical and virtual worlds introduces novel applications and methodologies. One such innovation is digital twins where companies, governments, and cities map real-world atom-based assets into their virtual bit-based counterparts. This mapping is achieved using technologies like LiDAR and Neural Radiance Fields (NeRFs). Additionally, the

[20] www.citigroup.com. (n.d.). Metaverse and Money. [online] Available at: https://www.citigroup.com/global/insights/citigps/metaverse-and-money_20220330 [Accessed 22 June 2024].

tokenisation of both physical and digital assets, which are then fractionalised, standardised, and made tradeable, further bridges the gap between these two realms.

In virtual digital worlds, digital identity and avatars are becoming an economic cornerstone. They represent the initial point of entry into the Metaverse. Upon entering a virtual world, users must create or select an avatar to represent themselves. This avatar can act as a unique identifier facilitating financial transactions and social interactions. Alternatively, users may opt for multiple digital identities, varying according to the social network, game, business, or sport they are engaged in. Avatars have spawned an entire ecosystem centred around customisation, enhancements, and virtual goods, all typically taking the form of NFTs. This emerging market intersects with various industries, including fashion, entertainment, and advertising. In these sectors, digital personas play a crucial role in user engagement and brand representation, highlighting the growing influence of avatars in the virtual economy (Fig. 4.1).

The 8 billion people on Earth will each need a new identity or multiple identities.[21] AI-powered bots, necessitating their own identities, assets, and virtual goods, underscore why projections for the Metaverse's growth are immensely high. As these bots potentially become the predominant user base of the web, their influence

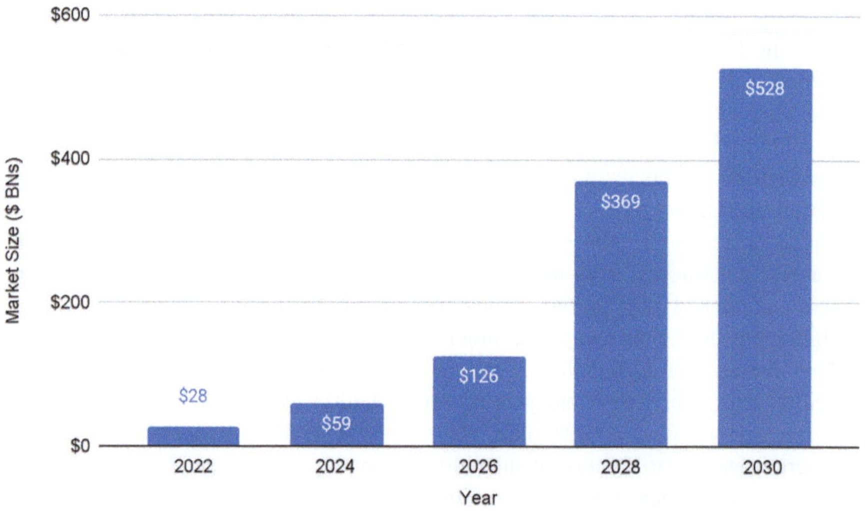

Fig. 4.1 Projected growth of the avatar market in billion USD (Avatars: Shaping Digital Identity in the Metaverse. (2023). Available at: https://www.blockchainresearchlab.org/wp-content/uploads/2020/05/Avatars-Shaping-Digital-Identity-in-the-Metaverse-Report-March-2023-Blockchain-Research-Lab.pdf. [Accessed 22 June 2024])

[21] www.citigroup.com. (n.d.). Metaverse and Money. [online] Available at: https://www.citigroup.com/global/insights/citigps/metaverse-and-money_20220330 [Accessed 22 June 2024].

will further amplify the demand for cryptocurrencies and NFTs. As Tyler Winklevoss, of crypto exchange Gemini, pointed out, cryptocurrencies are often described as the native currencies of machines and, given that machines vastly outnumber humans on Earth, their role in the Metaverse becomes even more significant. This trend suggests that AI bots could play a central role in shaping the economic model of the Metaverse marking a significant shift in how digital spaces are inhabited and utilised.

As the digital space continues to expand, it will inevitably give rise to new jobs and industries catering to its unique demands. Emerging roles such as digital fashion designers, avatar customisation specialists, and Metaverse security experts are expected to become commonplace. For perspective, the creator economy, valued at $250 billion in 2023, is projected to nearly double reaching $480 billion[22] by 2027. This growth trajectory is likely to be further propelled by the accelerating adoption of the Metaverse. Unshackled from the limitations of current technology, a surge of creativity is anticipated anchored in a blockchain-based model that redefines concepts of ownership and value. This evolution signals not just technological advancement but a significant shift in how people perceive and interact with digital environments.

However, there are risks. As Tim Sweeney, Epic Games CEO and creator of Fortnite, states, the "Metaverse is going to be far more pervasive and powerful than anything else. If one central company gains control of this they will become more powerful than any government and be a god on Earth". The potential commercialisation of the Metaverse plays into fears of a centrally controlled dystopian world as portrayed by science fiction films such as *The Matrix* and *Ready Player One*. Through enforcing app store commissions and technology, Apple and Google are already making a free, open Metaverse difficult for users and developers.

There are also technical challenges around interoperable decentralised identities which are yet to be solved. How is a single identity going to be represented across many different digital worlds that all look and feel different? There are also concerns around personal physical data. For example, a haptic suit provider will have a database of human biometrics while Worldcoin (founded by Sam Altman of OpenAI) has nearly 3 million human iris scans. Combined with AI- generated deep fakes, this could be a powerful weapon in the wrong hands. Lastly, the Metaverse will require huge amounts of compute and hardware which will further add to energy demand.

[22] Goldman Sachs (2023). The Creator Economy Could Approach Half-a-Trillion Dollars by 2027. [online] Goldman Sachs. Available at: https://www.goldmansachs.com/intelligence/pages/the-creator-economy-could-approach-half-a-trillion-dollars-by-2027.html [Accessed 22 June 2024].

4.5.3 Inclusivity and Accessibility in the Digital Space

Although the Metaverse has the potential to promote equality, diversity, and inclusion, there are near-term challenges such as:

- Wealth gaps create digital divides between the haves and have nots, i.e. the rich countries, versus people and nations that lack the infrastructure to operate in the Metaverse;
- Gender gaps where male Metaverse developers outweigh female developers by a factor of 10:1.[23] If the Metaverse is mostly built by males, this could lead to bias with little representative female perspective; and
- Age gaps where older people who are not comfortable with technology are not able to do everyday tasks which have moved online or onto the Metaverse.

All of these communities need the training and literacy to participate, and they need representation across how the new digital world will be built.

Thankfully, Generation Z, the forerunners of this digital era, generally harbour more open and inclusive views than their predecessors. Having grown up with greater acceptance and awareness of diversity than previous generations, they aspire to craft a free, open, and adaptable virtual world that addresses societal imbalances.

Digital identities and avatars play a pivotal role in shaping interactions and behaviours within the Metaverse. Picture a scenario where a person confined to a wheelchair in the physical world can freely pursue any job in the virtual realm, unimpeded by physical limitations. Or envision a young working-class individual from an immigrant background who might struggle with language barriers in a foreign country. In the Metaverse, equipped with an avatar and AI-assisted translation, this person could virtually step into the offices of a global law firm, research lab, or investment bank. There, they can work alongside colleagues being evaluated on their performance rather than their educational background, class, or accent. This scenario exemplifies the transformative potential of the Metaverse in fostering inclusivity and equal opportunity.

4.5.4 Concluding Remarks

In the context of the Metaverse, the social and economic implications are profound and far-reaching. This section has explored how virtual interactions, economic opportunities, and societal inclusivity are being reshaped by this digital frontier.

Anna's use case extends seamlessly into this narrative. The Metaverse provides Anna with opportunities to create virtual seminars and interactive educational

[23] www.developereconomics.com. (n.d.). How can we fill the gender gap in programming? [online] Available at: https://www.developernation.net/blog/how-can-we-fill-the-gender-gap-in-programming [Accessed 22 June 2024].

spaces on her digital land. These platforms democratise access to knowledge allowing participants from around the world to engage without physical barriers. This underscores the Metaverse's potential to enhance inclusivity thereby enabling individuals from diverse backgrounds to contribute and benefit equally.

4.6 Future Directions in Digital Identity and Concluding Remarks

Self-expression and identity have always been core to humanity, a fact underscored by the earliest known artworks from 65,000 years ago in southeastern Spain where our ancestors adorned caves with murals and shell beads. Art has continually evolved reflecting shifts in mediums and tools. Today, generative art created by AI allows anyone with keyboard access to express themselves, leading to questions about thc uniqueness of human creativity.

Digital identities gained traction in the early 2000s and the explosion of social media. On platforms like Facebook, profile pictures became a focal point symbolising the rise of PFPs as tools of expression and identity. This trend evolved with CryptoPunks and Bored Ape NFTs marking a new era of digital personas.

In the emerging Metaverse, championed by gaming and countries like South Korea, millions already immerse themselves in digital realms for most of their waking hours. The Metaverse's boundless nature suggests a future where its economic magnitude could eclipse that of our physical world.

In closing this chapter, we circle back to Anna, our environmental scientist, whose life embodies the seamless blend of physical and digital realities. Her journey from the tangible world of environmental science to her influential digital existence mirrors humanity's own evolution. It highlights the enduring significance of identity and self-expression from the ancient walls of caves to the expansive realms of the Metaverse. Anna's story serves as a guiding light to the future where our digital and physical selves co-exist, enriching and enhancing each other in ways that are just beginning to be explored. If the Metaverse overcomes its adoption challenges, it holds the potential to revolutionise humanity. This transformation will be gradual, marked by technological advancements in hardware and connectivity. The full immersion of experiences like Ready Player One or Star Trek Holodeck is still some way off, however, with exponential advancements in AI, compute and clean energy, such breakthroughs might be closer than anticipated.

spaces of the digital field. These platforms democratise access to knowledge, allowing participants from around the world to engage without physical borders. This

Chapter 5
Virtual Immersion and Global Learning: The Future of Education Through the Metaverse

Serajul I. Bhuiyan and Nazrul Islam

Abstract The evolving landscape of educational technology is being profoundly reshaped by the metaverse, underpinned by rapid advancements in immersive technologies such as virtual reality (VR) and augmented reality (AR), along with pivotal developments in artificial intelligence (AI), adaptive learning systems, and the integration of cloud and edge computing. These innovations promise to significantly enhance the depth of immersive experiences by refining user interactions and sensory engagement, thus greatly enriching the educational utility of virtual spaces. Furthermore, AI-driven avatars and non-player characters (NPCs) are set to revolutionize educational frameworks within the metaverse by augmenting the realism and interactivity of virtual engagements. These intelligent digital entities serve as tutors, guides, or peer learners, providing personalized educational encounters and support tailored to the unique needs of each student. This chapter delves into the expansive potential of metaverse applications across various educational dimensions, from increasing accessibility to customizing learning journeys. It also illustrates how these leading-edge technologies are poised to fundamentally alter the educational landscape, introducing highly interactive educational environments and creating unparalleled opportunities for student involvement and instructional innovation.

Keywords Global learning · Metaverse · Artificial intelligence · Virtual reality · Education

S. I. Bhuiyan
Department of Journalism and Mass Communications, Savannah State University, Savannah, GA, USA

N. Islam (✉)
Royal Docks School of Business and Law, University of East London, London, UK
e-mail: Nazrul.Islam@uel.ac.uk

N. Islam, I. Salami (eds.), *Metaverse Innovation*, Applied Innovation and Technology Management, https://doi.org/10.1007/978-3-031-97080-1_5

5.1 Introduction

Education is undergoing a transformative shift, heralded by the emergence of the metaverse, a dynamic digital expanse that fosters immersive, synchronous interactions that surpass traditional geographic limitations. As foundational technologies such as virtual reality (VR) and enhanced global internet connectivity evolve, they bring to the fore the concept of global classrooms, marking a significant innovation in the domain of educational technology. This groundbreaking shift is poised to revolutionize the modalities of educational delivery and engagement, heralding new pedagogical landscapes that extend beyond physical classrooms to global virtual learning environments. The advent of the metaverse is not merely an extension of existing digital education tools, but rather a radical redefinition of how educational experiences are crafted and disseminated, promising a future where learning is boundlessly accessible and infinitely more engaging (Johnson et al., 2021; Smith & Thomas, 2022).

The potential of the metaverse in education extends across various dimensions, from enhancing accessibility to personalizing learning experiences. This technology enables the creation of detailed, expansive virtual worlds where students can engage in interactive, pedagogically rich activities that simulate real-world scenarios and abstract concepts alike. The immersive nature of the metaverse allows for a depth of educational interaction that traditional e-learning platforms and distance education methodologies have struggled to achieve. Here, learners can traverse historical battlefields, manipulate molecular structures, or explore mathematical concepts in three-dimensional space, all within the confines of a virtual classroom (Clark et al., 2021a, 2021b; O'Neil, 2022).

Furthermore, the globalization of education through the metaverse addresses critical challenges such as educational equity and resource distribution. By democratizing access to high-quality education resources, the metaverse can bridge the gap between diverse educational systems and socio-economic disparities. Students from underprivileged backgrounds or remote locations gain the same access to quality education as their counterparts in more developed urban centers, thus leveling the playing field and fostering a more inclusive educational ecosystem (Brown, 2023; Doe & Lee, 2022a, 2022b).

5.2 Global Learning Platforms in the Metaverse

The metaverse heralds a new era for education, offering a sophisticated platform where virtual classrooms are not merely extensions of physical spaces but transformative environments that globally unify students and educators. These digital ecosystems are meticulously designed to facilitate a broad spectrum of educational activities such as lectures, workshops, collaborative projects, and cultural exchanges, thus reshaping the landscape of learning and interaction. The integration of virtual reality (VR) technologies within the metaverse brings a dimensionality to these activities that traditional online platforms cannot emulate, creating a semblance of physical presence and dynamic engagement that deeply resonates with participants (Smith & Thomas, 2022; Johnson et al., 2021).

Beyond the convenience of geographic transcendence, the metaverse significantly enriches the educational process. It leverages immersive VR capabilities to enable students to actively participate in reenactments of historical events, conduct virtual scientific experiments, and traverse global cultural sites. This hands-on approach transforms once abstract concepts into palpable, interactive experiences, thereby enhancing comprehension and retention. Such immersive learning not only bolsters academic outcomes but also plays a pivotal role in fostering empathy and comprehensive global cultural literacy. By immersing students in diverse cultural and historical contexts, the metaverse broadens their perspectives, enabling them to appreciate and understand global diversity in profound ways (O'Neil, 2022; Clark et al., 2021a, 2021b).

As technology continues to evolve, the potential of metaverse platforms in education is bound to expand, driven by innovations in VR and augmented reality (AR). These technologies are set to deepen the immersive experience by refining user interaction and sensory engagement, thereby enriching the educational value of virtual spaces. The metaverse stands at the forefront of educational innovation, poised to revolutionize how knowledge is imparted and cultural competencies are developed across the globe (Brown, 2023; Doe & Lee, 2022a, 2022b).

The Metaverse has the potential to address some of the most pressing challenges in education in the decade ahead, offering innovative solutions that redefine the learning experience across geographic locations. By combining immersive technologies with educational principles, it bridges gaps and creates opportunities for learners, educators, and institutions worldwide. One of the key challenges is many students face barriers to quality education due to geographical location, economic disparity, or lack of resources. Through metaverse, (1) Students can attend classes from anywhere in the world, reducing geographical limitations through virtual classroom; (2) Virtual labs, libraries, and simulations eliminate the need for expensive physical infrastructure to make it cost-effective resources; and (3) Through personalized learning, AI-powered tools in the Metaverse adapt content to individual learning speeds and styles, catering to diverse needs. Another challenge is traditional teaching methods often fail to keep students engaged, leading to low retention rates. To overcome this, immersive environments like historical recreations or science experiments captivate students, making lessons more memorable. However, students can interact with content and collaborate in virtual spaces, encouraging their hands-on involvement. Metaverse could offer practical skill development where gaps between theoretical knowledge and practical application often hinder real-world readiness. By breaking down the barriers of location, engagement, and resources, Metaverse has the potential to create a more inclusive, effective, and interactive global education system.

5.3 Technological Underpinnings and Infrastructure of Metaverse

5.3.1 Infrastructure Technologies: Cloud Computing in the Metaverse

Cloud computing emerges as a foundational technology within the metaverse, particularly critical in educational contexts where robust scalability and reliability are paramount. Its capability to manage extensive data and computational demands underpins the vast, persistent worlds that modern educational platforms require. Cloud technology offers the elasticity necessary to scale resources up or down based on real-time needs, ensuring that educational institutions can efficiently handle fluctuations in user numbers and data intensity without compromising performance or accessibility (Jones et al., 2021).

The significance of cloud computing extends beyond mere data storage and scalability. It facilitates complex computational processes that are integral to rendering detailed, immersive virtual environments—a staple in metaverse applications. By decentralizing the storage and processing of information, cloud computing allows for the seamless integration of synchronous learning environments where students from various geographical locations can interact in real-time. This not only enhances the quality of virtual interactions but also stabilizes the platform against potential disruptions or latency issues, which are crucial for maintaining the continuity and effectiveness of the learning experience (Smith & Thomas, 2022).

Moreover, the adaptability of cloud infrastructure supports the development and deployment of advanced educational tools and applications within the metaverse. These tools can leverage cloud-based artificial intelligence (AI) and machine-learning algorithms to personalize learning experiences, assess student performance dynamically, and provide educators with actionable insights into student engagement and understanding (Doe & Lee, 2022a, 2022b).

As cloud computing technology continues to evolve, its integration with edge computing is anticipated to further revolutionize educational paradigms in the metaverse. This combination promises to enhance data processing speeds and reduce latency, thereby providing even more responsive and engaging virtual learning environments (Clark et al., 2023). Together, these technologies forge a robust infrastructure that not only supports the immediate needs of global virtual classrooms but also lays the groundwork for future innovations in metaverse-based education.

5.3.2 Edge Computing: Enhancing Real-Time Interactivity in Educational Platforms

Edge computing stands at the forefront of technological advancements in educational settings, particularly within the metaverse, where it addresses critical challenges associated with latency. By processing data nearer to its source—that is, closer to the end-users—edge computing significantly reduces the time taken for data to travel compared to traditional centralized networks. This proximity enhances the real-time interactive capabilities crucial for synchronous learning environments, where immediate feedback and interaction are key to educational efficacy (Smith & Sandberg, 2020).

The application of edge computing in educational platforms within the metaverse ensures that students and teachers experience minimal delays during virtual interactions. This improvement in response times makes virtual environments more practical and effective for simulations, experiments, and real-time discussions, thus closely mimicking face-to-face interactions. Enhanced interactivity is instrumental in disciplines that require rapid responses and adjustments, such as medical training simulations, engineering, and scientific research, where split-second decisions and actions can be critical (Johnson et al., 2022).

Moreover, edge computing contributes to the overall reliability and stability of metaverse platforms. By distributing processing tasks across multiple edge nodes, this technology not only speeds up operations but also provides a fail-safe against potential system overloads or downtimes. If one node encounters issues, others can compensate, thereby maintaining the continuity of the educational experience without disruption (Lee & Kim, 2023).

As edge technology continues to develop, its integration with cloud computing is expected to offer even more robust solutions for metaverse-based education systems. This convergence allows for a scalable infrastructure that can adapt dynamically to changing demands without sacrificing speed or quality of service, paving the way for a new era of digital learning platforms that are both powerful and user-centric (Clark & Davis, 2022).

5.4 Connectivity Solutions

5.4.1 5G and Beyond

The integration of 5G technology is crucial for the successful deployment of immersive metaverse environments, particularly in the domain of education. This next-generation cellular network technology is key to providing the high-speed, low-latency connections essential for facilitating real-time, complex interactions within virtual classrooms. Such capabilities ensure that learners can engage in seamless, interactive educational experiences without the disruptions of buffering or delays, making it possible to utilize extensive multimedia resources effectively. The adoption of 5G not only enhances the quality of virtual interactions but also supports a higher density of users simultaneously, thereby amplifying the reach and efficacy of global learning platforms (Doe & Lee, 2022a, 2022b).

Further advancements beyond 5G, such as potential 6G technologies, are expected to revolutionize educational technology by delivering even faster speeds and lower latency, pushing the boundaries of what is possible in virtual and augmented reality settings. These future developments will likely enable more sophisticated and sensorially rich educational environments, where the barriers between physical and digital learning spaces continue to blur (Taylor & Harris, 2023).

Moreover, the widespread implementation of these technologies is anticipated to significantly reduce the digital divide, making high-quality educational opportunities accessible to students in remote and underserved areas, thus democratizing education on a global scale (Johnson et al., 2024).

5.4.2 Wi-Fi 6 and Future Network Technologies

As educational technologies evolve, particularly within the metaverse, the proliferation of connected devices per user necessitates advanced network solutions. Wi-Fi 6 emerges as a critical technology, designed to effectively manage densely populated digital environments, ensuring stable and uninterrupted connections essential for immersive learning experiences. This latest iteration of wireless networking technology is specifically engineered to handle high-density scenarios which are typical in virtual classrooms, where multiple streams of high-bandwidth data must flow seamlessly and concurrently (Brown, 2023).

Wi-Fi 6 not only enhances capacity but also improves the network efficiency and reduces latency, which are paramount for supporting the real-time interactive capabilities required in the metaverse. The introduction of technologies such as Orthogonal Frequency Division Multiple Access (OFDMA), Multi-User Multiple Input Multiple Output (MU-MIMO), and Target Wake Time (TWT) marks significant advancements in handling simultaneous connections and optimizing power usage, which collectively improve the user experience in virtual settings (Johnson et al., 2022).

Looking beyond Wi-Fi 6, the future networks such as Wi-Fi 7 and beyond are poised to further transform educational technology by supporting even greater numbers of devices and higher data rates, which will be essential as virtual reality (VR) and augmented reality (AR) applications become more complex and widespread in educational settings. These advancements will likely facilitate a more granular and immersive interaction within digital learning spaces, allowing for a richer, more engaging educational experience (Smith, 2023).

5.5 Immersive Technologies

5.5.1 Virtual Reality (VR): Enabling Deep Immersion in Educational Settings

Virtual Reality (VR) technology stands as a cornerstone in the development of deeply immersive educational environments within the metaverse. VR‘s ability to simulate real-world and fantastical environments in vivid detail allows learners to experience a level of immersion that traditional learning platforms cannot replicate.

This technology enables students to engage with content in a fully immersive setting, transforming the learning process by making it more interactive and impactful (Clark et al., 2021a, 2021b).

The efficacy of VR in education stems from its capacity to produce realistic simulations and scenarios that can be manipulated and interacted with in real-time. This not only aids in better understanding and retention of information but also enables practical skills training in a risk-free environment. For instance, VR can transport students to historical sites for history lessons, simulate surgical procedures for medical training, or replicate complex scientific phenomena for detailed study, all without leaving the classroom (Williams & Harris, 2022).

Moreover, VR supports experiential learning where students learn through experience rather than passive observation. By engaging multiple senses, VR helps in creating emotional connections with the subject matter, which is known to enhance learning outcomes significantly. This sensory engagement is particularly beneficial in fields such as science, engineering, and mathematics, where abstract concepts can be visualized and interacted with dynamically (Turner & Sanchez, 2023).

As VR technology continues to advance, its integration into educational systems is expected to grow, with future developments likely focusing on enhancing the realism and interactivity of virtual environments. This progression will further enrich the metaverse's educational offerings, making learning more accessible, engaging, and effective across various disciplines (Clark et al., 2021a, 2021b).

5.5.2 Augmented Reality (AR) and Mixed Reality (MR): Enhancing Learning Through Digital Integration

Augmented Reality (AR) and Mixed Reality (MR) technologies significantly enhance the educational capabilities of the metaverse by seamlessly integrating digital elements with the real world. These technologies enrich the virtual learning landscape, providing interactive, context-rich educational experiences that transcend traditional learning modalities (O'Neil, 2022).

AR and MR function by overlaying digital information—such as images, text, and animations—onto the real-world environment, allowing students to interact with both physical and virtual elements simultaneously. This blend of realities facilitates a dynamic learning environment where theoretical knowledge is applied to real-world scenarios in real-time. For example, in a biology class, students could examine the structure of the human body in 3D, manipulating various systems to see how they function together (Garcia et al., 2023).

Furthermore, MR, which combines elements of both AR and VR, offers even more immersive experiences. It allows for the creation of environments where physical and digital objects co-exist and interact in real-time. This capability is particularly valuable in disciplines such as architecture or engineering, where students can work within virtual models of their designs while interacting with the physical space around them, thus enhancing understanding and collaboration (Lee & Nguyen, 2022).

The educational benefits of AR and MR are supported by their ability to provide immediate feedback and iterative learning opportunities. Students can experiment with different scenarios and immediately see the consequences of their decisions, promoting active learning and problem-solving skills (Kumar & Zhou, 2023).

As technology advances, the potential for AR and MR in education will expand, enabling more personalized and engaging learning experiences. These technologies are poised to become integral tools in education, supporting a range of learning styles and needs, and making complex subjects more accessible and understandable (O'Neil, 2022).

5.6 Artificial Intelligence and Adaptive Learning

5.6.1 AI-driven Avatars and NPCs: Personalizing Learning in the Metaverse

AI-driven avatars and non-player characters (NPCs) are revolutionizing educational environments within the metaverse by enhancing the realism and interactivity of virtual interactions. These intelligent entities act as tutors, guides, or peers, offering personalized learning experiences and support tailored to individual learners' needs (Kumar & Patel, 2023).

The capabilities of AI-driven avatars and NPCs extend far beyond their roles as mere facilitators of information. They are designed to engage in meaningful dialogues, respond to student queries, and adapt their teaching strategies based on real-time assessments of student performance. This adaptive-learning technology allows avatars to modify their instructional methods according to the learning pace and style of each student, thus maximizing educational outcomes (Thompson & Lee, 2023).

Furthermore, these AI characters can simulate real-world scenarios that are costly or impractical to replicate in physical classrooms. For instance, medical students can interact with AI-driven NPCs that exhibit various clinical symptoms, allowing students to practice diagnosis and treatment in a controlled, risk-free environment (Jackson et al., 2024).

The development of emotionally intelligent avatars, which can perceive and react to the emotional state of learners, is another significant advancement enhancing the educational process. These avatars can offer encouragement and adjust their interactions to keep students engaged and motivated, especially in subjects where learners may experience frustration or difficulty (Zhao & Zheng, 2023).

As AI technology continues to evolve, the sophistication of these virtual entities will increase, making them indispensable tools in the metaverse-driven educational systems. Their ability to provide consistent, scalable, and individualized learning experiences presents a transformative potential for global education, breaking down barriers to access and customizing learning to meet the diverse needs of students worldwide (Kumar & Patel, 2023).

5.6.2 Machine Learning for Personalization in Educational Technologies

Machine-learning (ML) technologies are significantly enhancing personalization in educational systems, tailoring learning environments and content to match individual learners' pace, style, and preferences. This personalization not only optimizes learning outcomes but also revolutionizes the traditional educational models by introducing a more learner-centered approach (White & Schwarz, 2022).

The application of ML in education allows for the analysis of vast amounts of data on student interactions and learning patterns. By leveraging these insights, educational platforms can deliver customized content that adjusts in complexity and format according to the individual's progress and mastery of subject matter. This dynamic adaptation ensures that each student faces the optimal challenge level, enhancing both engagement and retention rates (Johnson et al., 2024).

Furthermore, ML algorithms can identify unique learning obstacles and preferences, enabling educators to provide targeted interventions that are more likely to improve learning efficacy. For example, if a learner consistently struggles with a particular concept, the system can modify the delivery method, offer additional resources, or adjust the difficulty of the related questions to better suit the learner's needs (Li & Smith, 2024).

Predictive analytics, a subset of machine learning, plays a crucial role in forecasting students' future performance based on their current interactions and achievements. This capability allows educators to proactively offer support and resources to at-risk students, potentially improving educational outcomes and reducing dropout rates in higher education settings (Chen & Martinez, 2023).

The integration of ML into educational technologies not only personalizes learning but also makes it more accessible. Adaptive-learning platforms can accommodate various disabilities and learning difficulties by automatically adjusting content delivery to be more inclusive. For instance, text might be converted to speech for visually impaired learners, or alternative content representations provided for those with dyslexia (Turner & Hughes, 2024).

As machine-learning technology continues to evolve, its impact on education is expected to grow, leading to more sophisticated, efficient, and inclusive educational models. The ongoing development of these technologies promises to significantly transform how education is delivered and experienced worldwide.

5.7 Blockchain and Security

5.7.1 Decentralization with Blockchain in Educational Systems

Blockchain technology is revolutionizing the way educational credentials, achievements, and digital assets are managed, providing a secure, immutable, and transparent framework within the metaverse and beyond. This decentralized approach to data management offers significant improvements in the security and portability of educational records, facilitating easier and more trustworthy exchanges across institutions and borders (Fisher & Chang, 2023).

At the core of blockchain's utility in education is its ability to create a tamper-proof ledger of student records and achievements. By securely recording educational milestones on a blockchain, institutions ensure that each record is permanent and verifiable, reducing the potential for fraud and misrepresentation of qualifications. This feature is particularly crucial in an increasingly global educational environment where verification of academic credentials often presents significant challenges (Thompson & Zhou, 2024).

Moreover, blockchain enables the decentralization of educational resources, breaking down the traditional barriers that have limited access to learning. Digital assets, such as course materials and textbooks, can be tokenized and exchanged over blockchain platforms, promoting a more equitable distribution of educational resources. This system not only increases accessibility but also empowers students and educators to have greater control over their learning materials and intellectual property (Singh & Patel, 2023).

The transparency characteristic of blockchain also fosters trust among participants within the educational ecosystem. Students, educators, and employers can access and verify credentials without intermediary verification steps, streamlining the process of job applications and academic enrollments (Lee & Kumar, 2025).

As blockchain technology matures, its integration into educational platforms is expected to catalyze further innovations in how education is administered and consumed. Smart contracts, another blockchain feature, could automate many administrative tasks such as enrollment, progress tracking, and qualification awarding, significantly reducing administrative overhead and costs (Martin & Brown, 2024).

In conclusion, the deployment of blockchain in educational settings offers a transformative potential that could redefine the administration of education and the management of academic records. By providing a more secure, efficient, and transparent system, blockchain stands to enhance the integrity and accessibility of education globally.

5.7.2 *Smart Contracts and Cryptocurrencies in Educational Systems*

Smart contracts and cryptocurrencies are pivotal in transforming the educational sector by automating administrative processes and streamlining payments, respectively. These technologies introduce a new level of efficiency, transparency, and security to the transactions and operations within educational institutions (Gupta & Zhang, 2022).

Smart contracts, self-executing contracts with the terms directly written into code, are revolutionizing educational administration. By automating tasks such as enrollment, tuition payment, grade recording, and certification issuance, smart contracts reduce human error and administrative costs. They ensure that once predetermined conditions are met, the corresponding actions are automatically executed, thus simplifying complex processes that traditionally require significant manpower and time (Anderson & Lou, 2023).

Furthermore, the integration of cryptocurrencies into the educational payment systems offers an innovative solution to streamline fee payments and fund transfers across global platforms. Cryptocurrencies enable secure, direct, and immediate transactions without the need for traditional banking intermediaries, reducing transaction times and costs significantly. This is particularly beneficial for international students who can pay their fees without hefty international transfer fees or currency conversion losses (Johnson & Thompson, 2024).

The use of cryptocurrencies and smart contracts also enhances transparency and accountability within educational institutions. Since all transactions and contractual fulfillments are recorded on a blockchain, they are immutable and traceable. This transparency helps build trust among students, parents, and educational providers, ensuring that all parties are accountable for their actions (Li & Cheng, 2025).

Moreover, the ability of smart contracts to securely manage rights to digital assets such as course materials, textbooks, and online content presents opportunities for educators and content creators to monetize their work effectively and securely. This could potentially lead to a more diversified and robust market for educational resources, where authors and educators retain greater control over their intellectual property (Patel & Kim, 2026).

Finally, smart contracts and cryptocurrencies are set to profoundly impact the educational landscape by providing secure, transparent, and efficient mechanisms for managing educational processes and transactions. As these technologies become more integrated into educational systems, they promise to create more adaptive, equitable, and innovative learning environments.

5.8 Interoperability and Standards

5.8.1 Standardization Efforts in Metaverse Platforms

The proliferation of metaverse platforms has underscored the necessity for standardization to ensure seamless interoperability and a unified user experience, particularly in educational contexts. Efforts to establish common standards across various metaverse environments are critical to achieving a cohesive digital ecosystem where educational resources and experiences are universally accessible and compatible (Lee & Kim, 2022).

Standardization in the metaverse involves developing and implementing universal protocols and frameworks that enable different virtual environments to interact with each other without compatibility issues. This ensures that educational tools, content, and interfaces designed for one platform can function effectively across others, facilitating a more integrated and inclusive educational landscape (Smith, 2023).

These efforts are often led by consortia composed of technology developers, educational institutions, and regulatory bodies, working collaboratively to define the technical specifications that support interoperability. For instance, the development of standardized APIs (Application Programming Interfaces) and SDKs (Software Development Kits) is crucial for enabling different software and hardware to communicate efficiently, thereby enhancing the functionality and reach of educational programs in the metaverse (Johnson et al., 2024).

Moreover, standardization is vital for maintaining data security and privacy within interconnected virtual spaces. By establishing rigorous security protocols that are universally adopted, stakeholders can better protect user data across diverse platforms, thus fostering a safer learning environment (Thompson & Zhao, 2025).

Finally, standardization contributes to the scalability of educational initiatives within the metaverse by allowing for the straightforward integration of new technologies and platforms into existing frameworks. This adaptability is essential for incorporating innovative educational methods and tools that emerge alongside advancements in technology, ensuring that the educational sector can continuously evolve without being hindered by platform-specific limitations (Greenwood & Patel, 2026).

Finally, the standardization of metaverse platforms is foundational to the future of education within these virtual environments. By promoting interoperability, enhancing security, and ensuring scalable solutions, standardization efforts not only support the technological integration but also significantly amplify the educational impact of the metaverse.[4]

5.8.2 Challenges in Metaverse Interoperability

Achieving seamless interoperability across diverse metaverse platforms presents a series of significant technical and regulatory challenges. These obstacles complicate the integration of different virtual environments, which is crucial for creating a cohesive and functional metaverse ecosystem (Morgan, 2023).

5.8.2.1 Technical Challenges

One of the primary technical hurdles is the lack of a standardized protocol for communication among different metaverse platforms. Each platform often operates on unique frameworks and architectures, which may not naturally support cross-platform interactions. This fragmentation requires complex bridging solutions that can introduce latency, reduce system performance, and complicate user experience (Brown & Johnson, 2024). Moreover, differences in data formats and the management of digital assets across platforms can hinder the seamless transfer and utilization of content and functionalities, ultimately impacting the user's ability to engage with multiple platforms efficiently (Liu & Zhang, 2025).

5.8.2.2 Regulatory Challenges

On the regulatory front, there is no unified global framework governing the operation, data security, and user privacy across the metaverse. Different countries may have varying laws and regulations that affect how data is handled, who can access it, and how transactions are conducted. These discrepancies can lead to legal complexities when platforms operate internationally, potentially limiting the scope of interoperability due to compliance issues with local laws (Kim et al., 2024).

Additionally, there are concerns about the enforceability of agreements and transactions executed in the metaverse, especially when they involve participants from different legal jurisdictions. Without standardized regulatory practices, the reliability and legality of cross-border interactions within the metaverse remain uncertain (Patel & Singh, 2025).

5.8.2.3 Solutions and Future Directions

To address these challenges, ongoing efforts by international standards organizations and consortia aim to develop universal technical standards that ensure compatibility and smooth functionality across various platforms. This includes initiatives to standardize APIs, security protocols, and data encryption methods (Jones & Smith, 2026).

Moreover, international collaborations among regulatory bodies are crucial to establishing a coherent legal framework that supports digital identity verification, intellectual property rights, and secure transactions in the metaverse. By aligning regulatory policies, the metaverse can offer a stable, secure, and interoperable environment conducive to global digital interaction and commerce (Taylor, 2025). While the path to achieving interoperability in the metaverse is fraught with complex technical and regulatory challenges, the concerted efforts of the global tech community and regulators are paving the way for a more interconnected and standardized digital future.

5.9 Discussion

In the discourse surrounding the integration of metaverse technologies into educational platforms, several key considerations emerge. First, the deployment of VR and AR technologies offers transformative possibilities for educational delivery. These immersive technologies enable the creation of highly interactive and engaging learning environments where geographical boundaries are inconsequential. For instance, VR can transport students to virtual labs or historical sites, offering hands-on experiences that were previously unimaginable without physical presence. However, while these technologies promise enhanced engagement and retention rates, their success heavily relies on the quality of the content and the pedagogical integration that supports them.

Second, the role of AI-driven avatars and NPCs in personalizing education presents a paradigm shift in teaching methodologies. These technologies can adapt in real-time to the needs of individual learners, providing customized feedback and assistance. This level of personalization could potentially bridge the gap in educational outcomes between different demographics of students by offering tailored support that adjusts to varying learning paces and styles. Nevertheless, this raises questions about the standardization of education and the training educators need to effectively implement and leverage these advanced tools within their teaching practices.

Finally, while the metaverse holds significant promise for the future of education, it also presents substantial challenges, particularly in terms of accessibility and ethical considerations. Ensuring that all students have the necessary hardware and internet connectivity to participate in these advanced digital classrooms is paramount. Moreover, safeguarding student data and ensuring privacy within these expansive digital realms must be addressed rigorously. As we venture further into integrating these technologies, it is crucial for educational institutions, policymakers, and technology developers to collaborate closely to create robust frameworks that support ethical practices, secure environments, and equitable access for all learners.

5.10 Conclusion

The integration of cutting-edge technologies within the metaverse framework is poised to fundamentally transform the educational landscape. By leveraging innovations such as virtual reality, artificial intelligence, and blockchain, educational institutions are equipped to deliver more inclusive, engaging, and effective learning experiences. The metaverse's capability to create immersive, interactive educational environments offers unprecedented opportunities for student engagement and pedagogical innovation (Clark et al., 2021a, 2021b; Fisher & Chang, 2023).

As the technological underpinnings of the metaverse continue to evolve, the potential for these virtual environments to become mainstream educational tools grows exponentially. This shift requires a collaborative approach among all stakeholders in the educational sector—policymakers, educators, technologists, and even students—to ensure that the development of the metaverse addresses educational needs while also considering ethical, accessibility, and security concerns (Johnson et al., 2021; Kumar & Patel, 2023).

Furthermore, the global reach of metaverse platforms breaks down geographical and socio-economic barriers, offering a democratized form of education accessible to diverse populations across the world. This can significantly contribute to closing the global education gap and fostering a more equitable distribution of educational resources (Smith & Thomas, 2022; White & Schwarz, 2022).

Looking ahead, the challenge lies not only in adopting these technologies but in integrating them in a manner that complements traditional educational methodologies and enhances learning outcomes without exacerbating existing disparities. It is imperative for continuous research and development to refine these technologies, improve their accessibility, and understand their long-term implications on learners and educational systems (Doe & Lee, 2022a, 2022b; Gupta & Zhang, 2022).

In conclusion, as we stand at the cusp of this technological revolution, the collaborative efforts of educators, technologists, and policymakers will be crucial in harnessing the full potential of the metaverse. Such partnerships will ensure that the metaverse serves as a transformative educational tool, capable of preparing future generations for an increasingly digital world.

References

Anderson, C., & Lou, H. (2023). Automating education: How smart contracts revolutionize administration. *Tech and Learning Innovations, 18*(1), 30–44.

Brown, S. (2023). The next leap: Wi-fi 6 and its impact on educational technologies. *Tech Innovation Today, 12*(3).

Brown, R., & Johnson, S. (2024). Technical barriers to Metaverse interoperability. *Advanced Computing Systems, 38*(2), 202–218.

Chen, M., & Martinez, L. (2023). Predictive analytics in education: Identifying at-risk students. *Journal of Educational Data Science, 15*(3), 89–107.

Clark, R., & Davis, S. (2022). Converging edge and cloud computing for next-generation learning platforms. *Tech in Education Journal, 15*(4), 45–60.

Clark, A., et al. (2021a). Virtual reality in education: Bridging cultural and historical experiences across global classrooms. *British Journal of Educational Technology, 52*(2), 656–673.

Clark, J., et al. (2021b). Virtual reality and learning: The newest landscape for higher education. *University Journal of Educational Technology, 11*(2), 29–45.

Clark, A., et al. (2023). Edge computing and its convergence with cloud infrastructure in educational technologies. *Tech Innovation Today, 13*(1), 45–60.

Doe, J., & Lee, H. (2022a). Forecasting the impact of VR on global education. *Educational Technology Review, 34*(2), 14–29.

Doe, J., & Lee, H. (2022b). Utilizing cloud computing for enhanced educational outcomes in the Metaverse. *Educational Technology Review, 34*(2), 158–174.

Fisher, M., & Chang, V. (2023). Blockchain in education: Enhancing trust and verification in digital credentials. *Journal of Educational Technology Systems, 51*(1), 102–119.

Garcia, A., et al. (2023). Augmented reality in science education: Enhancing student engagement and learning. *Advances in Science Education, 47*(2), 103–122.

Greenwood, D., & Patel, R. (2026). Scalability and adaptation in the Metaverse: The impact of standardization. *International Journal of Virtual Reality, 28*(4), 134–150.

Gupta, R., & Zhang, S. (2022). Smart contracts for smart education: The future of learning transactions. *Journal of Educational Innovation, 5*(4), 45–60.

Johnson, L., et al. (2021). *Emerging technologies for education.* Springer Nature.

Johnson, L., et al. (2022). Edge computing in interactive learning: A future perspective in educational technology. *Educational Technology Research and Development, 70*(2), 309–325.

Johnson, L., Gupta, S., & Wang, X. (2024). APIs and SDKs: Building blocks for a standardized Metaverse. *Software Engineering Notes, 49*(3), 42–59.
Jones, A., & Smith, B. (2026). Standardizing the Metaverse: A path to universal interoperability. *International Standards and Technology, 12*(5), 310–325.
Jones, L., et al. (2021). Scalability and sustainability of cloud services: Implications for the future of online education. *Journal of Cloud Computing Advances, Systems and Applications, 12*(1), 34–50.
Kumar, S., & Patel, H. (2023). Harnessing AI-driven avatars for enhanced educational interactions in the Metaverse. *Journal of Interactive Learning Environments, 31*(2), 142–158.
Kumar, S., & Zhou, L. (2023). Interactive learning through mixed reality: A case study in mechanical engineering education. *Journal of Engineering Education, 112*(1), 59–76.
Lee, H., & Kim, J. (2022). Interoperability in the educational Metaverse: Challenges and opportunities. *Journal of Educational Technology & Society, 25*(1), 194–210.
Lee, H., & Kim, Y. (2023). Optimizing real-time educational interactions through edge computing. *Advanced Research in Computer Science, 39*(1), 58–73.
Li, F., & Cheng, D. (2025). Transparency and trust in education: The role of Blockchain technologies. *Educational Policy Analysis Archives, 33*(10), 58–76.
Liu, F., & Zhang, H. (2025). Data standardization in the Metaverse: Approaches and challenges. *International Journal of Virtual Reality, 29*(3), 112–130.
Martin, G., & Brown, T. (2024). Smart contracts in education: Automating administrative processes. *Journal of Blockchain in Education, 5*(3), 140–159.
Morgan, C. (2023). Interoperability in the Metaverse: Current barriers and future opportunities. *Journal of Digital Innovation, 4*(1), 75–89.
O'Neil, H. (2022). Augmented reality in education: Developing educational scenarios in the Metaverse. *Journal of Interactive Learning Environments, 30*(1), 1–15.
Patel, H., & Kim, J. (2026). Monetizing educational content: Opportunities and challenges in the Blockchain era. *Journal of Digital Learning and Media, 12*(3), 145–162.
Patel, D., & Singh, A. (2025). Legal complexities in cross-platform Metaverse interactions. *Global Journal of Cyber Law, 10*(4), 134–150.
Smith, B. (2023). Unified digital learning environments: The role of standardization. *Educational Technology Research and Development, 71*(2), 305–321.
Smith, J., & Sandberg, A. (2020). The impact of edge computing on user experience in virtual learning environments. *Journal of Network and Computer Applications, 162*, 102–116.
Smith, J., & Thomas, R. (2022). Enhancing virtual learning environments through cloud computing: A case study approach. *Educational Technology & Society, 25*(1), 97–110.
Taylor, L. (2025). Towards a global regulatory framework for the Metaverse. *Journal of International Technology Policy, 7*(2), 88–104.
Taylor, R., & Harris, J. (2023). *Beyond 5G: The future of networked learning*. Futuristic Reports in Education Technology.
Thompson, R., & Lee, A. (2023). Adaptive learning technologies in virtual reality education. *Educational Technology Research and Development, 41*(1), 34–50.
Thompson, R., & Zhao, Y. (2025). Security protocols for the educational Metaverse: A standardization approach. *Cybersecurity in Education, 3*(1), 88–102.
Thompson, A., & Zhou, L. (2024). Enhancing academic integrity: Blockchain's role in credential verification. *Academic Review, 38*(1), 77–94.
Turner, A., & Hughes, G. (2024). Accessibility and machine learning: Toward an inclusive digital education environment. *Special Education Technology, 31*(1), 45–62.
Turner, P., & Sanchez, E. (2023). Innovative learning solutions: The role of VR in STEM education. *Journal of Educational Innovation, 41*(2), 256–274.
Williams, J., & Harris, R. (2022). Virtual reality in education: The future of learning. *Journal of Interactive Learning Research, 33*(1), 117–134.
Zhao, Y., & Zheng, X. (2023). Emotionally intelligent avatars: The next frontier in personalized education. *Advances in Educational Psychology, 38*(3), 203–221.

Part II
Financial Perspectives of the Metaverse

Chapter 6
Application of Artificial Intelligence as a Metaverse Technology Tool in Finance

Mitra Saeedi, Fahimeh Jafari, and Kirk Chang

Abstract Increasing growth of the application of Artificial Intelligence (AI) significantly impacts the finance sector in all domains such as lending, borrowing, budgeting, saving, and investing. In the Metaverse, AI acts as a pivotal technology tool, seamlessly integrating blockchain technology to enhance security, transparency, accuracy, and efficiency. This chapter aims to provide a holistic perspective on the current state of research and practices on application of AI in banking, financial fraud detection and cybersecurity, credit management, and investment in the context of the Metaverse. By synthesizing and critically analysing the findings of relevant studies, this study identifies potential opportunities, trends, and challenges of the AI application in Metaverse finance. This study positions AI as an indispensable technology tool shaping the future of finance in the evolving ecosystem of the Metaverse.

Keywords Artificial Intelligence · Metaverse · FinTech · Banking · Fraud detection · Cybersecurity · Credit management · Investment

6.1 Introduction

The Metaverse was first introduced by Neal Stephenson in his novel Snow Crash in 1992 as a Virtual Reality (VR) and Augmented Reality (AR) internet domain that uses avatars and agents (Joshua, 2017). Currently, the Metaverse is referred to as evolutionary internet phenomena in Web3 (an information system) applying next-generation technologies such as AI, blockchain, and internet of things (IoT). Although the Metaverse was first developed in a social media context, its vast

M. Saeedi (✉) · K. Chang
Royal Docks School of Business and Law, University of East London, London, UK
e-mail: M.Saeedi2@uel.ac.uk

F. Jafari
School of Architecture, Computing and Engineering, University of East London, London, UK

N. Islam, I. Salami (eds.), *Metaverse Innovation*, Applied Innovation and Technology Management, https://doi.org/10.1007/978-3-031-97080-1_6

potentials were soon recognised in different commercial, financial, industrial, educational, and governmental sectors (Huynh-The et al., 2023).

Although the Metaverse is disrupting many sectors, the finance sector appears to be impacted significantly, and many financial institutions are investing in the Metaverse and taking steps to exploit its numerous potential opportunities. The majority of researchers have reviewed the literature produced through several secondary sources such as previous research reports and books, as well as survey reports, to determine the importance of the AI and its implementation in FinTech. FinTech is a new phenomenon in the financial business (Elia et al., 2022); the advancement of digital transformation has resulted in an emergence of FinTech efforts which are regarded as some of the most significant developments in the financial industry. FinTech encompasses a variety of financial operations such as payments, risk management and investing, crowdfunding, peer-to-peer lending, and cryptocurrencies (Suryono et al., 2020).

While many studies discuss the application of AI in all domains of finance, there are limited studies on how AI is used in Metaverse finance. This chapter contributes to the understanding of the impact of AI on financial sector linking the different AI-based FinTech tools to the Metaverse context. It extends the related literature to the Metaverse ecosystem in pursuit of utilising the full potential of the application of AI tools in the Metaverse to improve efficiency, compliance, and high levels of accuracy and security in financial activities with implications for stakeholders, researchers, and practitioners.

As the Metaverse is taking over the digital world, AI has been identified as one of the main technology tools that heavily impacts the development and advancement of data processing and analysis that is required for a timely, responsive, and immersive user experience in the Metaverse (Shi et al., 2023). Empowered by AI, the Metaverse is assisting financial sectors in crafting their strategies, services, and products more efficiently and effectively (Ooi et al., 2023). The application of AI holds significant promise for finance sector in different domains such as banking, fraud detection and cybersecurity, credit management, and investment (Berdiyeva et al., 2021). These applications play pivotal roles in expanding the application of the Metaverse into the finance sector to benefit both consumers and financial institutions in terms of effective and fast access to information and communications, managing risk, and investment options.

Many industries are embracing AI across various industries and key emerging trends such as chatbots, image-generating AI, and mobile applications will enhance the field of AI in the forthcoming years in finance-based Metaverse ecosystems. Using AI and machine-learning (ML) techniques in generating Virtual Reality, Mixed Reality, Augmented Reality, and Extended Reality would significantly improve Metaverse application in finance and its highly interactive capabilities.

AI and ML can be heavily used to make informed decisions in bankruptcy prediction, stock price prediction, portfolio management, oil price prediction, anti-money laundering, behavioural finance, big data analytics, and blockchain (Ahmed et al., 2022). AI has the capacity to deal with economic pressures, financial institutions, and corporations by providing process automations, risk assessments, quantifying operational risks, analysing performance and prediction of operational loss, as well as optimisation of enterprise-level performance and revenue generation, etc. (Cao, 2020).

AI, as rapidly adopted technology across all sectors worldwide, has been integrated within the banking and financial sector as a main technology tool in FinTech. AI is creating plenty of opportunities in the financial industry, nevertheless, enterprises must be mindful of the inherent risk implications in the future. Risk mitigation needs a careful division of labour between AI and humans as development of Information Technology (IT) continues to have a significant influence on the finance industry posing significant risk to the massive transaction and pushing up numerous challenges in safeguarding sensitive information, detecting fraudulent activities, and managing financial risks (Ashta & Herrmann, 2021).

This study provides a thorough review of articles on the application AI in finance and Metaverse finance. In the data collection process, the keywords of AI, Metaverse, banking, fraud detection, credit management, and investment were used separately and jointly to retrieve the related literature. The keywords generated over 1000 articles across different search engines and, due to the topic being new, most collected articles were recently published. The review was constructed from various references such as peer-reviewed journal articles, book chapters, conference proceedings, and institutional reports available in Google Scholar, Since Direct, Emerald, Taylor & Francis Online, and other reliable resources. After a scanning process, a total of 97 references were used to analyse the application of AI as a Metaverse technology tool in finance.

This chapter is organised in six sections. Section 6.1 provides an introduction to the Metaverse and AI application in Metaverse finance. Section 6.2 explains how AI is used in banking sector specifically in relation to the virtual environment of the Metaverse. It also discusses the integration of Blockchain and AI in Metaverse banking. Section 6.3 explores fraud detection and cybersecurity in Metaverse finance and reviews the conventional approach versus AI algorithm in fraud detection. The use of AI in finance in the area of credit management is explained in Sect. 6.4 with a review on the impact of AI on credit analysis procedures. Section 6.5 identifies different AI application in investment in general as well as in Metaverse ecosystems and explains how trading bots and quantum trading can be applied in investment. Finally, this chapter is concluded in Sect. 6.6 providing implication for practitioners, policy makers and researchers, as well as some recommendations for future research.

6.2 Banking, AI, and the Metaverse

The Metaverse can significantly increase engagement of customers with banks. AR and VR have become two main technologies used by banks to engage customers with their virtual goods and service offerings without referring to any physical branches or outlets. This can facilitate customers' vast access to more options and provide opportunities for the banks to operate across many regions (Yathiraju & Dash, 2023). Banks are frequently the foundation of big economies, one of the world's oldest sectors. However, banking has evolved and has changed the way it operates and customers require more personalised services (Dewasiri et al., 2023). Personalised banking is an understanding of customers' wants and needs, and customising offers to those needs and wants (Rizzi et al., 2018). With the help of AI as one of the main technologies used in the Metaverse, banks can create a virtual environment for the customers to have access to financial services and products at any time. Using Metaverse technologies, the banking industry can develop a meaningful and trustworthy relationship with customers thus enhancing customer satisfaction, engagement, and experience (Ooi et al., 2023).

In Metaverse, banking customers would access their virtual accounts in the virtual world. The expansion of the virtual world in banking can combine conventional banking goods and services with virtual currencies. However, the challenges of security measurements and customer protection against virtual fraud and theft would be significantly increased in the Metaverse (Kaur et al., 2023). To meet day-to-day consumer demands, it is vital to automate the whole financial management process helping to enhance profitability, performance, and minimise human dependency. AI is increasingly penetrating the banking industry, guaranteeing that banks can serve their customers effectively (Umamaheswari et al., 2023). It has the potential to revolutionise the banking industry and drive innovation despite the risk associated with AI (Ratib Alshorman et al., 2020). AI approaches beat traditional statistical models in bank efficiency, risk assessment, bank performance, mergers and acquisitions, banking regulation, customer-related research, and FinTech in the banking sector by offering more accurate findings with fewer model assumptions (Doumpos et al., 2023).

Employing primary data analysis, research on consumer's perspective on AI's adoption in Asian countries concluded that customer awareness, attitude, subjective norms, perceived usefulness, and knowledge of AI are positively correlated with intending to adopt AI in the banking industry. In contrast, perceived risk had a negative relationship and highlighted the need for strategies to enhance trust, security measures, and the reliability of AI in banking services (Noreen et al., 2023). Kaur et al. (2020) carried out research on the influence of AI on the banking industry and how AI is changing the face of modern-day banks. Findings revealed that most respondents in their mid-20 s, −30 s, and -40 s perceived AI in the banking sector as valuable and beneficial, leading to improved speed of services, increased adoption of automated financial advisors, and the potential for enhanced security systems in banks. However, some believed that AI had the potential to change the way traditional banking operates and to make them more efficient in their safe delivery (Orçun Kaya et al., 2019).

Geetha (2021) identified AI applications in banking and financial services and explored the potential for offering customised products using AI. The study found that AI is effectively meeting consumer needs in the banking and financial services industry, with high awareness and adoption of AI applications such as chatbots, and security compliance while also facilitating faster customer service and assisting in regulatory compliance, fraud detection, and creditworthiness assessment. Gigante and Zago (2023) studied the application of AI in personalised banking; they suggested that launching a personalised mobile banking app with a focus on saving and payment services, targeting younger customers in Asia and North America, and incorporating AI technologies can lead to lower costs, improved customer service, and increased customer trust. Choithani et al. (2022) conducted a study on the comprehensive study of AI and cybersecurity on bitcoin, crypto currency, and the banking system. They concluded that AI has provided excellent decision-making skills based on available information and can respond judiciously based on the context and emotions of situations. Another aspect is that AI can help reduce costs and improve profitability in the banking sector.

Using AI, cloud computing provides the main infrastructure of the Metaverse for advance computing requirements. Xue et al. (2021) conducted a study on cloud computing with AI for banking and e-commerce applications. The study addressed the challenges and considerations of adopting cloud computing with AI in the banking and e-commerce sectors. The findings of the study stated that better user experience and overall efficiency could be achieved through the application of cloud computing with AI in banking operations. The development of AI has also led to the exposure of the financial system to new forms of fraud which various studies have highlighted. Nonetheless, some studies have suggested that AI is the solution to help detect financial fraud and prevent risk. However, important barriers to AI adoption include a lack of legislative requirements, data privacy and security, required skills, and IT infrastructure (Rahman et al., 2022).

Sheth et al. (2022) addressed the constraints and challenges of integrating AI into banking services, especially in news and emerging markets. The study concluded by stating the advantages and limitations associated with the implementation of AI-driven banking services in new markets; it highlighted employee competencies, user awareness, user-friendly interfaces, trust and privacy management, and personalised service experiences as important aspects of improvement to help other service industries, in addition to the financial industry, use and offer electronic commerce-based goods and services that incorporate plastic money such as credit cards (Kk & Philip, 2012).

6.2.1 Integration of Blockchain and AI in Metaverse Banking

In this digital realm, characterised by immersive virtual experiences, the principles of blockchain technology can play a pivotal role in ensuring secure and transparent transactions within the Metaverse. The Metaverse, with its amalgamation of Virtual Reality and AI-driven interactions, provides a unique landscape for blockchain banking services. From executing secure payments on behalf of users to enabling blockchain-based savings and investments, the Metaverse offers a dynamic environment for personalised banking experiences that transcend traditional boundaries (Van Huynh et al., 2022; Nair et al., 2023). The contribution of blockchain and AI to the Metaverse is further discussed by highlighting aspects such as handling and reusing high-quality/rich data, stabilising decentralised networks, ensuring data privacy, and managing economic-related data (Duan et al., 2021).

Blockchain is an innovative technology enabling the distribution and synchronisation of data among multiple participants. Guo and Liang (2016) referred to blockchain as a concept that combines different computer technologies including distributed data storage, point-to-point transmission, consensus mechanisms, and encryption algorithms. However, blockchain banking is all banking services and activities that are related to blockchain, for instance the execution of payments on behalf of a customer in blockchain, saving for the customer in blockchain, making investments in blockchain, etc. As the financial industry continues to undergo transformative shifts driven by technological advancements, the integration of AI and blockchain technologies is poised to extend its influence into the Metaverse, marking a next frontier for banking innovation. Through the clever use of cryptography, including encryption, it guarantees data security and detects any attempts at tampering. Blockchain is a cutting-edge technology that facilitates the secure exchange of information (Rizzi et al., 2018).

Alshorman et al. (2020) explored how blockchain technology is used in improving the quality and security of banking services, however, there are challenges such as scalability, governance, interoperability, privacy, and regulations that need to be addressed for successful implementation. Vedapradha and Ravi (2021) analysed the advantages of disruptive technological innovations such as AI and blockchain on qualitative service delivery and their impact on investment banks' employee performance. The study concluded that disruptive technology positively impacted the provision of unique services and technological innovations on service delivery and better employee performance. However, it emphasised that technology could be the key to achieving efficiency in operations and customer service delivery. Garg et al. (2021) carried out a study on measuring the perceived benefits of implementing blockchain technology in the banking sector. They explored the potential benefits that blockchain technology can provide to the banking industry and assessed how these perceived benefits influenced the decision-making and adoption of blockchain technology in banks. They highlighted the practical consequences of implementing blockchain technology in the banking industry. It emphasised its potential to solve various challenges and its ability to optimise banking operations.

Meghani (2020) investigated the areas where banks utilise AI and blockchain and examine their applications in leading commercial banks in India. Findings indicated that AI is shaping the future of banking by enhancing data analytics, combatting fraud, improving compliance, and meeting customer demands while blockchain technology is revolutionising the financial world through secure and non-centralised digital currency. Furthermore, AI has mostly been perceived to be a tool to help improve banking services and operations. Nevertheless, customers of financial institutions mostly prefer interaction with humans. In the emerging digital era, humans would work alongside advanced AI-driven technologies in Industry 5.0. In this context, the Metaverse provides a human-centric virtual universe that promotes the real-time interaction between human and disruptive technologies fostering efficiency, personalised value, and productivity (Mourtzis, 2023).

Dewasiri et al. (2023) identified the challenges banks face in adapting AI and blockchain technology and provided new insight into future banking in Industry 5.0 in this digital era. They investigated the recent application of AI and blockchain within the banking sector with regard to its challenges, potential, and the determinants for its adoption from the customers' points of view. However, the study's conclusion focused on using virtual robots and their potential to shape the banking industry.

Through a systematic exploration of blockchain from both technical and use case perspectives, it has been demonstrated that there is significant potential in revolutionising immersive experiences with virtual applications and services. This convergence of AI, blockchain, and the Metaverse not only aligns with the evolving demands for personalised banking but also introduces novel dimensions to security and user experiences. While challenges and considerations need to be addressed, recent studies highlight the potential transformative impact of AI and blockchain technologies in crafting secure and engaging financial interactions within the Metaverse (Xu et al., 2023).

6.3 Fraud Detection and Cybersecurity in Metaverse Finance

As the use of the Metaverse provides customers with many opportunities within the financial sector, many criminal activities have also expanded into the Metaverse's financial system. These financial crimes have significantly impacted customers' confidence in Metaverse finance. Governments and legislative bodies around the world have started introducing new policies and regulations to prevent financial crimes as much as possible (Wu et al., 2023).

AI and ML can help mitigate current global economic and financial issues (Milojević & Redzepagic, 2021). Banking sectors use internet payment techniques to boost efficiency; however, this exposes clients to fraudulent activity. The intentional misappropriation of others' property is a big problem, and it is becoming more common. FinTech solutions are jeopardising consumer protection and financial stability. A close collaboration and open discussion among academics, FinTech experts, and regulators can aid in the development of FinTech risk management models that, while limiting the negative impact of disrupting technologies, encourage the development of practises that could be used to offer automated risk management tools for both SupTech and RegTech purposes thus making FinTech innovations competitive and sustainable (Giudici, 2018; Nasir & Saeedi, 2019).

AI has had a substantial impact on the financial industry which includes financial markets, institutions, and regulations. The processing of data, improved productivity, and cost reductions will be significant benefits for risk management by automating day-to-day assistance, predictive data analytics, and business decisions. The financial system must completely understand AI in order to guide the whole process in its development, implementation, management, and control, as well as to carefully encourage its utilisation in the field of financial risk management. In order to ensure the authenticity of information collection, the use of AI for information collecting must comply to specific standards (Božić, 2023; Naim, 2022). To optimise shareholder wealth, the bank must take lucrative risks. With the rise of financial technology, there has been a spike in interest in investigating how AI may be created and used to better support more conventional financial services and operations (Swankie & Broby, 2019).

In Metaverse finance blockchain, smart contracts, internet of things, and AI solutions have distinct functionality and can effectively solve a variety of financial reporting and audit-related problems while addressing the major concern of financial fraud and audit scandals in technology. Roszkowska (2021) discovered that these technologies are capable of improving the integrity of financial statements and, more widely, to influence how organisations operate. Sirohi et al. (2023) suggested adopting a robust design and structured risk assessment considering the security and privacy elements in order to handle financial fraud.

It is argued that this virtual and implicit fraud causes greater risk to the sustainability of the digital system or Metaverse; in a future where everyone is showing a preference for digital finance, the problem of cyber fraud would go deeper and put everyone at risk of losing their money. However, AI may help with compliance management by automating regulatory document interpretation, monitoring transactions for suspicious activity, and ensuring regulatory requirements are followed. This helps financial institutions comply with rules and decreases the danger of penalties. While AI has various benefits, its adoption should be complemented by rigorous data security measures and adherence to ethical norms to retain consumer confidence and privacy (Btoush et al., 2021).

To minimise the risk, many researchers generated the algorithms based on the techniques of machine language to detect fraudulent activities (Raudha & Saeedi, 2019). However, the data sets of credit card transactions are relatively skewed and difficult to discriminate using a number of algorithms. Therefore, it becomes difficult to achieve efficiency in identifying cyber fraud. Overall, the growing concern is related to massive volume and unbalanced data which either is incorrectly identified or undergoing frequent changes in transaction types (Carcillo et al., 2021; Dal Pozzolo et al., 2018; Al Rubaie, 2021; Sethi & Gera, 2014).

Typical fraudulent activities and financial crimes can include scams, money laundry, wash trading, and cyber-attacks, etc. These activities can not only bring a significant amount of loss to users but it can also negatively impact the economic ecosystem. In conventional financial systems, fraudulent transaction and fraud identification has been always a major issue. Although AI and blockchain, the two main technologies in Metaverse finance, can identify and prevent fraudulent activities much faster and more efficiently, unfortunately, due to a lack of effective regulation in the newly evolved Metaverse, financial crimes such as identity theft, money laundry, and scams have been on the rise (Wu et al., 2023). The rise of online deception or fraud in the scope of e-commerce has significantly increased making it challenging to prevent. In the United States of America (USA), instances of fraud have been detected at a rate 15 times higher than the actual deception rate. The accessibility of AI has played a crucial role in this context. By utilising statistical analysis, AI systems can now detect fraudulent transactions without relying solely on human experts. This advancement in real-time authentication accuracy has led to a reduction in false positives (Fathi Eletter et al., 2010).

Ngai et al. (2011) demonstrated that data-mining tools (as main components of AI) such as logistic models, neural networks, the Bayesian belief network, and decision trees detect four forms of fraud: bank, insurance, securities, and commodities fraud. However, the present study primarily looked at corporate and credit card fraud with little data on money laundering, mortgage securities, and commodities fraud.

The cyber security sector has grown rapidly in recent years and online transactions are attractive to hackers; they are looking to access data to get easy money around the world. Hence, banking institutions are vulnerable and at the forefront of enterprise cyber security. Integration of various AI techniques as a mandatory component can increase the strong control and monitoring system irrespective of cost and benefit (Jiang & Broby, 2021; Morgan, 2021).

Cybercriminals utilise AI-based techniques to threaten victims and automate their attacks in order to gain access to their money. AI is one of the most effective technologies for preventing unanticipated dangers. Cyberattack problems may be classified and handled using the suggested approach which encrypts and decrypts data using the enhanced encryption standard.

Real-time frauds can be predicted with the combination of supervised and unsupervised AI models (Aschi et al., 2022). The Metaverse can benefit from leveraging ML algorithms, natural language processing, anomaly detection techniques, and advanced data analytics; AI-driven cybersecurity systems have the potential to fortify defined mechanisms, identify vulnerabilities, and mitigate risks associated with data breaches, ransomware attacks, identity theft, and other malicious activities. Similarly, fraud detection within the banking sector has become a paramount concern.

Cyber security is a defensive method to protect financial systems, digital data, networks, servers, and unwanted access to cyberspace. The finance industry is challenged by the digital innovations in their systems, processes, operations, and transaction volume. Additionally, due to their implementational reliance on third parties, they are frequently vulnerable to cyber-attacks. Therefore, it is critical to protect clients' personal and confidential information and to ensure its availability and integrity (Adel & Sara, 2020).

6.3.1 Conventional Approaches and AI Algorithms

With the rapid development in technological implementation, it is vital to comprehend the characteristics of the product to enhance and apply effective preventative measures. It is critical to pick an appropriate method; the ideal features may be selected using a genetic algorithm, and classifiers such as Random Forest, Decision Tree, logistic regression, artificial neural network, and Nave Bayes can be tested against the current system to carefully assess performance (Ileberi et al., 2022).

Cybersecurity has vaulted to the top of the banking industry's risk priority list, particularly in the fight against cyber-attacks and credit card fraud. Traditional rule-based systems have shown to be limited in their capacity to analyse massive amounts of data, discover trends, and identify abnormalities. However, identifying fraudulent activity with greater accuracy and efficiency offers considerable potential. Neural networks, support vector machines, and random forests are examples of ML models that can learn from previous data and make intelligent judgements in real time, successfully limiting financial losses associated with fraud (Btoush et al., 2023).

The typical and conventional techniques of detecting cyber fraud are no longer useful and sufficient to meet organisational needs. Many industries are using deep learning (DL) and ML due to its robustness, effectiveness, efficiency, and enhanced accuracy. Digital automation is linked to a variety of elements including safe communication between people, processes, and systems, which is crucial for protecting the privacy and security of distributed digital identities. Unquestionably, individual security breaches harmed billions of people globally in 2018 and the development of blockchain technologies for identifying systems may give beneficial answers to some of the problems that most centralised databases confront. Criminals commit a wide range of cybercrimes where physical devices and human resistance are insufficient to reduce attacks. AI in cybersecurity helps to handle some cybersecurity challenges and numerous new tough vulnerabilities that emerge every day. Most conventional vulnerability management systems react to events only after the vulnerability has been exploited (Azhar Mohammed, 2020). Despite external factors such as the General Data Protection Regulation (GDPR) Act 2018, European policymakers have introduced measures to increase AI activities. Data is essential to almost all business lines, including banks and financial institutions, and has attracted significant investment in the United States and China. As a result, autonomous data management without human intervention provides significant opportunity for banks to enhance speed, accuracy, and efficiency. AI application in banking focuses on customer, operation, trade, and regulatory compliance. For example, robo-advisors and online asset management services and financial planning tools assist users in making better and more efficient consumption and saving decisions. However, legislative regulations concerning data protection, as well as the highly regulated structure of banking, may pose challenges to AI application (Orçun, 2019).

Mhlanga (2020) investigated the substantial effect of AI on digital financial inclusion from the standpoint of risk identification, measurement, and addressing to the appropriate department to provide prompt assistance via chatbots, fraud detection, and cybersecurity. Furthermore, risk in digital banking is dependent on third parties utilising agent networks. AI is capable of improving the security of online finance and offering end consumers with safe payment confidence. Data security and maintenance of trust level is one of the major components to attain and retain customers. Due to rapid advancements in technology, traditional banks are under pressure to deal with the digital transformation, adoption of AI, and cybersecurity (Rodrigues et al., 2022).

Although banks are using technology to remain competitive in the industry, present hazards are growing and new risks are being discovered as business processes change. Following the global financial crisis, banks are subject to more stringent capital adequacy standards. ML, deep learning, speech recognition, natural language processing, and picture recognition are all examples of AI techniques in this regard (Swankie & Broby, 2019).

The 2008 global financial crisis exposed the digital economy to systemic weaknesses in the banking system, prompting regulatory agencies to work to improve financial stability. In light of the economy's globalisation and digitisation, the banking sector is actively evolving, transforming into infrastructural platforms and, as a result, regulation and supervision in this field are changing. According to international banking research, digitisation and globalisation of the economy encourage processes of international regulatory cooperation and law harmonisation. The increased digitisation of banking relationships will aid in the efficient application of prudential standards, notably those relating to the requirement to defend public interests (Tsindeliani et al., 2022).

Fraud incidents are growing as the amount of internet transactions grow, and credit card fraud has increased dramatically with the introduction of contemporary technology. Credit card fraud costs consumers and financial institutions millions of dollars each year. Fraud detection systems should be able to distinguish between legitimate and suspicious fraud and illegitimate transactions by using a variety of technologies (Raudha & Saeedi, 2019; Sethi & Gera, 2014; Trivedi et al., 2020).

The significance of cybersecurity and fraud detection in the Metaverse cannot be overstated; it is a pivotal factor that could determine the viability and success of this virtual space. Users must have confidence that their data, identities, and interactions are adequately safeguarded for the Metaverse to achieve widespread acceptance. Traditional methods of fraud detection may struggle to adapt to the dynamic and interconnected nature of transactions in the Metaverse. AI, with its ability to analyse vast data sets and detect anomalies, is positioned as a key enabler in fortifying financial systems against fraud within the Metaverse. AI algorithms, particularly ML models, can play a vital role in enhancing fraud detection capabilities. These algorithms can analyse user behaviour, transaction patterns, and other relevant data points to identify potentially fraudulent activities within the Metaverse (Chow et al., 2023). By leveraging AI, financial institutions operating in the Metaverse can stay ahead of evolving fraud tactics and ensure the security of digital transactions.

6.4 Credit Management, AI, and the Metaverse

In real-world finance, people often participate in all sorts of financial activities. Same activities apply in the Metaverse as customers engage in the virtual world with the same purpose of lending, borrowing, saving, investments, or use of other financial products and services. In the context of credit management and lending, the Metaverse can extensively use credit scoring models using blockchain and AI technologies to minimise the risk of lending (Truong et al., 2023).

The two main activities banks conduct include accepting deposits and disbursing loans. Loans are a type of consumer credit contract that serves as assets for banks since they make money from the interest that customers pay on long-term loans. Determining the feasibility of the loan and its accompanying terms, such as interest rates, requires rigorous analysis of financial data and other relevant information when banks contemplate providing a loan (Mishkin, 2019).

Banks and insurance businesses are part of the financial services sector which work in a competitive and complicated business climate and are under intense pressure to reform in order to stay relevant. According to Ansari and Riasi (2016), it is crucial to retain customer loyalty which includes satisfaction, trust, commitment, and perceived value. Modern companies have already shown how the use of contemporary technology and a constant customer-focused approach can reinvent financial service operations. Traditional service providers frequently lack the adaptability and creativity needed to satisfy the requirements of their consumers. As a result, FinTech has become a disruptive innovation that has the potential to transform established financial markets (Lee, 2016).

For a bank to be profitable, selecting the correct borrowers is essential, especially given the low-profit margins in retail banking and the requirement to reduce risks (Mishkin, 2019). Technically, it is essential for banks to conduct a thorough assessment of the creditworthiness of consumers before approving or modifying credit contracts. Traditionally, bank officers would personally evaluate loan applications based on the applicant details such as income, savings, and relying on their own experiences. However, the introduction of new data and analytics necessitates a review of the underlying challenges in this decision-making process.

6.4.1 *The Impact of AI on Credit Analysis Procedures*

Apart from the question of whether AI is more predictive than conventional statistical risk analysis models, AI-based techniques for evaluating banking risk provide an undeniable benefit over classic parametric scoring systems (Bedi et al., 2020). Berg et al. (2020) discovered that integrating a fingerprint of the customer considerably improved the predicted accuracy of scoring models. This study focuses on an e-commerce firm that extends credit to customers until products are delivered. Financial sector companies are anticipated to gain a competitive edge by utilising

AI/ML and big data, leading to enhanced operational efficiency and improved quality of financial services for customers.

The influence of AI on improving the making of financial decisions is an intensely debated issue. Companies like Big Data Scoring and Lenddo heavily support the use of AI algorithms to evaluate massive volumes of resources; this is critical to their fundamental operations. It is crucial for investors of all generations to not only carefully analyse potential companies but also remain vigilant to avoid deceptive practices in the market. Evaluating the authenticity of financial reports and data can be a daunting task for human resources alone. Experts believe that the use of AI (especially algorithms) can help mitigate some of these hazards (Killeen & Chan, 2018).

Predictive models for AI and ML can help in credit-rating procedures by allowing lenders to identify the risks of default payments and prepayment more accurately. Khandani et al. (2010) argued that ML could cut banks' losses on past-due clients by up to 25%. Additionally, there is proof that automated financial underwriting systems help underrepresented applicants by raising borrower acceptance rates due to their increased accuracy in anticipating defaults (Gates et al., 2002). These methods also make it possible to automate the appraisal of small borrowers at a reasonable cost (Bazarbash, 2019).

The mix of conventional and alternative sources of information frequently results in significant data volumes that are difficult to assess using classic credit scoring models. Researchers have been investigating the advantages of using AI and ML approaches for credit risk assessment to solve this problem. When trained just on publicly available data, ML models perform better outside of samples (Moscatelli et al., 2020). These ML models perform on par with conventional models when data from the credit registry is available. The benefits of employing ML-based credit scoring models rather than conventional models become more apparent when the lender-borrower relationship is short (Dragomir, 2010). These models consider a multitude of factors unique to the virtual space including the liquidity of virtual assets and the intricacies of digital commerce in the Metaverse.

6.5 Investment, AI, and the Metaverse

The integration of AI into investment strategies within the burgeoning Metaverse has become a focal point for financial innovation. As the Metaverse continues to evolve, AI plays a pivotal role in analysing vast data sets, identifying emerging trends, and making real-time investment decisions. Investors are increasingly leveraging ML algorithms to sift through the complexities of virtual economies, anticipating shifts in user behaviour, and optimising their portfolios for maximum returns. Notable developments include the use of AI-driven predictive analytics to assess the potential value of virtual assets and the application of natural language processing (NLP) algorithms to analyse social sentiment within virtual communities, thus influencing investment decisions. This intersection of AI and the Metaverse has garnered attention from both traditional and crypto-centric investors, showcasing a dynamic landscape where technological advancements shape the future of financial engagement in virtual environments.

AI has evolved tremendously over the past decade and is widely spread in the financial sector due to its benefits of cost reduction, synergies, and less time consumption (Bhagyesh Patel, 2018). Dandapani (2017) concluded that AI has caused major changes in the trading and investment sector through the adoption of automatic trading systems, robo-advisory services, and algorithm developments for trade execution. Some of the existing literature on the market movers will be analysed further in this section. Traditional quantitative trading involves the development of trading strategies using trader's perspectives of stock prices and other analysis tools, whereas intelligent quantitative trading operates using a broader scope and volumes of data. Traditional methods use mathematical formulas and models to analyse the market and gradually derive investment decisions. However, with the use of AI-based quantitative trading predictions are based on algorithms and knowledge graphs to develop strategies that minimise losses and automatically accommodate for changes in the market.

The recent growth in the use of big data has fuelled quantitative transactions due to the volume and range of data availability to analyse and evaluate data patterns. ML, an integral segment of AI, assists in the extraction of data, processing of the extracted data, and strategy development to maximise returns from quantitative trading decisions. Some of the widely discussed algorithms adopted in ML include Traditional ML algorithms, deep-learning algorithms, reinforcement-learning algorithms and deep-reinforcement-learning algorithms (Zhang, 2023).

However, when it comes to investment in virtual assets in the Metaverse environment, settling and comparing the values of the virtual assets could be challenging as these are not physical assets and determination of their fair value at the transfer point might be quite difficult. Furthermore, their values might be reported differently in different organisations (Pandey & Gilmour, 2023). Moreover, Yang et al. (2020) highlighted that ML algorithms need to be maintained and handled appropriately to produce a successful strategy as minor errors can cause models misfit for use.

6.5.1 Trading Bots

Automated trading systems (ATS) operate with trade rules embedded into a programme which begin to learn the structure of the data and forecasts trends that are yet to occur. ATs are widely used and make fast trade decisions through the use of trading bots. They have expanded and are growing to different trading platforms. Algorithmic trading is stated to execute trades at the most ideal rates with less errors and improved accuracy and minimise subjectivity and human errors while adjusting to market conditions automatically (Buchanan, 2019). In an attempt to maximise returns with minimum effort, Mathur et al. (2021) highlighted the benefits of a trade bot to a trader in trade execution. The authors specified that the algorithmic trading market would expand significantly between 2018 and 2026. Bhagyesh Patel (2018) described the use of AI in securities investments through the use of a computerised system structured to forecast the ideal circumstances at which shares could be bought or sold so that the profits outweigh potential losses.

Azhikodan et al. (2019) analysed the use of reinforcement-learning algorithms in stock value predications and proves its ability in doing so. Additionally, further suggestions by the author are determined to benefit from a master network which could be structured to predict stock values of multiple companies derived through individual networks to maximise the output from existing resources. In addition, the role of AI in effective investment portfolio management was studied through a framework discussed by Kristjanpoller et al. (2021) that involved a virtual expert pool providing stock recommendations and using AI through the wisdom of artificial crowds in decision implementation.

Rundo et al. (2019) proposed the Grid Trading System Robot (GTSbot), i.e. a trading bot used in the foreign exchange market to minimise experiencing financial risk associated in Forex trades. The author specifies that the forex market is exposed to high instability with lower opportunities for returns thereby increasing inefficiencies. Hence, the use of GTSbot would materialise returns of the highly liquid Forex market while mitigating potential incompetencies in the market. Robo-advisory is a software designed through the generation of algorithms to provide automated financial advisory to potential investors based on their requirements such as expected risk-return, investment objectives, risk appetite, and income levels while adopting to market fluctuations (Jung et al., 2018).

The process would include the investor answering a questionnaire stating their expectations and from which potential investment options are generated. The system would evaluate and assign an appropriate class of assets to invest in and the weightage allocated to each asset based on the investor preferences. A rational portfolio is created through the software, and an algorithmic rebalancing is continuously formed to accommodate for changes in the portfolio weights of assets (Jung et al., 2019). Additionally, changes to the portfolio would be adjusted through rebalancing based on variations in individual investor preferences over time. Generally, the algorithms that generate portfolio allocation through robo-advisors are derived from the Modern Portfolio Theory (Abraham et al., 2019). Jung et al. (2019) explained that the growth of robo-advisory services is triggered by the automated investor assessment and lower minimum investment attached to lower transaction fees compared to the traditional financial advisory services. Moreover, the authors discussed the potential scope for growth in robo-advisory among the tech savvy millennials and believe robo-advisors would cater to budget-friendly investors which was not catered to by the traditional financial advisors. They further stated that, through the use of robo-advisors, an opportunity to create an all-inclusive tool can be created in the future.

Shanmuganathan (2020) focused on the actual and potential implications of AI-based applications and technical issues that are related to behavioural finance. The study found that AI-based robo-advisors provide financial literacy instruction and impartial expert advice, which may offer solutions, based on clients' requirements. Tao et al. (2021) discussed the performance of AI-based advisors and conventional funds, i.e. equity, fixed income, money market, and hybrid funds during the period 2016 and 2019 in the United States. The survey resulted in robo-advisors outperforming these funds. The author specifies that the survey is restricted due to the data available being not exhaustive and recommend reassessing with a broader scope of data.

A survey that analysed the demand for financial advisory services due to robo-advisory services presented a strong negative relationship and highlighted a substitution effect on financial advisory (Brenner & Meyll, 2020). Furthermore, the use of robo-advisory was shown among investors who fear fraud and investors preventing conflict of interest. The author suggests developing relationships with clients based on trust and accompanying robo-advisors to financial advice.

Bhatia et al. (2021) analysed the opinions and knowledge of Indian investors regarding FinTech innovations and identified pointers that significantly influenced their views on inventions, such as robo-advisors. Furthermore, suggestions to improve the awareness of investors were discussed, and it was concluded that, at present, robo-advisors are considered a supplementary service rather than a substitute for financial advisory services in the Indian Stock Market thereby contradicting the conclusions of Brenner and Meyll (2020).

A robo-advisory service is an AI-driven service in its infancy. Despite the threats of competition and regulations, the on-going trend towards technological advancements across industries with tech savvy youngsters accepting AI-based trading and investments would contribute to the long-term growth of robo-advisory.

6.5.2 Quantum Trading

Beyond the on-going scope of online trading, the industry is underway to quantum computing. Dandapani (2017) discussed quantum computing as theoretical computation systems with faster processing capacity as opposed to the existing systems. This would be revolutionary as it enhances the scientific approach to trading. Execution of trades and examination of data at the speed of light would automatically develop an edge for quantum trading. Dandapani (2017) believed implementation of quantum trading would be time consuming but is expected to minimise existing systemic flaws in trading and investments in the new era of electronic trading. However, the development of quantum computing would increase the risk of layoffs thus causing a rise in costs and privacy concerns.

AI is a powerful and valuable tool to various industries in the twenty-first century. Automation that is driven by AI has evolved significantly over the last decade and further investigations such as quantum computing are underway to maximise and enhance the generated output. The trading and quantitative investment market has changed drastically in comparison to the market prior to automation with cost savings, less human errors, maximum wealth creation, and catering to different niche markets. However, Yampolskiy (2019) argued that, despite its benefits, AI has led to failures and inefficiencies in the past. The author recalled an instance that was relevant to investment and quantitative trading, the market crashes caused by trading software and thereby emphasised the importance of AI safety. The need to understand that system failures could occur due to misinterpretation of the user requirement and development of systems based on correlated functions was further elaborated upon. Therefore, the gaps in the learning curve need to be identified and developed over time with newer versions and updates of algorithms.

Recent references supporting this trend include reports from leading financial institutions, such as J. P. Morgan, discussing the impact of AI on asset management in virtual spaces. Additionally, insights from AI-focused companies like IBM encourage investment in Augmented Reality (AR) solutions due to the clear benefits they can provide in the Metaverse ecosystem. Den Yeoh et al. (2023) considered the Metaverse in investment using sentiment analysis and ML. They analysed time series data for crypto price and text where information like news, articles, and feedback from social media can use the input to generate the sentiment score to understand the crypto trends.

6.6 Conclusion

The Metaverse is disrupting many sectors including the finance sector, and different industries are investing in the Metaverse and taking steps to exploit its numerous opportunities. AI is one of the main technology tools in Metaverse finance, and it is assisting the finance industry in crafting its strategies, services, and products more efficiently and effectively. The application of AI holds significant promise for the finance sector in different domains such as investing, lending, borrowing, budgeting, saving, and forecasting. AI is a powerful and valuable tool used in banking, fraud detection and cybersecurity, credit management, and investment. Automation that is driven by AI has evolved significantly over the last decade, and further investigations and research on Industry 5.0 are underway to maximise and enhance the output generated. The finance sector has been drastically changed compared to the era prior to automation with cost savings, less human errors, maximum wealth creation, and catering to different niche markets, and the application of AI significantly impacts the finance sector in all domains of finance. The contribution of AI to Metaverse finance has been revolutionary and would further mitigate bureaucratic and inefficient operations in the industry with the on-going developments. Overall, in Metaverse finance, like any other technology-based platforms, trust, transparency, accuracy, security, and privacy are the key factors in customer satisfaction and success of adaptation. So far AI is proven to be one of the best technologies to make this transformation smoother, however, it has its own challenges regarding huge data processing, massive transaction, cyber-attacks, regulatory compliance, and virtual asset pricing. It is crucial for financial institutions to understand customers' needs and apply suitable techniques and technologies carefully in the Metaverse context. Consideration of security breaches, regulatory compliance, and personal data privacy should be at the top of implementational strategies since the advancement of technology can also pose a significant risk to the massive transaction and data transfer pushing up numerous challenges in safeguarding sensitive information, detecting fraudulent activities, and managing financial risks. AI plays a significant role in expanding Metaverse finance for consumers, financial institutions, and policy makers with regard to effective, efficient, and fast access to information and communications in banking operations, managing risk, cybersecurity, compliance, and investment options. Existing literature presents the need for further research surrounding the application of AI in Metaverse finance and its importance in connections and trust with customers, accuracy of price predictions derived from algorithms, assessment and inclusion of customer requirements, fully automated investment and trading reliability, and AI safety in future analysis. Continuous assessment of the fast-evolving new technologies regarding the application of AI and other new technologies in Metaverse finance is highly recommended for future research. Meanwhile, thorough research in adapting new technologies from a behavioural finance perspective can significantly help practitioners and policy makers to recognise the strengths and challenges of this transition.

References

Abraham, F., Schmukler, S. L., & Tessada, J. (2019). *Robo-advisors - Investing through machines*. Orld Bank Chile Center and Malaysia Hub: World Bank Group.

Adel, I., & Sara, A. (2020). The significance of cybersecurity system in helping managing risk in banking and financial sector. *Journal of Xidian University, 14*(7). https://doi.org/10.37896/jxu14.7/174

Ahmed, S., Alshater, M. M., El Ammari, A., & Hammami, H. (2022). Artificial intelligence and machine learning in finance: A bibliometric review. *Research in International Business and Finance, 61*, 101646. https://doi.org/10.1016/j.ribaf.2022.101646

Al Rubaie, E. M. H. (2021). Improvement in credit card fraud detection using ensemble classification technique and user data. *International Journal of Nonlinear Analysis and Applications, 12*(2), 1255–1265. https://doi.org/10.22075/IJNAA.2021.5228

Ansari, A., & Riasi, A. (2016). Modelling and evaluating customer loyalty using neural networks: Evidence from startup insurance companies. *Future Business Journal, 2*(1), 15–30. https://doi.org/10.1016/j.fbj.2016.04.001

Aschi, M., Bonura, S., Masi, N., Messina, D., & Profeta, D. (2022). Big data and artificial intelligence in digital finance. In J. Soldatos & D. Kyriazis (Eds.), *Big data and artificial intelligence in digital finance* (Vol. 1). Springer. https://doi.org/10.1007/978-3-030-94590-9

Ashta, A., & Herrmann, H. (2021). Artificial intelligence and fintech: An overview of opportunities and risks for banking, investments, and microfinance. *Strategic Change, 30*(3), 211–222. https://doi.org/10.1002/jsc.2404

Azhar Mohammed, I. (2020). Artificial intelligence for cybersecurity: A systematic mapping of literature. *SSRN Electronic Journal, 7*(9).

Azhikodan, A. R., Bhat, A. G. K., & Jadhav, M. V. (2019). Stock trading bot using deep reinforcement learning. *Lecture Notes in Networks and Systems, 32*, 41–49. https://doi.org/10.1007/978-981-10-8201-6_5

Bazarbash, M. (2019). *FinTech in financial inclusion machine learning applications in assessing credit risk*. IMF working paper monetary and capital markets department FinTech in financial inclusion: Machine learning applications in assessing credit risk.

Bedi, P., Goyal, S. B., & Kumar, J. (2020). Basic structure on artificial intelligence: A revolution in risk management and compliance. In *Proceedings of the 3rd International Conference on Intelligent Sustainable Systems, ICISS 2020* (pp. 570–576). Institute of Electrical and Electronics Engineers. https://doi.org/10.1109/ICISS49785.2020.9315986

Berdiyeva, O., Islam, M. U., & Saeedi, M. (2021). Artificial intelligence in accounting and finance: Meta-analysis. *International Business Review, 3*(1), 56–79.

Berg, T., Burg, V., Gombović, A., & Puri, M. (2020). On the rise of FinTechs: Credit scoring using digital footprints. *Review of Financial Studies, 33*(7), 2845–2897. https://doi.org/10.1093/rfs/hhz099

Bhagyesh Patel, K. (2018). Artificial Intelligence in finance, *4*. https://doi.org/10.13140/RG.2.2.11073.30560

Bhatia, A., Chandani, A., Atiq, R., Mehta, M., & Divekar, R. (2021). Artificial intelligence in financial services: A qualitative research to discover robo-advisory services. *Qualitative Research in Financial Markets, 13*(5), 632–654. https://doi.org/10.1108/QRFM-10-2020-0199

Božić, V. (2023). The role of artificial intelligence in risk management. *ResearchGate*. https://doi.org/10.13140/RG.2.2.29886.77126

Brenner, L., & Meyll, T. (2020). Robo-advisors: A substitute for human financial advice? *Journal of Behavioral and Experimental Finance, 25*, 100275. https://doi.org/10.1016/j.jbef.2020.100275

Btoush, E., Zhou, X., Gururajan, R., Chan, K. C., & Tao, X. H. (2021). A survey on credit card fraud detection techniques in banking industry for cyber security. In *Proceedings of 2021 8th IEEE international conference on Behavioural and social computing, BESC 2021*. Institute of Electrical and Electronics Engineers. https://doi.org/10.1109/BESC53957.2021.9635559

Btoush, E., Zhou, X., Gururajan, R., Chan, K. C., Genrich, R., & Sankaran, P. (2023). A systematic review of literature on credit card cyber fraud detection using machine and deep learning. *PeerJ Computer Science, 9*, e1278. https://doi.org/10.7717/PEERJ-CS.1278

Buchanan, B. G. (2019). *Artificial intelligence in finance*. The Alan Turing Institute. https://doi.org/10.5281/zenodo.2612537

Cao, L. (2020). *AI in finance: A review*.

Carcillo, F., Le Borgne, Y. A., Caelen, O., Kessaci, Y., Oblé, F., & Bontempi, G. (2021). Combining unsupervised and supervised learning in credit card fraud detection. *Information Sciences, 557*, 317–331. https://doi.org/10.1016/j.ins.2019.05.042

Choithani, T., Chowdhury, A., Patel, S., Patel, P., Patel, D., & Shah, M. (2022). A comprehensive study of artificial intelligence and cybersecurity on bitcoin, crypto currency and banking system. *Annals of Data Science*. https://doi.org/10.1007/s40745-022-00433-5

Chow, Y. W., Susilo, W., Li, Y., Li, N., & Nguyen, C. (2023). Visualization and cybersecurity in the Metaverse: A survey. *Journal of Imaging*. https://doi.org/10.3390/jimaging9010011

Dal Pozzolo, A., Boracchi, G., Caelen, O., Alippi, C., & Bontempi, G. (2018). Credit card fraud detection: A realistic modeling and a novel learning strategy. *IEEE Transactions on Neural Networks and Learning Systems, 29*(8), 3784–3797. https://doi.org/10.1109/TNNLS.2017.2736643

Dandapani, K. (2017). Electronic finance – Recent developments. *Managerial Finance*. https://doi.org/10.1108/MF-02-2017-0028

Den Yeoh, E., Chung, T., & Wang, Y. (2023). Metaverse in investment using sentiment analysis and machine learning. In *Strategies and opportunities for technology in the Metaverse World* (pp. 78–113). IGI Global. https://doi.org/10.4018/978-1-6684-5732-0.ch006

Dewasiri, N. J., Karunarathne, K. S. S. N., Menon, S., Jayarathne, P. G. S. A., & Rathnasiri, M. S. H. (2023). Fusion of artificial intelligence and blockchain in the banking industry: Current application, adoption, and future challenges. In *Transformation for sustainable business and management practices: Exploring the Spectrum of industry 5.0* (pp. 293–307). Emerald Group. https://doi.org/10.1108/978-1-80262-277-520231021

Doumpos, M., Zopounidis, C., Gounopoulos, D., Platanakis, E., & Zhang, W. (2023). Operational research and artificial intelligence methods in banking. *European Journal of Operational Research*. https://doi.org/10.1016/j.ejor.2022.04.027

Dragomir, L. (2010). *European Prudential banking regulation and supervision*. Routledge. https://doi.org/10.4324/9780203856413

Duan, H., Li, J., Fan, S., Lin, Z., Wu, X., & Cai, W. (2021). Metaverse for social good: A university campus prototype. In *MM 2021 - Proceedings of the 29th ACM international conference on multimedia* (pp. 153–161). Association for Computing Machinery. https://doi.org/10.1145/3474085.3479238

Elia, G., Stefanelli, V. and Ferilli, G.B. (2022), "Investigating the role of Fintech in the banking industry: what do we know?", *European Journal of Innovation Management*, Vol. 26, https://doi.org/10.1108/EJIM-12-2021-0608

Fathi Eletter, S., Ghaleb Yaseen, S., & Awad Elrefae, G. (2010). Neuro-based artificial intelligence model for loan decisions. *American Journal of Economics and Business Administration, 2*(1), 27–34.

Garg, P., Gupta, B., Chauhan, A. K., Sivarajah, U., Gupta, S., & Modgil, S. (2021). Measuring the perceived benefits of implementing blockchain technology in the banking sector. *Technological Forecasting and Social Change, 163*. https://doi.org/10.1016/j.techfore.2020.120407

Gates, S. W., Perry, V. G., & Zorn, P. M. (2002). Automated underwriting in mortgage lending: Good news for the underserved? *Housing Policy Debate, 13*(2), 369–391. https://doi.org/10.1080/10511482.2002.9521447

Geetha, A. (2021). *A study on artificial intelligence (AI) in banking and financial services*.

Gigante, G., & Zago, A. (2023). DARQ technologies in the financial sector: Artificial intelligence applications in personalized banking. *Qualitative Research in Financial Markets, 15*(1), 29–57. https://doi.org/10.1108/QRFM-02-2021-0025

Giudici, P. (2018). Fintech risk management: A research challenge for artificial intelligence in finance. *Frontiers in Artificial Intelligence, 1*. https://doi.org/10.3389/frai.2018.00001

Guo, Y., & Liang, C. (2016). Blockchain application and outlook in the banking industry. *Financial Innovation*. https://doi.org/10.1186/s40854-016-0034-9

Huynh-The, T., Gadekallu, T. R., Wang, W., Yenduri, G., Ranaweera, P., Pham, Q. V., da Costa, D. B., et al. (2023). Blockchain for the metaverse: A review. *Future Generation Computer Systems, 143*, 401–419. https://doi.org/10.1016/j.future.2023.02.008

Ileberi, E., Sun, Y., & Wang, Z. (2022). A machine learning based credit card fraud detection using the GA algorithm for feature selection. *Journal of Big Data, 9*(1). https://doi.org/10.1186/s40537-022-00573-8

Jiang, C., & Broby, D. (2021). *Mitigating cybersecurity challenges in the financial sector with artificial intelligence*.

Joshua, J. (2017). Information bodies: Computational anxiety in Neal Stephenson's Snow Crash. *Interdisciplinary Literary Studies, 19*(1), 17–47. https://doi.org/10.5325/intelitestud.19.1.0017

Jung, D., Dorner, V., Glaser, F., & Morana, S. (2018). Robo-advisory: Digitalization and automation of financial advisory. *Business and Information Systems Engineering, 60*(1), 81–86. https://doi.org/10.1007/s12599-018-0521-9

Jung, D., Glaser, F., & Köpplin, W. (2019). *Robo-advisory: Opportunities and risks for the future of financial advisory* (Contributions to management science) (pp. 405–427). Springer. https://doi.org/10.1007/978-3-319-95999-3_20

Kaur, N., Sahdev, S. L., Sharma, M., & Siddiqui, L. (2020). Banking 4.0: 'The influence of artificial intelligence on the Banking Industry & how AI is changing the face of modern day banks'. *Mechanical Engineering EJournal*.

Kaur, N., Saha, S., Agarwal, V., & Gulati, S. (2023). Metaverse and Fintech: Pathway for innovation and development. In *Proceedings of 2023 3rd international conference on innovative practices in technology and management, ICIPTM 2023*. Institute of Electrical and Electronics Engineers. https://doi.org/10.1109/ICIPTM57143.2023.10117956

Khandani, A. E., Kim, A. J., & Lo, A. W. (2010). Consumer credit-risk models via machine-learning algorithms. *Journal of Banking and Finance, 34*(11), 2767–2787. https://doi.org/10.1016/j.jbankfin.2010.06.001

Killeen, A., & Chan, R. (2018). Chapter 10 - Global financial institutions 2.011All views are those of the authors and do not reflect the views of the World Bank or its member countries. In D. Lee Kuo Chuen & R. Deng (Eds.), *Handbook of Blockchain, digital finance, and inclusion* (Vol. 2, pp. 213–242). Academic Press. https://doi.org/10.1016/B978-0-12-812282-2.00010-3

Kk, S., & Philip, N. (2012). *Credit card fraud detection based on behaviour mining.*

Kristjanpoller, W., Michell, K., Minutolo, M. C., & Dheeriya, P. (2021). Trading support system for portfolio construction using wisdom of artificial crowds and evolutionary computation. *Expert Systems with Applications, 177*, 114943. https://doi.org/10.1016/j.eswa.2021.114943

Lee, I. (2016). Fintech: Ecosystem and business models. *Advanced Science and. Technology Letters, 142*, 57–62. https://doi.org/10.14257/astl.2016.142.10

Mathur, M., Mhadalekar, S., Mhatre, S., & Mane, V. (2021). Algorithmic trading bot. *ITM Web of Conferences, 40*, 03041. https://doi.org/10.1051/itmconf/20214003041

Meghani, K. (2020). Use of artificial intelligence and Blockchain in banking sector: A study of scheduled commercial banks in India. *CompSciRN: Human-Robotic Interaction (Topic).*

Mhlanga, D. (2020). Industry 4.0 in finance: The impact of artificial intelligence (AI) on digital financial inclusion. *International Journal of Financial Studies, 8*(3), 1–14. https://doi.org/10.3390/ijfs8030045

Milojević, N., & Redzepagic, S. (2021). Prospects of artificial intelligence and machine learning application in banking risk management. *Journal of Central Banking Theory and Practice, 10*(3), 41–57. https://doi.org/10.2478/jcbtp-2021-0023

Mishkin, F. S. (2019). *The economics of money, banking, and financial markets* (12th ed.). Pearson.

Morgan, S. (2021). *Cyberwarfare in the C-suite cybercrime facts and statistics* (Vol. 21).

Moscatelli, M., Parlapiano, F., Narizzano, S., & Viggiano, G. (2020). Corporate default forecasting with machine learning. *Expert Systems with Applications, 161*, 113567. https://doi.org/10.1016/j.eswa.2020.113567

Mourtzis, D. (2023). The Metaverse in industry 5.0: A human-centric approach towards personalized value creation. *Encyclopaedia, 3*(3), 1105–1120. https://doi.org/10.3390/encyclopedia3030080

Naim, A. (2022). Role of artificial intelligence in business risk management. *American Journal of Business Management, Economics and Banking, 1.*

Nair, V. C., Munilla-Garrido, G., & Song, D. (2023). Going incognito in the Metaverse: Achieving theoretically optimal privacy-usability tradeoffs in VR. *Association for Computing Machinery (ACM)*, 1–16. https://doi.org/10.1145/3586183.3606754

Nasir, F., & Saeedi, M. (2019). 'RegTech' as a solution for compliance challenge: A review article. *Journal of Advanced Research in Dynamical and Control Systems, 11*(11), 912–919. https://doi.org/10.5373/JARDCS/V11SP11/20193115

Ngai, E. W. T., Hu, Y., Wong, Y. H., Chen, Y., & Sun, X. (2011). The application of data mining techniques in financial fraud detection: A classification framework and an academic review of literature. *Decision Support Systems, 50*(3), 559–569. https://doi.org/10.1016/j.dss.2010.08.006

Noreen, U., Shafique, A., Ahmed, Z., & Ashfaq, M. (2023). Banking 4.0: Artificial Intelligence (AI) in banking industry & consumer's perspective. *Sustainability (Switzerland), 15*(4). https://doi.org/10.3390/su15043682

Ooi, K. B., Tan, G. W. H., Aw, E. C. X., Cham, T. H., Dwivedi, Y. K., Dwivedi, R., Hughes, L., et al. (2023). Banking in the metaverse: A new frontier for financial institutions. *International Journal of Bank Marketing*. https://doi.org/10.1108/IJBM-03-2023-0168

Orçun, K. (2019). *Artificial intelligence in banking.*

Orçun Kaya, A., Jan Schildbach, E., DB Research Management, Schneider, S. (2019). *EU monitor global financial markets artificial intelligence in banking.*

Pandey, D., & Gilmour, P. (2023). Accounting meets metaverse: Navigating the intersection between the real and virtual worlds. *Journal of Financial Reporting and Accounting*. https://doi.org/10.1108/JFRA-03-2023-0157

Rahman, M., Ming, T. H., Baigh, T. A., & Sarker, M. (2022). Adoption of artificial intelligence in banking services: An empirical analysis. *International Journal of Emerging Markets*. https://doi.org/10.1108/IJOEM-06-2020-0724

Ratib Alshorman, A., Abushariah, M. A. M., Al Shorman, A. R., Eddin Sabri, K., & Qaimari, M. (2020). Blockchain for banking systems: Opportunities and challenges. *Journal of Theoretical and Applied Information Technology*, 15(23).

Raudha, F., & Saeedi, M. (2019). Artificial intelligence and machine learning as a tool in preventing and detecting financial fraud: A systematic literature review. *Journal of Advanced Research in Dynamical and Control Systems*. https://doi.org/10.5373/JARDCS/V11SP11/20193114

Rizzi, W., Schardin, S., Tanuwidjaja, I., & Wu, H. (2018). *Deep learning: The next frontier in personalized banking*. McKinsey.

Rodrigues, A. R. D., Ferreira, F. A. F., Teixeira, F. J. C. S. N., & Zopounidis, C. (2022). Artificial intelligence, digital transformation and cybersecurity in the banking sector: A multi-stakeholder cognition-driven framework. *Research in International Business and Finance, 60*, 101616. https://doi.org/10.1016/j.ribaf.2022.101616

Roszkowska, P. (2021). Fintech in financial reporting and audit for fraud prevention and safeguarding equity investments. *Journal of Accounting and Organizational Change, 17*(2), 164–196. https://doi.org/10.1108/JAOC-09-2019-0098

Rundo, F., Trenta, F., di Stallo, A. L., & Battiato, S. (2019). Grid trading system robot (GTSbot): A novel mathematical algorithm for trading FX market. *Applied Sciences (Switzerland), 9*(9). https://doi.org/10.3390/app9091796

Sethi, N., & Gera, A. (2014). A revived survey of various credit card fraud detection techniques. *International Journal of Computer Science and Mobile Computing, 3.*

Shanmuganathan, M. (2020). Behavioural finance in an era of artificial intelligence: Longitudinal case study of robo-advisors in investment decisions. *Journal of Behavioral and Experimental Finance, 27*, 100297. https://doi.org/10.1016/j.jbef.2020.100297

Sheth, J. N., Jain, V., Roy, G., & Chakraborty, A. (2022). AI-driven banking services: The next frontier for a personalised experience in the emerging market. *International Journal of Bank Marketing, 40*(6), 1248–1271. https://doi.org/10.1108/IJBM-09-2021-0449

Shi, F., Ning, H., Zhang, X., Li, R., Tian, Q., Zhang, S., Zheng, Y., et al. (2023). A new technology perspective of the Metaverse: Its essence, framework and challenges. *Digital Communications and Networks, 10*, 1653. https://doi.org/10.1016/j.dcan.2023.02.017

Sirohi, D., Kumar, N., Rana, P. S., Tanwar, S., Iqbal, R., & Hijjii, M. (2023). Federated learning for 6G-enabled secure communication systems: A comprehensive survey. *Artificial Intelligence Review, 56*, 11297. https://doi.org/10.1007/s10462-023-10417-3

Suryono, R. R., Budi, I., & Purwandari, B. (2020). Challenges and trends of financial technology (Fintech): A systematic literature review. *Information (Switzerland)*. https://doi.org/10.3390/info11120590

Swankie, G., & Broby, D. (2019). *Examining the impact of artificial intelligence on the evaluation of banking risk.*

Tao, R., Su, C. W., Xiao, Y., Dai, K., & Khalid, F. (2021). Robo advisors, algorithmic trading and investment management: Wonders of fourth industrial revolution in financial markets. *Technological Forecasting and Social Change, 163*, 120421. https://doi.org/10.1016/j.techfore.2020.120421

Trivedi, N. K., Simaiya, S., Lilhore, U. K., & Sharma, S. K. (2020). An efficient credit card fraud detection model based on machine learning methods. *International Journal of Advanced Science and Technology, 29*(5), 3414–3424.

Truong, V. T., Le, L., & Niyato, D. (2023). Blockchain meets Metaverse and digital asset management: A comprehensive survey. *IEEE Access, 11*, 26258–26288. https://doi.org/10.1109/ACCESS.2023.3257029

Tsindeliani, I. A., Proshunin, M. M., Sadovskaya, T. D., Popkova, Z. G., Davydova, M. A., & Babayan, O. A. (2022). Digital transformation of the banking system in the context of sustainable development. *Journal of Money Laundering Control, 25*(1), 165–180. https://doi.org/10.1108/JMLC-02-2021-0011

Umamaheswari, S., Valarmathi, A., & Lakshami, R. (2023). Role of artificial intelligence in The banking sector. *Journal of Survey in Fisheries Sciences, 10.*

Van Huynh, D., Khosravirad, S. R., Masaracchia, A., Dobre, O. A., & Duong, T. Q. (2022). Edge intelligence-based ultra-reliable and low-latency communications for digital twin-enabled Metaverse. *IEEE Wireless Communications Letters, 11*(8), 1733–1737. https://doi.org/10.1109/LWC.2022.3179207

Vedapradha, R., & Ravi, H. (2021). Innovation in banking: Fusion of artificial intelligence and blockchain. *Asia Pacific Journal of Innovation and Entrepreneurship, 15*(1), 51–61. https://doi.org/10.1108/apjie-09-2020-0142

Wu, J., Lin, K., Lin, D., Zheng, Z., Huang, H., & Zheng, Z. (2023). Financial crimes in Web3-empowered Metaverse: Taxonomy, countermeasures, and opportunities. *IEEE Open Journal of the Computer Society, 4*, 37–49. https://doi.org/10.1109/OJCS.2023.3245801

Xu, M., Guo, Y., Hu, Q., Xiong, Z., Yu, D., & Cheng, X. (2023). A trustless architecture of blockchain-enabled metaverse R. *Cryptography and Security, 3*, 88. https://doi.org/10.1016/j.hcc.2022.10

Xue, M., Xiu, G., Saravanan, V., & Montenegro-Marin, C. E. (2021). Cloud computing with AI for banking and e-commerce applications. *Electronic Library, 39*(4), 539–552. https://doi.org/10.1108/EL-07-2020-0207

Yampolskiy, R. V. (2019). Predicting future AI failures from historic examples. *Foresight, 21*(1), 138–152. https://doi.org/10.1108/FS-04-2018-0034

Yang, X., Liu, W., Zhou, D., Bian, J., & Liu, T.-Y. (2020), *Qlib: An AI-oriented quantitative investment platform.*

Yathiraju, N., & Dash, B. (2023). Big data and Metaverse revolutionizing the futuristic Fintech industry. *International Journal of Computer Science and Information Technology, 15*(1), 01–13. https://doi.org/10.5121/ijcsit.2023.15101

Zhang, K. (2023). *A survey of quantitative trading based on artificial intelligence* (pp. 171–177). Atlantis Press. https://doi.org/10.2991/978-94-6463-124-1_21

[illegible]

Chapter 7
FinTech and the Metaverse: Financial Inclusion Through GenAI, Blockchain, and Digital Banking

James Hutson and Gaurango Banerjee

Abstract The emergence of the Metaverse marks a transformative era in financial technology (FinTech), propelled by the integration of Generative Artificial Intelligence (GAI). This chapter explores how GAI enhances financial inclusivity and democratises access to financial services by merging with FinTech within the Metaverse. It highlights the synergy between these technologies, focusing on their potential to dismantle traditional barriers to financial access such as geographic and temporal limitations. This could lead to a more accessible and equitable financial ecosystem. Key advancements facilitated by GAI include significant reductions in operational costs—yielding lower fees and better rates for consumers—and the development of personalised financial literacy programmes that elevate consumer knowledge and decision-making capabilities. This chapter also examines GAI's role in fostering innovative financial products and services that may compel traditional financial institutions to adapt and expand their offerings. Furthermore, it delves into the potential for community-driven, decentralised financial systems within the Metaverse, underscored by the transparency and trustworthiness enhanced by blockchain technology. This environment is conducive to reducing entry barriers and fostering active financial participation. Ultimately, this discussion articulates a vision where the convergence of GAI and FinTech within the Metaverse drives a financially inclusive, user-focused, and innovative ecosystem. This chapter aims to map out the pathways through which these technologies could cultivate a prosperous financial landscape, positing the Metaverse as a frontier of synthesised prosperity in finance.

Keywords Generative Artificial Intelligence (GAI) · Financial technology (FinTech) · Metaverse · Financial literacy · Decentralised finances · Digital banking · Blockchain · Cryptocurrency

---

J. Hutson (✉) · G. Banerjee
Department of Finance, Lindenwood University, Saint Charles, MO, USA
e-mail: JHutson@lindenwood.edu

N. Islam, I. Salami (eds.), *Metaverse Innovation*, Applied Innovation and Technology Management, https://doi.org/10.1007/978-3-031-97080-1_7

7.1 Introduction

The term Metaverse has captivated the collective imagination, a testimony to which is its nomination as a finalist for the word of the year by Oxford University Press. The momentum behind this term was significantly fuelled by the strategic rebranding of Facebook to Meta, marking an investment of billions into the development of an immersive reality platform. Concurrently, projects such as Decentraland and The Sandbox have been pioneering Web3 versions of 3D social environments (Quiroz-Guitierrez, 2022). The cinematic visualisation of immersive virtual environments, notably depicted in Ready Player One (2018), has transitioned from the realm of fantasy to an attainable horizon, further propelling the Metaverse into the vanguard of popular discourse.

Ball (2022) delineated the Metaverse as an interoperable and scalable real-time network, accessible in 3D virtuality and experienced synchronously. This conceptualisation envisages a boundless user base engaging in a spectrum of interactions—social, financial, and beyond—within this unbroken virtual commune. However, the contemporary rendition of the Metaverse, as epitomised by entities like Meta, falls short of the ideals of interoperability and scalability. Rather than immersing in a singular virtual or 3D iteration of the Internet, users navigate through myriad portals leading to distinct virtual spaces hosted on divergent platforms. This scenario begets a multiverse of Metaverses coexisting in parallel yet encapsulated in silos (Valaskova et al., 2022). A crucial impediment to achieving interoperability stems from the realisation that technological innovation alone cannot orchestrate the Metaverse. The foundation of a stable and trustworthy economy is indispensable yet the extant digital economy predominantly orbits around centralised organisations, such as banks and corporations, which retain ownership of digital properties, thereby excluding users from proprietorship (Hollensen et al., 2022). In this context, blockchain-centric technologies emerge as a potential harbinger of decentralisation, representing a stride towards the actualisation of a true Metaverse (Berg et al., 2019).

Emerging from the origins of the Bitcoin cryptocurrency, blockchain technology has established itself as the foundational technology for the digital currency market due to its role in enabling a decentralised economic system (Gadekallu et al., 2022). Blockchain functions as a distributed ledger that records transactions across multiple computers to ensure no single point of failure can alter the data. This system enhances the traceability and security of digital assets within a financial network. Digital assets refer to digital representations of value or contractual rights that can be stored, traded, and transferred electronically. Common examples of digital assets include cryptocurrencies like Bitcoin and Ethereum, digital tokens, and non-fungible tokens (NFTs), each possessing unique ownership details verified by blockchain technology. NFTs are unique digital assets that represent ownership of specific items using blockchain technology which ensures each token is one of a kind and cannot be duplicated. NFTs can be associated with various forms of digital content, including art, music, video clips, and even virtual real estate, allowing them to be bought, sold, and traded on specialised platforms. Unlike cryptocurrencies such as Bitcoin, which are fungible and can be exchanged on a one-to-one basis, each NFT has distinct properties and values set by market demand, rarity, and the intrinsic value of the digital good it represents.

These assets can range from digital currency and securities to digital rights, virtual goods, and even digital versions of real-world assets, allowing for innovative uses in various industries beyond finance such as art, entertainment, and real estate. In blockchain, each transaction is recorded in a block and cryptographically linked to the previous transaction forming a secure, unalterable chain. This structural design ensures the immutability of the ledger, providing a trustworthy environment even in otherwise insecure commercial settings. A key characteristic of blockchain is its decentralised nature which operates without a central supervisory authority, thereby fostering a system where data integrity and trust are maintained collectively by all participants (Yang et al., 2022).

Employing proof of work as its consensus mechanism, blockchain is particularly suited for e-commerce platforms. In the context of the Metaverse, blockchain augments accountability within a nascent and volatile digital financial ecosystem. The visibility of ledgers to all stakeholders obviates the necessity of trust among parties, thereby bolstering cybersecurity and fortifying against data manipulation, with security undergirded by the collective network of participants and the inherent technology (Avital et al., 2016; Rückeshäuser, 2017; Weber et al., 2016). This framework renders traditional intermediaries—such as central banks and central counterparties which historically underpinned trust and security—redundant (Alt & Puschmann, 2016; Nakamoto, 2008). However, the promising avenues opened by blockchain are not devoid of challenges. Regulatory bodies across the globe grapple with the application of technology-neutral regulations to distributed ledger technology (DLT) within the financial sector. The advent of cryptocurrencies, with their capability to circumvent existing anti-money laundering legislations, has been leveraged to abet illicit activities (Fanusie & Robinson, 2018; Foley et al., 2018; Möser et al., 2013), thereby eliciting calls for enhanced regulatory frameworks (Auer & Claessens, 2018; Carstens, 2018; Landau & Genais, 2018).

Amidst the transformative potential of blockchain in reshaping financial models and posing substantial challenges to the centralised monitoring of transactions by banking systems, the impending metamorphosis anticipated with the advent of the Metaverse warrants equal contemplation, particularly in the realms of social, professional, and economic domains. Indeed, blockchain and the Metaverse are envisaged to collaboratively engender a novel paradigm through which global economic interactions, encompassing information exchange and monetary transactions, will be orchestrated in the near future. This evolving narrative mandates businesses to navigate a tri-dimensional commercial landscape. The erstwhile competitiveness afforded by brick-and-mortar establishments, which evolved to necessitate a digital presence with the proliferation of smartphones and online shopping, is now morphing once again with the emergence of the Metaverse. The erstwhile requisite of a website for professional and business credibility, legitimacy, and as a conduit for showcasing and transacting goods and services, is being transcended.

The narrative of retail has been evolving, where high-resolution imagery of products for consumer perusal is being overshadowed by the immersive retail theatre facilitated by the Metaverse. Here, three-dimensional representations of products are interacted with by consumer avatars within a 3D virtual milieu, elevating the shopping experience from a two-dimensional display to a multidimensional engagement. This trajectory, with antecedents traced back to platforms like Second Life since 2003, is being perpetuated by contemporary enterprises. From a marketing and advertising lens, the investment in the Metaverse's real estate of the future can be analogised to the value hitherto ascribed to a company's website domain. Similarly, the conceptualisation of a digital twin of a retail establishment in the Metaverse entails design, construction, hosting, and maintenance akin to a physical or web-based storefront. The discourse now transcends mere advertising in the Metaverse to deliberations on the economic viability of these digital twins of retail establishments. This unfolding scenario harbours profound implications for financial inclusivity. The democratisation of access to goods, services, and economic opportunities within the Metaverse, underpinned by blockchain's decentralised financial infrastructure, portends a paradigm where financial inclusivity is potentially ameliorated. The confluence of blockchain and the Metaverse could thus serve as a linchpin in bridging extant financial divides and fostering a more inclusive global financial ecosystem.

The burgeoning intersection of FinTech and the Metaverse unveils a spectrum of investment avenues that seemingly transcend traditional value propositions. The digital realm, characterised by exclusive online locations, has catalysed the emergence of digital real estate, thereby enabling creators to transact directly within the Metaverse. Emblematic of this trend is the acquisition of digital real estate for hosting virtual events or vending digital art as non-fungible tokens (NFTs). The allure of prospecting land within the Metaverse is being amplified with the advent of myriad platforms catering to this digital real estate market. A notable reflection of this trajectory in the tangible real estate sector is the marketing of newly constructed luxury homes through their digital twins within the Metaverse. A case in point is ONE Sotheby's International Realty's recent alliance with a general contractor and an NFT collector to proffer a virtual rendition of a real-world mansion on The Sandbox Metaverse platform. The transaction of the NFT asset, facilitated on the Ethereum blockchain, concurrently confers the rights to the physical property to the purchaser (PROFILEmiami, 2022).

The growing domain has witnessed firms channelling millions into acquiring space within the Metaverse, underpinned by a conviction in the blockchain-augmented technology morphing beyond a three-dimensional digital facade. Illustrative of this is a 2021 investment manoeuvre where a firm appropriated 2000 acres of virtual real estate, a venture amounting to around $four million, within The Sandbox Metaverse platform. This acquisition, transacted via 792 NFTs on the Ethereum blockchain, translated to the firm owning an expanse equivalent to 1200 city blocks within the virtual milieu (Marinotti, 2022). Another exemplar is evinced in the actions of the investment fund Republic Realm which, in June 2021, secured a digital land parcel within Decentraland for over US$900,000. The fund envisages transmuting this virtual plot into a digital mall dubbed Metajuku, modelled after Tokyo's Harajuku district (Ravenscraft, 2021). These ventures underscore a predilection among firms towards platforms with defined market caps, predicated on the principle that a cap on virtual real estate parcels inherently constrains supply. Platforms like Decentraland and The Sandbox, with their market caps, epitomise this scenario where escalating demand for digital real estate invariably propels the price per land parcel. This narrative accentuates the profound interlinkages between FinTech and the Metaverse, forging a digital frontier where financial transactions, augmented by blockchain technology, dovetail with virtual real estate endeavours. The ripple effects of these developments are anticipated to reverberate across the financial and technological landscapes, potentially redrawing the contours of investment, commerce, and digital interaction.

The modern history of finance is on the cusp of a new epoch marked by the confluence of Generative Artificial Intelligence (GAI) and financial technology (FinTech) within the immersive expanses of the Metaverse. This convergence heralds the potential to morph the architectural framework of financial services, laying the foundation for a democratised financial ecosystem. This chapter endeavours to traverse the multifaceted dimensions of this synergy, delineating the contours of a reimagined financial realm. At the nexus of GAI and FinTech lies the potential to transcend traditional financial boundaries, fostering a milieu of inclusivity and democratised access to financial services. GAI, with its prowess in data synthesis and trend prognostication, intertwines with FinTech's innovative financial solutions to engender a tapestry of opportunities within the Metaverse. This amalgamation not only augments the efficacy and accessibility of financial services but also propels the Metaverse into becoming a crucible for financial innovation and inclusion.

Key points encapsulated in this discourse encompass the transformative capability of GAI in forecasting market trends and engendering personalised financial services. The narrative delves into the realm of blockchain technology, elucidating its instrumental role in underpinning a decentralised financial ecosystem within the Metaverse. The discourse further navigates through the vistas of virtual real estate and digital assets, illustrating the burgeoning investment prospects and the paradigm shift in asset ownership and valuation. Additionally, the narrative elucidates the pivotal role of blockchain in fostering a transparent and secure financial milieu, mitigating the exigencies of trust and intermediaries. The intricacies of regulatory frameworks are also explored, underscoring the imperative for a collaborative approach in addressing regulatory challenges to ensure a stable and trustworthy digital economy.

This chapter endeavours to paint a comprehensive tableau of the multifarious facets of GAI and FinTech synergy within the Metaverse. Through a meticulous examination of emergent technologies and their potential to democratise financial services, the narrative aims to provide a panoramic view of a future where financial empowerment and inclusivity are not mere aspirations but attainable realities within a boundless digital realm. Through this exposition, a glimpse into a future of synthesised prosperity is unveiled, spotlighting the horizon of financial inclusion made conceivable through the harmonious melding of GAI, FinTech, and the boundless expanse of the Metaverse.

7.2 FinTech and Regulation

The anticipated path forward for regulation within a decentralised financial system fundamentally aligns with the concept of embedded supervision. Auer (2019) postulates that the rise of blockchain within the financial sphere augurs well for enhancing supervisory efficiency. At the heart of embedded supervision lies a regulatory architecture wherein a designated ledger's veracity is autonomously ascertained, courtesy of the inherent monitoring capabilities of blockchain. Nonetheless, the pragmatic realisation of such a framework remains contingent upon certain requisites, presently conjectural in nature (Elm & Montez, 2022). As delineated by Auer (2019), the edifice of embedded supervision necessitates:

1. A robust regulatory framework buttressed by a sound legal system.
2. Operationalisation aimed at attaining economic finality—ensuring a transaction, once consummated, remains irreversible.
3. Design predicated on economic consensus, undergirded by the assurance of automated supervision.
4. Advocacy for cost-effective compliance, fostering equitability across the spectrum of large and small enterprises.

The allure of such a supervisory paradigm emanates from its autonomous oversight capability akin to blockchain's inherent self-monitoring feature. Critics, however, pinpoint this very autonomy as a potential quandary. The alignment of embedded supervision with extant e-commerce stratagems within the gaming industry epitomises a tangible manifestation of this regulatory model. The amalgamation of blockchain technologies with gaming landscapes has spawned the advent of play-to-earn paradigms, characterised by tokenised economies and commerce (Chao et al., 2022).

Furthermore, the parallel evolution of the gaming industry and blockchain technology heralds an inexorable confluence, particularly within the realm of the Metaverse. Turdialiev (2022) elucidates several facets that underscore blockchain's suitability as a decentralised financial linchpin within the Metaverse:

1. *Digital proof of ownership*: digital wallets emblematic of ownership assertions pertaining to any blockchain-based asset.
2. *Digital collectability*: the emergence of NFTs facilitating the creation and collection of distinct digital assets.
3. *Transferable value*: the propensity for value transfer between users in online multiplayer games, a model adaptable to blockchain in the Metaverse.
4. *Governance*: the decentralisation ethos of blockchain supplanting centralised authority, ensuring adherence to established rules sans elected officials.

5. *Accessibility*: the democratisation of account creation, transcending conventional banking restrictions through digital wallet facilitation.
6. *Interoperability*: the advent of custom, interoperable blockchains, epitomised by Polkadot (DOT) and Avalanche (AVAX), accentuating blockchain's potential in fostering a seamlessly interconnected Metaverse.

As the Metaverse emerges as an alternate conduit for human interaction and economic exchange, its success is intertwined with the establishment of a resilient, secure, and robust economy. While the Metaverse economy may ostensibly diverge from contemporary economic models, Ball (2022) avers that the underlying economic dynamics would mirror real-world patterns. The proliferation of a vibrant economy within this sprawling digital space hinges on the interplay of competition, profitable enterprises, consensually acknowledged rules, a palpable sense of fairness, sustained consumer expenditure, and well-defined rights.

The concept of embedded supervision is gaining traction in response to the revolutionary shift towards decentralised finance (DeFi). DeFi refers to an emerging financial technology based on blockchain that operates independently of traditional centralised financial institutions like banks. By utilising smart contracts on blockchains, DeFi platforms enable users to lend, borrow, trade, and earn interest on their assets in a peer-to-peer manner, reducing reliance on intermediaries and potentially lowering costs for users. This paradigm aims to rectify the inherent limitations of the current financial system, which is dominated by central authorities, by offering a more open, accessible, and transparent financial ecosystem. Embedded supervision in this context refers to the integration of regulatory frameworks directly into blockchain networks, enhancing the oversight capabilities without the need for external enforcement bodies, thus aligning regulatory mechanisms with the decentralised and autonomous nature of DeFi.

The underpinnings of embedded supervision rest on leveraging blockchain technology to create a self-regulating, transparent, and efficient financial ecosystem, mitigating the need for centralised oversight. For instance, Mertzanis (2020) delineates the nexus between financial supervision structure and firms' financing constraints across 48 developing countries. The crux of this examination lies in discerning the impact of supervision structure—integrated, sectoral, or twin-peak model—on financing constraints of firms, accentuating the role of decentralised decision-making in prudential supervision and conduct of business supervision. The findings evinced that decentralised structures of prudential supervision are linked with more binding financing constraints in high-income developing countries and market-based financial systems. Conversely, decentralised structures of conduct of business supervision are associated with more stringent financing constraints across various economic landscapes. This underscores the pivotal role of decentralised decision-making in financial supervision, potentially abetting in mitigating financing constraints subject to the economic milieu (Abubakar & Abubakar, 2023).

The study by Chao et al. (2022) considers the burgeoning realm of DeFi in virtual communities, accentuating the quintessence of financial supervision amidst the ascendancy of blockchain technology. The discourse underscores the pervasive decentralisation and anonymity inherent in blockchain applications—from NFTs, DeFi, GameFi to DAOs and DEXs—necessitating a nuanced approach to financial supervision. The essence of decentralisation, encapsulated in the Ethereum Virtual Machine (EVM) and smart contracts, speaks to a new epoch of financial applications transcending the virtual-physical dichotomy. However, this decentralisation ethos also begets challenges for financial supervision necessitating a robust regulatory framework to assuage the risks entailed (White, 2023).

Schuler et al. (2023) also consider the potentialities of DeFi in engendering a new financial infrastructure, severing the chains of centralised service providers. The exposition elucidates the role of smart contracts in ensuring atomic transfers and holding collateral, epitomising the quintessence of blockchain technology in fostering a decentralised, transparent, and efficient financial ecosystem. The study lends credence to the potential of DeFi and blockchain technology in redefining financial infrastructure, heralding a new era of decentralised finance unshackled from the constraints of centralised oversight.

At the same time, the convergence of these discourses accentuates the imperative for a cogent regulatory framework—embedded supervision—to navigate the uncharted waters of decentralised finance. The ethos of decentralisation, embodied in blockchain technology, beckons a paradigm shift in financial supervision potentially heralding an epoch of self-regulated, transparent, and efficient financial ecosystems. The quest for financial inclusivity and democratisation, undergirded by blockchain technology, necessitates a nuanced approach to regulation, ensuring the equitable and sustainable growth of the decentralised financial landscape (Singh, 2023).

7.3 Impact of FinTech on Traditional Banking

The metamorphosis of digital realms, epitomised by the Metaverse, beckons a re-evaluation of traditional banking and financial systems. This section will consider the ramifications of this new virtual universe on these well-entrenched systems, navigating through the domains of user interactions, financial transactions, and the regulatory landscape. As a sprawling digital ecosystem, this immersive environment harbours the potential to redefine how individuals interact with financial instruments (Mozumder et al., 2023). Unlike the rigid structures that are characteristic of traditional banking, the Metaverse offers a flexible, interactive platform where financial transactions are not merely utilitarian but part of a broader experiential narrative. The potential for an immersive financial experience, where banking is not a stand-alone activity but intertwined with daily digital interactions, presents a paradigm shift. More specifically, the trajectory of the impact various kinds of FinTech will have on traditional banking is delineated through digital transformation, recalibrated customer expectations, innovative products and services, operational efficiency, competition and collaboration, regulatory compliance, financial inclusion, data analytics, cybersecurity, and market dynamics (Allen et al., 2021).

Furthermore, the Metaverse is poised to serve as a catalyst for financial inclusivity. Traditional banking systems, with their bureaucratic inertia and geographical limitations, often marginalise a segment of the population (Avanesh & Zachariah, 2023). The Metaverse, with its borderless nature, harbours the potential to democratise access to financial services. However, this digital leap necessitates robust cybersecurity frameworks to safeguard user data and financial assets thus posing a formidable challenge to both the Metaverse architects and traditional financial institutions (Sebastian, 2023). At the core of this digital transformation is the blockchain technology which promises to infuse transparency, security, and decentralisation into the financial transactions within the Metaverse. DeFi platforms, as discussed by Schuler et al. (2023), are at the vanguard of this transformation offering alternatives to centralised financial systems. The autonomous, smart contract-driven protocols of DeFi platforms encapsulate a move towards a more open financial system, albeit with challenges pertaining to regulatory compliance and consumer protection.

The juxtaposition of traditional and Metaverse-driven financial systems also invites a discourse on regulatory frameworks. The decentralised ethos of the Metaverse clashes with the centralised regulatory oversight characteristic of traditional financial systems (Koohang et al., 2023). The notion of embedded supervision, as posited by Auer (2019), presents a potential pathway to reconcile this dichotomy although the implementation of such a regulatory framework is laden with complexities. Moreover, the emergence of new financial instruments and assets unique to the Metaverse, such as NFTs and digital real estate, mandates a recalibration of financial valuation and assessment frameworks. The traditional financial systems, rooted in tangible assets, are now compelled to evolve methodologies to evaluate and integrate digital assets.

Moreover, the dynamism inherent in the realm of payment systems is emblematic of the broader shifts observed in the financial landscape heralded by the advent of FinTech. One pivotal determinant that is poised to sculpt the modalities of currency exchange for goods or services in the burgeoning digital domain is that of payment rails (Hutson et al., 2023). The proliferation of novel payment rails has been significantly propelled by advancements in communication technologies. Indeed, a discernible decline in cash utilisation as a medium of transaction has been noted. As noted by Ball (2022), the proportion of transactions in the United States of America (USA) employing cash plummeted from 40% in 2010 to a proximate 20% in 2021. New payment rails in the USA encompass the Clearing House Interbank Payment System (CHIPS), Fedwire (heretofore known as the Federal Reserve Wire Network), the Automated Clearing House (ACH), alongside a myriad of credit cards and peer-to-peer payment applications including PayPal and Venmo among others.

The pathway of transactions for acquiring software rights induces reflections on the expected flexible and innovative advancements in the virtual domain. For example, the year 2021 saw consumers directing over $50 billion towards digital-only video games while the Gross Domestic Product (GDP) of the virtual domain amplified fivefold since 2005 (Engelstätter & Ward, 2022). However, the payment channels pervading the virtual economy manifest a more restrictive demeanour compared to their real-world counterparts, predominantly owing to the enforced bundling of services. Examples encompass PlayStation's wallet, Apple's Apple Pay, and a variety of in-app payment facilities. Consoles like Xbox and PlayStation provide the capability for consumers to download game versions albeit confined to their specific hardware (Lehtonen et al., 2023). A divergent pathway was initiated in 2003 when Valve launched Steam as a Personal Computer (PC) alternative to the console economy. With the migration of many multiplayer online games towards a games-as-service model, Valve adeptly managed game updates and installations internally through a game launcher that meticulously indexed and centrally managed the game installer files. This framework also navigated a user's rights to the games, enabling automatic downloads as warranted. The economic model preserved a 30% revenue stream for Valve, akin to the console game platforms. This 30% paradigm also undergirds the economic models of Apple and Google regarding their app stores, further restraining virtual world platforms (Znica, 2022).

In the digital transition, the evolution of payment systems has been significant, marking a shift from traditional to more tech-driven solutions. The sphere of FinTech has seen the emergence of innovative payment mechanisms, largely driven by the proliferation of mobile instruments like smartphones and tablets (Danladi et al., 2023). These advancements have been instrumental in reducing resistance during the payment process, making transactions smoother and more accessible. Likewise, authentication, a cornerstone for secure payment processing in the FinTech environment, has garnered attention with studies like that of Bhat et al. (2023) delving into methods to bolster security and, by extension, trust in financial transactions. The pivotal role of ease in payment systems on user behaviour, especially in high-value and small-value payments, has been explored (Gomber et al., 2018), illustrating the importance of user-friendly interfaces in promoting the adoption of digital payment systems.

The discourse around payment systems in FinTech extends to the realm of blockchain where decentralisation emerges as a key theme. The potential of the technology in fostering a decentralised, financial solution in the Metaverse is underscored by attributes like digital proof of ownership, digital collectability, transferable value, and governance as elucidated by Turdialiev (2022). Moreover, the interoperability facilitated by blockchain, exemplified by platforms like Polkadot (DOT) and Avalanche (AVAX), holds promise in bridging the real and virtual worlds thus expanding the scope and functionality of payment systems in the digital age (Arslanian, 2022).

The foray of FinTech into the realm of traditional banking signifies a metamorphosis that is as profound as it is transformative. As conventional banks navigate the intricacies of contemporary financial conduct, the ramifications of these technologies loom substantial, casting an extended shadow on erstwhile established banking paradigms. In the ensuing discourse, a summation of the pivotal impacts FinTech is poised to impart on traditional banking will be meticulously reviewed. First, at the vanguard of this transition is the digital metamorphosis that FinTech facilitates. Traditional banking institutions, once the bedrock of brick-and-mortar financial transactions, find themselves at the cusp of an online revolution. The exigencies of modern banking now mandate a presence in the digital realm where transactions are executed at the click of a button and financial services are availed from the comfort of a user's home. The digital transition, however, is not merely a replication of traditional banking services on an online platform; it is an elevation, an enhancement facilitated by the seamless integration of technology (Breidbach et al., 2020).

As traditional banks tread the path of digital transformation, the spectre of customer expectations looms large. FinTech, with its penchant for tailor-made services, instant responses, and user-centric interfaces, has recalibrated customer expectations. The modern banking customer, now accustomed to the superior service standards set by FinTech, demands a similar level of service from traditional banking institutions (Barbu et al., 2021). Similarly, mention should be made of the innovative products and services it introduces into the financial ecosystem. Mobile banking, digital wallets, and peer-to-peer lending platforms—these are not mere services; they are harbingers of a new financial ethos that challenges, and often supersedes, the established norms of traditional banking (Guild, 2017; Wulandari et al., 2023).

Operational efficiency, emblematic of adept financial management, finds a formidable ally in FinTech. Through the avenues of automation and process streamlining, FinTech ameliorates operational impediments, fostering an ambience of efficiency and cost-effectiveness (Campanella et al., 2023). The interplay between competition and collaboration unfolds as a complex narrative wherein traditional banks and FinTech entities oscillate roles as adversaries and allies. On one hand, FinTech entities emerge as potent competitors yet, on the other hand, they unveil avenues for collaborative endeavours—a symbiotic rapport that enhances the service prowess of traditional banks. Regulatory compliance, a quintessential yet often onerous facet of financial management, is considerably simplified through the advent of FinTech. The stalwarts of this domain, blockchain technology and Artificial Intelligence, engender a seamless and efficacious mechanism for compliance and reporting (Gaviyau & Sibindi, 2023).

The aspiration of financial inclusion, noble in intent yet elusive in practice, discovers a viable conduit through FinTech. By extending its reach to the underbanked and unbanked demographics via mobile technology and digital platforms, FinTech endeavours to bridge the vast chasm of financial disparity. Data analytics, recognised as a potent tool in risk assessment and decision-making, is adeptly leveraged by FinTech to extract insights into customer behaviour and market trends (Ediagbonya & Tioluwani, 2023). When traditional banks adopt this data-driven modus operandi a significant augmentation in decision-making and risk assessment capabilities is observed. In an era where financial transactions are increasingly migrating to the digital sphere, the spectre of cybersecurity threats looms ominously. The exigency to safeguard sensitive financial data underscores the necessity for robust cybersecurity measures—a domain wherein FinTech's expertise shines (AlBenJasim et al., 2023). The market dynamics, hitherto the bastion of entrenched traditional banks, now experiences turbulence as FinTech diminishes entry barriers thereby enabling the foray of new market entrants. The erstwhile market hegemony and share of traditional banks now teeter on the brink of FinTech-induced disruptions, accentuating the imperative for traditional banks to adapt and evolve amidst this burgeoning landscape of financial technology.

In all, the trajectory of traditional banking is irrevocably altered by the advent of FinTech. As traditional banks navigate the complex landscape of modern financial conduct, the influence of FinTech is both a compass and a catalyst, guiding and goading them towards a new horizon of financial service delivery. The confluence of traditional banking and FinTech is not merely a meeting of technologies; it is a melding of old and new financial ethos, a confluence that holds the promise of a robust, inclusive, and efficient financial ecosystem.

The juxtaposition of traditional banking with FinTech in the context of payment systems unveils a tableau of contrasts and evolving paradigms. The centralised architectures and relatively rigid frameworks of traditional banking stand in stark contrast to the nimble, decentralised ethos of FinTech. As the Metaverse beckons a more integrated, seamless, and inclusive financial ecosystem, the innovation in payment rails fostered by FinTech emerges as a quintessential cog in this transformative wheel. Moreover, the trajectory of traditional banking and financial systems in the wake of the Metaverse evolution is contingent on the symbiotic relationship between technological innovation and regulatory adaptation. The potential for a more inclusive, transparent, and user-centric financial ecosystem is palpable yet hinges on the mitigation of cybersecurity risks and the formulation of robust regulatory frameworks.

7.4 Economic and Business Models in the Metaverse

The burgeoning Metaverse, characterised by its digital realms and virtual interactions, portends a revolution in the conventional frameworks of economic and business models. This digital frontier, integrated with blockchain technology, has catalysed the emergence of novel monetary systems, revenue streams, and financial instruments such as NFTs and digital currencies. These emergent paradigms are not only redefining the modalities of business operations but also engendering new avenues for revenue generation and value creation. The explorations by various scholars such as Li et al. (2023), Xu et al. (2023), and Zhou et al. (2023) elucidate the multifaceted impact of the Metaverse, NFTs, and digital currencies on the traditional economic and business models. The interaction between digital and physical assets, the coexistence of real-world and online activities, and the importance of property rights and monetary systems in the smooth functioning of the Metaverse economy are some of the critical areas of inquiry. These emergent paradigms are not only redefining the business models but also heralding a new epoch of digital economy characterised by innovation, inclusivity, and interactivity.

One of the seminal manifestations of this digital-economic nexus is the sale of digital art through NFTs. Metaverse galleries, flourishing as a natural confluence of digital art and blockchain technology, have emerged as prevalent business models (Hurst et al., 2023). NFTs, being unique digital assets verifiable via blockchain, facilitate the sale, and trade of digital art, thereby giving rise to new revenue streams. As these virtual spaces expand, the sale of NFTs is anticipated to unlock access to unique digital experiences such as virtual reality concerts or virtual product showrooms, thereby engendering a marketplace for unique digital experiences (Raad & Rashid, 2023). Furthermore, the exclusivity accorded to Metaverse lands through NFTs presents a novel paradigm of value and access. Certain realms within the Metaverse necessitate the possession of specific NFTs for entry, thereby creating a market for exclusive access to digital domains and real-life events organised by NFT collections. This exclusivity fosters a symbiotic rapport between brands and consumers, enriching community engagement and understanding of consumer preferences (Colicev, 2023).

The trading of virtual goods in cryptocurrencies is another dimension of this digital economy. According to data disseminated by crypto investment group Grayscale, the Metaverse could potentially engender a US$1 billion annual revenue market for enterprises adept at navigating this new commercial landscape. The willingness of individuals to transact in cryptocurrencies for virtual goods delineates a nascent market with substantial economic potential. Moreover, the integration of NFTs in loyalty programmes or reward systems presents an innovative avenue for customer engagement and retention. By issuing NFTs as digital tokens of value businesses can cultivate a new genre of loyalty programmes thereby fostering a digital economy of rewards and incentives (Kar & Varsha, 2023).

Although the term Metaverse has seemingly catapulted into financial discourse quite recently, its application to the retail sector traces back nearly two decades. Bourlakis et al. (2009) delved into the emergence of Metaverse retailing in the wake of the inaugural release of the smartphone, segmenting the evolution into three distinct phases: traditional, electronic, and Metaverse. The scrutiny was orientated towards elucidating the novel strategies retailers necessitated to navigate through three distinct, yet intertwined realms. Prominent promotional facets are delineated alongside the disparate challenges confronting traditional (brick-and-mortar retailers), e-retailers (leveraging the Internet), and Metaverse retailers. For the scope of the investigation, the scholars scrutinised the Metaverse phenomenon encapsulated by Second Life, while also acknowledging *World of Warcraft, Ever Quest, Eve Online,* and *Star Wars Galaxies* as the crucibles for the third dimension of commerce (Bizel, 2023). The exemplars underscored predominantly commenced as games or, more precisely, massively multiplayer online role-play games (MMORPGs). These gaming realms swiftly morphed into alternate universes, augmenting players' virtual and electronic domains. In light of the substantial consumer engagement, with individuals immersing for extensive durations (at times up to 12 h continuously) within these virtual environments, burgeoning social and business landscapes emerged to accommodate larger virtual expanses. The play-to-earn gaming model, encapsulated within virtual reality (VR) or augmented reality (AR), epitomises the amalgam of entertainment, digital assets, and economic value within the Metaverse. NFTs emerge as pivotal instruments in fostering a viable economy within these gaming realms, thereby unveiling investment avenues and engendering novel economic dynamics within the virtual domain (Prabadevi et al., 2023).

Amid such economic and social interchanges transpiring among players within these games and Metaverses, a pronounced crossover emerged between physical enterprises in the real world and virtual e-businesses. These advancements have birthed a multifaceted, multi-spaced economic milieu witnessing a significant amplification in complexity. The intertwined fabric of this nascent business environment encompassing electronic, virtual, and physical domains necessitates meticulous mapping to decipher the economic, social, and policy ramifications (Hackl, 2020). For triumph in this intricate landscape, Bourlakis et al. (2009) advocate for a comprehensive promotional strategy seamlessly operational across all three spheres.

The discourse looks back to the precursor of the contemporary Metaverse to frame the conversation. Unveiled in 2003, Second Life facilitated users in monetising their virtual endeavours. The copyright for content crafted by users on the platform was vested in the creators, thereby empowering them to monetise their content. Preceding the advent of NFTs and blockchain technology, Linden Lab's Second Life (https://www.lindenlab.com/) accorded content creators the leverage to shield their creations employing a triad of options—either permitting or obstructing owners to copy, modify, or transfer their creations or acquisitions (Rospigliosi, 2022). This system also chronicled items and their creators, functioning similarly in fabricating digital items that are unique and identifiable. All transactions within Second Life were predicated on the Linden Dollar which could be exchanged in-world for goods or services and could also be converted into real currency to financially benefit creators in the real world. Given the absence of a business licence requisite to function as an entrepreneur on the virtual platform, an accurate appraisal of the number of traders and the degree of their success remains elusive. Nonetheless, the Positive Linden Dollar Flow (PMLF) estimates there are over 66 million 'business owners' on the platform. Businesses discerned the allure of engaging customers on such a platform and commenced operations therein (Strobel & Hawkins, 2022). Exemplars of these real-world enterprises span a broad spectrum of markets and industries, inclusive of ABN AMRO, Adidas, American Apparel, Dell, Harvard Law School, IBM, Microsoft, Pontiac, Reuters, Sony Ericsson, the Swedish Government, and Toyota among others. While the majority utilised the platform predominantly for marketing endeavours, some have articulated intentions of actual trading within Second Life. Despite these strides, mainstream acceptance remains an aspiration yet to be fulfilled (Fernandes & Chatterjee, 2022).

The stark divergence between traditional or e-retailing and that witnessed in the Metaverse hinges on the anticipations of customers vis-a-vis their interaction with the brands they encounter. Unlike the conventional two-dimensional marketing and advertising realm where print, images, videos, and music are deployed to furnish a semblance of the product on offer, in the Metaverse customers envision engaging with it within a three-dimensional simulation. This modus operandi aligns with what Harris et al. (2001) envisaged as the advent of retail theatre. Papagiannidis and Bourlakis (2010) contend that certain retailers within Second Life crafted experiences that enable potential customers to interact with products thus fostering sales. Conversely, other retailers endeavour to cultivate a sense of community or belonging among their consumer bases. While this proffers enhanced access and the capacity to tailor marketing to specific customers, both Haig (2001) and Bourlakis et al. (2009) cautioned enterprises against the ramifications of excessively inundating potential customers. For instance, during visits to bustling locales within a Metaverse platform, automated systems might disseminate messages or notecards detailing products or services. Although users possess the option to mute a bot or automated agent, recurrent engagement in such activity can precipitate frustration (Ahn et al., 2022). Concurrently, if experiences are meticulously crafted, the augmented 3D information proffered could exert a positive influence on sales and the retail shopping excursion. Virtual retail unveils the potential to amalgamate augmented reality (AR) and virtual reality (VR) to fabricate a seamless shopping voyage. Virtual objects and digital information can be perused and revisited within a virtual milieu. The advantages are palpable; as opposed to beholding products on a flat screen, billboard, or sheet of paper, products could be translocated out of the catalogue and positioned in the real environment or clothes could be modelled for size and fit. Such product interactions could aid in facilitating a purchasing decision and engender enhanced confidence among customers (Popescu et al., 2022).

Therefore, the growing domain of the Metaverse unveils a paradigm of economic and business models that are as innovative as they are transformative. The sale and trading of digital art via NFTs herald a new era of digital ownership, underpinned by blockchain technology which is reshaping the contours of value and exchange within virtual spaces. The models of play-to-earn gaming exemplify the confluence of entertainment, digital assets, and economic value within the Metaverse, embodying a blend of economic and social engagement that extends beyond traditional frameworks of commerce.

The interactive dimension of Metaverse retailing represents a departure from conventional retail paradigms. Customers within the Metaverse expect a three-dimensional interaction with products, embodying a form of retail theatre where engagement transcends mere transactional exchange. The nuanced experiences within Metaverse retailing, encompassing a sense of community and interactive engagement with products, herald a novel consumer-business interaction paradigm. However, the challenges of potential information overload and the necessity for judicious design of interactive experiences underscore the fine balance that needs to be struck to enhance customer engagement without engendering disaffection.

Furthermore, the discourse surrounding the economic structures within the Metaverse, particularly in the context of NFTs, unveils a new frontier of the digital economy that transcends traditional boundaries of commerce. The potential of NFTs in facilitating unique, identifiable ownership of digital assets, coupled with the capacity for real-world monetisation, presents a novel, multifaceted economic environment. The crossover between physical businesses and virtual enterprises within the Metaverse elucidates a hybrid economic ecosystem, characterised by a fluid interchange between digital and physical assets.

The intricacies of economic and business models within the Metaverse elucidate a dynamic, evolving landscape of commerce and social interaction. The synergy between AR and VR in enhancing retail experiences, the evolving norms of digital ownership through NFTs, and the innovative revenue streams embodied in play-to-earn gaming models collectively signify a transformative shift in economic paradigms as they meld with digital innovation. The Metaverse, thereby, stands as a harbinger of a nuanced, multidimensional economic landscape, promulgating new vistas of value creation, consumer engagement, and entrepreneurial endeavour in the digital epoch.

7.5 FinTech and Cybercrime

The ensuing discourse will delve into the critical domain of cybersecurity, a realm of paramount importance in the contemporary financial landscape. The confluence of financial technology and digital innovation, while propelling economic mechanisms into a new era, also engenders a host of cybersecurity challenges. The sanctity of data, the robustness of financial transactions, and the trust imbued in digital financial platforms are undergirded by the efficacy of cybersecurity measures. As financial transactions increasingly traverse the digital domain the imperatives of cybersecurity become ever more pronounced. The narrative ahead will explore the multifaceted dimensions of cybersecurity within this new financial realm, examining the challenges, the evolving norms of data protection, and the strategies imperative for fostering a secure, resilient financial digital infrastructure.

The nascent ascendancy of FinTech in the financial sector, while being a harbinger of innovation and efficiency, also opens up a new battleground for cybercrime. The allure of sensitive financial data is an irresistible draw for cybercriminals making FinTech a lucrative target. The global repercussions of cybercrime are becoming increasingly dire with projections suggesting a staggering cost of $15 trillion by 2025 (Banafa, 2023). The burgeoning FinTech industry, despite its innovative strides in payment systems and digital technologies, finds itself in a relentless race against cyber criminals who are evolving at a parallel pace. The sustenance and prosperity of FinTech hinge significantly on its ability to ward off cyber threats, thereby preserving the integrity of its technological infrastructure and the trust of its clientele.

A quintessential element of cybersecurity in FinTech pertains to proactive measures to pre-empt cyber-attacks. The implementation of rigorous cybersecurity protocols, encompassing penetration testing and modernised IT security infrastructures, is imperative for FinTech firms. Investment in innovative identity authentication technology is pivotal to thwarting high-impact digital breaches that could otherwise precipitate a mass migration of customers towards competitors. A report by authID.ai underscores this imperative revealing that a substantial 84% of FinTech and banking leaders are gearing up to bolster their investment in IT security, particularly in identity authentication, in the imminent future (Tian et al., 2023).

Moreover, the intersection of FinTech with the burgeoning Metaverse and blockchain technology augments the complexity of cybersecurity. The decentralised ethos of blockchain, while being a hallmark of transparency and trust, also posits challenges in regulatory and cybersecurity domains (Baliker et al., 2023). The advent of financial exchanges within the Metaverse heralds a new era where the limitations of physical property investment are transcended. However, this digital frontier is not immune to cyber threats, necessitating robust cybersecurity measures to safeguard financial transactions and data within the Metaverse.

Literature in this domain elucidates the myriad facets of cybersecurity in the FinTech realm. AlBenJasim et al. (2023) advocate for a fortified legislative framework and the establishment of trustworthy cybersecurity systems to combat cybercrime in FinTech. Wulandari et al. (2023) delineate the cyber challenges faced particularly by FinTech startups and their endeavours to safeguard data and infrastructure. Subramanian et al. (2023) accentuate the global array of cybersecurity threats besieging the FinTech sector, advocating for the adoption of rigorous threat modelling methodologies like PASTA. Kaur (2023) delves into the systemic risks and contagion channels associated with digital financial criminality in the FinTech sector, highlighting the dire need for upgraded defensive technological structures.

In all, the symbiotic relationship between FinTech and cybersecurity is indubitable. The burgeoning FinTech sector, with its profound potential to revolutionise financial transactions and services, must navigate the perilous waters of cybercrime. The onus is on FinTech firms to fortify their cyber defences, invest in state-of-the-art authentication technologies, and foster a culture of cybersecurity awareness. The nexus between FinTech, blockchain technology, and the Metaverse further accentuates the imperative for robust cybersecurity measures to ensure a secure, resilient, and trustworthy digital financial ecosystem.

7.6 GenAI and FinTech

Generative Artificial Intelligence (GenAI) denotes a significant stride in the broader field of Artificial Intelligence (AI), with a particular emphasis on the generation of novel and original content predicated on patterns discernible in existing data. The realm of FinTech stands at the cusp of a monumental transformation fuelled by the capabilities of GenAI. The International Monetary Fund (IMF) underscores the leap in technological prowess represented by GenAI, enhancing the spectrum of applicability within financial institutions. These entities, quick to adapt to the technological zeitgeist, are implementing GenAI across a myriad of applications thereby revolutionising the operational fabric of the FinTech industry (Shabsigh & Boukherouaa, 2023).

GenAI distinguishes itself from other forms of Artificial Intelligence (AI) through its unique capability to create new and original content from learned data patterns. Unlike traditional AI, which primarily focuses on analysing data and making predictions or decisions based on existing information, GenAI uses algorithms like Generative Adversarial Networks (GANs) and Variational Autoencoders (VAEs) to produce data that can mimic real-world artefacts be it text, images, or music. This ability to generate synthetic data is transformative, offering applications that range from creating digital art to simulating real-world scenarios for training AI without the need for real data inputs. Consequently, GenAI not only enhances the capabilities of machines in interpreting and responding to their environments but also empowers them to contribute creatively to areas previously dominated by human cognition. This evolution represents a significant leap from conventional AI's capabilities, pushing the boundaries of machine autonomy and creativity.

The manifold benefits of GenAI within FinTech encompass a spectrum ranging from streamlining financial processes and automating repetitive tasks, to crafting personalised financial solutions and recommendations (Kanbach et al., 2023). Enhanced automation and efficiency stand as pivotal areas where GenAI finds its forte, significantly reducing the manual effort traditionally required. Furthermore, the domain of risk management is poised for an advanced makeover with GenAI at the helm offering nuanced and data-driven strategies to mitigate financial risks. Fraud detection, credit scoring, and investment management are other arenas where new generative tools demonstrate their prowess as markedly evident, driving innovation and precision in these crucial financial activities (Pires et al., 2023). However, alongside the remarkable promise, the technology brings forth a set of challenges and risks, notably in the realms of embedded bias, privacy preservation, outcome opaqueness, and cyber threats. The technologically nuanced nature of GenAI could potentially exacerbate certain risks, notably those pertaining to financial sector stability. For instance, the opaque nature of algorithmic decision-making processes could engender systemic risks if not meticulously regulated and understood (Aggarwal et al., 2023).

Several studies clarify the profound intersectionality between AI and FinTech, with a notable emphasis on the disruptive potential of AI in reshaping the financial industry's landscape, particularly in the wake of the COVID-19 pandemic (Wójcik & Ioannou, 2020). The innovations driven by AI and FinTech, as delineated by Allen et al. (2021), span a gamut of financial activities including algorithmic trading, digital payments, and robo-advising, heralding a new era of digitised financial operations. Furthermore, studies accentuate the burgeoning influence of AI and FinTech within the banking sector, suggesting a trajectory towards maximised resources, diminished risks, and enhanced revenue generation (Kunduru, 2023).

Furthermore, scholarship surrounding GenAI and its interplay with FinTech extends into the realms of inclusivity and accessibility, core tenets imperative for fostering equitable financial ecosystems. The nexus of GenAI, FinTech, and inclusivity yields a potent potential to ameliorate historical financial exclusions thus engendering a broader spectrum of societal participation in financial frameworks. The scholarly expositions elucidated herein navigate through the intricate terrain of algorithmic fairness, regulatory scaffolds, and the consequential impact on digital financial inclusion thereby illuminating the pathway towards a more inclusive and accessible FinTech landscape.

Memarian and Doleck (2023) accentuate the quintessence of fairness, accountability, transparency, and ethics (FATE) within the AI domain positing these principles as indispensable for mitigating algorithmic disparities. The effective integration of these principles necessitates an inclusive engagement with a diverse array of communities thereby fostering a milieu of algorithmic inclusivity and accessibility. The narrative then unfolds into the legal and regulatory architectures governing AI within the financial services industry as elucidated by Firmansyah and Arman (2023). These regulatory frameworks are seminal for enhancing access to finance, particularly through the lens of Regulatory Technology (RegTech) which epitomises the confluence of AI, compliance processes, and financial accessibility. Firmansyah and Arman also delve into the multifaceted impact of AI on trading platforms, investment advisory paradigms, and compliance mechanisms thereby offering a nuanced understanding of the regulatory imperatives requisite for fostering financial inclusivity.

Venturing further into the realm of digital financial inclusion, Telukdarie and Mungar (2023) explore the multifarious influence of AI. The discourse traverses through crucial domains such as risk management, information asymmetry, customer support, fraud detection, and cybersecurity, highlighting the pivotal role of AI in bridging the financial inclusion chasm. The collective essence distilled from these scholarly endeavours underscores the imperativeness of responsible AI practices, meticulously crafted regulatory frameworks, and the judicious adoption of AI tools and applications. These elements are intrinsically linked to the aspirations of engendering accessibility, inclusivity, and financial inclusion within the FinTech ecosystem.

These studies posit a compelling argument for the integration of responsible AI practices within the FinTech industry. The promise of GenAI, when navigated with an informed and inclusive approach, holds the potential to significantly contribute to the amelioration of financial exclusions. However, the journey towards achieving this noble objective necessitates a collaborative, informed, and ethically grounded approach, ensuring that the technological advancements in GenAI and FinTech are harnessed for the collective good thereby fostering a more equitable and inclusive financial future.

As the integration of Generative Artificial Intelligence (GenAI) with financial technology (FinTech) continues to reshape the landscape, professionals within the sector are presented with a unique opportunity to harness these innovations for enhanced service delivery, improved efficiency, and more personalised customer experiences. The practical implications of these findings are significant, offering a pathway towards not only technological advancement but also a more inclusive financial ecosystem.

In the rapidly evolving landscape of financial technology, the adoption of GenAI represents a transformative shift with profound implications for service delivery, operational efficiency, and customer interaction. As one delves into how these can be implemented, strategic recommendations for FinTech professionals aiming to harness the innovative potential of GenAI are outlined. These strategies are designed not only to enhance the technical capabilities of financial institutions but also to ensure they are aligned with market demands and regulatory frameworks. By effectively leveraging GenAI FinTech professionals can unlock new levels of performance, tailor their services to better meet customer needs, and position their organisations at the forefront of the financial industry's future. Here are actionable strategies that can guide professionals in implementing GenAI to transform their operations and service offerings.

1. *Enhance personalisation and customer engagement*: by utilising GenAI, financial institutions can offer highly personalised financial advice, tailored investment solutions, and customised financial products. This can be achieved by analysing large datasets to identify individual preferences and behaviours, thereby providing services that meet specific customer needs, enhancing satisfaction, and fostering loyalty.
2. *Automate and optimise operations*: GenAI can automate complex and time-consuming processes such as risk assessment, loan underwriting, and fraud detection. By implementing these systems, FinTech companies can reduce operational costs, minimise human error, and increase processing speed leading to more efficient service delivery and improved profitability.
3. *Develop innovative financial products*: professionals can use GenAI to explore new financial products and services that were not previously feasible. For example, predictive models generated by GenAI could help in crafting investment strategies that adapt to market changes more dynamically or insurance products that more accurately reflect the risks of individual policyholders.
4. *Improve regulatory compliance and reporting*: GenAI can also be instrumental in enhancing the accuracy and efficiency of regulatory compliance and reporting. By automating data collection and analysis financial institutions can ensure more consistent adherence to changing regulations and standards, reducing the risk of non-compliance penalties.

Transitioning from theoretical understanding to practical application, the following provides a roadmap for professionals ready to integrate the technology into their financial operations. This segment is pivotal for those in the FinTech sector seeking to apply the insights discussed previously, ensuring that the adoption of GenAI is not only strategic but also effective and sustainable. Here, the focus is on specific steps that can be taken to operationalise GenAI within financial institutions, emphasising the importance of building robust infrastructures, nurturing skills, and fostering ethical practices. These strategies are designed to ensure that professionals can navigate the complexities of GenAI implementation with confidence and clarity, ultimately enhancing their capabilities and competitive edge in the financial marketplace.

1. *Investing in skills and training*: to fully capitalise on GenAI technologies firms should invest in training and developing their workforce to handle new tools and understand GenAI capabilities. This includes hiring data scientists and AI specialists who can bridge the gap between technical potential and practical financial applications.
2. *Building collaborative ecosystems*: establish partnerships with technology providers, academic institutions, and innovation hubs to stay at the forefront of GenAI development and application. These collaborations can provide access to the latest research, advanced technologies, and innovative methodologies.

3. *Prioritising ethical considerations*: as financial services become more reliant on GenAI, it is critical to address ethical concerns related to data privacy, security, and bias. Institutions should develop clear policies and frameworks to manage these issues ensuring trust and transparency with their customers.
4. *Adopting a phased implementation approach*: start with pilot projects to integrate GenAI applications in specific areas of operation. Evaluate the outcomes and scale up gradually, adjusting strategies based on feedback and results to mitigate risks associated with new technology deployments.

These strategies can allow FinTech professionals to implement the insights from this chapter leading to significant advancements in their operations and service offerings once implemented. The convergence of GenAI and FinTech not only promises substantial economic benefits but also a redefinition of how financial services are conceptualised and delivered in the digital age.

7.7 Conclusion

In the discussion on the transformative interplay between FinTech, Generative Artificial Intelligence (GenAI), and the Metaverse, this chapter has encapsulated the pivotal insights and forecast the trajectory of these converging technologies. The integration of GenAI within FinTech, facilitated by the expansive digital realms of the Metaverse, heralds a new era in financial services—one characterised by heightened personalisation, enhanced operational efficiency, and innovative financial products. The key contributions of this exploration include a detailed examination of how GenAI can drive significant advancements in financial inclusivity and literacy by democratising access to complex financial services and tailoring products to individual consumer needs. Future research should delve deeper into the ethical implications and governance challenges posed by these rapidly evolving technologies. The burgeoning integration of the Metaverse into everyday financial transactions and its potential to redefine traditional banking and investment paradigms invites rigorous scrutiny and proactive regulatory approaches to ensure consumer protection and system integrity.

Emerging trends indicate that the line between physical and virtual financial interactions will continue to blur with the Metaverse offering a new platform for secure, immersive, and engaging financial experiences. The potential for blockchain to further secure these interactions suggests a fertile area for innovation, particularly in developing robust protocols that enhance transparency and trust among users. By strengthening one's understanding of these dynamics, the financial sector can harness the full potential of these technologies ensuring that they not only lead to economic growth but also contribute to a more equitable financial ecosystem. The continued exploration of these themes will provide valuable insights into the resilience of financial systems and the adaptability of markets in the face of technological change, guiding stakeholders towards a future where finance is more accessible, inclusive, and aligned with the digital age.

References

Abubakar, A. G., & Abubakar, S. G. (2023). Revolutionary applications of trending block chain innovation in accounting and auditing. *World Journal of Advanced Engineering Technology and Sciences, 10*(1), 040–053.

Aggarwal, L., Vasisht, U., Kanwar, R., Kumar, A., & Goswami, P. (2023). *Analyzing Chatgpt based on large language model from industrial perspective*. Available at SSRN 4563696.

Ahn, S. J., Kim, J., & Kim, J. (2022). The bifold triadic relationships framework: A theoretical primer for advertising research in the metaverse. *Journal of Advertising, 51*(5), 592–607.

AlBenJasim, S., Dargahi, T., Takruri, H., & Al-Zaidi, R. (2023). FinTech cybersecurity challenges and regulations: Bahrain case study. *Journal of Computer Information Systems*, 1–17.

Allen, F., Gu, X., & Jagtiani, J. (2021). A survey of fintech research and policy discussion. *Review of Corporate Finance, 1*, 259–339.

Alt, R., & Puschmann, T. (2016). Bankmodell. In *Digitalisierung der Finanzindustrie* (pp. 55–117). Springer Gabler.

Arslanian, H. (2022). The emergence of new Blockchains and crypto-assets. In *The book of crypto: The complete guide to understanding bitcoin, cryptocurrencies and digital assets* (pp. 99–119). Springer International Publishing.

Auer, R. (2019). *Embedded supervision: How to build regulation into blockchain finance*.

Auer, R., & Claessens, S. (2018). Regulating cryptocurrencies: Assessing market reactions. *BIS Quarterly Review*.

Avanesh, N. M., & Zachariah, M. (2023). Bracing up for financial inclusivity: The CabDost way. *Emerald Emerging Markets Case Studies, 13*(1), 1–24.

Avital, M., King, J. L., Beck, R., Rossi, M., & Teigland, R. (2016). Jumping on the Blockchain Bandwagon: Lessons of the past and outlook to the future. In *Panel at: Proceedings of the 37thInternational Conference on Information Systems, Dublin, Ireland* (pp. 1–6).

Baliker, C., Baza, M., Alourani, A., Alshehri, A., Alshahrani, H., & Choo, K. K. R. (2023). On the applications of Blockchain in FinTech: Advancements and opportunities. *IEEE Transactions on Engineering Management*.

Ball, M. (2022). *The Metaverse and how it will revolutionize everything*. Liveright Publishing, co. W.W. Norton & Company.

Banafa, A. (2023). *Introduction to internet of things (IoT)*. CRC Press.

Barbu, C. M., Florea, D. L., Dabija, D. C., & Barbu, M. C. R. (2021). Customer experience in fintech. *Journal of Theoretical and Applied Electronic Commerce Research, 16*(5), 1415–1433.

Berg, C., Davidson, S., & Potts, J. (2019). Blockchain technology as economic infrastructure: Revisiting the electronic markets hypothesis. *Frontiers in Blockchain, 2*(2019), 22.

Bhat, J. R., AlQahtani, S. A., & Nekovee, M. (2023). FinTech enablers, use cases, and role of future internet of things. *Journal of King Saud University-Computer and Information Sciences, 35*(1), 87–101.

Bizel, G. (2023). A bibliometric analysis: Metaverse in education concept. *Journal of Metaverse, 3*(2), 133–143.

Bourlakis, M., Papagiannidis, S., & Li, F. (2009). Retail spatial evolution: Paving the way from traditional to metaverse retailing. *Electronic Commerce Research, 9*(1), 135–148.

Breidbach, C. F., Keating, B. W., & Lim, C. (2020). Fintech: Research directions to explore the digital transformation of financial service systems. *Journal of Service Theory and Practice, 30*(1), 79–102.

Campanella, F., Serino, L., Battisti, E., Giakoumelou, A., & Karasamani, I. (2023). FinTech in the financial system: Towards a capital-intensive and high competence human capital reality? *Journal of Business Research, 155*, 113376.
Carstens, A. (2018). *Money in the digital age: what role for central banks?, lecture at the House of Finance*. Goethe University.
Chao, C. H., Ting, I. H., Tseng, Y. J., Wang, B. W., Wang, S. H., & Wang, Y. Q. (2022). The study of DeFi in virtual community and financial supervision. In *The 9th multidisciplinary international social networks conference* (pp. 74–80).
Colicev, A. (2023). How can non-fungible tokens bring value to brands. *International Journal of Research in Marketing, 40*(1), 30–37.
Danladi, S., Prasad, M. S. V., Modibbo, U. M., Ahmadi, S. A., & Ghasemi, P. (2023). Attaining sustainable development goals through financial inclusion: Exploring collaborative approaches to Fintech adoption in developing economies. *Sustainability, 15*(17), 13039.
Ediagbonya, V., & Tioluwani, C. (2023). The role of fintech in driving financial inclusion in developing and emerging markets: Issues, challenges and prospects. *Technological Sustainability, 2*(1), 100–119.
Elm, M., & Montez, T. (2022). *The banking head of digital's five-year innovation strategy: A playbook for open finance, AI, the Metaverse and beyond.* Insider Intelligence,.
Engelstätter, B., & Ward, M. R. (2022). Video games become more mainstream. *Entertainment Computing, 42*, 100494.
Fanusie, Y. & Robinson, T. (2018). Bitcoin laundering: an analysis of illicit flows into digital currency services, *Center on Sanctions and Illicit Finance memorandum*, January.
Fernandes, A., & Chatterjee, S. (2022). Possibilities of metaverse: The second life. *International Journal of Engineering and Management Research, 12*(4), 79–82.
Firmansyah, B., & Arman, A. A. (2023). Generic solution architecture Design of Regulatory Technology (RegTech). *Indonesian Journal of Electrical Engineering and Informatics (IJEEI), 11*(2).
Foley, S., Karlsen, J., & Putniņš, T. (2018). Sex, drugs, and bitcoin: How much illegal activity is financed through cryptocurrencies? *Review of Financial Studies*. forthcoming.
Gadekallu, T. R., Pham, Q.-V., Nguyen, D. C., Maddikunta, P. K. R., Deepa, N., Prabadevi, B., Pathirana, P. N., Zhao, J., & Hwang, W.-J. (2022). Blockchain for edge of things: Applications, opportunities, and challenges. *IEEE Internet of Things Journal, 9*(2), 964–988.
Gaviyau, W., & Sibindi, A. B. (2023). Customer due diligence in the FinTech era: A *bibliometric analysis. Risks, 11*(1), 11.
Gomber, P., Kauffman, R. J., Parker, C., & Weber, B. W. (2018). On the fintech revolution: Interpreting the forces of innovation, disruption, and transformation in financial services. *Journal of Management Information Systems, 35*(1), 220–265.
Guild, J. (2017). Fintech and the future of finance. *Asian Journal of Public Affairs*, 17–20.
Hackl, C. (2020). The Metaverse is Coming and It's A Very Big Deal. *Forbes*. 2020, June 5. Retrieved December 3, 2022 https://www.forbes.com/sites/cathyhackl/2020/07/05/the-metaverse-is-coming%2D%2Dits-a-very-big-deal/?sh=1f4c347a440f
Haig, M. (2001). Talking to the teen generation. *InBrand strategy* (p. 30).
Harris, K., Harris, R., & Baron, S. (2001). Customer participation in retail service: Lessons from Brecht. *International Journal of Retail and Distribution Management, 29*(8), 359–369.
Hollensen, S., Kotler, P., & Opresnik, M. O. (2022). Metaverse–the new marketing universe. *Journal of Business Strategy*.
Hurst, W., Spyrou, O., Tekinerdogan, B., & Krampe, C. (2023). Digital art and the Metaverse: Benefits and challenges. *Future Internet, 15*(6), 188.
Hutson, J., Banerjee, G., Kshetri, N., Odenwald, K., & Ratican, J. (2023). Architecting the Metaverse: Blockchain and the financial and legal regulatory challenges of virtual real estate. *Journal of Intelligent Learning Systems and Applications, 15.*

Kanbach, D. K., Heiduk, L., Blueher, G., Schreiter, M., & Lahmann, A. (2023). The GenAI is out of the bottle: Generative artificial intelligence from a business model innovation perspective. *Review of Managerial Science*, 1–32.

Kar, A. K., & Varsha, P. S. (2023). Unravelling the techno-functional building blocks of Metaverse ecosystems–a review and research agenda. *International Journal of Information Management Data Insights, 100176.*

Kaur, G. (2023). Understanding the impact of CBDCs on financial stability: The shift towards a user-centric financial ecosystem. In *Concepts, technologies, challenges, and the future of web 3* (pp. 456–473). IGI Global.

Koohang, A., Nord, J. H., Ooi, K. B., Tan, G. W. H., Al-Emran, M., Aw, E. C. X., & Wong, L. W. (2023). Shaping the metaverse into reality: A holistic multidisciplinary understanding of opportunities, challenges, and avenues for future investigation. *Journal of Computer Information Systems, 63*(3), 735–765.

Kunduru, A. R. (2023). Artificial intelligence advantages in cloud Fintech application security. *Central Asian Journal of Mathematical Theory and Computer Sciences, 4*(8), 48–53.

Landau, J. P., & Genais, A. (2018). *Les crypto-monnaies, rapport au Ministre de l'Économie et des Finances*, 4 July.

Lehtonen, M. J., Gustafsson, R., & Hassan, L. (2023). The multiplex of value creation and capture logics in the video game industry: An integrative review of 20 years of studies and a future research agenda. *Technological Forecasting and Social Change, 195*, 122756.

Li, K., Lau, B. P. L., Yuan, X., Ni, W., Guizani, M., & Yuen, C. (2023). Towards ubiquitous semantic Metaverse: Challenges, approaches, and opportunities. *IEEE Internet of Things Journal.*

Marinotti, J. (2022). Can you truly own anything in the Metaverse? A law professor explains how blockchains and NFTs don't protect virtual property. *Market Watch.* Retrieved October 9, 2022: https://www.marketwatch.com/story/can-you-truly-own-anything-in-the-metaverse-a-law-professor-explains-how-blockchains-and-nfts-dont-protect-virtual-property-11650559724#:~:text=When%20you%20buy%20an%20item,a%20unique%20string%20of%20bits

Memarian, B., & Doleck, T. (2023). Fairness, accountability, transparency, and ethics (FATE) in artificial intelligence (AI), and higher education: A systematic review. *Computers and education. Artificial Intelligence, 100152.*

Mertzanis, C. (2020). Financial supervision structure, decentralized decision-making and financing constraints. *Journal of Economic Behavior & Organization, 174*, 13–37.

Möser, M., Böhme, R., & Breuker, D. (2013). An inquiry into money laundering tools in the Bitcoin ecosystem in *Proceedings of the APWG eCrime Researchers Summit (ECRIME),* San Francisco (pp. 1–14).

Mozumder, M. A. I., Theodore, A. T. P., Athar, A., & Kim, H. C. (2023). The metaverse applications for the finance industry, its challenges, and an approach for the metaverse finance industry. In *2023 25th international conference on advanced communication technology (ICACT)* (pp. 407–410). IEEE.

Nakamoto, S. (2008). Bitcoin: A peer-to-peer electronic cash system. *Decentralized Business Review, 21260.*

Papagiannidis, S., & Bourlakis, M. A. (2010). Staging the new retail Drama: At a Metaverse near you! *Journal of Virtual Worlds Research, 2*(5), 425–446.

Pires, P. B., Santos, J. D., Pereira, I. V., & Torres, A. I. (Eds.). (2023). *Confronting security and privacy challenges in digital marketing.* IGI Global.

Popescu, G. H., Valaskova, K., & Horak, J. (2022). Augmented reality shopping experiences, retail business analytics, and machine vision algorithms in the virtual economy of the Metaverse. *Journal of Self-Governance & Management Economics, 10*(2).

Prabadevi, B., Deepa, N., Victor, N., Gadekallu, T. R., Maddikunta, P. K. R., Yenduri, G., & Liyanage, M. (2023). Metaverse for Industry 5.0 in NextG Communications: Potential Applications and Future Challenges. *arXiv preprint arXiv:2308.02677.*

PROFILEmiami. (2022). *Take a First Look at 'Metareal' Mansion to be Sold via NFT as Real Home and Digital Twin in the Metaverse*. 2022, August 11. Retrieved 2022, December 3: https://profilemiamire.com/miamirealestate/2022/8/11/take-a-first-look-at-metareal-mansion-to-be-sold-via-nft-as-real-home-and-digital-twin-in-metaverse

Quiroz-Guitierrez, M. (2022). This week in the Metaverse: 'Metaverse' could be word of the year, Johnnie Walker launches an NFT, and Mattel creates an NFT marketplace. *Fortune Crypto*. 2022, November 25. Retrieved 2022, December 4 https://fortune.com/crypto/2022/11/25/this-week-in-the-metaverse-johnnie-walker-oxford-rockstar-games/

Raad, H., & Rashid, F. K. M. (2023). The Metaverse: Applications, Concerns, Technical Challenges, Future Directions and Recommendations. *IEEE Access*.

Ravenscraft, E. (2021). The metaverse land rush is an illusion. *Wired*. (December 26, 2021). https://www.wired.com/story/metaverse-land-rush-illusion/

Rospigliosi, P. A. (2022). Metaverse or simulacra? Roblox, Minecraft, meta and the turn to virtual reality for education, socialisation and work. *Interactive Learning Environments, 30*(1), 1–3.

Rückeshäuser, N. (2017). Do we really want Blockchain-based accounting? Decentralized consensus as enabler of management override of internal controls. In *Proceedings of the 13th International Conference on Wirtschaftsinformatik* (pp. 16–30).

Schuler, K., Nadler, M., & Schär, F. (2023). Contagion and loss redistribution in crypto asset markets: Modelling the intersection of DeFi and CeFi. *Available at SSRN 4499113*.

Sebastian, G. (2023). A descriptive study on metaverse: Cybersecurity risks, controls, and regulatory framework. *International Journal of Security and Privacy in Pervasive Computing (IJSPPC), 15*(1), 1–14.

Shabsigh, G., & Boukherouaa, E. B. (2023). Generative Artificial Intelligence in Finance. *FinTech Notes, 2023*(006).

Singh, S. (2023). The emergence of web 3 and its Core building blocks: Understanding the third iteration of the internet. In *Concepts, technologies, challenges, and the future of web 3* (pp. 1–22). IGI Global.

Strobel, J., & Hawkins, C. (2022). Designing in second life: Identity construction and learning in a virtual informal environment. *Journal of Online Engineering Education, 1*(1).

Subramanian, M., Malathi, S., Shajahan, U. S., Dhinakaran, D. P., Kaur, K., & Lakshmi, M. R. (2023). Fintech and the future of financial services. *Journal of Survey in Fisheries Sciences, 10*(3S), 6620–6627.

Telukdarie, A., & Mungar, A. (2023). The impact of digital financial technology on accelerating financial inclusion in developing economies. *Procedia Computer Science, 217*, 670–678.

Tian, S., Zhao, B., & Olivares, R. O. (2023). Cybersecurity risks and central banks' sentiment on central bank digital currency: Evidence from global cyberattacks. *Finance Research Letters, 53*, 103609.

Turdialiev, M. A. (2022). The legal issues of the Metaverse and perspectives of establishment of International Financial Center in Metaverse. *Oriental Renaissance: Innovative, Educational, Natural and Social Sciences, 2*(8), 239–249.

Valaskova, K., Machova, V., & Lewis, E. (2022). Virtual marketplace dynamics data, spatial analytics, and customer engagement tools in a real-time interoperable decentralized Metaverse. *Linguistic and Philosophical Investigations, 21*, 105–120.

Weber, I., Xu, X., Riveret, R., Governatori, G., Ponomarev, A., & Mendling, J. (2016). Untrusted business process monitoring and execution. In *Proceedings of International Conference on Business Process Management* (pp. 329–347).

White, E. (2023). What does finance democracy look like?: Thinking beyond fintech and regtech. *Transnational Legal Theory*, 1–25.

Wójcik, D., & Ioannou, S. (2020). COVID-19 and finance: Market developments so far and potential impacts on the financial sector and centres. *Tijdschrift voor Economische en Sociale Geografie, 111*(3), 387–400.

Wulandari, R., Susilowati, E., Safitri, N., & Ikhsan, M. (2023). A literature review on Fintech innovations: Examining the evolution, impact, and challenges. *SEIKO: Journal of Management & Business, 6*(2), 438–448.

Xu, M., Guo, Y., Hu, Q., Xiong, Z., Yu, D., & Cheng, X. (2023). A trustless architecture of blockchain-enabled metaverse. *High-Confidence Computing, 3*(1), 100088.

Yang, Q., Zhao, Y., Huang, H., Xiong, Z., Kang, J., & Zheng, Z. (2022). Fusing blockchain and AI with metaverse: A survey. *IEEE Open Journal of the Computer Society, 3*, 122–136.

Zhou, Z., Chen, Z., & Jin, X. L. (2023). A review of the literature on the metaverse: Definition, technologies, and user behaviors. *Internet Research.*

Znica, O. (2022). Video game streaming: How poor licensing undermines creators. *Interactive Entertainment Law Review, 5*(1), 32–45.

Chapter 8
National Strategies and Practices for the Metaverse Development: The Case of Finland

Jussi S. Jauhiainen

Abstract This chapter explores Finland's national Metaverse strategy including the perspectives of pivotal technology developers and users. The strategy, launched in December 2023, is the first national Metaverse strategy in Europe. It is structured around five core themes: technology enablers, business networks, Metaverse society, Metaverse health, and industrial Metaverse. To unravel the intricacies, a content analysis of Finland's national Metaverse strategy report was analysed and a semi-structured survey was conducted with 20 prominent enterprises actively engaged in the development and application of virtual, augmented, and extended reality technologies within Finland.

This analysis sheds light on the opportunities and challenges inherent in governance for advancing the Metaverse through national strategies. It also provides insights into how private-sector enterprises in Finland perceive the public sector's role in shaping Metaverse-related development practices within this technology-intensive realm. Moreover, this chapter expands its horizon by incorporating references to other national, local, and private Metaverse strategies and practices worldwide, contributing to a nuanced understanding of the global landscape in this transformative technological domain. Through a synthesis of these elements, a comprehensive view of Finland's pioneering efforts in the Metaverse strategy and its implications for broader international developments is presented.

Keywords Metaverse · Finland · Strategy · XR · Governance

J. S. Jauhiainen (✉)
Department of Geography and Geology, University of Turku, Turku, Finland

Institute of Ecology and the Earth Sciences, University of Tartu, Tartu, Estonia
e-mail: jusaja@utu.fi

N. Islam, I. Salami (eds.), *Metaverse Innovation*, Applied Innovation and Technology Management, https://doi.org/10.1007/978-3-031-97080-1_8

8.1 Introduction

In December 2023, Finland achieved a historic milestone by becoming the first European country to formally introduce a national Metaverse strategy. The strategy was a collaborative effort involving key stakeholders in Finland's Metaverse landscape encompassing businesses, universities, associations, and individuals. The impetus for the strategy's development and funding originated from the national government's technology development agency Business Finland (Metaverse Initiative, 2023).

This chapter explores the nuances of Finland's national Metaverse strategy and also provides insights into the viewpoints of pivotal technology developers and users regarding this pioneering initiative, including how governance of the Metaverse is addressed in the strategy. The context derives from related technology developments within the country and national technology policies including initiatives by Business Finland.

The tangible manifestation of this strategy is a comprehensive 23-page report organised into four distinct sections (Metaverse Initiative, 2023). To analyse this material, key themes and keywords pertaining to the Metaverse were identified within existing research literature and a theory-driven content analysis was employed to assess the extent to which these elements were present in the national strategy. The empirical findings are then subjected to discussion and complemented by personal reflections. Importantly, the chapter author followed the strategy formation process taking part in open gatherings and following relevant themes in thematic email groups associated with the strategy.

The Metaverse is, in practice, developed in Finland and other countries by private enterprises. Therefore, a semi-structured survey was conducted with 20 influential enterprises deeply engaged in the development and application of virtual, augmented, and extended reality technologies in Finland. The survey explored the enterprises' comprehension of the content and significance of the national Metaverse strategy as well as the level of their involvement in the strategy formulation process. This comprehensive examination illuminated both opportunities and challenges associated with policy guidance and governance of the Metaverse in Finland and what can be learned from the interaction between the private sector, public sector, and civil society in shaping the development practices of this technology-intensive domain.

Besides Finland, this chapter incorporates references to Metaverse strategies embraced by other nations and cities within and beyond Europe as well as to digital platforms that are currently referred to as the Metaverse, for example in digital social interaction and gaming fields. The latter engages millions of people in these digital realms daily. This broader contextualisation serves to illuminate the interconnected landscape of Metaverse strategies, contributing to a comprehensive analysis of Finland's strategic positioning in this emerging technological domain.

There is not yet any comprehensive and extended Metaverse anywhere in the world. According to Andrew McStay (2023), there is almost a fatalistic sense that an

XR-based Metaverse is inevitable. Therefore, there will be a need to govern the Metaverse in one way or another. On one hand, the governance refers to imagined and suggested futures about what the Metaverse could be. Such governing of the future of the Metaverse is about selecting and de-selecting development trajectories of related technologies and their potential impacts. This extends to the broader ecosystem that supports the development of the Metaverse. On the other hand, governance refers to digital platforms that contain features of the Metaverse and which are in use as of 2024 (Egliston et al., 2024). This pertains to what is done within the Metaverse.

As discussed in various chapters of this book, the Metaverse, characterised by a vast, three-dimensional (3D) computing network, integrates various technologies. It merges physical and digital realms within the online sphere, spanning the Internet, social networks, and innovative technologies. Positioned for significant expansion throughout the 2020s, the forthcoming development of the Metaverse will be driven by advancements in digital, virtual, and immersive technologies. These include Artificial Intelligence (AI), the Internet of Things (IoT), Big Data, Edge Computing, Blockchain, 5G and 6G networks, Digital Twins, and spatial computing technologies. The latter include augmented reality (AR) and virtual reality (VR), which are commonly grouped under the labels of mixed reality (MR), as well as extended reality (XR), which is the most advanced form of digitally mediated realities (Bibri, 2022; Egliston et al., 2024); Khestri, 2025). To support their development strategies, policies and practices are needed for the overall successful governance of the Metaverse.

The key novelty in the Metaverse is that it opens up exhilarating possibilities for enriched human experiences, collaboration, and engagement that transcend the limitations of physical environments and traditional face-to-face interactions. Furthermore, the recent development of chatbot generative AI suggests that intensive human–machine interaction, collaboration, and cocreation will happen in the Metaverse (Jauhiainen, 2024). These enhance automated content production and novel experiences in the Metaverse (Lv, 2023). With the advent of 6G networks in the 2030s, seamless transmission of vast amounts of data will become achievable thanks to features such as ubiquitous connectivity, ultra-low latency, ultra-high capacity, reliability, and stringent security measures (Tang et al., 2023). These advancements will pave the way for the realisation of myriad facets of the Metaverse.

As discussed later, various public and private stakeholders and people are already exploring the potential of the Metaverse. The potential of forthcoming major economic opportunities has so far been the key driver to foster the development of the Metaverse. Projections suggest that by 2030 the global Metaverse market could attain a value of 400 billion dollars, contributing 1–2% to the global gross domestic product (Globenewswire, 2023). Beyond its economic implications, the Metaverse is poised to exert a profound impact on social networking dynamics. As the accessibility of Internet continues to expand and global digital divides diminish between various geographical areas, the Metaverse can become a truly global platform in the 2030s.

8.2 Governance of the Metaverse

Governance of the Metaverse can be defined as the framework of legal, political, and economic relationships that shape the interconnected actions among Metaverse-related technology companies, governments, users, and other stakeholders. Governance encompasses both restrictive dimensions that limit the Metaverse-related actions of individuals and entities belonging to the Metaverse ecosystem and enabling dimensions that provide freedom and avenues for individual or collective action regarding the Metaverse.

There are not yet globally extended Metaverse laws, regulations, or policies. Individuals and entities may be subject to regulation through external governance such as laws and public policies regarding the use of the Metaverse within specific territorial administrations such as countries. That governance might be quite different or not exist in another country (Egliston et al., 2024). It is to be determined who has jurisdiction in the Metaverse. Virtual worlds and online communities cross international boundaries and involve multiple legal systems (Kalyvaki, 2023).

At the core of the global Metaverse, when such a global platform would appear, lies data-driven corporate-led technocratic governance. This governance extends not only within the Metaverse itself but also across the broader ecosystem connected to it. Andrew McStay (2023) argues that, so far, the Metaverse has been created to serve the plutocratic ends of technology corporations rather than to be good for the general public. Given that digital technologies permeate all aspects of modern digitalised society, there arise issues and critical concerns about the Metaverse. These consist of, among others, surveillance, control, freedom, personal autonomy, privacy, cybersecurity, discrimination, and social exclusion. Therefore, it is imperative to comprehensively understand and address the risks and impacts associated with the governance of the Metaverse (Bibri, 2022).

When external governance of the Metaverse is lacking, or enterprises, governments and/or users consider it otherwise necessary, they may voluntarily adhere to related self-governance principles. Ben Egliston et al. (2024) underscore that governance related to the Metaverse is influenced by governments, civil society, and industrial entities. National governments, alongside non-governmental organisations (NGOs) and civil society, propose laws and regulations but it is predominantly private enterprises and corporations that practically develop the Metaverse. They offer voluntary and non-binding suggestions on governance arrangements for both the broader Metaverse ecosystem and within the Metaverse itself.

These key stakeholders in the Metaverse may also engage in co-governance, collaboratively determining regulatory approaches and practices for the Metaverse (Egliston et al., 2024). Lijuan Yang (2023) highlights the necessity of cooperation among governments, standard-setting organisations, and enterprises to expedite the establishment of standards for the Metaverse and to facilitate their effective dissemination. The compatibility and security of these technical standards greatly influence the depth and breadth of the Metaverse. They are paramount for the transformation from smaller Metaverse platforms to broader interconnected Metaverse

(Hyun, 2023; Yang, 2023). However, according to Goldberg and Schär (2023), while open standards and blockchain-based governance are necessary conditions, they are not enough to form a decentralised Metaverse without power hierarchies within it.

8.2.1 Metaverse Horizontal Layers

Governance of the Metaverse is related to the various vertical layers it consists of as well as to the horizontal ecosystem that the Metaverse covers. According to Lee et al. (2023), the Metaverse consists of technology and ecosystem. With technology, one can refer to vertical socio-technological layers with different digitally mediated realities and functional interconnected spheres. By ecosystem, one can refer to the horizontal Metaverse ecosystem with environmental, social, and economic dimensions along which a variety of data is collected, analysed, and made for the use of decision-making.

From the horizontal perspective, the Metaverse can be seen from a narrower or broader perspective. From a geographically narrower scope, the Metaverse is a smart city (Fig. 8.1). This includes the city's 3D semantic model in which the data's meaning is related to the real world. The material city's development is significantly impacted by the continuously collected, analysed, and monitored digitalised data about the smart city such as the digital twin of a material city. The data regards functional aspects of urban areas in their economic, social, and environmental aspects. These include smart safety and security, smart traffic mobility, smart health and welfare, smart energy, smart city education, and smart community and social network, as well as smart environmental monitoring and control (Allam et al., 2022; Aloqaily et al., 2022; Kshetri, 2023; Kuru, 2023; Singh et al., 2021).

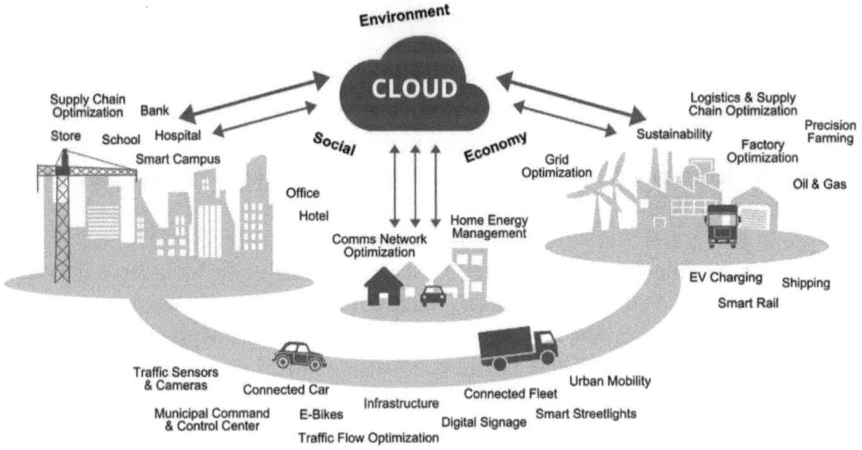

Fig. 8.1 Metaverse ecosystem of a smart city. Modified from Nopanen (2022)

In fact, globally, the most practical Metaverse solutions so far regard digital twins of existing cities. Examples of such smaller or larger smart cities with Metaverse functions can be found in many technologically developed regions of the world. The most commonly mentioned cities discussed with the Metaverse dimension include Seoul, Dubai, Shanghai, Santa Monica, Tokyo, New York City, London, Singapore, and Helsinki (Bibri, 2022; de Almeida, 2023). Besides using the data for their development, these cities also actively promote, advertise, and brand these Metaverse functions (Kuru, 2023). The governance of this geographically narrower horizontal Metaverse refers to the public policies on how these digital twins are utilised for the benefit of their material counterparts. Often these digital twins also include the support for developing leading companies in the Metaverse sector in that smart city (Kshetri, 2023).

The broader perspective of the Metaverse refers to geographically wider territories than just cities and urban areas. As the global political system consists of countries, then this Metaverse refers to how independent countries launch and implement the Metaverse for their benefit. The case of Finland will be discussed at length later in this chapter (see Metaverse Initiative, 2023), but there are also many other countries that have specific strategies, policies, and practices for the Metaverse.

China is one of the key systematic proponents of the Metaverse for national development. It has two main scopes. On the one hand, it has identified a huge market potential in the digital sector related to the Metaverse. In 2021, a national document stated that digital reality, digital twins, and blockchain are the key technologies to be developed. This was followed by the government's action plan for 2022–2026 for the integration and development of VR and digital industry applications. This plan also focused on VR, digital twins, and blockchain, but it also included MR, AI, and cloud computing for industrial applications. In 2023, the supreme political regime of the country, the Chinese Communist Party launched the action plan for 2023–2025 regarding industrial innovation and development of the Metaverse (Gong, 2024). On the other hand, an idea is to use the virtual dimension to enhance the material reality and to use the real dimension to strengthen the strictly regulated and controlled virtual context (Kshetri, 2023).

South Korea was one of the early movers to the Metaverse and became one of the global Metaverse leaders. Its K-Metaverse was launched in 2022 to promote the country's globally competitive companies in the Metaverse sector. This includes the systematic development of Seoul's digital twin that extends beyond purely economic interests. It provides access to municipal services for the city's inhabitants and promotes virtual tourism to it (de Almeida, 2023; Kshetri, 2023).

The rich Middle Eastern countries have become active in Metaverse development. The United Arab Emirates (UAE) strengthens the role of Dubai as a technological and economic hub for the broader Metaverse ecosystem. It provides government services, real estate business, tourism, and education in the Metaverse aiming to make Dubai one of the leading Metaverse economies in the world. In addition, the Metaverse is part of Saudi Arabia's Vision 2030 in which digital gaming and e-sport platforms are seen to generate significant economic turnover. Furthermore, the futuristic megacity NEOM will contain its own Metaverse platform. This digital twin is going to be used from the early development phase onward. It will make it possible for people from anywhere to visit it virtually before making an investment or migrating there (Kshetri, 2023).

8.2.2 Metaverse Vertical Layers

Besides the above-discussed horizontal features of the Metaverse ecosystem, the Metaverse can also be seen to encompass the interconnected vertical layers of the 3D Internet and their connections to physical space. These layers tightly intertwine the virtual and material worlds within their economic, social, and identity systems (Yang, 2023; Fig. 8.2). These layers identify key aspects within the Metaverse and their relevance when considering the overall governance of the Metaverse.

At the foundation of the vertically composed Metaverse lies the essential layer of material technological infrastructure that enables data movement and storage. The development of this infrastructure is subject to various national technology policies and regulations. Enterprises develop required technologies, and business operations are another of their key targets. The Metaverse is built on technical standards, shared technical facilities, and the successful integration of tools and platforms. Metaverse standards come from enterprises, industry alliances, and government bodies such as government departments and standardisation agencies (Yang, 2023). In fact, among the key challenges to the current state of the Metaverse is the lack of shared standards. This limits interoperability between several digital platforms so that they would enable people to move from one platform to another with their avatars and virtual property. Another challenge of this still early development stage is the limited synchronicity that is needed to make the Metaverse sufficiently seamless to attract its users (Mosco, 2023).

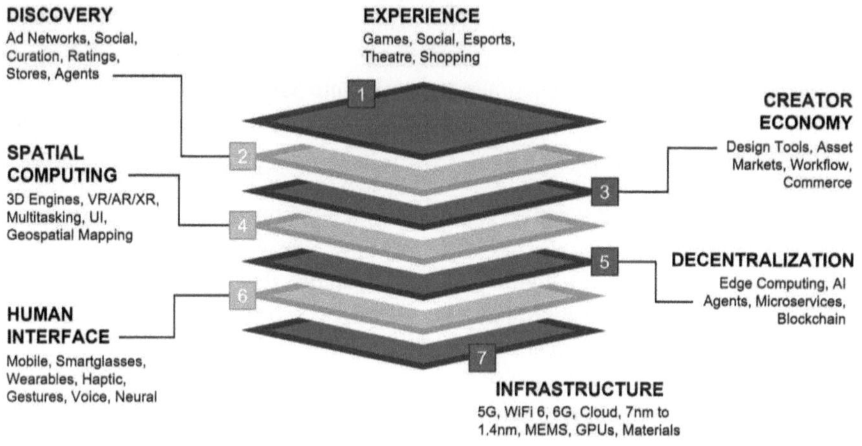

Fig. 8.2 Layers of the Metaverse. Modified from Radoff (2021) and Datta (2022)

The subsequent layer of the human interface involves human interaction within the Metaverse. This necessitates devices and modes of operation linked to the technological infrastructure. The production of devices is the task of private enterprises. While AR and VR devices serve as access points to the Metaverse, they also serve various unrelated tasks, underscoring their versatility and potential impact beyond immersive experiences.

The above-mentioned human interaction necessitates a layer of decentralised computational tasks. It incorporates edge computing, blockchain, AI agents, and other tools. While the private sector is responsible for their development, the initial skills required for this development are supported by higher education policies.

The layer of spatial computing constitutes another layer, encompassing different dimensions of digitally mediated realities, geospatial mapping, and associated technologies that are core competencies of high-technology enterprises. One reality within it is AR, where real-world environments are enhanced with digital 3D elements. AR creates an immersive and interactive experience where virtual content is spatially integrated into the real world, offering users a profound sense of presence in a combined real/virtual space. AR experiences are often accessible through a wide range of devices, e.g. computers, gaming consoles, VR headsets, smartphones, tablets, and compatible applications (Goldberg & Schär, 2023) making it the most prevalent form of blended reality environments so far (Statista, 2023b). However, it is expected that the Metaverse will distance itself from such direct dependence on the physical material environment. Alternatively, the operator could require a specific device to be used by the end users.

Another dimension of the spatial computing layer is VR, where users immerse themselves in simulated environments through digital devices like VR glasses. VR provides an immersive and interactive experience that fosters a strong sense of presence. However, the adoption of VR devices still remains relatively low. It is estimated that in 2024, 14.3 million VR devices would be sold globally, indicating a growing but still niche market (Statista, 2023a). VR provides an environment that is not necessarily connected to a material physical environment anymore. However, it is mostly based only or mostly on visualisation, thus it does not sustain deeper multi-sensory immersion that would be important if one fully expects to feel in the Metaverse. AR and VR are sometimes combined into MR, further bridging the gap between physical and digitally created realities and suggesting a more feasible path for the expansion of the Metaverse.

While AR and VR primarily engage one or two senses, limiting their immersion effect, the development of XR presents a promising advancement. XR integrates physical environments, people, and MR, offering a more immersive and multi-sensory experience. As XR technologies evolve rapidly, they are expected to play a pivotal role in the advanced Metaverse. However, broader XR implementation requires robust telecommunication and data infrastructure to facilitate fast data transfer, computation, and storage (Egliston et al., 2024). Ultimately, the Metaverse aims to create a persistent and immersive simulated world where large groups of users can interact simultaneously, sharing a profound sense of presence in this blended environment.

The creator economy layer pertains to Metaverse content including design tools, asset markets, work environments, and commerce activities. Here an important role is played by legislation that sets the framework under which conditions economic transactions can happen and how ownership of digital goods is organised. On the business side, there is the industrial Metaverse that involves digital twins of the physical-material world entities. These are used for experimenting, simulating, and optimising production, service provision, training, and related decision-making. Rapidly expanding IoT is part of this sphere (Mystakidis, 2022).

Another business-orientated sphere is the enterprise Metaverse. It facilitates collaborative work, the building of teams across geographical distances in the physical world, and offers showrooms for enterprises to present their products and services. This has already become a significant dimension with digital fashion and digital assets purchased and sold every day. In this sphere, virtual land, goods, art, and accessories can be rented, bought, and sold. Increasingly, major brand companies are designing physical goods that are targeted to both material and digital environments. They merge products, people, and purpose with an immersive, blockchain-based digital world (Di Bartolo, 2023; Hollensen et al., 2023).

People and enterprises are connected to the governmental or administrative Metaverse. This non-business sphere refers to focused public sector services and activities provided for the people and enterprises. It may contain digital twins of existing public services that are then also provided virtually providing an option for users to use the service either materially or virtually. It can also substitute the existing physical world service so that it will be transferred exclusively to the digital sphere. It can also be a service that is new and only achievable in the digital sphere (Bibri, 2022).

The layer of discovery encompasses social curation, ratings, advertisements, stores, and agents present within this layer. Lastly, the layer of experience focuses on individuals' various social activities and interactions in the Metaverse including shopping, entertainment, e-sports, and gaming. Its provision is mainly the task of private enterprises, but individual consumers are those who make these services succeed or fail. This consumer or people's Metaverse is a virtual or blended digital-material environment for individuals to socially interact with other people and digital objects. With immersive images, sounds, and other sensations, it provides a sense of being there and offers various opportunities to play, create, and explore (Mystakidis, 2022). When the Metaverse advances substantially, some people might start to value being socially present in the Metaverse even more significantly than being socially present in the physical world. It might be so that being in the Metaverse creates a distinct value (McStay, 2023) with interoperable 3D avatars, digital services, and virtual real-world experiences (Kuru, 2023). The consumer Metaverse is connected to the enterprise Metaverse as people conduct economic activities within the Metaverse.

8.2.3 Metaverse Platforms Designed Privately

Privately designed and created popular Metaverse platforms include, for example, Roblox, Decentraland, The Sandbox, Metropolis, Minecraft, Somnium Space, CryptoVoxels, Fortnite, Upland, NeosVR, High Fidelity, and VRChat. These are developed by technology companies, and people are using them with governments remaining distant in the background with their legal, political, and economic regulations. Therefore, active governance is mostly about relationships between these companies and users, as well as stakeholders within these platforms.

Roblox, launched in 2006, is a leading online game platform and creation system with tens of millions of active users worldwide. Users can create and share their own games across various genres. In the 2020s, Roblox expanded into virtual reality (VR) and is evolving into a Metaverse platform. This vision includes 3D spaces for socialising, shopping, attending lectures, and conducting business meetings remotely. The platform provides intuitive tools, such as Lua scripting language, enabling users (developers) to craft interactive gameplay (Roblox, 2024).

The majority of games in Roblox are user-generated, fostering a diverse and dynamic library. Users can share, collaborate, and earn revenue through virtual sales and in-game purchases. Roblox functions as a social hub where users connect, join groups, and participate in virtual events. It supports chat, friends lists, and in-game communication, fostering a strong sense of community. Available on multiple platforms, including PC, mobile, and consoles, Roblox offers widespread accessibility and popularity (Roblox, 2024).

The main governance challenges that Roblox is facing centre on content moderation, user safety, and platform policies. There is a need to ensure that user-generated content aligns with community standards, addressing online harassment, and protecting younger users from inappropriate content. Safety measures include age-appropriate content filters and parental controls. Platform governance issues encompass policies on virtual transactions, intellectual property, and user rights. As Roblox grows, it must balance these concerns to maintain a safe and inclusive platform experience.

Decentraland, launched in 2017, is a blockchain-powered virtual reality platform where users can create, explore, and monetise digital experiences and assets in a decentralised virtual world. It operates on the Ethereum blockchain and utilises non-fungible tokens (NFTs) to represent ownership of virtual land and assets. Its users can purchase virtual land parcels using MANA, the platform's native cryptocurrency, and have complete control over their digital property. They can customise their land to create interactive games, art installations, shops, and social hubs which can be shared and monetised through in-world transactions. Users can own various digital assets, e.g. monetary units, land parcels, avatar apparel, usernames, or avatars. These assets are virtual and their ownership is usually stored on a database that is managed by the operator of a centralised ledger or the community in the case of a public blockchain system (Goldberg & Schär, 2023).

Decentraland functions as a decentralised autonomous organisation (DAO), allowing users to participate in governance decisions through decentralised voting. The platform supports social interaction, including voice chat, and offers various opportunities for users to earn and spend cryptocurrency within the ecosystem. However, centralisation and concentrated voting power may lead to dependencies, rent extraction behaviour, and create hold-up problems. Therefore, producers, service providers, and consumers must evaluate the governance structure of the platform (Goldberg & Schär, 2023).

Decentraland has attracted major brands and users can buy, sell, and create virtual wearables and accessories for their avatars. The platform's architecture aims to provide a foundation for businesses and developers to build and monetise applications without concerns of central control (Goldberg & Schär, 2023). As one example of a contemporary Metaverse platform, Decentraland relies on its community for governance across platform development, content moderation, and community management. Challenges include ensuring platform integrity while meeting community needs, moderating user-generated content to align with standards, and fostering inclusivity through community engagement.

The Sandbox was founded in 2011 as a mobile video game focused on world-building. Users create unique universes in this virtual world using digital elements like trees, fire, water, and mud to complete objectives. As of 2021, over 12,000 users own digital land on the platform. Users can create, play, and monetise games and experiences within the platform. They can build virtual worlds, characters, and assets. The platform ensures true ownership of digital assets through blockchain technology. The Sandbox offers a range of immersive experiences including gaming, virtual shopping, fashion shows, concerts, art exhibitions, and conferences. It incorporates play-to-earn mechanics, enabling users to earn cryptocurrency rewards. The platform is interoperable with other virtual worlds, fostering a vibrant community of creators, players, and developers collaborating and contributing to its growth (The Sandbox, 2024).

As in other current Metaverse platforms, in The Sandbox, governance issues also revolve around platform development, content moderation, and community management. Decisions on updates and features are community-driven, balancing desires with platform integrity. Content moderation ensures compliance with standards and regulations while effective community management fosters inclusivity and collaboration. Governance regards collaboration within its decentralised structure.

8.3 National Metaverse Strategy for Finland

As discussed above, the Metaverse is primarily spearheaded by leading technology companies but there is a growing interest within the public sector to support its potential applications. During the early 2020s, several countries and cities started formulating their own development strategies for the Metaverse.

In 2023, Finland achieved the milestone of becoming the first European country to officially launch a national Metaverse strategy (Metaverse Initiative, 2023). This initiative was led by Business Finland, the national governmental technology agency, which provided financial support for the strategy's development. However, the strategy itself was collaboratively crafted by key stakeholders in Finland with vested interests in the Metaverse including businesses, universities, associations, and individuals.

The report The Metaverse Strategy for Finland—Virtual Potential to Real-World Impact (Metaverse Initiative, 2023) outlines Finland's objectives for the year 2035 and details the action plan for achieving them. Like many other national Metaverse strategies globally, such as those of China, South Korea and UAE, Finland also has a primary objective to establish the country as a preeminent player in the global Metaverse industry. This requires harnessing the Metaverse's potential to foster the creation of new businesses, job opportunities, export opportunities, and innovations. However, at the same time, the strategy is underpinned by core values of well-being, freedom, openness, and trust. These have been much less often discussed in other national Metaverse strategies (de Almeida, 2023; Khestri, 2023; Gong, 2024).

8.3.1 Core Themes of National Metaverse Strategy for Finland

The strategy is organised through five core themes that discuss both the economic and softer values and potential of the Metaverse as well as the action plan and the key stakeholders for it. The core themes have been organised as technology enablers, business networks, Metaverse society, Metaverse health, and industrial Metaverse.

Technology Enablers This theme prioritises the development, standardisation, and support of essential technical infrastructure, standards, platforms, interfaces, and devices required for immersive and virtual experiences. It encompasses aspects such as interoperability, scalability, security, privacy, and accessibility. The strategy anticipates that the national technology development agency, Business Finland, will assume a leading supportive role. It can offer financial assistance to enterprises and research through its Immersive Digital Life mission and the program Enabling Technologies and Architectures for Immersive Experiences (Metaverse Initiative, 2023).

Business Networks Within this aspect of the strategy, the goal is to facilitate and coordinate the establishment of an autonomous Metaverse ecosystem that spans all critical segments of the value chain, fostering collaboration with European and global partners. This is aimed at ensuring technological independence in the evolving geopolitical landscape and fostering substantial business value within Europe. It encompasses aspects such as innovation ecosystems, business ecosystems, joint offerings, value chains, business models, and regulations. A primary focus is on identifying, developing, and supporting the business opportunities and networks arising from the Metaverse with significant involvement from large Finnish corporations and Business Finland's Immersive Digital Life mission (Metaverse Initiative, 2023).

Metaverse Society This theme revolves around familiarising Finnish society and the general population with the Metaverse, fostering an understanding of its use cases and business opportunities, and establishing the necessary framework for widespread adoption across all age groups. It encompasses the entire educational system, public services, media, arts, entertainment, gaming, and culture. Efforts will be made to ensure accessibility to the Metaverse for everyone through hubs, public libraries, or other public venues. Highly visible Metaverse events will be organised for the public, and Metaverse-related content will be disseminated through mainstream media channels. Finland aims to lead in the societal utilisation of the Metaverse, leveraging its robust education system, creative industries, and gaming sector. The strategy specifically highlights the crucial role of Tampere University and the Smart City working group in facilitating these endeavours (Metaverse Initiative, 2023).

Metaverse Health Focused on promoting physical, mental, and social well-being, this theme aims to harness Metaverse technologies to enhance the inclusion and well-being of citizens. The strategy posits that AR, VR, and Metaverse technologies can offer innovative approaches to improving health outcomes, reducing costs, and increasing access for all residents of Finland. The goal is to integrate Metaverse technologies into preventive healthcare and healthcare delivery nationwide. By leveraging these technologies, Finland seeks to cultivate a mentally healthier, cognitively sharper, and economically stronger populace, thereby contributing positively to the nation's economy. The strategy foresees the University of Oulu and Business Finland's OneHealth programme, as part of the health mission, leading this initiative (Metaverse Initiative, 2023).

Industrial Metaverse This theme focuses on supporting and accelerating the adoption of Metaverse technologies within Finnish industries to enhance productivity, efficiency, safety, and sustainability across various sectors, including manufacturing, maintenance, construction, built environments, defence, logistics, transportation, and sales. Metaverse technologies have the potential to enable human-centric remote work, teleoperation, digital twins, AI assistants, collaborative robotics, and situational awareness. This programme aims to bolster the integration of Metaverse technologies into Finnish industries. Key stakeholders for this initiative include the National Technology Research Centre VTT, large corporations, Robocoast EDIH, and Metaverse Hackathons for industrial innovation and development (Metaverse Initiative, 2023).

8.3.2 *Vision for the Year 2035 in the National Metaverse Strategy for Finland*

The strategy foresees that by the year 2035, i.e. within one decade, Finland will emerge as the foremost global influencer and facilitator of the Metaverse. Finland will be globally recognised for its leadership and the country will stand as a model society with complete integration of the Metaverse. In that context, Finland would boast a vibrant solution ecosystem, attracting significant Foreign Direct Investments across the Metaverse value chain, with an annual industry turnover exceeding €30 billion (Metaverse Initiative, 2023).

The national Metaverse ecosystem connects different actors, sectors, and domains and provides a favourable environment for standardisation, regulation, cybersecurity, and education. Finland's vision prioritises open standards and interfaces, ensuring individual and national autonomy without dominance by any single entity. This is expected to foster a thriving economy, empowering Finnish technology companies to thrive profitably. By demonstrating technological sovereignty and business excellence and by offering real-world testing grounds across various sectors including industry, education, gaming, and defence, Finland will lead globally in Metaverse innovation.

Finland is committed to enhancing well-being sustainably leveraging the Metaverse to reduce emissions, enhance circularity, improve well-being, and promote social cohesion. This would advance human rights and support global democratic development and cooperation. Finland would align closely with the United Nations Sustainable Development Goals and would become a global leader in achieving these. Addressing sustainability in the Metaverse strategy is not a common phenomenon as, globally, little research on the Metaverse has addressed sustainability (Jauhiainen et al., 2023).

In terms of freedom, it is expected that Finland will champion global efforts in diversity and accessibility in the Metaverse, ensuring inclusivity for all individuals regardless of background or abilities. This would be a major step forward as currently the inclusion of physically disabled individuals in the Metaverse remains distant with limited standards and regulations in place (Radanliev et al., 2023). Finland's cultural diversity and heritage would be celebrated in the Metaverse, enriching this virtual environment. It is suggested that citizens would benefit from quality services, entertainment, and education, enhancing their well-being and opportunities. As an open hub for innovation and creativity in the Metaverse, Finland nurtures a culture of experimentation, collaboration, and entrepreneurship. Talent, startups, and investors are supported in the Metaverse domain, offering a conducive national regulatory and funding environment.

The strategy also addressed the aspects of concern regarding the Metaverse including digital rights and ethics, safeguarding users' privacy, security, and autonomy (Fernandez & Hui, 2022). Emphasising trust within the Metaverse, Finland is seen as a global advocate for these. The nation upholds democratic values, transparency, and accountability in Metaverse governance and development. Furthermore,

Finland promotes digital literacy and responsibility among its citizens, empowering them to make informed and ethical choices in the Metaverse.

8.3.3 VR, AR, and XR Technology Enterprises Viewpoints on the National Metaverse Strategy

As previously discussed, the development of the Metaverse is, in practice, the task of private enterprises (Bibri, 2022; Egliston et al., 2024; Mystakidis, 2022). In Finland, the formation of the national strategy for the Metaverse involved stakeholders from various sectors including the public sector, private sector, NGOs, and individuals. To gain further insights into the strategy's impact a survey was conducted with 20 key Finnish companies operating in the VR, AR, and XR sectors. Participants received the strategy report before completing the survey.

Overall, two-thirds of the surveyed key companies in Finland in the VR, AR, and XR sectors considered Metaverse development central to their operations both in the industrial and consumer-orientated sectors. This was true for both the industrial Metaverse (65% agreed, 20% disagreed, 15% did not know) and the people-orientated consumer Metaverse (70% agreed, 10% disagreed, 20% did not know).

For these 20 companies, the Metaverse represents the fusion of existing real-world and virtual digital content incorporating various technologies such as VR, AR, XR, digital twins, and environments. It serves as an interactive platform for multi-user experiences integrating diverse visual technologies and presenting a 3D form of the Internet, including a digital parallel. While some viewed the concept as a promising buzz term with future potential, others saw it as a true opportunity for consumers to explore, experience, and purchase products without physical contact and for companies to operate, design, develop, and sell without physical products. This indicates a comprehensive understanding of the Metaverse's dimensions among the surveyed companies.

Nearly all companies (90%) were familiar with Finland's Metaverse strategy, with 35% being well-informed and 55% somewhat familiar. Half of these enterprises (50%) had some level of involvement in the strategy's preparation during the autumn of 2023. More than half (60%) of the respondents expressed a positive view of Finland's Metaverse strategy. The remainder were neutral, and none of the respondents viewed the strategy negatively. The positive attitude was evident as half of the companies (50%) intended to incorporate the strategy into their operations although a significant portion (45%) remained unsure about its utilisation due to the novelty of the strategy.

Nearly half (45%) of responded companies believed that the national Metaverse strategy would impact their operations, while 35% were unsure, and 20% believed that it would have no impact. Companies expressed varying levels of interest in the different themes of the strategy with the majority (80%) showing interest in technological developments and innovations in the Metaverse (Technology Enablers), followed by two-thirds (65%) expressing interest in the industrial Metaverse, and more than a half (55%) on the business networks theme. There was less interest in the remaining themes of the Metaverse society (35%) and the Metaverse health (25%).

8.4 Conclusions

The overarching term Metaverse encapsulates the amalgamated and immersive material-digital realm. However, as of 2024, rather than a singular Metaverse, multiple distinct Metaverses now exist and this will also be the case in the near future. Each platform provides slightly different environments for user engagement. From a co-creative governance viewpoint, it is crucial to preserve the digital-material identity in the Metaverse platforms while ensuring the accessibility of individual avatars across different platforms.

Due to the lack of overall commonly shared standards, it is challenging to move easily from one Metaverse platform to another. However, governments can manage the standardisation strategies, compatibility, and security of core standards to prevent a monopoly in the Metaverse. They can encourage rapid responses to meet the standardisation needs in specific technical fields, ensure fairness and consensus in standards for rules and procedures, and encourage the establishment of alliances (Hyun, 2023; Yang, 2023). Furthermore, ethical, legal, and security deliberations are needed to guarantee the safe and motivated presence of individuals within a meaningful Metaverse. In fact, ownership of standards and protocols is crucial in deciding the nature of the Metaverse experience. It is problematic if Metaverse's core languages, protocols, standards, and laws of digital reality are subject to property rights (McStay, 2023).

Finland's Metaverse strategy was launched at the end of 2023 (Metaverse Initiative, 2023). The main objective of the strategy was to form a common vision for the Metaverse in Finland covering the entire value chain and to gain international attention for the expertise in the extended technology made in Finland. The goal was that Finland would be one of the world's leading countries developing and utilising the Metaverse by 2035. However, in addition to Finland, almost all countries that have launched broader Metaverse strategies foresee that their country will be among the leading Metaverse nations in the future (de Almeida, 2023; Gong, 2024; Kshetri, 2023).

As discussed earlier, the Metaverse can also be seen more narrowly as a digital twin of a smart city. Finland's strategy addressed some aspects of a horizontal Metaverse ecosystem but not many details of the various layers on which the Metaverse is developed. Overall, as external governance of the Metaverse is lacking, enterprises and users tend to voluntarily adhere to self-governance principles. There is still much to be studied about the governance relationships between enterprises, the public sector, NGOs, and individuals in the strategies and practices of the Metaverse development.

References

Allam, Z., Sharifi, A., Bibri, S., Jones, D., & Krogstie, J. (2022). The Metaverse as a virtual form of smart cities: Opportunities and challenges for environmental, economic, and social sustainability in urban futures. *Smart Cities, 5*, 771–801. https://doi.org/10.3390/smartcities5030040

Aloqaily, M., Bouachir, O., Karray, F., Ridhawi, I., & Saddik, A. (2022). Integrating digital twin and advanced intelligent technologies to realize the Metaverse. *IEEE Consumer Electronics Magazine*. https://doi.org/10.1109/MCE.2022.3212570

Bibri, S. (2022). The social shaping of the Metaverse as an alternative to the imaginaries of data-driven smart cities: A study in science, technology, and society. *Smart Cities, 5*, 832–874. https://doi.org/10.3390/smartcities5030043

Datta, A. (2022). Metaverse for building next-gen infrastructure. *Geospatial World* 7 November, 2022.

de Almeida, G. (2023). Cities and territorial brand in the Metaverse: The Metaverse SEOUL case. *Sustainability, 15*(13), 10116. https://doi.org/10.3390/su151310116

Di Bartolo, T. (2023). How phygital takes the Metaverse into mass adoption, and what that means for businesses. *Forbes* 8 February, 2023.

Egliston, B., Carter, M., & Clark, K. (2024). Who will govern the metaverse? Examining governance initiatives for extended reality (XR) technologies. *New Media & Society*. https://doi.org/10.1177/14614448231226172

Fernandez, C., & Hui, P. (2022). Life, the Metaverse and everything: An overview of privacy, ethics, and governance in Metaverse. In *IEEE 42nd international conference on distributed computing systems workshops (ICDCSW), Bologna* (pp. 272–277). https://doi.org/10.1109/ICDCSW56584.2022.00058

Globenewswire. (2023). *Metaverse economy set to reach $400 billion by 2030 but struggles to live up to initial hype*. 5 December 2023. https://www.globenewswire.com/news-release/2023/12/05/2791147/28124/en/Metaverse-Economy-Set-to-Reach-400-Billion-by-2030-But-Struggles-to-Live-Up-to-Initial-Hype.html

Goldberg, M., & Schär, F. (2023). *Metaverse governance: An empirical analysis of voting within Decentralized Autonomous Organizations*. https://doi.org/10.2139/ssrn.4310845

Gong, X. (2024). Turning the virtual into reality: China's role in the Metaverse. *Asia Policy, 19*(1), 8–20. https://doi.org/10.1353/asp.2024.a918867

Hollensen, S., Kotler, P., & Opresnik, M. (2023). Metaverse—The new marketing universe. *Journal of Business Strategy, 44*(3), 119–125. https://doi.org/10.1108/JBS-01-2022-0014

Hyun, W. (2023). Study on standardization for interoperable Metaverse. In *25th international conference on advanced communication technology (ICACT)* (pp. 319–322). https://doi.org/10.23919/ICACT56868.2023.10079642

Jauhiainen, J., Krohn, C., & Junnila, J. (2023). Metaverse and sustainability: Systematic review of scientific publications until 2022 and beyond. *Sustainability, 15*, 346. https://doi.org/10.3390/su15010346

Jauhiainen, J. (2024). The Metaverse: Innovations and generative AI. *International Journal of Innovation Studies* 8 (3), 262–272.

Kalyvaki, M. (2023). Navigating the metaverse business and legal challenges: Intellectual property, privacy, and jurisdiction. *Journal of Metaverse* 3 (1), 87–92.

Kshetri, N. (2023). National Metaverse strategies. *Computer, 56*(2), 137–142. https://doi.org/10.1109/MC.2022.3227681

Khestri, N. (2025). *The Rise of Web3 and the Metaverse*. Edward Elgar, Cheltenham.

Kuru, K. (2023). MetaOmniCity: Toward immersive urban Metaverse cyberspaces using smart city digital twins. *IEEE Access*. https://doi.org/10.1109/ACCESS.2023.3272890

Lee, L., Braud, T., Zhou, P., Wang, L., Xuo, D., Lin, Z., Kumar, A., Bermejo, C., & Hui, P. (2023). All one needs to know about Metaverse: A complete survey on technological singularity, virtual ecosystem, and research agenda. *Journal of Latex Class Files, 14*(8) arXiv:2110.05352. https://doi.org/10.48550/arXiv.2110.05352

Lv, Z. (2023). Generative artificial intelligence in the metaverse era. *IEEE Cognitive Robotics, 3*, 208–217. https://doi.org/10.1016/j.cogr.2023.06.001

McStay, A. (2023). The metaverse: Surveillant physics, virtual realist governance, and the missing commons. *Philosophy & Technology, 36*, 13. https://doi.org/10.1007/s13347-023-00613-y

Metaverse Initiative. (2023). *The Metaverse Strategy for Finland—Virtual Potential to Real-World Impact*. https://www.digitalfinland.org

Mosco, V. (2023). Into the Metaverse: Technical challenges, social problems, utopian visions, and policy principles. *JANVOST, 30*(2), 161–173. https://doi.org/10.1080/13183222.2023.2200688

Mystakidis, S. (2022). Metaverse. *Encyclopaedia, 2*, 486–497. https://doi.org/10.3390/encyclopedia2010031

Nopanen, V. (2022). Metaverse city—smart city and place. *My Metaverse Day* 14 September 2022.

Radanliev, P., De Roure, D., Novitzky, P., & Sluganovic, I. (2023). Accessibility and inclusiveness of new information and communication technologies for disabled users and content creators in the Metaverse. *Disability and Rehabilitation: Assistive Technology*. https://doi.org/10.1080/17483107.2023.2241882

Radoff, J. (2021). The seven layers of the Metaverse. *Medium* 7 April 2021.

Roblox. (2024). *Roblox*. www.roblox.com

Singh, M., Fuenmayor, E., Hinchy, E., Qiao, Y., Murray, N., & Devine, D. (2021). Digital twin: Origin to future. *Applied System Innovation, 4*(2), 36. https://doi.org/10.3390/asi4020036

Statista. (2023a). *Volume of the VR headsets market worldwide from 2018 to 2028*. https://www.statista.com/forecasts/1331896/vr-headset-sales-volume-worldwide

Statista. (2023b). *Number of mobile augmented reality (AR) active user devices worldwide from 2019 to 2024*. https://www.statista.com/statistics/1098630/global-mobile-augmented-reality-ar-users/

Tang, F., Chen, X., Zhao, M., & Kato, N. (2023). The roadmap of communication and networking in 6G for the Metaverse. *IEEE Wireless Communications Letters*. https://doi.org/10.1109/MWC.019.2100721

The Sandbox. (2024). *What is the Metaverse? A guide to the future of the web*. https://www.sandbox.game/en/blog/what-is-the-metaverse-a-guide-to-the-future-of-the-web/3362

Yang, L. (2023). Recommendations for metaverse governance based on technical standards. *Humanities and Social Sciences Communications, 10*, 253. https://doi.org/10.1057/s41599-023-01750-7

Chapter 9
Convergence of Metaverse, AI, Blockchain, Web3, and CBDC

Sharjil Ahmed

Abstract Financial innovation and fintech bring new offerings which potentially support financial inclusion by offering fast payment systems, using basic banking app services instead of visiting branches, etc. However, have the key problems which still exist in the system, such as a significant segment of the society remaining unbanked or underbanked and lacking basic banking financial services such as payments, savings, and credit facilities been addressed? Financial services are underutilised due to expensive transactions resulting in low customer satisfaction. Lastly, connectivity, especially for cross-border transactions, remains weak. These issues have multifaceted impacts on both the economy and people's day-to-day existence. They impede economic growth, disrupt credit allocation, exacerbate income inequality, and incentivise financial activities to shift towards unregulated shadow intermediaries.

This chapter explores the converging forces advancing the Metaverse, Artificial Intelligence, Blockchain, and Web3 technologies in multiple dimensions. It explores their interconnections, obstacles, and opportunities to understand how these advances will change human interaction, creativity, and expression in the digital age.

Keywords Metaverse · Blockchain · Artificial Intelligence · CBDC · Web 3.0

9.1 Introduction

Advancements in computing power and new algorithms, along with access to extensive data, have led to the development of highly robust and realistic systems. These advancements prompt fundamental inquiries about how society will operate and function in the future.

S. Ahmed (✉)
Cykube, London, Middlesex, UK
e-mail: sharjil.ahmed@cykube.com

N. Islam, I. Salami (eds.), *Metaverse Innovation*, Applied Innovation and Technology Management, https://doi.org/10.1007/978-3-031-97080-1_9

A few years ago, envisioning computer programs capable of assimilating nearly all the accumulated knowledge of humanity would have seemed unimaginable. The idea that these programs could be employed to automate intricate tasks, handle routine activities, and even address previously unanswerable questions was beyond contemplation. It remains uncertain how much further these systems will progress in a short time.

First of all, there is a need to identify why these problems exist. One of the key reasons is the way the financial system has evolved over the years in silos and by tweaking existing systems and processes to achieve their results without considering its impact on the wider financial system. Legacy systems and infrastructure remain one of the biggest challenges in the adoption of emerging technologies for financial institutions because they were adopted when computing power was slow and inefficient. This created an issue of having separate proprietary databases and ledgers for money and assets which is still the case even today. These databases are interconnected using third-party messaging systems that require messages to traverse a convoluted network of bilateral links distinct from the path corresponding to money or other financial assets. Hence, almost all the transactions need to be reconciled before achieving a final settlement which, of course, delays the process significantly. That, in turn, increases the cost of the transaction and makes the current settlement process more expensive. When it comes to cross-border transactions, it increases the cost even more as systems must be linked through international messaging networks in addition to domestic ones which naturally brings compliance and legal challenges. In conclusion, it is not only making the current system inefficient and expensive, but sometimes the transactions never even happen due to the cost and complexity of the transaction.

Would emerging technologies be able to make the transactions efficient? This chapter is going to explore how Artificial Intelligence (AI), Blockchain, Web3, the Metaverse, and Central Bank Digital Currencies (CBDCs) will affect financial transactions and e-commerce.

In recent years, technological advancements have propelled humanity into a new era marked by the convergence of the Metaverse, Artificial Intelligence (AI), Blockchain, and Web3 technologies. This chapter serves as a gateway to understanding the profound impact and intricate interplay of these cutting-edge innovations.

The Metaverse, once confined to the pages of science fiction, has now become a tangible reality offering immersive digital exposure to physical limitations. The Metaverse is becoming mainstream worldwide as it offers large virtual landscapes and endless social, commercial, and entertainment potential. As this chapter progresses, one will see how the Metaverse can change how people live, work, and connect in the digital age.

AI and the Metaverse are key to technological progress, transforming industries, and enhancing human capacities. AI is everywhere, from intelligent virtual assistants to autonomous systems that can make complex decisions. It promises efficiency and ethical issues.

Blockchain technology is a decentralised ledger system that underpins digital trust, security, and transparency. Blockchain's immutable record-keeping and peer-to-peer transactions have enabled innovation beyond cryptocurrencies, including smart contracts, decentralised finance (DeFi), and non-fungible tokens (NFTs). This chapter will reveal Blockchain's disruptive potential in creating Metaverse infrastructure and promoting digital sovereignty.

Finally, Web3 depicts the Internet's transformation into a user-centric, decentralised environment with interoperability, data ownership, and decentralisation. Web3 promotes user empowerment and community governance as centralised platforms confront privacy breaches and content control. This chapter will study Web3 and Metaverse synergies to picture a future where people have more control over their digital identities and experiences.

9.1.1 Why Emerging Technologies Now?

Before these technologies are explored, one needs to take one step back and start thinking about why these technologies are becoming so important, how these technologies are becoming so addictive, and why it is becoming difficult for society to live without adopting these technologies.

The financial crisis in 2008 not only impacted the housing sector but also impacted the broader global economic activity. It triggered central banks and regulators to start identifying the root cause of the crisis, and they naturally started reforming the financial sector with depth supervision and regulatory reforms. The whole purpose was to avoid similar events in the future.

The financial crisis caused lots of mayhem, and, unfortunately, some of the large banks started filing for bankruptcy which started destabilising the global financial economic system. Additionally, some of the major investment and retail banks, insurance companies, asset managers, insurance companies, and savings and loan providers filed for solvency which caused a global recession. Once the leading financial institutions started filing for bankruptcy, it triggered consumers' distress and their trust in banks was hugely impacted. Traditionally, banks act as trustees for consumers' funds, but, after the crisis, consumers started losing their trust and confidence in banks due to a lack of transparency regarding their own funds.

To protect the financial system, global and local regulators brought new reforms, policies, and procedures along with new reporting mechanisms. Banks and financial institutions have been obliged to embrace new rules and regulations and to come out of their comfort zone. Some of the banks got huge penalties for non-compliance which triggered a new wave of discomfort to the financial institutions globally. All the banks and financial institutions started working on getting their house in order and complying with the new regulations. In some cases, some of the major banks have started the re-compliance of their clients with even stricter due diligence and even stopped onboarding new partners for some time.

While banks were busy sorting out their internal issues, consumers (who had already lost their trust in banks) were busy exploring Facebook, Twitter (now X), WhatsApp, Amazon, and other social media channels. This started to change their habits and service level expectations from the banks. For example, in addition to solely being a social media channel, Facebook started to offer money transfer services in the United States in 2014, and WeChat became one of the biggest remittance services in China. Post-financial crisis, regulatory changes opened up the market for new service providers as can be noticed by the evolution of Bitcoin followed by many other cryptocurrencies that have been introduced, all of which were built on blockchain technology. In parallel, it is important to remember that mobile banking started picking up since 2007, as consumers became more tech-savvy and started using mobile phones for their mobile top-ups and day-to-day banking services.

9.2 What Is Blockchain?

9.2.1 Definition

'Blockchain is a decentralised, distributed ledger technology (DLT) that records transactions across multiple computers in a way that makes them tamper-resistant and transparent. In essence, it is a chain of blocks where each block contains a list of transactions. These transactions are validated by network participants, often referred to as nodes or miners, through a process known as consensus. Once a transaction is validated and added to a block, it is cryptographically linked to the previous block thereby forming a chain. This linking ensures that any attempt to alter a transaction in a block would change all subsequent blocks making it highly impractical and virtually impossible to tamper with the data. One of the key aspects of blockchain is immutable means, once data recorded goes into the blockchain it cannot be altered, changed, or deleted from the system'. (Built In, n.d.; Stephen, 2021).

Blockchain technology has gained significant attention due to its potential applications beyond cryptocurrencies like Bitcoin. It is being explored for use cases such as supply chain management, voting systems, healthcare records management, and identity verification where secure, transparent, and immutable record-keeping is crucial.

9.2.2 Types of Blockchain

There are three types of blockchain:

- Public blockchain.
- Private blockchain.
- Consortium blockchain (also known as federated blockchain).

9.2.2.1 Public Blockchain

Public blockchains are open networks where anyone can join, participate, read, and write transactions without any permissions. The uniqueness of this model is that anyone from any part of the world can send the transaction through the network, and all the stakeholders can view the transaction on the distributed ledger once it is approved or considered valid across the network. Anyone can commit transactions on the public blockchain but the data within the blocks and the identity of the individual will remain anonymous. Some of the examples are Bitcoin and Ethereum.

9.2.2.2 Private Blockchain

Private blockchains are permissioned networks where access is restricted to certain users and they need to have a special set of rules and permissions. Once it is approved, only they can participate, read, and write transactions on the network. They are specifically used in enterprise settings for specific purposes such as financial transactions on a need-to-know basis.

9.2.2.3 Consortium Blockchain

A consortium blockchain is a semi-decentralised blockchain where a group of organisations controls the network. It is more decentralised than a private blockchain but less decentralised than a public one. Consortium blockchains are useful for industries or sectors where collaboration is necessary.

Use Case: Cross-Border Currency Remittance and Settlements Using Blockchain

Just imagine, one needs to transfer funds from the United Kingdom (UK) to the United Arab Emirates (UAE). What does one need to keep in mind per the current infrastructure and state of play? Infrastructure is relying on business, financial institutions, government, regulatory bodies, and brokers. Generally, banks handle the data and transactions per the regulatory requirements which takes longer for the transaction to be fully processed.

Suppose one need to send funds from a UK bank account to a friend in the UAE, into their local bank account. a transfer of £100 would be initiated through the UK bank to the beneficiary's bank account in the UAE. Despite being initially informed that the transaction would be completed within 3 days it took nearly a week. The bank manager explained that their bank lacks a correspondent relationship with the UAE bank, necessitating the transfer of funds to their correspondent bank in the UAE. Once the correspondent bank verifies the transaction, the amount is then transferred to the beneficiary bank's account with fees deducted. This entire process incurs additional time, costs, and introduces uncertainty for the sender. Another crucial aspect to consider is that the funds become immobilised within the bank without generating any economic value, thus creating liquidity problems for both the sender and the beneficiary. If this liquidity were readily accessible it could potentially have significant effects on both the economy and the individual's well-being.

Will the identical transaction occur through a consortium model based on blockchain? This approach unites all relevant parties including banks in the UK and UAE, regulators, and other necessary stakeholders for remittance transactions, ensuring their pre-qualification and inclusion in the platform. Should senders wish to transfer funds from the UK to the UAE, they can utilise this blockchain-based platform to directly transfer funds to the recipient's bank account in the UAE in real-time and at a predetermined cost (Fig. 9.1).

9.2.3 *Benefits of Using Blockchain*

Some of the benefits of blockchain can be understood from this real-life example.

1. *Transparency*: It brings transparency to the level of the cost and timing it takes for beneficiaries to receive funds. It also reduces fraud risks.
2. *Decentralisation*: Blockchain uses a decentralised network of computers (nodes) to store and govern data. This decentralisation enhances security and transparency by eliminating the need for a central authority.

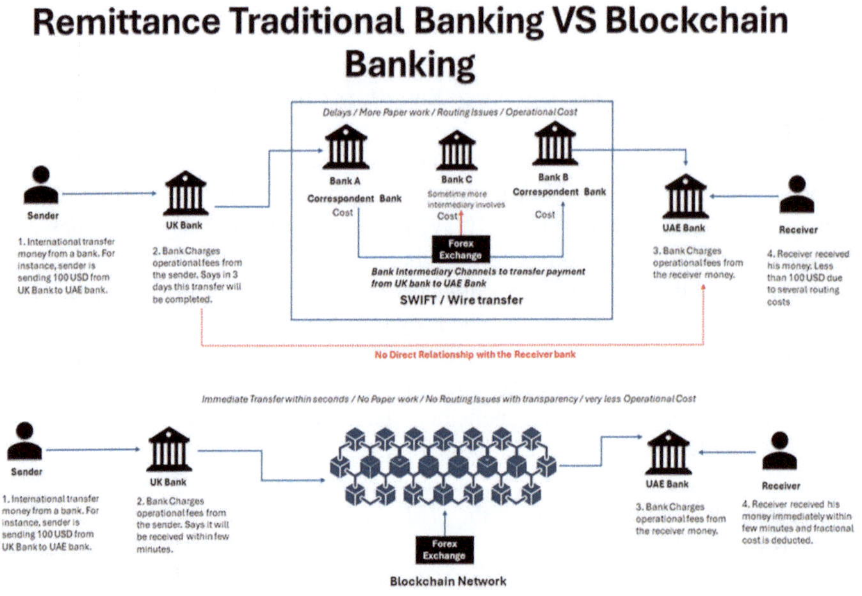

Fig. 9.1 Flow chart comparing traditional banking and blockchain banking for remittance. Author's creation (no external source)

Fig. 9.2 Flow of smart contract

3. *Immutability*: Blockchain transactions cannot be changed or removed.
4. *Traceability*: All of the transactions on the blockchain are immediately traceable.
5. *Cost reduction*: It brings the sender and beneficiary onto the same platform which reduces the intermediary cost which is significant in these transactions.
6. *Disintermediation*: Blockchain disintermediates by removing the requirements for intermediaries like banks, financial institutions, or centralised authorities in various processes. It also established a decentralised network which brings transparency to all the transactions on the network as it gets verified, recorded, and executed between the parties eliminating the need for any intermediary.
7. *Efficiency*: Transactions can be done in real time.
8. *Security*: All the transactions on the blockchain are cryptographically secured.
9. *Smart contracts*: Smart contracts are nothing but a programming code automatically executed once certain criteria are met. It is a form of one-sided promise that is filled once a computer program receives certain instructions. In the above example, if the smart contracts are set, then the entire process can be automated (Fig. 9.2).

The next section will look at cryptocurrency, how it is revolutionising the financial market, and what its wider impact will be going forward.

9.3 What Are Cryptocurrencies?

There is a common misconception that Bitcoin and blockchain are the same thing. This is not the case.

Bitcoin is one of the applications that have been built on blockchain.

9.3.1 Definition and Understanding of the Bitcoin

Bitcoin enables blockchain-based peer-to-peer cash transactions directly between parties without the involvement of a bank. The introduction of Bitcoin seems like it might change the financial world by completely revolutionising payment technology. It is supposed to provide low transaction costs, trustless ownership, transparency by providing real-time transactions, pseudonymity, and exchange without any government or financial institutions involved. Since its original launch, many more cryptocurrencies and crypto assets have flooded the market. At this juncture, it is important to have an understanding of the differences between cryptocurrency and crypto assets (Bonomi et al., 2023).

9.3.2 Cryptocurrency

Digital currencies that use cryptography for security and run on blockchain-based decentralised networks are called cryptocurrencies. Exchange, account, and value storage are common functions of these currencies. Examples of cryptocurrencies include Bitcoin, Ethereum, Litecoin, and many others. Cryptocurrencies are primarily designed for use as currencies or payment systems.

9.3.3 Crypto Assets

Crypto asset is a broader term that encompasses all digital or virtual assets that utilise cryptographic techniques for security and are based on blockchain or distributed ledger technology. Cryptocurrencies are a type of crypto asset, but the term crypto asset may include tokens, digital securities, utility tokens, non-fungible tokens (NFTs), and other digital assets that reflect ownership or rights. Crypto assets can serve numerous purposes beyond serving as currencies including showing ownership of a digital asset, granting access to a service or platform, or enabling participation in a decentralised network.

To summarise, cryptocurrencies are a subset of crypto assets that are mainly meant for use as digital currencies. However, crypto assets include a wider range of digital assets that utilise encryption and blockchain technology for purposes beyond cash.

The increasing popularity of cryptocurrencies has raised concerns among investors due to the absence of regulatory control. Simultaneously, malicious individuals took advantage of this scenario thus resulting in an increase in fraudulent actions. Regulators were aware of these developments as these developments posed risks to the stability of financial systems in several countries.

Real-World Use Cases

Peer-to-peer payments: These are a popular bitcoin use case. Individuals can send cryptocurrency directly without a bank or third party. Regional areas without typical financial services benefit from this.

Remittance: Cryptocurrencies allow migrant workers to transfer money home faster and cheaper than traditional remittance providers.

Online purchases: Many online merchants accept cryptocurrencies. Consumers can shop anonymously and securely without disclosing financial information.

Investment: Cryptocurrencies have also evolved into asset class. Investors can buy and hold cryptocurrencies in the hope that their value will increase over time, similar to stocks or commodities.

As cryptocurrencies are being explored, it is essential to develop an understanding of the new player in the digital currency arena: Central Bank Digital Currencies.

9.4 Central Bank Digital Currencies

9.4.1 Background and Introduction

The success and popularity of cryptocurrencies have spurred central banks to explore similar digital currency solutions, thereby leading to the development of CBDCs.

According to the Atlantic Council report, 130 countries are investigating central bank digital currency, representing 98% of global GDP. Approximately 64 countries are in advanced exploration including launch, pilot, or development. As highlighted, central banks worldwide are actively assessing whether to issue CBDCs or not. This consideration comes amidst the increasing adoption of digital banking and economies, thus reducing reliance on physical currency notes and coins.

During a recent trip to the Middle East, the author of this chapter experienced firsthand the diminishing need for physical bank cards or cash as most transactions were seamlessly embedded and did not require their use. This underscores the necessity for a currency that provides public access to money, a gap that CBDCs have the potential to fill.

9.4.2 Key Challenges in CBDC Policy Making

One of the primary challenges policymakers are facing in issuing CBDCs is its impact on macroeconomic policies, particularly monetary policy and the financial stability of the economy. To address this, central banks globally are conducting research and developing pilot programs to gain practical insights into CBDCs'implications (Auer et al., 2022).

It is evident that central banks recognise the growing need for CBDCs and are proactively preparing themselves for its potential mainstream adoption. While the precise timing for CBDC launches remains uncertain for many central bankers, recent trends suggest that CBDCs could become mainstream sooner rather than later.

In-depth analysis and impact of CBDC on monetary policy is not the focus of this chapter but the key is to understand the need and potential use of CBDC going forward.

CBDCs have maintained momentum in the second half of 2023. New analysis shows 130 countries, representing 98% of global GDP, are exploring CBDCs. A record of 64 countries are in advanced exploration. The European Central Bank

(ECB) launched a preparation phase for a digital Euro, and PetroChina performed the first international crude oil exchange utilising the digital Yuan.

CBDC represents the next phase in the evolution of money along with the benefits of digital technology with the stability and trust of fiat currency. CBDC is a digital representation of a country's first central bank-issued currency, making payment and settlement secure and efficient.

CBDCs build upon the foundation laid by fiat currency, leveraging advancements in blockchain technology and digital infrastructure to enhance the efficiency, transparency, and inclusivity of the monetary system. By digitising fiat currency, CBDCs offer new opportunities for financial innovation, inclusion, and economic development.

9.4.3 How Are Central Bank Digital Currencies Defined?

CBDC has been defined differently by various stakeholders.

BIS says 'CBDC is not a well-defined term'. Most expect it to be new central bank money. That is, a central bank debt denominated in an existing unit of account that acts as a store of value and medium of exchange.

Brooking wrote that CBDC is an electronic record or digital token of a country's official currency. State monetary authority or central bank issues and regulates it. The issuing government guarantees CBDCs.

Another definition is digital money denominated in the national unit of account that is a central bank liability. CBDCs match the pricing of their physical counterparts. This contrasts with Bitcoin and Ethereum whose values are not tied to fiat currencies.

From the above, the following points on CBDC can be extracted:

1. Alternative form of currency.
2. Authorised by central banks as the central authority.
3. Central bank obligation, expressed in an established unit of account.
4. CBDCs serve as both a medium of exchange and a store of value.
5. Its value reflects the fiat currency of the nation.

9.4.4 Types of CBDC

Two types of CBDCs exist.

1. *Retail CBDC*: It is a form of CBDC issued by the central bank for use by the general public including individuals and institutions for their everyday transactions.
2. *Wholesale CBDC*: It is used by banks and licensed financial institutions for interbank settlements, payments, and securities transactions.

It is still in the early stages of CBDCs, and there is a need to determine the demand and supply for CBDCs. Whether it will be based on blockchain or another centralised technology is yet to be determined. Some of the potential challenges that may be encountered include scalability and efficiency, especially in the case of retail CBDCs. While CBDCs can enhance efficiency, scalability and security remain uncertain when considering their widespread use.

It is worth understanding the evolution of money.

History and Evolution of Money

The history of money is a long and complex one spanning thousands of years and involving various forms of currency and exchange systems. Here is a brief overview of the evolution of money.

Barter system: In ancient times, people engaged in barter where goods and services were exchanged directly for other goods and services without using money. This method succeeded for simple transactions but had divisibility, transportability, and value consistency concerns.

Commodity money: Commodity money evolved with complex cultures. Grains, cattle, precious metals (gold, silver), and shells were commodity money. Early currencies were based on these goods which were universally accepted.

Metal coins: Metal coins became standard forms of money around 600 BCE. Governments and rulers began minting gold, silver, and other metallic coins with symbols or images to verify their legitimacy and value. Metal coins encouraged trade and were used across civilisations.

Paper money: The tang dynasty (seventh century CE) introduced paper money to China along with metal coins. Paper money was once backed by precious metals or other valuable commodities and was handier than metal coinage. Paper money spread across cultures and civilisations.

Fiat currency: Fiat currency is government-issued money without actual backing. Central banks managed monetary policy and regulated the money supply as governments abandoned the gold standard over generations.

Digital money: With modern technology, digital money is becoming common. Digital money, like credit cards, cryptocurrency, online banking, and electronic transactions, has changed financial transactions.

Cryptocurrencies: Blockchain-based cryptocurrencies like bitcoin, Ethereum, and others are decentralised in nature. Cryptocurrencies offer decentralisation, security, and anonymity without traditional banks. Money has evolved with human civilisation and its increasingly complex exchange and commerce systems. Money has always facilitated economic activity and shaped society, from barter systems to digital currencies.

It is important to explore Web3 and the Metaverse while studying blockchain, cryptocurrencies, and CBDCs. By comprehending these interrelated factors, one can more fully understand digital finance and the virtual environment.

9.5 Web3

Web3 improves, opens, and secures the Internet for everyone. Although it is still evolving, it is already changing how people use the Internet.

For understanding, let us look at past Web versions.

9.5.1 Web 1.0

Web 1.0 was a read-only Web designed to help users access data, news, and emails. Its main goal was to improve user data discovery.

9.5.2 Web 2.0

The Internet today is full of user-generated content. Since technology adoption began with the Internet, one now lives in the digital age. The Internet is mostly used for transactions and data sharing. Modern Internet use includes shopping, music/movie streaming, banking, and social media—all transaction-based.

The Internet is essential to society's daily lives and businesses. Centralisation has resulted from Internet dependence. Internet use has led to the rise of Apple, Facebook, Google, Microsoft, Amazon, Uber, Airbnb, and others. These firms dominate Internet interactions.

Corporate companies own Internet data and transactions thus diminishing individual control. Power concentration among a few technology companies has given them significant influence over governments and society. They influence government policy and people's daily lives, showing their grip over digital landscapes. After establishing the existing status of the Web, it is exciting to examine the need for Web 3.0.

9.5.3 Web 3.0

Web 3.0 centres on decentralisation to encourage consumers by giving them data control. This paradigm prohibits data use without consent. Users are free to sell their data without losing ownership or being tracked.

Decentralisation allows customers to directly engage with suppliers and buyers with blockchain technology. A notable use case of Web 3.0 is its facilitation of direct dealings between users and service providers, thereby eliminating the need for intermediaries. Users can provide genuine feedback based on their experiences which can be verified. This enables users to make informed decisions when purchasing products or services as all comments are authentic without any tampering. Bitcoin is one of the working examples of Web 3.0.

9.5.3.1 Characteristics of Web 3.0

Some of the key features of Web 3.0 can be gauged from the above discussion.

Data ownership: Users will have full control over their data, allowing them to determine how their information is used and monetised. It allows more power and control back into the hands of users. Instead of big companies owning and controlling a person's data, Web3 is all about giving people more ownership and privacy over their online lives.

Peer-to-peer networks: It enables direct peer-to-peer interaction between the users without any intermediaries which allows more efficient and secure transactions and communication.

Trust and transparency: It promotes trust and transparency between the parties with the help of blockchain which allows data and transactions to be verified in real time without the need of any third party.

Immutable data: It allows data integrity and permanence through immutable data storage on a distributed ledger thus preventing the alteration of records.

Decentralisation: This means that instead of having one central authority in charge of everything online, power is spread out across many different computers and networks. This makes it harder for anyone to control or manipulate the Internet. For example, while Web 2.0 also allows for feedback, it is common to encounter biased product reviews or manipulated feedback, either in favour or against, often orchestrated by large groups of individuals.

User empowerment: It empowers users by providing greater control over their online experiences, data, and interactions, ultimately promoting a more open democratic and inclusive Internet ecosystem.

Use Case: Web3, Real Estate Tokenisation: A Perfect Use Case of Web3
What is the problem statement here and how would Web3.0 be beneficial?

If a property owner is looking for funds but cannot access banks or other financiers what would be their options?

With the development of Web3, powered by blockchain technology, an individual has the opportunity to tokenise their property. This involves dividing the property into smaller fractions and allowing other investors to become partial owners represented by the token and earn rental yield based on their investment, all without the need for intermediaries like banks.

For example, if a person sells 10% of their property and 100 investors purchase fractional shares, they become partial owners alongside them. They can then receive rental income from the property proportionate to their ownership share. These investors have the flexibility to buy or sell their fractional shares on the platform as needed. Some of the benefits are as follows:

1. Investors can invest from any part of the world.
2. It allows 24/7 instant trading and liquidity.
3. Trading on secondary exchange without any fear.
4. Enables financial inclusion by opening investment opportunities to small investors which were previously limited to an elite group.
5. Property viewing can be done virtually 24/7.
6. Cost would be reduced as one of the essences of blockchain is disintermediation.
7. The entire process may be automated with smart contracts.

It introduces fresh investment prospects for small investors by democratising the financial landscape and promoting financial inclusion. There are numerous other potential use cases.

The next section will look at the Metaverse. These foundational technologies have set the stage for a new era in digital innovation where the lines between the physical and virtual worlds blur and exciting immersive experiences become more abundant.

9.6 The Metaverse

The Metaverse is an expansion of Web3 into a virtual realm, utilising blockchain technology to deliver a more immersive and user-driven experience.

The Metaverse is a combined virtual space formed through the fusion of digitally improved physical reality and persistent virtual reality. It represents a future iteration of the Internet, comprising virtual environments, augmented reality (AR), and virtual reality (VR). In this digital realm, users can engage with one another and digital entities in real time. Envisioned as a fully immersive and interactive digital universe, the Metaverse allows individuals to work, socialise, play, and undertake various activities, blurring the boundaries between the physical and virtual realms. In a simple word, the Metaverse facilitates the dematerialisation of elements from the physical world into the digital realm.

Metaverses use a variety of unique upcoming technologies and trends. These include VR, AR, flexible work arrangements, HMDs, an AR cloud, the IoT, 5G, AI, and spatial computing.

Use Cases of the Metaverse

Some of the used cases are virtual banks, virtual gaming, health surgery, 3D training, and social events. For example:

- JP Morgan becomes the first bank to establish its existence on the Metaverse.
- Virtual meetings and workspace platforms have the potential to revolutionise how employees and individuals interact, connect, and collaborate.
- Games can be created to train individuals in equipment operation and hazard management without direct exposure to those hazards.
- Customisation of cars would be increased as the Metaverse allows car dealers to use spatial computing and AR to customise the interior and exterior per individual requirements.
- Similarly, customisation of real estate would allow developers to develop an individual property per the client's interior and exterior requirements using both spatial computing and AR.
- XYZ realty streamlines offsite construction inspections using advanced AR technology for engineering. It brings precision and accuracy of up to 3–5 mm and ensures the whole structure aligns flawlessly.
- Metamajlis is an app that brings together the virtual and real world by connecting family and friends in different parts of the world. They can customise their meeting room and food menu per your requirements before inviting guests into their virtual room.
- It also allows even the smallest transaction payments to be made without the need for cards. Imagine purchasing items online without repeatedly entering credit card details; instead, simply use one's Metaverse wallet for payments. Meanwhile, blockchain technology ensures that consumers can execute transactions safely and without any alteration (Fig. 9.3).

Financial institutions

- Interactive virtual branches for personalised financial advice for their retail customers.
- Gamified financial education experiences to engage younger generations.

Organisations

- Host interactive product launches and conferences within the Metaverse.
- Provide virtual training simulations for employees in a safe and immersive environment.
- Showcase products and services in 3D environments to enhance customer experiences.

Malls and retail stores

- Create virtual storefronts with 3D product visualisation and customisation.
- Offer interactive shopping experiences where customers can try on clothes virtually or explore furniture arrangements within a 3D space.
- Host virtual events, sales, and promotions within the Metaverse to attract customers.
- Develop a social shopping experience where avatars can interact and browse together.

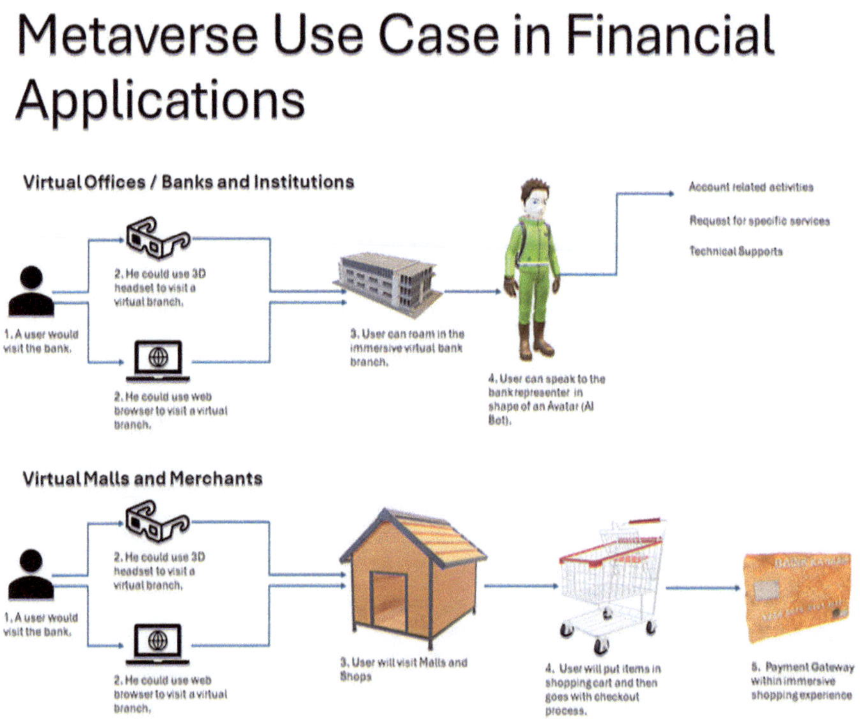

Fig. 9.3 Flow chart illustrating metaverse use cases in financial applications. Author's creation (no external source)

9.6.1 What Are the Hurdles in Metaverse Adoption Currently?

- *Headset Cost*
- Presently, users use VR headsets, smart glasses, phones, and PCs to access two- and three-dimensional virtual worlds. However, for widespread adoption, the cost of VR headsets needs to be adjusted to match market affordability as their current prices act as a barrier to mass adoption.
- *Bandwidth.*
- The second big issue is bandwidth in some parts of the world which is still not up to speed to ensure a smooth user experience.
- *Discomfort.*
- It has also been noted that during experiments of people using VR headsets; they have felt nausea, migraine, discomfort, and anxiety. These side effects should improve as the technology matures.

9.7 Societal, Ethical, and Economic Impact of These Technologies

The integration of AI, blockchain, Web3, and the Metaverse presents a transformative convergence with various impacts across society, ethics, and the economy.

9.7.1 Societal Impact

Societally, it offers the potential for increased digital inclusion through decentralised access to financial services, information, and opportunities. However, disparities in accessing technology due to digital literacy also need to be addressed. Concerns about digital identity and privacy in virtual environments cannot be neglected.

9.7.2 Ethical Impact

Ethically, this convergence challenges traditional notions of transparency, accountability, and fairness. One of the inherent characteristics of blockchain is immutability which enhances accountability. AI is dependent on modelling and could potentially bring algorithmic biases and discriminate against certain groups leading to ethical concerns about fairness and inclusivity.

The Metaverse, enabled by AI-driven interactions and blockchain-based economies, could foster the creation of virtual communities where individuals can interact, collaborate, socialise, and conduct business. It has the potential to reshape how people connect and engage with each other. One of the disadvantages would be it limits physical human interaction with each other.

9.7.3 *Economic Impact*

Economic impact of these technologies could be significant. Decentralised finance disrupts traditional financial business models and democratises financing by eliminating intermediaries. Equally, one needs to be careful of the unethical behaviour of bad actors which raises the regulatory challenges. The Metaverse will bring completely new opportunities in the virtual world such as virtual real estate, digital assets, virtual shopping, and immersive experiences which were not available previously.

9.8 Issues and Challenges Integrating Technologies

9.8.1 *Regulatory Challenges*

Understanding changing regulations is crucial. Data sovereignty, IP rights, digital asset legislation, and monetary policy must be considered as the regulatory landscape is still evolving for emerging technologies. Multinational convergence deployments face jurisdictional regulations. Innovation, compliance, and accountability require clear regulatory and legal frameworks.

9.8.2 *Financial Stability*

Emerging technologies create new financial stability and systemic vulnerabilities that central banks must address. Rapid tokenisation of assets inside the Metaverse, vulnerabilities in blockchain smart contracts, and algorithmic trading in AI-driven financial markets have the potential to increase market volatility and liquidity risks. Given the phenomenon of technological convergence, it is crucial for central banks to establish robust risk assessment and regulatory frameworks in order to safeguard financial stability.

9.8.3 *Cross-Border Issues*

The absence of borders in the Metaverse and blockchain networks weakens the control over currency and the ability to move capital across borders. Central Bank Digital Currencies (CBDCs) operating within interconnected networks may encounter situations where different regulations are exploited to gain an advantage, as well as complications related to legal jurisdictions, which can make cross-border monetary policy more complex. In order to overcome these challenges and incorporate CBDCs into the worldwide financial system, it is essential to encourage international collaboration and establish standardised protocols.

9.8.4 *Monetary Policy*

The convergence of evolving technologies presents innovative monetary policy possibilities to enhance financial inclusion and accessibility. Metaverse digital identification solutions, AI-powered credit scoring algorithms, and blockchain-based remittance systems have the potential to enable financially disadvantaged communities to get financial services. Central banks must prioritise inclusive monetary policy frameworks that use technology convergence to decrease financial access inequities and empower the economy.

9.8.5 *Design and Implementation*

CBDC design and implementation is difficult. CBDC integration with financial infrastructures and interoperability with other emerging technologies are technological challenges for central banks. To meet monetary policy goals, CBDC architecture, governance, and privacy must be carefully considered.

9.8.6 *Security*

Payment infrastructure security is critical. Web3 and the Metaverse provide additional security threats due to their decentralisation. Coding faults and vulnerabilities can affect smart contracts on the blockchain. Blockchain transactions are pseudonymous, therefore making it hard to track and retrieve stolen cash after a security compromise. Digital identities and assets can be stolen or manipulated in the Metaverse. Blockchain networks and AI algorithms can threaten privacy through data breaches. To reduce these effects, strong security and privacy-enhancing technologies are needed.

9.8.7 *Standardisation*

Technology interoperability and standardisation are crucial. The Metaverse, AI algorithms, Blockchain protocols, Web3 platforms, and CBDC infrastructures have different technical requirements and frameworks, thus making data transmission and integration difficult. This obstacle must be overcome to maximise convergence.

9.9 Conclusion

It is important to understand how these new technologies can be used and how they are connected. There is a lot of work happening and, as all of these emerging technologies are developing in parallel, they will only come to the mainstream once they all converge and build a strong ecosystem.

Blockchain is a technology enabler for both Web 3.0 and the Metaverse. Blockchain will provide data storage and an immutable analysis, distributed, and shared ledger. Web 3.0 will be the new Internet where individuals will be able to interact with each other in real time without reliance on any big tech giant and without any intermediaries. It also facilitates buying, selling, and owning assets in addition to creating new things. More importantly, people will have control of their own data which they can monetise for their own benefit.

CBDC will be used as a digital currency in addition to cryptocurrency and stablecoins.

Artificial Intelligence becomes the central intelligence, which constantly analyses information and makes decisions based on the actual continuous flow of data. The Metaverse will be society's new immersive world where people interact with each other, explore different places, and even play games with each other in real time.

Blockchain benefits are not technology-led; they are more about business processes. The combination of blockchain and other emerging technologies will significantly affect how business is currently conducted. A more transparent, smarter, more cost-effective, interoperable, and efficient solution will be seen going forward which ultimately facilitates financial inclusion and privacy.

While the full impact of these emerging technologies is still yet to be proven, it seems to be going in the right direction but it certainly requires continuous research and development along with active management.

References

Auer, R., et al. (2022). Central bank digital currencies: Motives, economic implications, and the research frontier. *Annual Review of Economics, 14*, 697–721.

Bonomi, A., Lehmann, M., & Lalani, S. (Eds.). (2023). *Blockchain and private international law.* Brill | Nijhoff. https://doi.org/10.1163/9789004514850

Built In. (n.d.). *Blockchain.* https://builtin.com/blockchain. Accessed 20.04.24.

Stephen, M. (2021). *Modern forms of money and the development of the concept of legal tender*. University of Johannesburg. https://ujcontent.uj.ac.za/esploro/outputs/graduate/Modern-forms-of-money-and-the/9912331107691#file-0

References

Part III
Legal and Regulatory Perspectives of the Metaverse

Chapter 10
Intellectual Property and NFT Use in the Metaverse: A Global Approach to Regulation

Miroslava Marinova

Abstract This chapter offers an introduction to the emerging use of non-fungible tokens (NFTs) in the Metaverse and their implications for intellectual property (IP) rights. It aims to provide new researchers with a clear foundation in this technically complex area, while also challenging traditional IP frameworks, such as copyright and trademark, by questioning the traditional notions of ownership and authorship in decentralised virtual realms. This chapter identifies issues with the disparity between territorial intellectual property rights and the borderless nature of blockchain technologies, the treatment of AI-generated works, and the uncertainty surrounding licensing and enforcement. From the UK and comparative perspectives, the article identifies gaps in regulation and calls for a more harmonised global initiative in law reform.

Keywords Non-fungible tokens (NFTs) · Intellectual property law · Copyright · Trademark · Metaverse · AI-generated content · Digital art

10.1 Introduction

NFTs, or non-fungible tokens, are digital assets that have gained significant attention in recent years as a new way to monetise digital assets such as digital art and collectibles in a virtual reality called the Metaverse (Mujević & Mujević, 2023). Digital art creation starts with an entry in the blockchain ledger called mining; the entry itself is called a token (Roose, 2021; Moringiello & Odinet, 2022). NFTs are unique as they have unique identification codes and metadata that distinguish them and cannot be replicated (Sharma, 2021). They can be traded online with

M. Marinova (✉)
Royal Docks School of Business and Law, University of East London, London, UK

GW Competition and Innovation Lab, George Washington University, Washington, DC, USA
e-mail: M.Marinova@uel.ac.uk

N. Islam, I. Salami (eds.), *Metaverse Innovation*, Applied Innovation and Technology Management, https://doi.org/10.1007/978-3-031-97080-1_10

cryptocurrency and encoded with the same software as many cryptos (Conti & Schmidt, 2022). Due to their ability to increase in value, they are attractive for investments and creating and developing digital art within the set market (Multazam, 2022; Zhang, 2022). Some commentators predict that tokenisation will change significantly everyday transactions (Moringielo & Odinet, 2022). These assets can be traded across platforms in virtual reality without country-specific domains or territorial connecting factors that usually exist on the Internet which makes the Metaverse a borderless virtual world (Saw & Chan, 2023). According to the Merriam-Webster dictionary, an NFT 'is a unique digital identifier that cannot be copied, substituted, or subdivided, that is recorded in a blockchain, and that is used to certify authenticity and ownership as discussed by the authors (as of a specific digital asset and specific rights relating to it)'.

A critical characteristic of NFTs is that they offer ownership or proof of authenticity of digital assets through blockchain-stored tokens including tweets, videos, and artworks (Ante, 2022). The question of ownership in the virtual space known as Metaverse is complex and still in the early stages of development (Yemenici, 2022). Indeed, the research has focused on Bitcoin and other cryptocurrencies rather than on NFTs (Bao & Roubaud, 2022). However, studies report legal implications surrounding using NFTs in the Metaverse including intellectual property rights, jurisdiction, privacy, and contractual obligations (Kasiyanto & Kilinc, 2022; Kalyvaki, 2023). However, one of the main challenges is the ownership of digital assets and issues related to copyright and trademark rights, mainly due to the borderless nature of the Metaverse which contrasts the conventional territorial nature of intellectual property rights (Saw & Chan, 2023). This means that copyright and trademark laws may be difficult to enforce in the Metaverse, given the decentralised and virtual nature of the platform (Saw & Chan, 2023).

As the NFTs prove ownership but do not grant copyright or trademark rights, buyers and sellers must understand their legal rights and obligations and avoid infringing the asset's creator or owner's intellectual property rights which can lead to legal disputes (Lehdonvirta, 2011). In some cases, creators of virtual assets in the Metaverse may own the rights to their creations and, when the NFT is sold, there is a transfer of ownership but this is different from the transfer of IP rights (Sheldon, 2007). If the owner of the NFT also holds the IP rights then an explicit IP licensing agreement must be implemented. However, before that, it is essential to determine whether the NFTs are eligible for IP protection in the first place. This becomes even more complex in scenarios where Artificial Intelligence (AI) systems generate NFTs. Based on that, it seems that the legal status of NFTs within existing IP frameworks remains a subject of debate as it presents novel challenges for IP law requiring innovative approaches to address issues of jurisdiction, enforcement, and governance (Fairfield, 2005).

Additional uncertainty with the ownership of NFTs arises from the terms of service of many virtual worlds, platforms, and games as they may specify that the creators of virtual assets do not own their rights but instead grant a license to the platform or game owner to use the assets (Cornelius, 2011). This means that the platform or game owner may have the right to sell, license, or otherwise profit from the assets while the creator of the assets may not have any right to do so. However, it is also possible that the user who creates an asset might not be the valid owner of it but rather the virtual platform or game itself as the terms of use might indicate that the platform or game retains ownership of all virtual assets (Belk et al., 2022). This suggests that the question of ownership and the right to exercise this ownership is not the only controversy surrounding the NFTs.

This background reveals many uncertainties related to the legal status of NFTs and IP law implications associated with the notion of ownership, transfer of ownership, IP protection of NFTs, and whether NFTs created by AI can benefit from IP protection.

This chapter aims to conduct a comprehensive review of the literature concerning NFTs to provide insights into the evolving landscape of NFTs with a particular focus on their implications on intellectual property rights. Given its inherent technical complexity, the analysis also aims to provide new researchers in the field with a foundational understanding of this subject matter. Secondly, this chapter will identify gaps in intellectual property law implications within NFTs and propose future research exploration. This comprehensive analysis will provide valuable insights for legal scholars, practitioners, and policymakers navigating the evolving landscape of intellectual property in the Metaverse. NFTs also have tax issues because their taxation is unclear as a novel asset class. They might have money-laundering compliance considerations as well. In addition, there are copyright issues with AI content creation, difficulties in obtaining licenses for large datasets that create potential threats to creators' interests, and the application of exceptions (Vesala, 2023). However, examining these implications lies beyond the scope of this chapter and will not be addressed herein.

10.2 Overview of NFTs and Their Increasing Use in the Metaverse

10.2.1 The Concept of Metaverse

The term 'Metaverse' was popularised by Neal Stephenson in his 1992 cyberpunk novel Snow Crash. In the book, Stephenson described his concept of Metaverse as a virtual reality space where users could interact with each other in digital environments using avatars. Stephenson's vision served as an inspiration that expanded on the idea of the Metaverse by imagining more considerable and more complex virtual environments (Hollensen et al., 2022). The Oxford English Dictionary definition of Metaverse is: 'A (hypothetical) virtual reality environment in which users interact with one another's avatars and their surroundings in an immersive way, sometimes posited as a potential extension of or replacement for the Internet, World Wide Web, social media, etc. Also, more generally, the notional environment in which users of networked computers interact = cyberspace'. The Oxford Learner's

Dictionary's definition of Metaverse is shorter. It reads as: '(Metaverse is) … a virtual reality space in which users can interact with an environment generated by computer and with other users'. Recently, a more advanced definition was given by Mezei and Arora (2023) as follows: 'Metaverse as a horizontal virtual collaborative space which merges the advancements of software and hardware technology (especially high-speed networks, blockchain/web3, Artificial Intelligence, and extended reality), platformisation, datafication, and social changes'.

Following these definitions, it can be concluded that Metaverse includes a space where people can engage in different activities like socialising, gaming, doing business, and even creating digital artwork. Essentially, it is like traditional online platforms but with a virtual setting that blurs the distinction between the natural world and the digital realm. In essence, the Metaverse represents virtual spaces for people to interact, communicate, and use as a commercial forum in the digital era going beyond physical space and time constraints.

The advancement of technology, the creation of digital markets, and changing consumer behaviour have resulted in a more significant role of commerce within the Metaverse. Users can participate in various economic activities within this virtual space, from purchasing to selling to trading virtual products and services. One of the main factors driving commerce growth in the Metaverse is the abundance of trading options available. Users can design and exchange digital assets such as virtual properties, clothing, accessories, and artwork within virtual worlds. These virtual products hold value in the virtual realm and can be purchased, sold, or bartered using virtual currencies or cryptocurrency, thus transforming the landscape of virtual social interactions (Zhang, 2022). Cryptocurrencies like Bitcoin, Ethereum, and others are commonly used for transactions within virtual worlds (Humayun & Belk, 2022). Blockchain technology, which supports most cryptocurrencies, provides a transparent way to record all transactions within the virtual environment. This ensures that ownership of digital assets is securely recorded, preventing fraud and counterfeiting. One of the digital assets that has gained popularity in recent years is non-fungible tokens (NFTs). Thus, the next section of this chapter will explain the NFTs, their main characteristics, and the difference between fungible and non-fungible tokens before exploring the implications of intellectual property law for NFTs.

10.2.2 What Are NFTs?

One of the digital assets that have gained significant attention in recent years is the so-called NFTs or non-fungible tokens. NFTs represent ownership or proof of authenticity of a particular item or piece of content due to their unique ability to define ownership and authenticity of art in virtual reality (Koster 2000). NFTs are extremely important for the Metaverse because they create a new virtual economy and make it possible to show who owns an asset, create scarcity, and make money from content (Moringiello & Odinet, 2022a, 2022b).

In the context of the Metaverse, NFTs can represent virtual real estate (Hutson et al., 2023), digital artwork (Martins et al., 2020), collectibles, and other unique digital assets (Lennard, 2023). For example, one of Beeple's famous NFT-based digital art pieces was sold for millions. NFTs can represent digital collectibles like trading cards, virtual pets, or in-game items (Dowling, 2022). 'CryptoKitties' is a well-known example of how users can buy, sell, and breed virtual cats as NFTs (Qin et al., 2021). Musicians and artists can release albums, songs, or concert tickets as NFTs, enabling fans to own a unique piece of music or access exclusive content. Moments from sports events, movies, or historical events can be tokenised as NFTs. Some blockchain projects offer NFT-based domain names, which allow users to register and trade unique blockchain domain addresses (Raman & Raj, 2021). Comic book publishers and trading card companies have explored NFTs to create digital versions of their products with collectible value (Craig, 2021). NFT-based virtual pet games and platforms allow users to own and trade virtual pets. Another example of an NFT is the CryptoPunks which is the largest single traded market in NFTs where unique digital characters were created, registered, and traded as individual assets on the Ethereum blockchain (as of March 2021, individual CryptoPunks were trading at between $20,000 and $100,000) (Dowling, 2022). These examples demonstrate the diverse applications of NFTs as tokenised digital assets, giving them ownership characteristics on blockchain platforms (Kuntze et al., 2013).

Recent empirical studies have discussed the potential of NFTs to change how many industries operate. They highlight that art, sports, digital collectibles, and gaming are the most impacted, but this could soon extend to the entire digital market (Bao & Roubaud, 2022). Certain studies suggest that the introduction of NFTs in the art industry has revolutionised the secondary market leading to a significant shift in the funding mechanisms for individual artists and collectives (van Haaften-Schick & Whitaker, 2022).

By utilising blockchain technology, NFTs offer a transparent and safe platform for purchasing, selling, and exchanging digital assets, opening up new markets for investors, collectors, and creators to sell artwork, music, images, or collectibles in the virtual economy (Maouchi et al., 2022). For instance, in the case of art, NFTs eliminate the need for galleries, agents, and specialists to verify authenticity, and digital currencies eliminate the need for federal reserves, banks, and credit card firms (Belk et al., 2022). Since a blockchain ensures the validity of the painting anyone can now purchase it online. Artwork listed on the Internet reaches a broader audience than just those who attend galleries and exhibitions (King et al., 2021). Additionally, an NFT may include a smart contract that guarantees the artist a predetermined share of any future sales of their creations.

10.2.3 The Difference Between Fungible and Non-Fungible Tokens

As explained, NFTs are digital assets representing ownership or proof of authenticity of a unique item or piece of content such as digital art, collectibles, and virtual real estate. NFTs hold unique characteristics and cannot be exchanged on a like-for-like basis (Borri et al., 2022). In contrast, fungible tokens like cryptocurrencies (e.g. Bitcoin or Ethereum), which are interchangeable, can be traded on a one-to-one basis. The critical differences between NFTs and fungible tokens can be summarised as follows (Iredale, 2021). The first one is related to the uniqueness of the NFTs. Each NFT is distinct and unique, representing a specific digital item or piece of content while fungible tokens are identical and interchangeable (Fairfield, 2022). The second one is related to ownership and authenticity. NFTs provide a mechanism for establishing ownership and proof of the authenticity of digital assets (Taherdoost, 2022). This is possible because the ownership history and transaction details are recorded on the blockchain technology of each NFT (Moringiello & Odinet, 2022a, 2022b). On the other hand, fungible tokens represent a quantity of a specific cryptocurrency and do not have unique ownership records. The next difference is related to NFTs' value and scarcity derived from their uniqueness. This is the characteristic that makes them valuable for collectors and investors. Fungible tokens, on the other hand, derive their value from market demand and supply dynamics, which are similar to traditional commodities or currencies (Cellini et al., 2023). Finally, NFTs are primarily utilised in digital art, gaming, entertainment, and collectibles, focusing on uniqueness and ownership rights (Fairfield, 2022). On the other hand, fungible tokens serve as a means of exchange, store of value, or unit of account in blockchain ecosystems and decentralised finance applications (Bamakan et al., 2022). Viewed in this light, NFTs present a fresh approach to representing and exchanging one-of-a-kind digital assets on blockchain platforms, opening up new opportunities for ownership, authenticity, and value generation in the digital space. However, the increasing popularity of NFTs brings some legal issues related to the transfer of ownership and this is the question of ownership of IP rights associated with NFTs. This is because when an NFT is sold it is not an automatic transfer of the IP rights to the buyer which suggests that an explicit IP licensing agreement is an integral part of the process. Prior to this, it is essential to determine whether the NFTs are eligible for IP protection in the first place. This becomes even more complex when AI systems have generated the NFTs.

10.3 NFTs and Intellectual Property Law Implications

10.3.1 Intellectual Property Law Basics

In a legal context, property refers to the collection of rights that allow an individual to possess, control, and exclude others from using and controlling a specific thing or item—this grants the owner a comprehensive monopoly over the use and exploitation of the property. Intellectual property law applies when the property in question is intangible and results from intellectual efforts which is the ownership of creation of the mind (Ochoa et al., 2020). However, with intellectual property (IP) (pure intangible), these distinctions might not be made until they are legally challenged.

Several types of intellectual property can be protected through various legal mechanisms, each with its legal principles and protections. These include patents, trademarks, copyrights, designs, and trade secrets (Siegel & Wright, 2007). Patents grant inventors exclusive rights to their inventions for a specified period while trademarks protect distinctive signs identifying goods or services in the marketplace (Dinwoodie & Janis, 2008). Copyrights safeguard literary, artistic, and musical works, while designs protect the visual appearance of products. Additionally, trade secrets provide confidential information with legal protection against unauthorised use or disclosure.

The overarching goal of intellectual property law is to strike a balance between providing creators with incentives to innovate and ensuring that society benefits from disseminating knowledge and information (Blackburn, 2003). While intellectual property rights confer monopoly power to creators, thereby restricting imitation and duplication, they also promote creativity and economic development by encouraging investment in research and development (Vaidhyanathan, 2017).

Despite the diversity of subject matter covered by intellectual property law, its fundamental principles centre on establishing property protection over intangible assets. This protection encourages individuals and businesses to invest time, resources, and effort into creating new ideas, inventions, and works of art, ultimately driving innovation and progress.

NFTs allow creators to tokenise digital assets and assert ownership over unique digital creations. As a result, the NFTs have reshaped traditional notions of ownership in the digital realm (Gürkaynak et al., 2018). While NFTs enable creators to monetise their digital works and establish provenance, they also raise questions about the application of IP law, particularly regarding digital asset ownership and licensing. In the context of the Metaverse, the role of IP law becomes even more critical. Moreover, the Metaverse blurs the boundaries between physical and digital realms, raising complex questions about ownership, licensing, and infringement (Flanagan & Maniatis, 2008).

IP laws can provide creators and owners of virtual assets and experiences exclusive rights to use, sell, and license their works. For example, patents can protect the functional aspects of virtual objects such as the technology used to create them (Mesevic, 2023; Siegel & Wright, 2007). Trademarks' role is safeguarding virtual enterprises' identity and visual representations such as logos and branding. In contrast, copyrights protect the original and creative aspects within virtual environments including 3D models, avatars, and various digital creations (Noveck, 2005).

10.3.2 NFTs and Copyright Issues

A particular area of IP law, namely copyright law, is one of the most debatable areas of intellectual property law in the context of NFTs and the Metaverse (He, 2022; Lapatoura, 2022). This is because the essence of copyright law is to grant creators exclusive rights over their original works of authorship, including literary, artistic, musical, and dramatic works, which cover the existence of copyrights. However, copyright also deals with the enforcement of copyright in case of infringement, the remedies against the infringement, and the exercise of the copyrights related to the transfer and licensing of copyright. When people create digital assets, they tokenise their digital artworks as NFTs (Hugenholtz et al., 2006). From this perspective, copyright ownership over creative content is asserted, raising questions about the enforceability of copyright claims and the authenticity of digital assets in blockchain technology (Stokes, 2019). The emergence of NFTs in the Metaverse introduces novel considerations for copyright law, particularly regarding ownership and the transfer and licensing of digital assets (Bartle, 2004).

10.3.2.1 Fundamentals of Copyright Law

Copyright law in the United Kingdom is primarily governed by the Copyright, Designs and Patents Act 1988 (CDPA). This act grants legal protection to creators of original literary, artistic, musical, and dramatic works. Section 1 of the CDPA states that copyright is a property right which subsists in an exhaustive, or closed, list of eight different categories of work in the following categories: (a) original literary, dramatic, musical or artistic works; (b) sound recordings, films or broadcasts; and (c) the typographical arrangement of published editions. This is in contrast with the approaches followed by some EU countries where the list of protected subject matter is the open versus the exhaustive (closed) list in the UK legislation. Under UK legislation, computer-generated work ranging from literature, computer games, and even medical diagnostic programs can also be protected by copyright (Section CDPA 9(3) 1988). In addition, Section 178 CDPA defines computer-generated as 'the work [that] is generated by computer in circumstances such that there is no human author of the work' (Section 178 CPDA 1988). The United Kingdom's position regarding the authorship of computed generated output was clearly expressed in the Whitford Committee Report on Copyright and Designs Law as follows: 'The author of the output can be none other than the person, or persons, who devised the instructions and originated the data used to control and condition a computer to produce a particular result' (Dworkin, 1977).

The main aim of copyright law is to give creators exclusive rights over their works, allowing them to control how they are used and distributed. One important aspect of copyright law is the concept of originality which is also considered the core of copyright (Gervais, 2004). However, there is no definition of originality in the UK legislation; the case law developed the standard of originality (Rahmatian,

2013). In the United Kingdom, copyright protection automatically applies to an original work once created if it meets specific criteria. These criteria can be summarised as follows. Firstly, it is essential to establish whether the work fits into one of the defined categories of protected material as outlined in copyright legislation (Section 1 of the CDPA 1988). These categories cover various creative forms such as literary, dramatic, musical, and artistic creations. As outlined above, the originality of the work is a crucial consideration, especially for literary, surprising, and musical pieces as well as artistic endeavours. In addition, literary, dramatic, and musical creations and artworks need to be recorded in a fixed format (Section 3(2) of the CDPA 1988). This ensures that the work is preserved in a physical format like writing, recording, or painting, allowing it to be reproduced and shared. This requirement does not cover artistic work (Section 3(2) of the CDPA 1988). Furthermore, the jurisdiction is a significant factor in determining copyright protection, especially regarding the work's connection with the United Kingdom. Suppose the work is associated with the United Kingdom (first published or first broadcast) regardless of the author's nationality or residence. In that case, it is covered by UK copyright law (Sections 154–156 of the CDPA 1988). In the end, if a piece of work meets specific requirements—fitting into a known category, showing creativity, being documented tangibly, and having ties to the United Kingdom—copyright protection is granted automatically. This means that, unlike with patents or trademarks, creators do not need to formally register their works to receive copyright protection (Sections 154–156 of the CDPA 1988). Instead, protection is granted when the work is created, allowing authors to manage how their creations are used and distributed.

According to the CDPA, copyright protection usually lasts for the author's life plus 70 years (Section 12 CDPA 1988). However, specific works, such as sound recordings and broadcasts, have different durations. Creators have the exclusive rights to reproduce, distribute, perform, and adapt their works during the copyright protection period with some exceptions relating to research and private study, criticism or review, or news reporting.

Another critical issue in copyright law is the question of ownership. According to Section 9(1) CDPA 1988, the author of a work is the person who creates it. The Act specifically refers to work that is computer generated in the case of a literary, dramatic, musical, or artistic work, specifying that the author shall be taken to be the person by whom the arrangements necessary for the creation of the work are undertaken (Section 9(3) CDPA 1988). Moreover, the Act refers to a work of unknown authorship if the author's identity is unknown and a person cannot ascertain his identity by reasonable inquiry (Section 9(4) and 9(5) CDPA 1988).

In the United Kingdom, copyright law is influenced not just by domestic laws such as the Copyright, Designs and Patents Act (CDPA) but also by international agreements like the Berne Convention (1886) and the Agreement on Trade-Related Aspects of Intellectual Property Rights (TRIPS). The Berne Convention, now ratified by 179 countries, lays down fundamental rules for copyright protection among its member nations. It guarantees that creators of literary and artistic works receive automatic protection in other member countries without requiring procedures like registration. Moreover, the convention upholds the principle of national treatment ensuring that foreign creators are given the same rights as local creators in each member country. Signed by more than 160 countries including the United Kingdom, TRIPS mandates that member states must offer copyright protection for at least 50 years after the author's death and implement measures to combat copyright infringement. By following the guidelines of these global treaties, the United Kingdom guarantees that its copyright regulations are in line with international norms and ensures that creators and copyright holders receive reliable protection at home and abroad. These accords are vital in unifying copyright laws internationally, making it easier to enforce and recognise copyright globally and fostering the exchange of cultural and creative works globally.

In the European Union, copyright law is governed by directives that aim to align intellectual property rights among member states. The primary directive, the Copyright Directive, sets out basic protection standards for authors and creators across the European Union (Directive (EU) 2019/790 of the European Parliament and of the Council of 17 April 2019 on copyright and related rights in the Digital Single Market and amending Directives 96/9/EC and 2001/29/EC). This directive grants creators exclusive rights to their works including reproduction, distribution, and communication to the public. It also includes provisions for exceptions and limitations to copyright, striking a balance between the needs of creators and those of users and the general public (Art. 4 of the Directive).

Copyright laws differ significantly among countries globally influenced by legal traditions, cultural norms, and economic levels. Despite these variations, international treaties and agreements exist to establish copyright protection worldwide. The Berne Convention for the Protection of Literary and Artistic Works is one of the most crucial agreements setting minimum standards for copyright protection among its member nations. This convention guarantees that works created in one member country are protected under copyright law in all other member countries without the requirement for formal registration or notice. Additionally, the Agreement on Trade-Related Aspects of Intellectual Property (TRIPS) significantly shapes global copyright laws. International agreements ensure copyright is recognised and enforced worldwide, supporting cultural exchange and innovation.

From the above, it can be concluded that copyright law provides a framework for protecting creative works and ensuring that creators have control over their intellectual property. However, the emergence of NFTs in the Metaverse introduces new challenges in defining ownership because of the decentralised nature of virtual worlds (Fairfield, 2005).

10.3.2.2 NFTs Implications on Copyright Law

Originality

One of the fundamentals of copyright is related to the concept of originality. This is because the copyright protects the original expression of ideas. To qualify for copyright protection a piece of work must meet specific standards of originality which can differ based on the location. Typically, originality involves the creation of a piece through independent intellectual effort and possessing a certain level of creativity. Regarding copyright laws, being original does not necessarily mean being wholly new or one-of-a-kind. It mainly pertains to the author's independent creation and the use of skill, labour, and judgment in the creation process. Essentially, the work should not be a direct copy of something else but instead originate from the author's endeavours. Several judgments set up the criteria for originality (Ladbroke v William Hill p 291: Interlego v Tyco [1989] AC 217 at 262.; Infopaq International A/S v Danske Dagblades Forening (C-5/08) EU:C:2009:465 [2012]; Bus. L.R. 102 [2009]; 7 WLUK 441 (ECJ (4th Chamber); C-145/10 Eva-Maria Painer v Standard VerlagsGmbH and Others 9Third Chamber) [2011] ECR I-12533; Foorball et al. and others v Yahoo! UK Ltd and others, Case C-604/10; Temple Island Collection v New English Teas [2012] EWCA 890 Civ).

In the Metaverse, especially where NFTs are concerned, the idea of being original is crucial in determining if digital assets can be copyrighted. NFTs often represent digital pieces like art, virtual property, or collectibles which copyright laws could potentially protect. For instance, imagine a digital artist who designs a one-of-a-kind art piece specifically to be sold as an NFT. In this situation, the uniqueness of the artwork would be evaluated based on whether it showcases the creator's creative vision and demonstrates a significant amount of originality. If the artwork meets the criteria for being original it might be eligible for copyright protection.

Determining the originality of digital assets in the Metaverse can be tricky, especially when dealing with derivative works or collaborations. Using AI-generated content adds another layer of complexity to this issue, blurring the lines between algorithms and human creativity. Copyright law values originality but applying it in the Metaverse calls for a deeper understanding of digital creations and NFTs' challenges.

Ownership

One of the fundamentals of copyright law is the concept of ownership which determines who holds the rights to utilise and profit from work. In general, this means that the artists who create virtual assets such as NFTs should have ownership rights over their creations. However, this does not automatically grant them copyright or intellectual property rights to the content within their creations.

In virtual reality, owning NFTs does not always mean owning the rights to intellectual property. For instance, having an NFT of digital art does not automatically provide copyright or reproduction rights to the art. NFTs are traded on blockchain platforms and ownership is recorded on a decentralised ledger. Verifying the ownership chain can be difficult especially when transactions involve multiple platforms or have gaps in the record.

The ownership issue becomes complex in the Metaverse due to the lack of clear legal guidelines in decentralised virtual environments. This uncertainty can lead to disputes over ownership mainly when creators assert rights over assets they believe belong to them.

Who Can Exercise the Ownership?

Another issue is related to the exercise of ownership by the creators of NFTs (Lee, 2023; Murray, 2022a). There are various rules and regulations regarding the ownership and transfer of digital assets set by different Metaverse platforms and NFT marketplaces. These rules can vary significantly and might involve giving the platform some control over user-generated content or limiting asset usage and transfer (Dharma, 2023). This raises concerns about how much control creators genuinely have over their virtual assets (Blazer, 2006). A recent study evaluating the terms of service from major NFT minting platforms revealed that they are contradictory and do not grant meaningful ownership rights to NFT holders over the associated digital content because the platforms can remove access to the NFT and underlying content at their discretion (Moringielo & Odinet, 2022). The results of this study suggest that even though the individual/the creator created the content, the platform or game owner could potentially benefit from or use these assets without the creator's consent. Additionally, the terms of service may state that the platform or game has ownership rights over all virtual assets created within its platform regardless of the creator's involvement (Moringielo & Odinet, 2022). From the above, it seems that the question related to the exercise of ownership by the creators of NFTs is an unsettled area that needs more research.

10.3.2.3 NFTs and AI-Generated Content

Copyright issues surrounding AI-generated NFTs are complex and pose new questions regarding authorship, ownership, and legal responsibilities.

Distinction Between AI Creation and Human Tokenisation

Although the exact definition of AI remains a topic of debate, it is commonly viewed as intelligence created by computer software and hardware (Helm et al., 2020). AI can produce original work through the demonstration of intelligence (Simon, 1995). Modern AI programs have expanded beyond just creating written content; they can now compose music, paint pictures, and more, often with minimal human input. The question arises of whether these creations should be protected by copyright and, if so, who would hold the rights to them which invites a comparison between NFTs and AI-generated items. As explained above, NFTs are cryptographic tokens that symbolise ownership or authentication of a one-of-a-kind digital item like digital artwork, collectibles, or virtual properties. They are commonly utilised to trade digital assets within digital art. In contrast, AI-generated work encompasses creative content generated by Artificial Intelligence algorithms often without direct human involvement. This category includes AI-generated art, music, literature, and other creative expressions. While NFTs can facilitate the buying and selling of AI-generated work, it is crucial to note that they are distinct entities. NFTs primarily signify ownership or origin of digital assets, including those produced by AI but they do not create content themselves.

NFTs can blend the boundaries between ownership and creation when they represent AI-created content. The key distinction lies in the creative process. With AI-generated content, the content is created by Artificial Intelligence algorithms without direct human involvement. This content can encompass art, music, writing, or any other form of creative expression. Conversely, NFTs are tokens that symbolise the ownership or origin of digital assets. When AI-generated content is tokenised as an NFT, it indicates that someone, whether a human creator or an AI developer, has chosen to tokenise that content to establish ownership.

While AI can generate the content it is ultimately up to humans to decide whether to tokenise it as an NFT (Battah et al., 2022). This distinction is crucial because it determines who holds the rights and responsibilities related to the NFT such as copyright ownership and the ability to sell or transfer it. It also raises questions about authorship and the worth of AI-generated works in art and digital collectibles. When AI-created content is tokenised as an NFT it can blur the lines between human-created and AI-generated works regarding ownership and value (Sharp, 2022). The main idea is that NFTs can demonstrate ownership and authenticity regardless of whether humans, AI, or a combination of the two produced the content (Grba, 2023). However, there is a difference in the creative process. Regarding AI-generated content, Artificial Intelligence algorithms primarily drive the creative process without direct human input (Anantrasirichai & Bull, 2022). NFTs serve as a way to establish ownership and provenance. Still, the decision to tokenise a piece of content (whether AI-generated or not) and attribute value to it is ultimately a human decision. While AI may create the content, human intervention is necessary to designate it as an NFT, determine its value, and address copyright and intellectual property considerations (Hutson & Lang, 2023). The main point is that NFTs can represent ownership of AI-generated content but the creative process and value assessment still require human involvement.

Copyright Authorship in AI-Generated Content

Traditional copyright laws protect original works created by human authors. However, the emergence of AI algorithms that independently generate digital content challenges the concept of authorship. AI algorithms can autonomously produce creative works, raising questions about who should be considered the author for copyright purposes—the human programmer, the AI system itself, the user, the AI company, or all creative participants.

The academic literature is divided into two camps on this point. The first camp advocates that AI-produced work is original and deserves copyright protection (Aziz, 2023). Their position is based on the understanding that the test for originality, as one of the fundamentals of copyright, is a universal test for protecting literary and artistic work. From this perspective, if AI creates the work and represents an original expression of an idea it should be copyright-protected (Aziz, 2023).

Some scholars believe AI systems should be considered authors if they show independence and innovation in creating art content (Mazzone & Elgammal, 2019). An exciting topic of discussion on this point is the project known as The Next Rembrandt in which a group of researchers utilised machine learning algorithms to study and imitate the artwork of the famous Dutch painter Rembrandt van Rijn to produce a new painting in his signature style. Another example is the situation surrounding the AI-produced art piece Edmond de Belamy, crafted by the collective Obvious in Paris using a Generative Adversarial Network (GAN). In 2018, this artwork was purchased at auction for a hefty sum and sparked debates around ownership and copyright. Although these artworks did not directly lead to a legal battle they did generate discussions regarding the concept of authorship and the impact of AI on artistic creation. The advocates of the first camp consider that if the test for originality is applied to the AI-generated portrait of Edmond de Belamy it will meet the criteria for originality developed by the courts (Aziz, 2023). This is because AI created Emond de Belamy by using the following ten human characteristics: (1) innovative, (2) autonomous, (3) unpredictable, (4) independent, (5) rational-intelligent, (6) evolving and capable of learning, (7) efficient, (8) accurate, (9) goal-oriented, and (10) capable of processing free choice (Heath, 2020).

According to other scholars, the significance of human participation in the creative process is a requirement because 'creativity is a fundamental feature of human intelligence and a challenge for AI', which indicates that human input may still be required for copyright protection (Boden, 1998). Recent legal advancements, like the European Parliament's resolution on IPRs for AI technology development, illustrate the continuing discussions surrounding authorship and copyright in AI-generated works.

In a notable legal case known as Naruto v. Slater, the Ninth Circuit Court of Appeals dealt with a unique situation involving the copyright of nonhuman authorship for a selfie taken by a crested macaque named Naruto (Naruto v. Slater, United States Courts of Appeals (9th Circuit 2018), No. 16-15469). The controversy started when wildlife photographer David Slater left his camera unattended during a photo session in Indonesia. The macaque, Naruto, managed to snap a few pictures of himself, one of which became famous as the monkey selfie. The People for Ethical Treatment of Animals (PETA) took legal action against Slater for allegedly infringing on Naruto's copyright by displaying, advertising, and selling the book. This case garnered global attention and sparked discussions about copyright laws and authorship. Ultimately, the Ninth Circuit decided against Naruto, ruling that animals are not eligible for copyright protection under US law. The court discussed how the US Supreme Court and Ninth Circuit have consistently referred to persons or human beings in copyright authorship analysis without expanding the definition to include animals. They also mentioned that the Copyright Office will not register works created by 'nature, animals, or plants', like a 'photograph taken by a monkey'. Therefore, Naruto could not be considered the author of the photographs because he was not human and the copyrights belonged to Slater. Although the Naruto v. Slater case did not involve AI-generated content, it highlighted judicial views on authorship in works not created by humans. The decision highlights the fundamental principles of copyright law which are built on human creativity. It also raises significant concerns about how copyright regulations must adapt to keep up with technological advancements and innovative forms of expression (Palace, 2019).

However, in some jurisdictions such as the United Kingdom, New Zealand, and Ireland, the legislation gives special ownership provisions for computer-generated work (as for example Section 9(3) from the CDPA 1988 in the United Kingdom). Others, such as Germany (§ 31 of the German Copyright Act (UrhG)) and France (The droit d'auteur or French authors' rights law, Art. 112-1), have specific requirements in the national legislation that only allow a natural person to be considered the author of the copyright-protected work. Some other jurisdictions do not have specific provisions that will enable or forbid copyright protection for nonhuman creators. In addition, there is no clear position on international agreements. For example, the Berne Convention does not clearly define who can be considered an author or explicitly prohibits copyright protection for non-human creations. The convention also acknowledges that different countries interpret the concept of authorship differently with some recognising individuals as authors and others not. In many countries with copyright laws, organisations are often seen as the owners of copyrighted works. In addition, the TRIPs agreement sets global copyright protection standards but it does not explicitly approve or disallow non-human or artificial entities from being recognised as authors. This debate in the scholarship will continue. Meanwhile, courts may have to determine whether AI-generated works are eligible for copyright protection and, if so, who should be recognised as the author.

Copyright Ownership in AI-Generated Content

When owning an NFT representing an AI-generated digital product a few factors must be considered. These factors include the NFT's structure and the content's associated rights. If a creator uses AI to make a digital product the ownership of the copyright for that product could be influenced by the jurisdiction and the terms of use for the AI software used. Essentially, tokenising an AI-generated digital product as an NFT creates a digital certificate on a blockchain that proves ownership and origin. This process involves the creator asserting ownership of the token representing the digital product.

When one owns an NFT, one might not automatically own the copyright or intellectual property rights to the AI-generated content it represents. This largely depends on how the NFT is set up and the specific terms that were established when creating it. When minting the NFT, certain usage rights, licenses, or restrictions can be specified. The legal framework and regulations in different jurisdictions can also play a role in determining ownership and associated rights related to NFTs and AI-generated content. Copyright laws differ from country to country and can impact who has the copyright and which rights are passed on with the NFT.

NFTs frequently include making or sharing derivative works derived from copyrighted content. When AI programs produce or alter copyrighted material creators must handle the legal limits of fair use, transformative use, and making derivative works. Unauthorised copying or changing of copyrighted material could lead to copyright infringement allegations. AI-generated NFTs may include elements from copyrighted works like images, music, or text. Creators must get the proper licenses or permissions to use these materials legally. Not doing so could result in claims of infringement and legal trouble.

10.3.3 NFTs and Trademark Law

Similar to the exchange of tangible things in the real economy, the rise of the Metaverse has created new channels for trading digital goods. As a result, brands are now more actively involved in the Metaverse economy's growth and development than in the real world (Balis, 2022). This has prompted brands to become increasingly involved in developing and expanding the Metaverse economy, similar to their engagement in the physical world (Balis, 2022). With the increased use of NFTs to represent ownership of digital assets trademark issues have become particularly relevant. Trademark use in the context of the Metaverse presents one such problem (Murray, 2022a, 2022b). Due to their establishment and business operations, companies operating in virtual worlds may have their trademarks replicated or cited in various digital contexts. Suppose consumers become confused about the source or endorsement of digital goods or services due to the unauthorised use of a brand within the Metaverse. In that case, it may give rise to concerns regarding trademark infringement. Some studies examine the interaction of NFTs and trademark law concerning subject matter that exists only in cyberspace (Murray, 2022a, 2022b).

The trade of NFTs that use branded content or logos raises concerns about brand protection and intellectual property rights. If individuals or entities tokenise digital assets that incorporate trademarked elements without proper authorisation it could result in trademark infringement, diminishing the brand's distinctiveness or reputation.

Moreover, the decentralised nature of blockchain technology, which underpins NFT transactions, complicates traditional methods of enforcing trademark rights. Identifying and holding accountable individuals or entities responsible for trademark infringements within the Metaverse presents unique challenges requiring innovative approaches to enforcement by both brand owners and legal authorities. Addressing these issues effectively will require a nuanced understanding of trademark law and the development of tailored strategies to safeguard brand identity and intellectual property rights in the evolving landscape of the Metaverse.

10.3.3.1 Fundamentals of Trademark Law

Intellectual property law encompasses various intangible concepts and rights including trademarks, copyrights, patents, rights of publicity, moral rights, economic rights, and trade secrets. It was also outlined that the primary interaction between NFTs and intellectual property law is in copyright law. However, it is crucial to recognise that NFTs also might have trademark law implications (Murray, 2023). Thus, it is essential to differentiate between legal frameworks that govern trademarks instead of copyrights, patents, and other forms of intellectual property. This understanding is necessary for navigating the legal landscape surrounding NFTs effectively.

Trademark law exists to safeguard unique symbols that can be visually represented and differentiate the products or services of one company from another. A trademark can include words (such as personal names), designs, letters, numbers, colours, sounds, or the shape of goods or their packaging. Note that the phrase 'may consist of' suggests possibilities, meaning it does not cover every potential trademark option. According to Section 1(1), TMA 1994 trademark means any capable sign:

(a) of being represented in the register in a manner that enables the registrar and other competent authorities and the public to determine the clear and precise subject matter of the protection afforded to the proprietor, and
(b) of distinguishing goods or services of one undertaking from those of other undertakings.

In trademark law, a fundamental principle is the requirement of distinctiveness. Trademarks need to differentiate one company's products or services from those of others. This is important so that consumers are not deceived or unsure about where products or services come from. This requirement is specified in Section 1(1): 'a trademark means any sign capable of ... distinguishing goods or services of one undertaking from those of other undertakings'. It suggests that any sign that is capable of distinguishing goods or services can be used as a trademark.

Another critical aspect of trademark law is the likelihood of confusion. This rule prevents trademarks from being registered or used if they may be mistaken for existing trademarks owned by others. Such safeguards are in place to ensure consumers are not misled and to maintain the integrity of established trademarks (Firth et al., 2005). Moreover, trademark law acknowledges the significance of safeguarding well-known trademarks regardless of potential confusion. These trademarks receive enhanced protection and are shielded from actions that may diminish their value or unfairly benefit others irrespective of their registration status or usage in a specific jurisdiction (Michaels & Norris, 2002).

In the United Kingdom, trademark rights are typically obtained by registering with the Intellectual Property Office (IPO). To receive legal protection trademarks ought to be registered. Whether a trademark is capable of registration depends on three requirements. First, the subject matter of the application must satisfy the definition of trademark in Section 1 of the Trademarks Act 1994 (TMA). Second, whether there are any objections to the application under the absolute grounds for refusal in Section 3, and last, whether any prior rights could prevent registration under the relative grounds for refusal in Section 5.

For this analysis, it is essential to note that trademark protection is territorial. This means that trademark protection is limited to specific geographic territories or jurisdictions, indicating that legal rights and enforcement are only valid within those boundaries. This implies a trademark registered in one country does not automatically receive protection in other countries. Instead, trademark owners must apply for registration or recognition in each jurisdiction where they want their trademark protected. The territorial nature of trademark protection has important implications. Businesses or individuals looking to protect their trademarks in multiple countries must go through the registration process for international trademark registration.

The process of getting an international trademark registration involves a few steps. Firstly, the trademark registration should be completed in the home country of the trademark owner, for example, the United Kingdom. Once the registration is completed, the trademark owner can ask the trademark application to be treated as an International Registration through the World Intellectual Property Organisation (WIPO) before applying to the WIPO. The specific countries where trademark protection should also be specified from a list of 98 countries that are part of the Madrid Protocol, an international treaty about trademarks. Once an application is submitted, WIPO reviews the trademark to ensure it complies with relevant regulations and standards. If the application meets the necessary criteria, WIPO publishes the trademark in the WIPO Gazette of International Marks. This publication notifies designated countries and allows them to review the trademark and raise any objections within 18 months. If no objections are raised within the specified timeframe the trademark is granted protection in those jurisdictions. However, each designated country has the right to refuse or object to the registration.

After registration, the trademark owner has the exclusive right to use it for specific goods or services. This prevents others from using a similar mark that could confuse consumers. Trademark law in the United Kingdom is regulated by laws such as the Trademarks Act 1994 and the Trademarks Rules 2008. These laws set out the trademark registration process and the legal options available to trademark owners in infringement cases.

10.3.3.2 NFTs Implications on Trademark Law

Trademark law plays a significant role in the Metaverse when NFTs are involved as conflicts may arise over branding and identity in virtual spaces (Christodoulou et al., 2022). This connection between trademark law and NFT issues in the Metaverse is essential to consider as improper use of registered trademarks can lead to trademark infringement lawsuits. For example, in the Nike v StockX lawsuit, Nike brought legal action against StockX, a popular online sneaker reseller, for launching an NFTs series based on Nike's shoes thereby allowing customers to buy NFTs tied to a physical product. Nike claimed the NFTs infringed on its trademarks and would be confusing to customers (see Nike, Inc. v. StockX LLC, United States District Court, S.D. New York, Apr 7, 2023, 22-CV-00983 (VEC)(SN) (S.D.N.Y. Apr. 7, 2023)). Another case is Hermès Int'l v. Rothschild. In this case, Rothschild created NFTs linked to images of handbags marketed with a similar name, MetaBirkin, and a similar appearance to the famous Hermès handbags (No. 22-cv-00384 (S.D.N.Y.)).

In the Metaverse, companies and people can make virtual products, services, and experiences that need branding to set them apart. NFTs showing these virtual assets might have logos, symbols, or other unique marks acting as trademarks (Noveck, 2005). However, issues could arise if these trademarks are too similar or copy existing trademarks in the real world or the Metaverse (Bell, 1997). Branding can be easily seen through the use of trademarks. For example, a virtual clothing store in the Metaverse might create a unique logo to show its brand. This logo could be used on virtual clothes or shown in the store. Similarly, a virtual gaming platform may use a recognisable symbol as its trademark to stand out from competitors in the gaming industry (Ung, 2008). However, problems may occur if these virtual trademarks resemble existing trademarks in the real world or within the Metaverse (Bell, 1997). For instance, if a virtual clothing brand's logo closely mimics that of a famous fashion house in reality it could confuse customers and weaken the uniqueness of the original trademark (Dougherty & Lastowka, 2007).

With the rise of NFTs in the Metaverse, there is a risk that virtual items with similar trademarks could confuse users. For instance, if different creators make NFTs for virtual clothing lines resembling logos or brand names, users might have difficulty distinguishing them which could result in trademark conflicts. Imagine if several artists design NFTs of virtual clothing collections, each featuring similar logos or brand names (Divea & Surjit, 2022). This could confuse users exploring the Metaverse, as they may struggle to differentiate between these virtual items and become unsure of their origins. Such confusion presents problems for creators aiming to create unique brand identities in the Metaverse and for users trying to make educated choices about the virtual products they interact with or buy. Moreover, the increase in NFTs with comparable trademarks raises worries about possible trademark disputes among creators resulting in disagreements regarding ownership, infringement, and brand erosion. Academic works in intellectual property law and digital spaces frequently delve into these matters analysing how the likelihood of confusion standards are applied to virtual trademarks and NFTs.

Protecting well-known trademarks is a significant issue in the digital world as popular brands try to find their way into online spaces. These trademarks, known for their wide recognition and unique qualities, face difficulties preserving their value and avoiding unauthorised use in virtual worlds (Look, 1999). In the digital realm of NFTs and virtual environments, unauthorised use of well-known trademarks is possible, potentially harming the brand's identity and taking advantage of its established reputation for financial gain. For example, individuals or companies might include famous logos in NFTs or virtual worlds without permission, using the brand's popularity to attract users and make money (Dougherty & Lastowka, 2007). This unauthorised use damages the well-known brand's reputation and poses legal issues under trademark law. Brand owners could argue that using their logos without permission in virtual reality violates or dilutes their trademark, potentially causing customer confusion or weakening the brand's unique identity (Noveck, 2005).

The criteria for the likelihood of confusion, a crucial aspect of trademark law, is critical in the Metaverse as NFTs become more common (Santiago, 2022). In this online world, where virtual items and activities are often branded, users are more likely to be confused by similar trademarks from different sources (McKenna, 2009). For example, well-known trademarks such as Second Life (owned by Linden Research, Inc.) and Minecraft (owned by Microsoft) stand out (Chin, 2006; Shapiro, 2008). Second Life is a trademark linked to a virtual world platform that Linden Research, Inc. created. This platform allows users to design custom avatars, build virtual settings, and interact socially with others. Used extensively for education, business, and entertainment, Second Life offers a diverse virtual space supporting various activities and connections. In the same way, Minecraft is a trademark owned by Microsoft and is a well-known Sandbox video game created by Mojang Studios, later acquired by Microsoft (Bergquist, 2011; Lastowka, 2012). In Minecraft players can freely build and explore virtual worlds made up of block-like elements with gameplay choices ranging from solo to collaborative modes (Lane & Yi, 2017). This digital gaming world has gained significant popularity across different audiences for its creativity and engaging atmosphere. Another example is Roblox, created by the Roblox Corporation. It is a famous trademark among children and teenagers that allows users to create and share their games and play games created by other users. World of Warcraft is a game developed by Blizzard Entertainment, Inc., set in the Warcraft universe. This multiplayer online role-playing game (MMORPG) lets players create characters and engage with others in a virtual environment. Known for its popularity, World of Warcraft has a devoted player community and obvious rules about using the trademark. Moreover, the guidelines specify the exact trademarks and the jurisdiction where they are registered.

In summary, the principles of trademark law including distinctiveness, likelihood of confusion, and protection of well-known trademarks play a significant role in utilising NFTs in the Metaverse. As virtual worlds progress and NFT adoption grows, it is crucial for individuals involved to remember trademark issues to prevent possible disputes and preserve brand integrity in the online space. The examples of famous virtual trademarks show that companies have well-established guidelines that help users understand how and when to use the trademark. However, the lawsuits discussed above are ongoing so how the courts will apply the existing legal framework is about to be seen (Murray, 2022a, 2022b).

10.3.4 Evaluation of Approaches to Address Ownership and Copyright Issues in AI-Created NFTs

Some NFTs might be AI-created. However, whether they can benefit from copyright protection is a question that needs more clarification as there are differing views on the level of human involvement required to classify copyright protection. The different positions of the various jurisdictions reflect this controversy. For example, the United Kingdom's current position is that AI-generated content can be copyright-protected. Some other countries adopted a similar approach to the United Kingdom, such as Hong Kong, Ireland, New Zealand, Ireland, and India (see for example

Section 5 of the New Zealand Copyright Act (1994); Section 11(3) of the Hong Kong Copyright Ordinance (CO) (Cap. 528); Section 21(f) of Irish Copyright and Related Rights Act (2000)). As explained above, the CDPA contains a provision for protecting computer-generated work (Section 9(3) CDPA 1988). It also provides clarification that the author should be considered to be 'the person by whom the arrangements necessary for the creation of the work are undertaken' (Section 9(3) CDPA 1988). It is also accepted that the copyright owner should be the AI system's owner or user.

In 2021, the UK government's call for views on Artificial Intelligence and intellectual property response revealed that many respondents emphasised prioritising human creators. Some suggested that works generated solely by AI should not receive copyright protection while others proposed granting AI-generated works a distinct copyright category with reduced duration and coverage. This is because some believe that creations produced by AI should be acknowledged as genuine artistic expressions and, therefore, qualify for copyright protection. They argue that even though AI is not controlled directly by humans during the creative process, humans design and teach these systems providing them with the algorithms, data sets, and parameters that influence their output. Consequently, the end products can be viewed as indirectly influenced by human creativity and intellectual labour thus warranting legal protection.

Furthermore, several respondents acknowledged the significance of copyrighted material in training AI systems. Some argued that copyright constraints hindered this process, potentially leading to bias. Conversely, others contended that licensing arrangements adequately addressed these concerns. Additionally, comments addressed the challenges of discerning which works were utilised for training AI and determining authorship by human or machine.

In response, the UK government considered that there is no need to adjust the current copyright protection legislation as the current protection of computer-generated work is sufficient and can be adapted for work that AI creates. This was based on the observation that AI is still in its early stages so a proper evaluation of the options is impossible. With regard to the licensing or exceptions to copyright for text and data mining (TDM), it was considered reasonable to introduce a new copyright and database exception that allows TDM for any purpose which would allow the rights holders to have safeguards to protect their content including a requirement for lawful access. The introduction of this exception suggests that the rights holders will no longer be able to charge for UK licenses for TDM of material already available legally. In response to this proposal for legislative changes, on 17 January 2023, the House of Lords Communications and Digital Committee (the Committee) issued a report on the creative industries in which it recommended that the IPO 'pause its proposed changes to the text and data mining regime immediately'. The broader TDM copyright and database rights exception was withdrawn based on that.

However, the lack of differentiation between computer-generated and AI-generated work might create issues regarding authorship claims and the relevance of the originality requirement and, specifically, how this requirement can be applied in the case of AI-generated work (Section 1 (1) CDPA 1988). This is because, for the authorship of computer-generated work, the legislation envisages 'the person by whom the arrangements necessary for the creation of the work are undertaken'. In contrast, AI-generated work includes machine learning software which replaces the user participation in creating the work and nevertheless puts the originality requirement for copyright protection into question (Burylo, 2022). The requirement for originality is linked to a natural person which means that individual effort and creative work must be present in computer-generated work (Maggiore, 2018). When it comes to works generated by AI the unique aspect is that the AI system itself conducts the creative process and is programmed to create content autonomously. This poses a significant challenge to the applicability of existing copyright legislation primarily designed to protect the creative output of human authors.

A recent judgment from China recognised copyright in an AI-assisted image, suggesting that human involvement can be in prompting and controlling the AI which, according to the court, was sufficient for originality (the Beijing Internet Court's recent judgment in Li v Liu; Re Spring Breeze Has Brought Tenderness (case number (2023) Jing 0491 Min Chu No. 11279). This indicates that the level of human involvement is a factor that determines the case's outcome and it will remain a barrier to copywriting in AI-generated content. However, the Chinese court's judgment gives hope to some who believe that if a human being uses the prompts to guide the AI it means there is human involvement. However, some might consider that the prompts are only suggestions as the same prompt might generate different outcomes and there is no creativity. This is because the AI system creates input from text and data mining, which contains other creative work, in response to the prompt, which nevertheless puts into question the originality of AI-generated content. However, using copyrighted works as input for text and data mining without authorisation creates a different controversy as it has been addressed differently across jurisdictions. For example, the European Union introduced a mandatory exception in 2019 that allows TDM of copyrighted works for commercial or non-commercial purposes as long as the user has lawful access to the works. This position indicates the European Union's broader approach towards TDM exceptions to facilitate AI innovation. Other jurisdictions like the United Kingdom have decided not to broaden the exception to keep the balance between supporting AI and protecting creative industries. The current exemption for using copyrighted work for non-commercial research is in Section 29 (1) CDPA 1988. In 2022, the government proposed expanding it to permit TDM for any purpose, including commercial use, to support AI development and innovation. This proposal faced opposition from creative industries who argued it could harm their interests (see n186). Consequently, in early 2023, the UK withdrew plans for a broader TDM exception retaining only the existing limited exception for non-commercial research. The fact that the different jurisdictions treat the use of copyrighted works as input for text and data mining without authorisation differently indicated another issue with the copyright of AI-generated content.

However, while UK copyright legislation protects AI-generated work, most countries do not (Gaffar & Albarashdi, 2024). This has been the position of the US

Copyright Office, which refuses to register works without a human author, as recently confirmed by the federal district court which affirmed that the US Copyright Office's position that AI-generated artwork is not eligible for copyright protection under US law stands (Thaler v. Perlmutter, No. CV 22-1564 (BAH), 2023 WL 5333236 (D.D.C. Aug. 18, 2023)). The Australian Court expressed the same position in a recent case, Acohs Pty Ltd v Ucorp Pty Ltd, where the court held that a work generated with computer-intervention could not be protected by copyright because a human did not produce it (Federal Court of Australia, Acohs Pty Ltd v Ucorp Pty Ltd [2012] FCAFC 16). Similarly, in other jurisdictions like Spain (Law No. 22/1987 of November 11, 1987, on Intellectual Property, Spain) and Germany, it is accepted that only works created by humans can be protected by copyright (Copyright law, Part 1—Copyright (§§ 1–69g), Section 3—The author (§§ 7–10), § 7 The author is the creator of the work). On the other hand, some people believe that not granting copyright for works created by AI could hinder investment in AI creative technologies. The court's position in these jurisdictions might be based on the understanding that even though AI can mimic human creativity, it lacks the consciousness, intentionality, and emotional depth in human works.

This raises concerns about granting copyright protection to AI-generated works, as it may go against the fundamental principles of copyright law that seek to promote and reward human creativity. Although EU copyright law does not expressly state that copyright requires a human creator, the focus on human authorship can be found in the case law of the Court of Justice of the European Union (CJEU) (Hugenholtz et al., 2006). According to the CJEU, works need to be created by humans to be recognised as the author's intellectual property (Case C-5/08, Infopaq International v Danske Dagblades Forening Infopaq International [2009] ECR I-6569). This means that non-human entities cannot be considered authors. This is because originality involves work independently created by the author and not copied, requiring creativity or intellectual effort. The CJEU confirmed this in the case of Levola Hengelo BV v Smilde Foods BV, where the CJEU clarified the two cumulative conditions must be satisfied, i.e. originality (it must be the result of the author's intellectual creation) and that the work must be the expression of the author's intellectual creation (Case C-310/17, Levola Hengelo BV v Smilde Foods BV [2018] ECLI:EU:C:2018:899, paragraph 34–37). The CJEU provided more clarification in the case of Eva-Maria Painer v Standard Verlags GmbH and Others where it held that:

> …a portrait photograph can … be protected by copyright if, as the national court will determine in each case, such photograph is an intellectual creation of the author reflecting his personality and expressing his free and creative choices in producing that photograph (C-145/10 Eva-Maria Painer v Standard Verlags GmbH and Others (Third Chamber) [2011] ECR I-12533).

The position of the CJEU establishes that for copyright protection the work must be the original result of the creator's intellectual creation. The originality requirement is clearly defined in the EU legislation as evident from the text of the Directives. Art.3 (1) from the Database Directive states: 'By this Directive, databases which, because of the selection or arrangement of their contents, constitute the author's intellectual creation shall be protected as such by copyright' (C-145/10 Eva-Maria Painer v Standard Verlags GmbH and Others (Third Chamber) [2011] ECR I-12533).

Art 1(3) from the Computer Programs Directive states: 'a computer program shall be protected if it is original in the sense that it is the author's intellectual creation…' Art 6 from the Term Directive states: 'photographs which are original in the sense that they are the author's intellectual creation shall be protected … Member States may provide for the protection of other photographs'. This indicates that only works created by human creativity are eligible for copyright protection under EU copyright law even if technical aids such as cameras are employed in the creative process. This raises the question as to what extent the AI systems can be considered a technical aid if they not only help with creativity but also make the decisions involved in the creative process. The answer to this question will depend on the degree of human involvement in the creative process. A closer examination of the case law of the CJEU in cases involving the application of the originality criteria to AI-generated work reveals that a work can be considered an intellectual creation if it reflects the personality of the author which means that the author is free to exercise creative choices in the development of the work (Gaffar & Albarashdi, 2024). The CJEU confirmed this in the case of Football Dataco Ltd v Yahoo! UK Ltd (Case 604/10 ECLI:EU:C:2012:115). Another example that provides additional insight into the notion of originality concerning works generated by AI is the Cofemel v G-Star case (C-683/17 Cofemel v G-Star Raw ECLI: EU:C: 2019:721, para 31). In this case, the CJEU considered that a creation cannot be deemed original if AI developed it without creative expression. Thus, creative expression is crucial for a creation to be eligible for copyright protection. From the above, it can be concluded that works resulting from human creativity and creative choices made with AI assistance or other technical tools might be eligible for copyright protection under EU law. However, works generated entirely by AI systems without human creative input would likely not qualify for such protection. In general, the courts have ruled out the idea of giving copyright protection to works solely based on technical rules or considerations without any creative input from a human.

10.4 Conclusion

This chapter aimed to comprehensively review the literature concerning NFTs to provide insights into their evolving landscape, focusing on their implications for intellectual property rights. This chapter explored the characteristics of NFTs and their increasing use in the Metaverse. It was found that the potential of NFTs to change some industries is significant, which indicates that the legal status of NFTs and their use in the Metaverse has to be clarified.

The analysis in this chapter identified a few gaps related to uncertainties regarding the legal status of NFTs, the notion of ownership, the transfer of ownership, and the availability of IP protection for NFTs. The analysis started with an overview of the implications of NFTs on intellectual property law, particularly in the context of copyright, especially regarding digital asset ownership and licensing. The analysis revealed that copyright law is a mainly debated area in the context of NFTs and the Metaverse as it grants creators exclusive rights over their original works. Still, the enforceability of copyright claims and the authenticity of digital assets in blockchain technology introduce novel considerations. The traditional application of copyright law was discussed with the view of positioning the NFTs within this framework. It was highlighted that critical aspects of copyright law include the concept of originality which is fundamental in establishing minimum standards for copyright protection which are recognised globally.

While copyright law provides a framework for protecting creative works the emergence of NFTs in the Metaverse introduces new challenges in defining ownership due to the decentralised nature of virtual worlds. This is mainly because determining the originality of digital assets like NFTs in the Metaverse can be challenging, especially with AI-generated content. Ownership of NFTs does not automatically grant the owner the copyright or intellectual property rights to the content within the NFT. The issue of ownership in the Metaverse is complex due to the lack of clear legal guidelines.

Another identified issue concerns the extent of creators' control over their virtual assets as NFT platforms may retain the ability to remove access to the NFT and underlying content.

The issue of copyright authorship in AI-generated content is debated. Some argue that AI-produced work should be eligible for copyright protection if it meets the originality criteria. In contrast, others believe human participation in the creative process is still required. While NFTs can represent ownership of AI-generated content, the creative process and value assessment still require human involvement. Legal cases like Naruto v. Slater have highlighted the challenges of applying traditional copyright laws to non-human authorship and the need for copyright regulations to adapt to technological advancements.

The possibility of copyright protection for NFTs is a complex issue, especially when an AI system creates the NFT. While the legal landscape is evolving, the prevailing view is that some level of human authorship and creative involvement is necessary for AI-generated works to qualify for copyright protection. The critical determinant is whether the work exhibits originality through human creative choices despite technical constraints or AI assistance. However, one question that still lacks a clear answer is whether using prompts to guide AI can be considered sufficient to determine human involvement. However, some may view these prompts as mere suggestions since the same prompt can generate different outcomes due to the lack of creativity in the AI system's input generated from text and data mining. This raises questions about the originality of AI-generated content, particularly when it incorporates copyrighted works. Different jurisdictions have taken varying approaches to this issue. Some, like the European Union, have introduced a mandatory exception that permits the text and data mining of copyrighted works for commercial or non-commercial purposes. Others, like the United Kingdom, have chosen not to broaden the exception to maintain a balance between supporting AI and protecting creative industries. Different jurisdictions treat copyrighted works as input for text and data mining differently, highlighting another issue in the copyright of AI-generated content.

The analysis also outlined the significant implications of NFTs on trademark law in the Metaverse. Trademark law is crucial in the Metaverse as conflicts may arise over branding and identity in virtual spaces. Improper use of registered trademarks can lead to trademark infringement lawsuits as seen in cases like Nike v StockX and Hermès Int'l v. Rothschild. In the Metaverse, companies and individuals can create virtual products, services, and experiences that require branding and trademarks to differentiate them. However, issues can arise if these virtual trademarks are too similar or copy existing trademarks in the real world or the Metaverse.

The rise of NFTs in the Metaverse increases the risk of virtual items with similar trademarks confusing users, as they may struggle to differentiate between these virtual items and their origins. Protecting well-known trademarks is a significant challenge in the digital world as unauthorised use of famous logos in NFTs or virtual worlds can damage brand identity and reputation. The criteria for the likelihood of confusion, an essential aspect of trademark law, is critical in the Metaverse as users are more likely to be confused by similar trademarks from different sources. Examples of well-known virtual trademarks include Second Life, Minecraft, Roblox, and World of Warcraft. The analysis revealed that the principles of trademark law including distinctiveness, likelihood of confusion, and protection of well-known trademarks play a crucial role in using NFTs in the Metaverse, and ongoing legal cases will shape how the existing legal framework is applied in this new digital landscape.

Next, the analysis discussed the challenges of enforcing intellectual property rights in the Metaverse, particularly the global reach of NFTs and the decentralised nature of the Metaverse. It highlighted the difficulties in determining jurisdiction and applicable laws for infringement and the complexities of applying current IP regulations to NFTs. The analysis also addressed the challenges of identifying and locating copyright or trademark law infringers in the Metaverse and the complications of cross-border disputes related to copyright and trademark infringements.

The application of current IP regulations to NFTs presents several legal complexities. One major challenge is determining jurisdiction and choice of law based on the identity of infringing users in the Metaverse. The borderless and decentralised nature of the Metaverse makes it challenging to identify and locate copyright or trademark law infringers due to anonymity and the use of pseudonym identities in virtual reality. Additionally, enforcing copyright and trademark rights in the Metaverse is complicated because traditional IPRs are territorial, conflicting with the borderless nature of the Metaverse. This creates challenges in asserting rights, handling infringement problems, and determining which country's law applies to the infringement of IPRs in the Metaverse. Furthermore, copyright ownership of digital content transformed into NFTs can be complex especially when dealing with AI-generated or joint works. These complexities require thorough examination and possible revisions to keep up with technological advancements and evolving legal matters.

Based on the contributions including clarification of copyright implications, examination of ownership issues, and trademark law implications, the analysis in this chapter also provided future research direction related to the evolution of legal frameworks and how to be adapted to better address the unique challenges posed by NFTs and the Metaverse and assessment of the implications of AI-generated content in the context of copyright law, mainly focusing on the criteria for originality and human involvement.

References

Anantrasirichai, N., & Bull, D. (2022). Artificial intelligence in the creative industries: a review. *Artificial Intelligence Review, 55*(1), 589–656.

Ante, L. (2022). The non-fungible token (NFT) market and its relationship with Bitcoin and Ethereum. *FinTech, 1*(3), 216–224.

Aziz, A. (2023). Artificial intelligence produced original work: A new approach to copyright protection and ownership. *European Journal of Artificial Intelligence and Machine Learning, 2*(2), 9–16.

Balis, J. (2022). How brands can enter the Metaverse. *Harvard Business Review*. Retrieved from https://hbr.org/2022/01/how-brands-can-enter-the-metaverse

Bamakan, S. M. H., Nezhadsistani, N., Bodaghi, O., & Qu, Q. (2022). Patents and intellectual property assets as non-fungible tokens; key technologies and challenges. *Scientific Reports, 12*(1), 2178.

Bao, H., & Roubaud, D. (2022). Non-fungible token: A systematic review and research agenda. *Journal of Risk and Financial Management, 15*(5), 215.

Bartle, R. A. (2004). Pitfalls of virtual property. *Np, Apr.*

Battah, A., Madine, M., Yaqoob, I., Salah, K., Hasan, H. R., & Jayaraman, R. (2022). Blockchain and NFTs for trusted ownership, trading, and access of AI models. *IEEE Access, 10*, 112230–112249.

Belk, R., Humayun, M., & Brouard, M. (2022). Money, possessions, and ownership in the Metaverse: NFTs, cryptocurrencies, Web3 and Wild Markets. *Journal of Business Research, 153*, 198–205.

Bell, T. W. (1997). Virtual trade dress: A very real problem. *Maryland Law Review, 56*, 384.

Bergquist, M. S. (2011). *Economics in the small and independent game industry*. Master's thesis, Institutt for Telematikk.

Blackburn, R. (2003). *Intellectual property and innovation management in small firms*. Routledge.

Blazer, C. (2006). The five indicia of virtual property. *Pierce Law Review, 5*, 137.

Boden, M. A. (1998). Creativity and artificial intelligence. *Artificial Intelligence, 103*(1–2), 347–356.

Borri, N., Liu, Y., & Tsyvinski, A. (2022). The economics of non-fungible tokens. Available at SSRN: https://ssrn.com/abstract=4052045.

Burylo, Y. (2022). AI-generated works and copyright protection. *Entrepreneurship, Economy and Law, 3*, 7.

Cellini, R., Cuccia, T., & Lyrvall, J. (2023). On the price dynamics of non-fungible tokens: The 'Bored Apes' case. *PLoS One, 18*(11), e0287881.

Chin, B. M. (2006). Regulating your second life-defamation in virtual worlds. *Brooklyn Law Review, 72*, 1303.

Christodoulou, K., Katelaris, L., Themistocleous, M., Christodoulou, P., & Iosif, E. (2022). NFTs and the Metaverse revolution: research perspectives and open challenges. In M. C. Lacity &

H. Treiblmaier (Eds.), *Blockchains and the token economy: Theory and practice* (pp. 139–178). Springer Nature.
Conti, R., & Schmidt, J. (2022). What is an NFT? Non-fungible tokens explained. *Forbes Advisor,* 8.
Cornelius, K. (2011). Responsibility under criminal law in virtual worlds. In K. Cornelius & D. Hermann (Eds.), *Virtual worlds and criminality* (pp. 95–119). Springer.
Craig, J. (2021). Comic books are going digital & venturing into NFTs: What does it mean? Retrieved April 11, 2024, from https://phemex.com/blogs/crypto-comics-nft.
Dharma, D. S. (2023). Regulating the Metaverse: ensuring legal protection and intellectual property rights in the digital landscape. *Indonesian Law Journal, 16*(2), 161–184.
Dinwoodie, G. B., & Janis, M. D. (Eds.). (2008). *Trademark law and theory: A handbook of contemporary research.* Edward Elgar Publishing.
Divea, K., & Surjit, R. (2022). Blockchain utility by pioneers in fashion and apparel industry. In S. S. Muthu (Ed.), *Blockchain technologies in the textile and fashion industry* (pp. 81–108). Springer Nature.
Dougherty, C., & Lastowka, G. (2007). Virtual trademarks. *Santa Clara Computer & High Technology Law Journal, 24,* 749.
Dowling, M. (2022). Is non-fungible token pricing driven by cryptocurrencies? *Finance Research Letters, 44,* 102097.
Dworkin, G. (1977). The Whitford Committee report on copyright and designs law. *The Modern Law Review, 40*(6), 685–700.
Fairfield, J. A. T. (2005). Virtual property. *Boston University Law Review, 85,* 1047.
Fairfield, J. A. T. (2022). Tokenized: The law of non-fungible tokens and unique digital property. *Indiana Law Journal, 97,* 1261.
Firth, A., Lea, G., Cornford, P., & Lingren, K. (2005). *Trademarks: Law and practice.* Jordans.
Flanagan, A., & Maniatis, S. M. (2008). *Intellectual property on the Internet.* University of London Press.
Gaffar, H., & Albarashdi, S. (2024). Copyright protection for AI-generated works: Exploring originality and ownership in a digital landscape. *Asian Journal of International Law,* 1–24.
Gervais, D. J. (2004). The compatibility of the "skill and labour" originality standard with the Berne convention and the TRIPs agreement. *European Intellectual Property Review, 26*(2), 75–80.
Grba, D. (2023). The transparency of reason: ethical issues of AI art. In S. Lindgren (Ed.), *Handbook of critical studies of artificial intelligence* (pp. 504–514). Edward Elgar.
Gürkaynak, G., Yılmaz, I., Yeşilaltay, B., & Bengi, B. (2018). Intellectual property law and practice in the blockchain realm. *Computer Law & Security Review, 34*(4), 847–862.
He, T. (2022). From single-player games to Metaverse: A futuristic analysis of challenging legal issues in the video game industry in China. *GRUR International, 71*(10), 952–966.
Heath, G. C. (2020). Patents and AI inventions. In *Intellectual property law and the fourth industrial revolution* (pp. 153–177). Wolters Kluwer Law.
Helm, J. M., Swiergosz, A. M., Haeberle, H. S., Karnuta, J. M., Schaffer, J. L., Krebs, V. E., Spitzer, A. I., & Ramkumar, P. N. (2020). Machine learning and artificial intelligence: definitions, applications, and future directions. *Current Reviews in Musculoskeletal Medicine, 13*(1), 69–76.
Hollensen, S., Kotler, P., & Opresnik, M. O. (2022). Metaverse—The new marketing universe. *Journal of Business Strategy, 44*(3), 119–125.
Hugenholtz, P. B., van Eechoud, M., Van Gompel, S., & Helberger, N. (2006). The recasting of copyright & related rights for the knowledge economy. *Report to the European Commission, DG Internal Market,* 308.
Humayun, M., & Belk, R. (2022). How brand hive minds thrive: Understanding Bitcoin's resilience. *Cryptoeconomic Systems, 2*(1).
Hutson, J., Banerjee, G., Kshetri, N., Odenwald, K., & Ratican, J. (2023). Architecting the Metaverse: Blockchain and the financial and legal regulatory challenges of virtual real estate. *Journal of Intelligent Learning Systems and Applications, 15.*

Hutson, J., & Lang, M. (2023). Content creation or interpolation: AI generative digital art in the classroom. *Metaverse, 4*(1), 13.

Iredale, G. (2021). The difference between fungible and non-fungible tokens.

Kalyvaki, M. (2023). Navigating the Metaverse business and legal challenges: Intellectual property, privacy, and jurisdiction. *Journal of Metaverse, 3*(1), 87–92.

Kasiyanto, S., & Kilinc, M. R. (2022). Legal conundrums of the Metaverse. *Journal of Central Banking Law Institutions, 1*(2), 299–322.

King, E., Smith, M. P., Wilson, P. F., & Williams, M. A. (2021). Digital responses of UK museum exhibitions to the COVID-19 crisis, March–June 2020. *Curator: The Museum Journal, 64*(3), 487–504.

Koster, R. (2000). A declaration of the rights of Avatars. In *Cross currents: Cultures, communities, technologies*, pp. 203–207.

Kuntze, R., Crudele, T. R., Reynolds, D., & Matulich, E. (2013). The rise and fall of virtual reality retailing in second life: An Avatar's perspective. *Journal of Management and Marketing Research, 13*, 1.

Lane, H. C., & Yi, S. (2017). Playing with virtual blocks: Minecraft as a learning environment for practice and research. In *Cognitive development in digital contexts* (pp. 145–166). Academic Press.

Lastowka, G. (2012). Minecraft as Web 2.0: Amateur creativity and digital games. In *Amateur Media* (pp. 153–169). Routledge.

Lapatoura, I. (2022). Fashion beyond physical space: NFTs and intellectual property challenges in the Metaverse. *Entertainment Law Review, 33*(6), 197–202.

Lee, E. (2023). NFTs as decentralized intellectual property. *University of Illinois Law Review*, 1049.

Lehdonvirta, V. (2011). Real-money trade of virtual assets: Ten different user perceptions. *SSRN Electronic Journal*. https://doi.org/10.2139/ssrn.1351772

Look, J. J. (1999). The virtual wild, wild west (www): Intellectual property issues in cyberspace-trademarks, service marks, copyrights, and domain names. *UALR Law Review, 22*, 49.

Maggiore, M. (2018). Artificial intelligence, computer-generated works and copyright. In E. Bonadio & N. Lucchi (Eds.), *Non-conventional copyright* (pp. 382–399). Edward Elgar.

Maouchi, Y., Charfeddine, L., & El Montasser, G. (2022). Understanding digital bubbles amidst the COVID-19 pandemic: Evidence from DeFi and NFTs. *Finance Research Letters, 47*, 102584.

Martins, T., Correia, J., Rebelo, S., Bicker, J., & Machado, P. (2020). Portraits of no one: An internet artwork. In *Proceedings of the 28th ACM international conference on multimedia* (pp. 4392–4393).

Mazzone, M., & Elgammal, A. (2019). Art, creativity, and the potential of artificial intelligence. *Arts, 8*(1), 26.

Mezei, P., & Arora, G. C. (2023). *Copyright and metaverse*. https://papers.ssrn.com/sol3/papers.cfm?abstract_id=4444608. Accessed 5 April 2024.

McKenna, M. P. (2009). Trademark use and the problem of source. *University of Illinois Law Review, 773*.

Mesevic, I. R. (2023). Intellectual property rights in the Metaverse. *Regional Law Review, 345*.

Michaels, A., & Norris, A. (2002). *A practical guide to Trademark Law*. Sweet & Maxwell.

Moringiello, J. M., & Odinet, C. K. (2022a). Blockchain real estate and NFTs. *William & Mary Law Review, 64*, 1131.

Moringiello, J. M., & Odinet, C. K. (2022b). The property law of tokens. *Florida Law Review, 74*, 607.

Mujević, B., & Mujević, M. (2023). NFTs and copyright law. *Science International Journal, 2*(2), 15–20.

Multazam, M. T. (2022). Exploring the legal and policy implications of non-fungible tokens. *Jurnal Politik dan Pemerintahan Daerah, 4*(2), 293–303.

Murray, M. D. (2022a). NFT ownership and copyrights. *Indiana Law Review, 56*, 367.

Murray, M. D. (2022b). Trademarks, NFTs, and the law of the Metaverse. *Arizona Law Journal of Emerging Technologies, 6*.

Murray, M. D. (2023). Trademarks, NFTs, and the law of the metaverse. *Arizona Law Journal of Emerging Technologies, 6*, 3.

Noveck, B. S. (2005). Trademark law and the social construction of trust: Creating the legal framework for online identity. *Washington University Law Quarterly, 83*, 1733.

Ochoa, T., Ghosh, S., & LaFrance, M. (2020). *Understanding intellectual property law*. Carolina Academic Press.

Palace, V. M. (2019). What if artificial intelligence wrote this: artificial intelligence and copyright law. *Florida Law Review, 71*, 217.

Qin, W., Li, R., Wang, Q., & Chen, S. (2021). Non-fungible token (NFT): Overview, evaluation, opportunities and challenges. *arXiv Preprint*. https://doi.org/10.48550/arXiv.2105.07447

Rahmatian, A. (2013). Originality in UK copyright law: The old "skill and labour" doctrine under pressure. *IIC-International Review of Intellectual Property and Competition Law, 44*(1), 4–34.

Raman, R., & Raj, B. E. (2021). The world of NFTs (non-fungible tokens): The future of blockchain and asset ownership. In A. B. Mnaouer & L. C. Fourati (Eds.), *Enabling blockchain technology for secure networking and communications* (pp. 89–108). IGI Global.

Roose, K. (2021). Buy this column on the blockchain!. *New York Times*. https://www.nytimes.com/2021/03/24/technology/nft-column-blockchain.html. Accessed 11 April 2024.

Santiago, M. L. (2022). The legal challenges of the Metaverse: Business trademarks. In *8th international scientific-business conference LIMEN 2022-leadership, innovation, management and economics: Integrated politics of research conference proceedings* (pp. 357–370). Udruženje ekonomista i menadžera Balkana.

Saw, C. L., & Chan, S. (2023). *The subsistence and enforcement of copyright and trademark rights in the Metaverse* (SMU Centre for AI & Data Governance Research Paper, 03).

Sharma, R. (2021). Non-fungible token definition: Understanding NFTs. *Investopedia*. Retrieved July 5, 2021, from https://www.investopedia.com/non-fungible-tokens-nft-5115211.

Sharp, A. J. (2022). Head in the BitCloud: A discussion on the copyrightability and ownership rights in generative digital art and non-fungible tokens. *San Diego Law Review, 59*, 637.

Shapiro, B. (2008). Trademark arbitration: A first rate change for a second life future. *Chicago-Kent Journal of Intellectual Property, 8*, 273.

Sheldon, D. P. (2007). Claiming ownership, but getting owned: Contractual limitations on asserting property interests in virtual goods. *UCLA Law Review, 54*(3), 751–787.

Siegel, D. S., & Wright, M. (2007). Intellectual property: the assessment. *Oxford Review of Economic Policy, 23*(4), 529–540.

Simon, H. A. (1995). Artificial intelligence: an empirical science. *Artificial Intelligence, 77*(1), 95–127.

Stokes, S. (2019). *Digital copyright: law and practice*. Bloomsbury.

Taherdoost, H. (2022). Non-fungible tokens (NFT): A systematic review. *Information, 14*(1), 26.

Ung, M. (2008). Trademark law and the repercussions of virtual property (IRL). *Commlaw Conspectus, 17*, 679.

Vaidhyanathan, S. (2017). *Intellectual property: A very short introduction*. Oxford University Press.

van Haaften-Schick, L., & Whitaker, A. (2022). From the artist's contract to the blockchain ledger: New forms of artists' funding using equity and resale royalties. *Journal of Cultural Economics, 46*(2), 287–315.

Vesala, J. (2023). Developing artificial intelligence-based content creation: Are EU copyright and antitrust law fit for purpose? *International Review of Intellectual Property and Competition Law, 54*(3), 351–380.

Yemenici, A. (2022). Entrepreneurship in the world of Metaverse: Virtual or real? *Journal of Metaverse, 2*(2), 71–82.

Zhang, Z. J. (2022). Cryptopricing: Whence comes the value for cryptocurrencies and NFTs? *International Journal of Research in Marketing*. https://doi.org/10.1016/j.ijresmar.2022.08.002

Chapter 11
Financial Services in the Metaverse: Legal and Regulatory Considerations

Iwa Salami

Abstract The Metaverse is still in its nascent stages and, while businesses (B2C companies) continue to build a presence in the Metaverse and virtual world investments have surged, truly immersive experiences are still not achievable with current technologies. While there is potential for a fully functioning virtual world with some applications—particularly in the fields of education, healthcare, and gaming—its application in finance is still emerging. Therefore, the existence of virtual bank branches currently seems quite far-fetched. Also, what constitutes a fully functioning Metaverse/virtual world with an inbuilt financial system would need to be characterised by the absence of fragmentation or domination of the space by a few powerful players. This, however, would only be possible if it is a regulated space, but this is currently not the case since there are growing numbers of platforms operating in virtual spaces that are not subject to regulation.

This chapter seeks to investigate the key legal and regulatory issues that would need to be addressed for financial transactions in the Metaverse to be truly global and interoperable between different types of Metaverse and blockchain environments. This chapter considers legal issues that may arise in enforcing contracts in a Metaverse context. It also considers regulatory concerns raised by potential financial services activities occurring in the Metaverse such as data protection, privacy, investor protection, financial crime, and financial stability, and how these may be mitigated. It begins with the evolution of the concept of the Metaverse and considers the possible types of Metaverses focusing on decentralised and centralised Metaverse spaces. Next, it assesses the legal challenges in decentralised Metaverse spaces and compares this to the state of enforcement in Metaverse spaces owned and controlled by regulated institutions, it reviews key regulatory and policy issues and how they impact financial services. It also looks at United Kingdom (UK) regulators (Information Commissioner's Office (ICO), the Competition and Markets Authority (CMA), the Financial Conduct Authority (FCA), and the Bank of England) con-

I. Salami (✉)
Royal Docks School of Business and Law, University of East London, London, UK
e-mail: i.salami@uel.ac.uk

N. Islam, I. Salami (eds.), *Metaverse Innovation*, Applied Innovation and Technology Management, https://doi.org/10.1007/978-3-031-97080-1_11

cerning services in Metaverse spaces and calls for coordination of activities at a global level. This chapter concludes with some reflections.

Keywords Financial services · Metaverse · B2C companies · Legal issues · Regulatory aspects

11.1 Introduction

Although there is no standard definition for the Metaverse it is generally accepted as an immersive computer-generated environment existing purely in the virtual space where the user uses a personal avatar. Also, its definition may change depending on the enabling technologies and ecosystems where the technologies are applied.

Metaverse technology is likely to be a significant contributor to the digital transformation sweeping the globe. This digital transformation has had a massive impact on the financial industry which has witnessed significant transformation in dimensions including payments and settlement, capital markets/investment services, banking, and insurance. The technologies that have thus far contributed to this process include Web3 such as blockchain, Artificial Intelligence (AI), machine learning, big data, cryptography, and biometrics. These have made financial services more inclusive, cheaper, and more efficient.

It is fitting to mention that although the primary subject domain of the Metaverse is computer science with the earliest work published in 2013 (Dionisio et al., 2013), numerous Metaverse studies have also been found in other fields such as education (Akour et al., 2022; Kye et al., 2021; Suh & Ahn, 2022), medicine (Almarzouqi et al., 2022; Skalidis et al., 2022), and the arts (Baía Reis & Ashmore, 2022; Lee et al., 2022; Strutt, 2022).

The literature review studies on Metaverse have, however, mainly concentrated on medicine and health, focusing on the application of Metaverse technology for the prevention and treatment of diseases (Garavand & Aslani, 2022; Petrigna & Musumeci, 2022). Suffice to say that there has also been a literature review study in marketing, exploring Metaverse studies in the virtual advertisement space (Shen et al., 2021) which reveals a significant literature review in this field. With respect to the specific area of finance, there is a small amount of literature on finance and the Metaverse and one of the first is the study by Kappe and Steurer (2010). This research aims to design a micropayment system that can be used in virtual worlds. The study highlighted that numerous virtual worlds have already embraced the idea and made use of the integrated micropayment system. Additionally, recent research by Belk et al. (2022) explored the potential for fractional ownership and fractionalised property rights as well as the theoretical and practical concerns of the new digital ownership resulting from the acceptance of the Metaverse. Nakavachara and Saengchote (2022) looked at whether the choice of settlement influences a person's willingness to pay in the Metaverse. They discovered that the use of crypto assets in the Metaverse affects people's willingness to pay due to their volatility. Finally,

Vidal-Tomás (2022) published a paper on finance in which he highlighted some of the features of 84 Metaverse tokens and 129 play-to-earn tokens and described the bubble indicators for them which investors should keep a close eye on.

However, no studies specifically address the legal and regulatory issues raised by financial transactions in different types of Metaverse spaces and the significance of the need for a holistic approach in regulating financial services in Metaverse spaces. It is this gap that this chapter seeks to address. This chapter investigates the key legal and regulatory issues that would need to be addressed for financial transactions in the Metaverse to be truly global and interoperable between different types of Metaverse and blockchain environments—blockchain being a key technology at the heart of Metaverse developments. This chapter considers legal issues that may arise in enforcing contracts in a Metaverse context. It also considers regulatory concerns raised by the potential financial services activities occurring in the Metaverse such as data protection, privacy, investor protection, financial crime, and financial stability and how these may be mitigated. It begins with the evolution of the concept of the Metaverse and considers the possible types of Metaverses, focusing on decentralised and centralised Metaverse spaces. It then assesses the legal challenges in decentralised Metaverse spaces such as the enforcement of financial transactions on blockchains and compares that to the state of enforcement in Metaverse spaces owned and controlled by regulated institutions. It moves on to consider key regulatory and policy issues and how they impact financial services, it looks at UK regulators (ICO, CMA, FCO and the Bank of England) concerning services in Metaverse spaces and calls for coordination of activities and suggests that a similar coordinated approach among diverse regulators be taken at global level. This chapter concludes with some reflections.

11.2 Key Milestones in the Evolution of the Metaverse

The idea of a Metaverse has existed for many years. In his 1992 book Snow Crash, Neal Stephenson first used the term Metaverse to refer to a three-dimensional virtual environment. It was envisioned as a virtual environment where people could escape reality and establish distinctive online personalities (Team Mudrex, 2023). However, due to technological breakthroughs like augmented reality (AR) and virtual reality (VR), it has recently attracted increased attention. Suffice to mention that what is now generally accepted to be the Metaverse is a combination of developments dating back to as far back as the seventeenth century where, in 1838, scientist Sir Charles Wheatstone outlined the concept of binocular vision, where two images were combined—one for each eye—to make a single 3D image (Marr, 2022). It should be added that this Metaverse concept is still emerging to date.

The earlier 2000s saw the launch of Second Life, a free 3D virtual environment where users may create, interact, and have voice and text conversations with people all around the world. Ball (2022) highlighted that it offered a proto-Metaverse where users could interact with one another, exchange virtual products, and live without constraints (Ball, 2022). However, it was never widely used as it was difficult for new users to navigate and create content within the platform as it frequently experienced technical issues and meltdowns. Nonetheless, subsequent virtual gaming environments like Roblox and Fortnite, launched in 2004 and 2017, respectively, attract millions of users as they are more engaging.

In 2010, Palmer Luckey, an 18-year-old inventor and entrepreneur, designed the Oculus Rift VR headset prototype. VR has gained popularity again thanks to the groundbreaking headset which uses computer processing power and has a 90-degree field of vision. 2014 saw Facebook purchase Oculus VR for a reported $2 billion. Mark Zuckerberg, the creator of Facebook, said at the time that the two companies would collaborate to expand the Oculus platform and create partnerships to enable new games (Marr, 2022).

In 2016, Microsoft released its HoloLens headset, introducing mixed reality (VR and AR) to the public for the first time. A holographic image can be generated in front of users using a HoloLens which can be projected into the actual environment and augmented reality can be used to alter it. Also, at the corporate level, the rebranding of Facebook as Meta Platforms in late October 2021 as an indication of its intentions to explore opportunities in the Metaverse was one of the significant announcements that caused a spike in attention (Marr, 2022). Google Trends data highlights how the Metaverse became the subject of a massive explosion in popular conversation in October 2021.

Despite the fact that investment in virtual worlds has grown rapidly, the technology still falls short of achieving fully immersive experiences; despite the exaggerated predictions, it is believed that interest has fallen in 2022 and 2023 (BIS, 2024).

11.2.1 Evolution of Financial Technology and Linkages with Metaverse Technologies

The conversations around the financial services and the Metaverse find themselves as part of the narrative of the evolution of Financial Technology (FinTech).

FinTech, the application of technology to finance, evolved as part of the response to the radically changed regulatory and compliance landscape that emerged after the 2007 financial crisis. The use of technology in finance transcends the term FinTech, which was coined almost a decade ago.

11.2.1.1 The 1960s

According to a thorough historical account of the application of technology in finance by Arner et al. (2017), the adoption of technology in finance dates back to the 1960s when advanced markets made the switch from an analogue to a digital financial industry with the introduction of the handheld financial calculator and the automated teller machine. They account that this was followed by decades of swift technological developments and that while the introduction of technology in finance has brought about extensive changes to the financial sector, the two main areas that have been significantly transformed by technology have been payments and capital markets.

11.2.1.2 The 1970s and 2000s

Arner et al. (2017) state that the most significant developments in payments took place in the early 1970s with electronic payment systems in developed markets and cross-border payment systems, such as SWIFT (Society for Worldwide Interbank Financial Telecommunications), VISA, the establishment of RTGS (real-time gross settlement systems) in the 1980s and 1990s, and the creation of Continuous Linked Settlement (CLS), all of which have contributed to today's $6.6 trillion-a-day global foreign exchange markets (Debnath & Barton, 2019). Debnath and Barton (2019) observed that these developments took place through a progressive collaboration between major central banks and financial institutions intended to facilitate the globalisation of finance and, at the same time, reduce the inherent systemic risks in cross-border payments. They conclude that these global payment infrastructures have also been the platform for the development of new technology-driven payment systems, such as PayPal, Alipay (Arner et al., 2017), and WeChat Pay.

In considering the application of technology to securities markets, recount that, since the early 1970s, markets have transformed from nineteenth-century paper-based physical systems to today's virtual electronic markets, characterised by high frequency and algorithmic trading which began in 1971 with the establishment of NASDAQ, the first fully electronic securities market. They account that this transformation stemmed from an interaction between major market participants and regulators focused on improving efficiency and risk management while seeking to control risks to investors and markets. They claim that this interaction resulted in the National Market System (NMS) in the United States of America (USA) and the Investment Services Directive (ISD), Markets in Financial Instruments Directive (MiFID), and European Market Infrastructure Regulation (EMIR) in the European Union (EU). They also conclude that this is the reason the majority of securities trading in advanced markets today involves computers transacting and trading with each other with less involvement of humans.

11.2.1.3 2007–2009

The years which immediately followed the financial crisis (which was largely the result of the collapse of subprime mortgages that were then collateralised as debts, held by banks that then became worthless, causing the banks to be bailed out by taxpayers' money) saw a shift from Web2-based Internet providers to Web3-based Internet operations—Web3 being a term used to describe the next iteration of the

Internet, one that is built on blockchain technology and is communally controlled by its users. This was born largely from the dissatisfaction over the role banks played in this process leading to the crisis, which was deemed as exploitative. Interests by libertarians spurred the notions of a preferred and alternative and decentralised financial system where users could exchange value and conduct other financial activities without banks and facilitated by Web3 technology—a key one being blockchain. Simply put, Web2 has been described as the Internet that enabled the acquisition of information and the exchange through third-party media—otherwise known as the era of read-and-write engagement with the Internet that saw the development of Facebook, X, blogs, Wikipedia, etc. Web3 was based on peer-to-peer transactions and involves individual control of personal data and the use of crypto assets without the interference of intermediaries, all facilitated through technologies such as blockchain, which is a type of distributed ledger technology.

Transactions in crypto assets as a form of exchange or payments were conducted through centralised or decentralised exchanges. The facilitation of payments and other financial transactions on a peer-to-peer basis through non-custodial finance and without intermediaries (including crypto asset exchanges) was promoted in DeFi (decentralised finance).

Decentralised Finance (DeFi) finds a natural home in the Metaverse. Smart contracts and blockchain-based protocols have the potential to facilitate decentralised lending, borrowing, and investing in virtual worlds. This could present novel prospects for individuals to engage in international financial markets and obtain an extensive array of financial services directly within the Metaverse (City of Dreams, 2023).

By blurring the lines between real and virtual assets, the Metaverse creates opportunities for investment, wealth creation, and ownership. Creative platforms and virtual worlds offer areas for creating original virtual environments, artwork, and experiences. It is a place where concepts become reality, where artists can collaborate with others on their creations and even make money from them. The ability to purchase, sell, and exchange these virtual goods as non-fungible tokens (NFTs) within the Metaverse opens up new investment and revenue-generating opportunities. Examples of these virtual assets include digital art, virtual real estate, and in-game items. Although the idea of the Metaverse has been around for decades, there was a spike in interest in the concept at the end of 2021 when sales of NFTs increased and major tech companies like Facebook/Meta made announcements about their interest and investment in the virtual world.

The Metaverse provides a means of storing and sharing information, and it also clears the path for the emergence of a new kind of economics in the future. Intangible goods like NFTs in the arts and fashion, as well as virtual travel, events, and real estate, are traded in this economy. Therefore, to monetise transactions in this digital environment, it would rely on blockchain technology as well as digital assets and currencies (LeewayHertz, 2022). Additionally, millions of dollars are being invested in virtual experiences that are only accessible online, and, as a result, the Metaverse is becoming increasingly profitable. These dynamics shape the financial industry overall and generate career opportunities within the Metaverse.

11.3 Two Approaches: Financial Transactions in Centralised and Decentralised Virtual/Metaverse Spaces

Financial transactions involving digital assets and currencies can be conducted through centralised or decentralised virtual platforms or ecosystems. Their occurrence in Metaverse ecosystems will depend on the type of Metaverse space. Thus, it is conceived that decentralised finance would only be able to exist in a decentralised Metaverse space (where transactions are not regulated and occur between unregulated participants/entities and through unregulated institutions known as decentralised autonomous organisations (DAOs)) (Ogundare, 2023). Transactions (on regulated platforms) involving regulated crypto asset activities, however, would only be able to interface with regulated companies operating in regulated Metaverse spaces.

11.3.1 Fully Decentralised Metaverse Spaces and Financial Activities

As noted above, financial transactions on fully decentralised Metaverse spaces (involving the facilitation of payments and other financial transactions without intermediaries) would be through what is purely referred to as decentralised finance.

Decentralised finance (DeFi) is an ecosystem of financial applications that are built on top of blockchain networks. DeFi aims to create an open-source, permissionless, and transparent financial system that operates without any central authority. Instead, a smart contract—a self-executing contract with the terms of the agreement between transacting parties written into lines of code—replaces financial institutions in the transaction (Salami, 2021). As a result, DeFi is available to everyone with reliable access to electricity and Internet connectivity. It also serves as a form of non-custodial finance since users maintain full control of their assets and carry out transacts through smart contract programmes that facilitate peer-to-peer interactions. DeFi has also been defined as, 'decentralised apps (Dapps) providing financial services on a blockchain settlement layer including payments, lending, trading, investments, insurance, and asset management' (Wharton, 2021).

DeFi occurring in these decentralised Metaverse spaces attracts any individual who can engage in transactions through different DeFi platforms with unknown individuals and is facilitated through smart contracts. For this reason, DeFi can be deemed as inclusive but operates with no clear standards on data privacy, digital ownership, and consumer protection. Decentralised applications, or DAOs, such as Decentraland and Sandbox are examples of Metaverse projects and DAOs built on the Ethereum blockchain. Axie Infinity is another Metaverse project that runs on its own Ethereum sidechain called Ronin (Zeuch, 2023).

Decentralised finance (DeFi) applications run on DAOs and a DAO can be defined as 'the entity created by the deployment of an autonomous and self-executing software running on a distributed system, such as blockchain, that allows a network of participants to interact and manage resources on a transparent basis and in accordance with the rules defined by the software code' (Riva, 2020). The participants of a DAO benefit from the pseudonymity of the blockchain environment and can only be identified by their public key (their wallet address) (De Filippi & Wright, 2018). There is no link to their real identity except in circumstances where they are using regulated services that require Know Your Customer (KYC) identification. With pseudonymity, the only barrier to becoming a member of a DAO is usually economic meaning that DAOs can potentially be joined by anyone from anywhere in the world. As such, a DAO must be considered as a community of unreliable members and for DAOs to function their architecture must take this key characteristic into account. Hence, they are entities whose rules are defined and enforced in the form of smart contracts which, as stated above, are blockchain-based software codes that carry out, control, and document relevant events and actions according to predefined terms and rules.

11.3.1.1 Legal Challenges of DeFi: Legal and Enforcement Requirements of Decentralised Autonomous Organisations (DAOs)

As DAO transactions are conducted over public blockchains, they are, by nature, international. This makes their existence completely viable without the need for physicality, location, or connectivity thus making the application or intervention of a state's judiciary nearly meaningless or unfeasible. Since it does away with the idea that Internet transactions can always be connected to a state's territory in some way, the use of blockchain technology further complicates the application of private international law rules. This is because a fundamental tenet of private international law is that commercial agreements should have a territorial connection. However, like any technology created by humans, smart contracts have flaws. Errors can happen when translating the legal contract's terms into the smart contract's code. Unwanted results may arise during the smart contract's execution due to defects or coding errors as well as unanticipated events that were not planned for. Disagreements over how the smart contract's code should be interpreted can potentially result in conflict. This could happen, for instance, when an external source (sometimes referred to as an oracle) verifies factual components that the smart contract relies on to perform its function. A grievance may occur if a smart contract follows its instructions exactly yet the outcome goes against justice and fairness. In conclusion, the automated operation of smart contracts does not completely remove the possibility of legal action (Rabinovich-Einy & Katsh, 2019).

DAO maintenance and operation are likewise entirely dependent on the smart contract architecture. Smart contracts, which define the DAO's governance structure and dictate how its members relate to one another, are the code that encodes its internal governance. Smart contracts may be the best way to increase the effectiveness of corporate governance because they rely solely on the code and eliminate the need for human intervention during execution. The automation and transparency of internal operations lower the expenses associated with agent supervision and monitoring (Kaal, 2021). There may be disagreements among DAO members even in cases where the code operates as intended. Such conflicts may arise when a minority shareholder believes that the majority shareholders have violated its rights. Moreover, DAOs are vulnerable to errors in the smart contracts that specify their governance framework and operational procedures. The more complicated a DAO structure is, the more likely it is to have these issues. The example of the DAO case highlights how a flaw in the code can lead to a DAO's downfall.

Given that smart contracts are not immune to conflict and that decentralised autonomous organisations (DAOs) may experience internal conflicts within their own membership as well as external conflicts with third parties, it is yet unclear whether state courts will have the authority to settle these disputes. Determining whether current connecting factors can connect DAO issues to a state and whether that state's private international law regulations give its courts jurisdiction over those conflicts is crucial. In the event that this is not the case, participants in the blockchain ecosystem may encounter circumstances where they are denied justice. These problems actually arose with the first decentralised autonomous organisation (DAO), which gave rise to a heated disagreement between parties with conflicting interests that needed to be settled quickly without the assistance of the government or a formal dispute resolution process. The possibility of disputes in the blockchain ecosystem, the legal ambiguity surrounding cryptocurrency transactions, and the potential for disputes to be resolved in this setting were all made clear by this case.

11.3.1.2 Unregulated DAOs Operating Within Unregulated Metaverse Spaces

Unregulated DAOs are not incorporated under a state's jurisdiction and are established outside of the law and current legal frameworks. They are the type that would function in a fully decentralised Metaverse. They operate outside of the law which exposes their members and those who enter into contracts with them to huge levels of legal uncertainty.

The fundamental question is whether an unregulated DAO should be viewed as a simple partnership, in which case the relationships among the members of the DAO would be of a contractual nature, or whether it should be regarded as a company (or another form of organisation), in which case the relationships among the members of the DAO would be governed by corporate law (and laws governing other forms of organisations) (Rolo, 2019). The main issue, however, is figuring out which laws apply and which laws should be used to decide whether a DAO qualifies as a company.

If a DAO is classified as a simple partnership, then each partner in a simple partnership is liable jointly and severally for all debts committed under the partnership's legal framework. Since it is impossible to hold unregulated DAO members accountable for anything beyond their initial contribution when they buy governance tokens that only grant them the ability to vote in the DAO's governance—especially when the DAO has thousands of members who use pseudonyms—this legal framework is inappropriate for decentralised autonomous organisations. In this instance, the status of DAO members is significantly closer to that of shareholders in a limited corporation than it is to that of ordinary partnership members. The main developers of those DAOs may be considered as the executive board that is in charge of overseeing it and needs approval from its shareholders, or the DAO members, who vote on proposals.

Finding a forum for actions pertaining to the governance of unregulated DAOs is almost impossible when attempting to attach corporate law disputes involving those DAOs to a state using all the connecting criteria of private international law. This is true since uncontrolled DAOs operate without being subject to any laws. They are registered and managed only on the blockchain, and most of their operations take place in the blockchain ecosystem. Furthermore, the anonymity that their users experience when using and transacting on the blockchain makes it even more difficult to establish connectivity to choose a dispute resolution forum.

Therefore, when it comes to unregulated DAOs, connection criteria that use the DAO's seat or the home or regular abode of its members to link a dispute to a state's territory are inappropriate. Consequently, conflicts pertaining to the management of unregulated DAOs are outside the purview of governmental justice. This is the reason the goal of private international law, which is to connect legal transactions to a state, is challenged by blockchain technology, much like it was with the introduction of the Internet (Svantesson, 2017).

11.3.2 Fully Regulated Metaverse Spaces

Regulated Metaverse spaces (such as may occur from registered companies and firms in the real world seeking to explore opportunities in Metaverse spaces) would necessarily require the use of crypto assets (Ogundare 2023) through linked centralised and regulated crypto assets platforms or the use of tokenised deposits or central bank digital currencies. As such, retail central bank digital currencies, tokenised deposits, or other quick payment systems from central banks might all be made to enable Metaverse services.

However, having these two Metaverse spaces may mean that virtual environments and financial transactions in these spaces can become fragmented as it would be necessary that interoperability is enhanced between these two ecosystems for an integrated Metaverse ecosystem to exist.

The functioning of regulated and registered businesses in regulated Metaverse domains may lead to fragmentation. This could lead to strong private companies controlling such spaces (BIS, 2024). In order to ensure effective and interoperable payments, public policy must establish clear rules for data privacy, digital ownership, and consumer protection (BIS, 2024).

11.3.2.1 Regulated DAOs Operating in a Fully Regulated Metaverse Space

Regulated DAOs are subject to state corporate law requirements and use the blockchain infrastructure for their internal organisational structure. Their legal status and capacity are established by corporate law, and their governance is governed by their code. However, very few states have put up legislation to grant DAOs legal standing. In areas where establishing a DAO is permitted, members of the DAO can take advantage of the safeguards offered by the DAO's legal personality. This is especially significant in terms of minimising individual liability. Members who want their DAO to have legal personality in certain jurisdictions must follow specific legal procedures while founding the DAO such as registering the DAO with the state company register.

The US states of Vermont and Wyoming have passed the clearest legal framework making it possible for DAOs to operate within the confines of the law.

On August 28, 2018, the US state of Vermont introduced and passed legislation creating the blockchain-based limited liability company (BBLLC) (Vermont Act No 205 (S.269)). A DAO that is registered as a limited liability company (LLC) under Vermont law is called a BBLLC. This regulation allows a DAO to lawfully enter into contracts and shields its 'owners, managers, and blockchain participants from unwarranted liability'. Since BBLLCs are a specific kind of LLC they must adhere to the same rules as LLCs in general. The capacity to employ blockchain technology for all or part of a BBLLC's governance is the key innovation of that rule. Voting on a BBLLC's operations and activities can be recorded using smart contracts that are established on the blockchain. Under the moniker dOrg LLC, the first BBLLC was established in Vermont in 2019 (Goodenough & Burke, 2019). This organisation is the 'first legal entity that directly references blockchain code as its source of governance' (Goodenough & Burke, 2019). In light of this, BBLLCs have different legal status from their members and are covered by a limited liability regime for the DAO's debts which shields the members from liability for any commitments the DAO assumes. Within the BBLLC legal framework, DAOs can now do business, bring lawsuits and be sued, and sign contracts under their own names for the first time.

A DAO statute was passed by the US state of Wyoming in April 2021, and it went into effect on July 1 of the same year (Wyoming Act No. 73 (SF0038)). It established the DAO as a new class of organisation under Wyoming law (6 Title 17, Chapter 31 of the Wyoming Statutes (W.S.)). A Wyoming DAO is an LLC whose articles of organisation refer to a DAO's smart contract used for managing and running the business. By putting DAOs under the Decentralised Autonomous Organisation Supplement and the Wyoming Limited Liability Company Act, Wyoming took a position akin to that of Vermont. Regulated DAOs are like all other corporate forms. They are new forms of incorporated entities that use blockchain technology in their main body of legislation.

Since regulated DAOs function simultaneously in a state jurisdiction and on the blockchain they constitute a hybrid type of business. Despite being recognised by law as a single entity, a regulated DAO is actually made up of two very distinct components: the corporate body, such as an LLC, which gives the corporation legal substance, and the DAO, also known as the code, which organises the organisational structure of the business. The two parts of the company are linked by corporate law although being subject to vastly different sets of laws. Corporate law rules the entity and the state in which it is registered or incorporated has authority over it. There is a true relationship between that state and the entity through its corporate body. The two DAO rules that are currently in force—that is, that the entity must be established in a corporate register and that the DAO be represented by a minimum of one person who is legally liable for the DAO's decisions—make this relationship viable. On the other hand, the DAO can only be managed in accordance with its code which sets its rules. A legitimate connection to the blockchain is established by the DAO's registration in the ledger. The characteristic of being two distinct halves of one single entity, which is present in regulated DAOs, is absent from unregulated DAOs. Unregulated DAOs lack a corporate body subject to corporation law because they are not regulated by state law.

Only regulated DAOs can function both on-chain and off-chain. These traits, which are related to their organisational structure, need to be considered whenever a DAO gets into a dispute. Therefore, for a DAO transaction to be enforced off-chain it must be regulated.

11.4 DAOs and Private International Law in Metaverse spaces

As considered above, DAOs use smart contracts to enter into contractual agreements with third parties. Smart contracts do not prevent all disputes from happening even though they try to provide a strict structure with few conflicts. As a result, just like other entities DAOs can have disagreements with outside parties as well as with other members of the DAO. Not all disagreements can be avoided, even while the smart contract and blockchain architectures enable DAOs to be structured to minimise the number of disputes that arise both inside the entity and with outside parties. Whether or not they are subject to national legislation, DAOs are, by nature, international entities because they operate on public blockchains. The norms of private international law must be applied to establish which state a DAO can sue or be sued by.

The goal of private international law is to give individuals the legal certainty they need to create international relations. The fundamental elements of the private international law approach are the parties' locations and the conditions that link them. Determining which state the activity and the parties have the closest connections to, or at least enough connections to, is the first step toward coordinating the legal orders. When there are enough relationships between the parties or the dispute's subject and the state, the state will consent to offer the protection of its courts. Thus, the development of private international rules that definitively identify the courts having jurisdiction over a case confers legal certainty.

Neither the International Institute for the Unification of Private Law (UNIDROIT), the United Nations Commission on International Trade Law (UNCITRAL), or, indeed, any other international organisation has proposed any international instrument (such as a Model Law) to harmonise the legal framework of DAOs (UNCITRAL Model Law 1985). Nonetheless, by putting forth the Coalition of Automated Legal Applications (COALA) Model Law for Decentralised Autonomous Organisations (DAOs), the international working group COALA, which is made up of professionals in the legal and technological domains, is attempting to harmonise the legal framework of DAOs at the international level (COALA, 2021).

The Model Law provides uniform legal parameters that national lawmakers can utilise if they intend to enact significant national law governing DAOs. In a state that has incorporated the Model Law into its national legal system, a DAO established in accordance with the provisions of the transposed or accepted Model Law will be acknowledged as a legitimate legal body. Giving the DAO legal existence and legal personality in every state that has adopted, the Model Law will guarantee that the DAO's acts have legal consequences (COALA, 2021). In other words, if the Model Law is approved, it will provide global requirements that DAOs have to meet to become recognised as legal entities (like Limited Liability Companies). However, this is not the case yet as the Model Law has not received worldwide recognition.

Nonetheless, this could be the necessary initial steps required for preparation for the operation of a regulated Metaverse; a Metaverse that would facilitate interoperability between different Metaverses or virtual platforms. This is so that transactions happening in those spaces would be global and facilitated by DAOs and real-world companies operating in Metaverses or virtual spaces, and, as such, there would be a need for dispute resolution mechanisms to be built into their operation. The Model Law would provide a level playing field for all DAOs to be regulated and fall within the national legal framework of the country where they are registered. This would prove useful for determining the place where disputes would be heard, that is, finding a court with jurisdiction over the matter.

11.4.1 Enforcement of DAO-Related Disputes in the Metaverse

When it comes to obstacles to obtaining justice in a DAO dispute, it is important to note that locating a court having jurisdiction over the issue is simply one stage in the legal procedure. Even if a state court has jurisdiction and issues a verdict, the party that was wronged may not be able to pursue the enforcement of the decision on the blockchain if the losing party refuses to cooperate. The content of the blockchain cannot be changed by any authority due to the immutability inherent in blockchain technology. State agencies are unable to enforce rules pertaining to assets in the crypto asset industry because blockchain technology is impenetrable.

The DAO's crypto asset holdings cannot be stolen, frozen, or seized, and no enforcement entity may compel it to do anything. A DAO cannot therefore be the target of any coercive actions. The DAO project highlighted the risks associated with using DAOs and showed how, because of their peer-to-peer decentralised architecture, they are immune to state power. As DAO members enjoy pseudonymity on the network, enforcement agencies are also unable to force them to take action either on or off the blockchain. State authorities have less enforcement power over the organisation, its assets, or its members when it comes to unregistered DAOs.

According to some writers, 'Courts cannot require a retroactive change in the blockchain because that is computationally near impossible' (Kaal & Calcaterra, 2017–2018). This would go against the immutability of the blockchain (De Filippi & Wright, 2018). Even if a smart contract falls under the jurisdiction of state enforcement, they are unable to stop its execution or seize the crypto assets it contains. This is because, once they are deployed on the blockchain, smart contracts' code cannot be changed (Templin, 2019). A blockchain community's members are the only ones who can have such authority. The DAO case study showed that, in extreme cases, the community might choose to change the ledger's state. Such a judgement to impose a court verdict on a DAO's straightforward contractual arrangement is incredibly unlikely.

One thing is certain for the Metaverse to evolve into an inclusive ecosystem that benefits all parties involved, industry participants, regulators, and consumers must work together to shape its future.

11.5 Regulatory Interests and Dimensions in Financial Services Operating in Metaverses Spaces

The potential effects of the Metaverse on data, competition, finance, and content make it imperative that regulators collaborate when interacting with and learning about these technologies. For this, the UK-based Digital Regulation Cooperation platform (DRCF) is an excellent platform. The DRCF is a collaborative effort between a few UK regulators. Together, these authorities handle different facets of online regulatory issues. The Competition and Markets Authority (CMA), the Information Commissioner's Office (ICO), and the Office of Communications (Ofcom) formed the DRCF in July 2020. The Financial Conduct Authority (FCA), which had previously been an observing member, became a full member in April 2021.

The goal of the DRCF is to achieve more collaboration between these regulators, particularly considering the unique challenges associated with regulating Internet platforms. It addresses issues including privacy, safety, algorithms, competition, and data protection.

These authorities must collaborate within the DRCF to make sure that the interests of citizens and consumers are at the centre of digital innovation as goods and services, along with the opportunities and hazards that go along with them, become more interconnected (DRCF, 2024).

Furthermore, if the Metaverse is the next generation of the Internet, governments, regulators, and legislators around the world will probably be watching it closely. Areas of interest to regulators for transactions happening on the Metaverse would include regulating crypto assets transactions against money laundering that could potentially occur through centralised and decentralised exchanges, and the classification and protection of property rights in Metaverse spaces would also be key to regulators (Citi GPS, 2022).

Four key regulators that would have an interest in the operation of financial services in Metaverse spaces would include central banks, financial services regulators, data protection authorities, competition, and market authorities. While there are others, these are the ones that have been considered in this chapter.

In the context of the UK, these regulators are the Information Commissioner's Office, Competition and Markets Authority, Financial Conduct Authority, and the Bank of England. Their interests would be assessed to the extent that transactions on the Metaverse have implications for areas for which the remit of their work covers.

11.5.1 Data Protection Concerns and Data Protection Authority (Information Commissioner's Office)

Although the Metaverse is generally accepted as a combined virtual space it is made up of individual technologies including Artificial Intelligence, head-mounted displays (HMDs), the Internet of Things (IoT), 5G, augmented reality (AR), virtual reality (VR), and spatial technologies. The whole Metaverse experience is provided by combining these technologies but these technologies will largely rely on data to deliver that experience, especially high-quality data (i.e. trusted data).

11.5.1.1 Why Data Is Key to the Metaverse

The Metaverse is powered by data. Without data, the Metaverse could not operate and a significant amount of that data will be personal data. Data is necessary to customise. One explanation for this is that, to prevent users from impersonating others and to create the most realistic digital portrait of every individual in the Metaverse, devices will read a baseline level of personal data as a security precaution. Furthermore, user data is needed for Metaverse enterprises to customise encounters with them and boost the probability that a purchase will be made. They therefore have a greater opportunity to provide highly targeted services the more user data they have. One may argue that other contemporary digital enterprises and social media platforms are comparable. The unprecedented amount of personal data that can be collected and the novel techniques employed in its collection. Thanks to websites and applications, businesses can now discover how individuals use their smartphones to explore the Web and use apps. In the future, organisations will have real-time access to data on individuals within the Metaverse through entry-point devices like VR and AR headgear. Thanks to developments in sensor, display, and optic technology, the Metaverse may soon be able to be experienced through glasses, contact lenses, and other embedded technology (Khan, n.d.).

Examples of the use of data in the Metaverse can be seen in the use of avatars and digital twins. Avatars, which individuals can have several of to reflect different aspects of their lives (both social and professional), can be created to be closely identical to our real selves using data facilitated by Artificial Intelligence (AI). By evaluating 2D user photos or 3D scans, AI will play a key role in producing accurately customised avatars of ourselves (Swaminathan, 2023). Digital twins, on the other hand, are digital representations of physical infrastructure and devices that data scientists and IT professionals can use to run simulations. Digital twins are continuously updated with historical as well as current data from various sources to create an up-to-date representation as soon as new information becomes available (Swaminathan, 2023).

A recent article (McKinsey, 2022), states that digital twin technology will play a major role in creating the enterprise Metaverse. The article claims that 'Dozens of interconnected digital twins will power the enterprise Metaverse. These digital twins will replicate everything from people (like customers and employees) to physical assets (like products and office buildings), to core business processes, and will frequently engage with the real-world/physical environment without the need for human interaction'. It is understood that, for developers to employ these technologies to create the platforms and applications that will enable the Metaverse to realise its full potential, they will need access to high-quality training data.

As such, regulators and authorities would be keen to ensure that the accessing, handling, processing, and use of this data is done in a way that does not violate the rights of individuals. The internationalisation of the data in the Metaverse space would also be a challenge. If the technology enables you to teleport your avatar to any area within the Metaverse, where exactly is your current position? It is currently unclear which national privacy laws will apply when navigating the Metaverse, as well as whether privacy laws based on physical jurisdiction are even relevant there.

Whatever the case, the ICO whose function is to uphold information rights in the public interest, is aware that digital identity is a critical part of virtual spaces, including the Metaverse, in the future (ICO, 2024). It has been acknowledged that developers of interoperable environments may look to digital identities to help provide a frictionless experience in moving between virtual worlds. Users may enter immersive virtual worlds or Metaverses using portable, unique identities which may be lifelike representations of themselves or may be intentionally not lifelike at all.

Platforms will need to find a balance between accountability and privacy, as many users may seek to be anonymous while online for a variety of reasons. While this challenge is one that is faced by platform providers today, the potential to interact via visible avatars in immersive virtual worlds adds a new dimension to this conversation.

Even though no formal plan exists to regulate data privacy in these settings, the ICO will keep a close eye on advancements in the immersive virtual worlds industry and assess the market as new services and products are introduced and use cases arise (ICO, 2024). As laws and standards are developed, the ICO will also stay in touch with other regulators operating in various digital services, nations, and industries. Considering this, the ICO and their DRCF counterparts have jointly released an Immersive Technologies Foresight Paper (DRCF, 2023). The ICO also warns that new privacy issues may surface as Metaverse technology develops. It will be necessary for organisations to integrate privacy-by-design strategies into the Metaverse's architecture as it grows and industry standards are established. This will guarantee that solutions are developed with strict guidelines and security protocols for data protection (ICO, 2024). It is thought that transactions in the Metaverse are unlikely to be suitable for the current system.

11.5.1.2 Financial Services and the Use of Data

The use of data in financial services in the Metaverse would depend on what type of Metaverse is being built. In a truly decentralised Metaverse where blockchains and DLT-based systems are used, there is no regulation for the use of data in financial transactions. In this ecosystem, parties are not obligated to prove their identity nor is anything known about them. As such, the Metaverse could comprise a truly decentralised Metaverse or one that conforms with regulation. For the truly decentralised Metaverse (run through decentralised organisations and networks) using crypto assets, transactions would be stored on public blockchains. Crypto assets and other forms of digital assets could be designed to support services in the Metaverse.

However, achieving interoperability between transactions in unregulated decentralised Metaverse spaces and regulated financial services operating in the Metaverse would be problematic without a coordinated plan for enabling regulation to facilitate interoperability. This would result in two key areas of challenge: first, the traditional finance regulatory obligation to fulfil Know Your Customer (KYC) requirements for all transactions with customers and clients (which is not a requirement in decentralised ecosystems) (Salami, 2021) and second, regulated financial institutions have a longstanding duty of confidentiality towards their clients. This duty ensures that customer information remains private and is not disclosed without proper authorisation. Confidentiality extends to personal financial details, transaction history, and other sensitive data. This would be a challenge to achieve as all the transactions in the decentralised space are recorded on publicly available blockchains. Therefore, although traditional financial institutions and banks here can be supported by tokenised deposits for transactions in Metaverse spaces (since they have not been permitted to use or hold crypto assets), the KYC and privacy issue would be a huge challenge.

As such, clear rules and regulations on investor protection, fulfilment of KYC requirements, and data privacy—governing the way financial services would be delivered and the way data would be provided, used, stored, shared, and processed—would need to be in place to have fully interoperable and inclusive financial services in Metaverse spaces. As such, traditional financial institutions such as banks, who may be keen to deliver services via the Metaverse, would be restricted both by client confidentiality provisions and the current requirements for data protection as governed by the data protection laws under the current regime. For example, UK financial institutions would be permitted to handle the data of their clients as permitted by the UK GDPR, which implemented the EU GDPR regulations (which precisely govern the way that data is collected, processed, shared, and used).

There is also the cross-border dimension to this, which further complicates the regulatory process, so the challenge regarding the storage and accessibility of data in public blockchains is further complicated by the cross-border and global nature of operations that is expected to characterise the Metaverse. This particularly considers the various approaches to the use of data. For instance, the use of data is heavily regulated in Europe under GDPR which is not the case in the USA where the approach to data protection has been sectoral, meaning that different laws apply to different industries or types of data. This fragmented approach can lead to inconsistencies and gaps in privacy protections. The lack of a comprehensive federal privacy law has several implications: data fragmentation (companies collect and share vast amounts of data across various sectors, often without clear guidelines), data breaches (the absence of uniform standards can contribute to data breaches and leaks), consumer harm (individuals may suffer harm due to intentional or unintentional misuse of their data), and inequities (data can be used in ways that disproportionately affect certain groups (e.g. adjusting interest rates based on race)). In summary, the USA's data privacy landscape remains complex, and there is a growing consensus that a comprehensive federal privacy law is necessary to address the challenges posed by unregulated data. These different positions on data globally are bound to affect the free use/flow of data in the Metaverse.

11.5.2 Financial Stability Concerns and Central Banks

The Bank of England, or indeed any monetary authority, would be interested in the potential of financial services within Metaverse spaces to the extent that the financial activities facilitated on the Metaverse could have a systemic implication. So far, this is not a major issue as financial services have not started operating from the Metaverse or virtual platforms. However, this could be envisaged using tokenised deposits in permissioned blockchain settings and would attract the same types of regulation that currently exist for transactions happening with real-world financial systems.

What might be problematic could be transactions occurring in permissionless blockchains and with crypto assets and the use of stablecoins as they are currently in use. These may be more susceptible to all the risks already identified and seen through the collapse of Terra Luna (in the case of algorithmic-backed stablecoins) and the problematic nature of using over-collateralised crypto-backed stablecoins, or indeed the systemic risks associated with using fiat-backed stablecoins that are backed by commercial papers and which can have a devasting effect on the value of the assets backing the commercial paper should there be a run on the stablecoin to want to convert to fiat (Salami, 2021).

This dichotomy of approaches becomes more problematic when making the case for the interoperability of financial services in the Metaverse. It would warrant resurrecting Salami's (2020) argument for a need for a holistic approach to regulating transactions involving digital assets. The difference in approaches to regulating transactions involving centralised and decentralised virtual assets service providers would inhibit interoperability. This would be unworkable in a situation where you have financial services running on decentralised Metaverses and those run by regulated and financial institutions operating in a centralised Metaverse space. Standard banking regulations such as licensing, capital, and liquidity requirements, and fit and proper tests for directors and management (corporate governance) may be non-existent in decentralised Metaverse spaces. These regulations, which have been tried and tested in traditional finance as facilitating safety and soundness in the banking system, will still apply to traditional finance banks providing services in the Metaverse. Integrating the two systems would not be permitted by regulators.

Of course, for now, without full-fledged transactions in the Metaverse, there is hardly a concern about the interoperability of financial services in centralised and decentralised Metaverses. Nonetheless, the extent to which traditional financial institutions have exposure to crypto asset firms, some of which run on decentralised networks, would be more the area of concern. However, worrying about this too may not be immediately necessary as the entire crypto market's capitalisation is still less than $3 trillion. This amount is not enough to create any significant global financial instability. Also, risks are minimised as financial institutions are not allowed to trade in crypto assets that are hugely volatile. Transactions in more decentralised ecosystems may, however, pose a problem to the extent that fiat-backed stablecoins that are backed by commercial papers (representing real-world assets) are used. Huge sales of these commercial papers in the event of a run on stablecoins for fiat can result in the drastic depreciation of the value of the issuing firm, business, and/or industry it represents. This could potentially create a crisis (as this could significantly impact the assets class) where the commercial paper backing stablecoins had to be sold in multiples to repay or maintain convertibility; the value of the asset could easily become worthless in a short space of time which can then have an impact on industry. If property developers issued commercial paper, for instance, a sale of assets to maintain one-on-one convertibility by stablecoin issuers is likely to drive down the asset value of the property developers. This would have a knock-on effect on their finances, funding, resources, and balance sheet; if many property developers had commercial papers backing stablecoins, this could destabilise financial markets and lead to a crisis.

11.5.3 Competition Concerns and the Competition and Markets Authority (CMA): Standardisation and Interoperability

Some stress the importance of the technical solutions, protocols, and services that enable interoperability to build the Metaverse ecosystem but warn that this may lock in developers and limit consumer choice and the creation of competing innovations (Madiega et al., 2022).

Building the Metaverse environment will give some companies unparalleled opportunities to monopolise digital markets. It is believed big tech companies such as Alphabet (Google), Amazon, Apple, Meta, and Microsoft are likely to drive the Metaverse architecture in defining technical standards and protocols. The risk is that these companies may attempt to shape the emerging Metaverse standards to foster their business practices, with every incentive to perpetuate current anti-competitive practices, such as self-preferencing (i.e. favouring their own products) and dark patterns (i.e. designing websites and mobile application interfaces to influence users' behaviour and decision-making).

Also, the fact that the Metaverse environment requires competitors to communicate, collaborate, and ensure that platforms are interoperable could also potentially lead to a series of anti-trust challenges, for instance concerning the sharing of sensitive information, such as pricing or agreements between competitors subject to competition law scrutiny (Madiega et al., 2022).

In the UK, anti-competitive practices that can be detrimental to smaller firms and consumers are usually regulated by the Competitions and Markets Authority (CMA), an independent department of the UK government. Its primary focus is to ensure that competition and markets work in favour of consumers. The CMA's goals include enforcement, consumer protection, and ensuring that all UK business is conducted fairly and legally to the highest standards (CMA GOV.UK).

Therefore, where a few companies exert significant control over a given market (such as in an oligopoly) these companies may control prices by colluding with each other, ultimately providing uncompetitive prices in the market. In such markets, few large firms control a large market share leading to less competition. Should these firms engage in anti-competitive behaviour, such as price-fixing, the CMA can take legal action to rectify the situation. Investigations can result in penalties for breaching firms, thereby promoting fair practice and market competition (CMA GOV.UK).

The earliest work of the CMA on the Metaverse and immersive technologies has been around horizon scanning and in this vein on May 17, 2022, the CMA (through the DRCF Digital Regulation Cooperation Forum (DRCF) organised the Metaverse Symposium in partnership with Digital Catapult. The event brought together industry experts, analysts, academics, government representatives, and regulators. The focus was on exchanging ideas and perspectives regarding the potential implications of the Metaverse and immersive technologies for people, businesses, and the wider economy (CMA BLOG competition and markets.blog.gov.uk).

The CMA's interest in the Metaverse reflects its commitment to understanding and addressing the implications of emerging technologies. As the Metaverse evolves, regulatory frameworks will need to adapt to ensure consumer protection, competition, and innovation. In summary, the CMA is actively engaging with the Metaverse and immersive technologies and recognising their potential impact on the digital landscape and the economy.

11.6 Global Coordination of Regulators: The Digital Regulatory Cooperation Forum (DRCF) Approach

As noted above, the Digital Regulatory Cooperation Forum (DRCF), which was formed in 2020, is a collaborative effort between a few UK regulators including the Competition and Markets Authority (CMA), the Information Commissioner's Office (ICO), the Office of Communications (Ofcom), and the Financial Conduct Authority (FCA). Together, these authorities handle different facets of online regulatory issues. As stated above, the potential effects of the Metaverse on data, competition, finance, and content make it imperative that regulators collaborate when interacting with and learning about these technologies. For this, the UK-based Digital Regulation Cooperation platform (DRCF) is an excellent platform. Given that the Metaverse would have a strong global character of service providers, customers, consumers, and participants from all over the world there is a need to have a replica of the DRCF albeit from a global perspective. This forum should convene all data protection, competition, financial regulatory, and content authorities internationally since these authorities across the globe are most likely to handle these different aspects of online regulatory concerns.

The global forum should aim to achieve more collaboration between these regulators, particularly considering the unique challenges associated with regulating Internet platforms. It addresses issues including privacy, safety, algorithms, competition, and data protection. However, due to the disparity of regulatory approaches on these for areas across the world, this would be no small feat. As discussed, the different approaches to regulating data protection even in advanced markets such as in Europe and the USA is an example of where a lot of work and convergence would need to be achieved for us to build a truly integrated global Metaverse. Other quite complex aspects of coordination in the space would include coordinating the approach towards decentralised organisations operating in decentralised Metaverse spaces given the significance of interoperability between centralised and decentralised Metaverse spaces.

Since the Metaverse is envisaged to be the next generation of the Internet, governments, regulators, and legislators around the world are likely to be watching it closely and would need to prepare a coordination forum for regulating this global virtual space. This coordination would benefit from existing global coordination on regulating aspects of the Metaverse such as crypto assets transactions against money laundering that could potentially occur through centralised and decentralised exchanges and also the classification and protections of property rights in Metaverse spaces. It would benefit hugely also from a globally coordinated approach towards regulating DAOs such as is envisaged through the proposed Model Law for Decentralised Autonomous Organisations (DAOs) by the Coalition of Autonomous Legal Associations.

11.6.1 Practical Approaches to Achieving Coordination

Some practical solutions that can be brought on board immediately are creating a Regulators Sandbox (of sorts) where regulators come together and learn from each other and share best practices of how not to regulate, good practices, and a programme for sandbox regulators. This would help facilitate the levelling-up of jurisdictions with weak frameworks and would necessarily call for the global coordination of regulators.

Global cooperation among regulators would also be needed for agreeing on standards for the various areas of regulatory interests (that is data privacy, competition policies, financial regulations and content). Global cooperation would also be needed for agreeing standards around the sustainability implications of the Metaverse and data would be critical for how financial services operating from the Metaverse can engage in green financing.

The actions above would require convening all key stakeholders working on or interested in the Metaverse globally (such as experts, academics, technologists, innovators, bankers, investors, regulators, policymakers, and central banks) for teasing out the right approach that facilitates innovation. This should be done but not at the expense of financial stability, data privacy, investor protection, and market integrity.

11.7 Concluding Remarks

Metaverse technologies have an increasing potential to be the next generation of the Internet, with the potential of Metaverse and virtual spaces to be the venue for all types of business transactions including financial transactions. As such, it is important that governments, regulators, and legislators around the world keep an eye on these developments and start now to plan for such a situation.

This, of course, as assessed above, would require that both the legal and regulatory framework for the operation of financial services in Metaverse spaces is in place and is robust enough to avoid major disruptions to business and ultimately local and global economies. It began with the evolution of the Metaverse; it considered the possible types of Metaverse, focusing on decentralised and centralised Metaverse spaces. With respect to legal considerations, this chapter analysed that, while the offering of financial services by registered firms in regulated Metaverse/virtual spaces will not be problematic since real-world judicial intervention can be sought to resolve disputes and regulatory intervention can be brought on board for regulated institutions, there is a great need to work through the approaches for resolving disputes involving unregulated firms operating in unregulated Metaverse spaces. This chapter clearly highlights the legal challenges of the enforcement of financial transactions in decentralised Metaverse spaces and compares it to the state of enforcement in Metaverse spaces owned and controlled by regulated institutions. Making the point that smart contracts do not prevent all disputes from happening, it highlights the challenges of private international law given the global nature of these transactions and the absence of a unified global regime, such as a Model Law, for resolving disputes involving unregulated firms/decentralised autonomous organisations (DAOs) that operate globally. It also highlights that the international working group, Coalition of Automated Legal Applications (COALA) and Model Law for Decentralised Autonomous Organisations (DAOs), are attempting to harmonise the legal framework of DAOs at the international level. If this work is given global recognition, it would certainly contribute to the development of private international rules that definitively identify the courts having jurisdiction over a case and this will undoubtedly confer legal certainty for the operation and recognition of DAOs globally.

This chapter has considered key regulatory and policy issues and how they impact financial services, and it has identified key UK regulators (ICO, CMA, FCO and the Bank of England) concerning potential issues raised by services in the Metaverse and calls for coordination of activities. This chapter concluded that global cooperation and coordination would be key to establishing robust regulation for a fully functioning, integrated Metaverse, characterised by interoperability with other virtual spaces and adhering strongly to the principles of sustainability.

References

Akour, I. A., Al-Maroof, R. S., Alfaisal, R., & Salloum, S. A. (2022). A conceptual framework for determining Metaverse adoption in higher institutions of gulf area: An empirical study using hybrid SEM-ANN approach. *Computers and Education: Artificial Intelligence, 3*, 100052. https://doi.org/10.1016/j.caeai.2022.100052

Almarzouqi, A., Aburayya, A., & Salloum, S. A. (2022). Prediction of user's intention to use Metaverse system in medical education: A hybrid SEM-ML learning approach. *IEEE Access, 10*, 43421–43434. https://doi.org/10.1109/ACCESS.2022.3169285

Arner, D. W., Barberis, J. N., & Buckley, R. P. (2017). FinTech, RegTech and the reconceptualization of financial regulation. *Northwestern Journal of International Law & Business, 37*(3), 371–414.

Baía Reis, A., & Ashmore, M. (2022). From video streaming to virtual reality worlds: An academic, reflective, and creative study on live theatre and performance in the Metaverse. *International Journal of Performance Arts and Digital Media, 18*(1), 7–28. https://doi.org/10.1080/14794713.2021.2024398

Ball, M. (2022). *The Metaverse: And how it will revolutionize everything*. Liveright.

Bank for International Settlements (BIS). (2024, February 24). The economic implications of services in the Metaverse. https://www.bis.org/publ/bppdf/bispap144.html

Belk, R., Humayun, M., & Brouard, M. (2022). Money, possessions, and ownership in the Metaverse: NFTs, cryptocurrencies, Web3 and wild markets. *Journal of Business Research, 153*, 198–205. https://doi.org/10.1016/j.jbusres.2022.08.031

Citi Global Perspectives & Solutions (Citi GPS). (2022, March 30). Metaverse and money. https://www.citigroup.com/global/insights/citigps/metaverse-and-money_20220330

City of Dreams. (2023, July 15). Banking on the Metaverse: The future of financial services. *Medium*. https://medium.com/@COD_Metaverse/banking-on-the-metaverse-ed4b579f48

Coalition of Automated Legal Applications (COALA). (2021). *The model law for DAOs*. COALA.

Competition and Markets Authority. https://www.gov.uk/government/organisations/competition-and-markets-authority/about

Debnath, A., & Barton, S. (2019, September 16). Global currency trading surges to $6.6 trillion-a-day market. *Bloomberg*.

De Filippi, P., & Wright, A. (2018). *Blockchain and the law*. Harvard University Press.

Digital Regulation Cooperation Forum, About the DRCF, Digital Regulation Cooperation Forum, https://www.drcf.org.uk/aboutus (2024).

Dionisio, J. D. N., Burns, W. G., & Gilbert, R. (2013). 3D virtual worlds and the Metaverse: Current status and future possibilities. *ACM Computing Surveys, 45*(3), 1–38. https://doi.org/10.1145/2480741.2480751

Garavand, A., & Aslani, N. (2022). Metaverse phenomenon and its impact on health: A scoping review. *Informatics in Medicine Unlocked, 32*, 101029. https://doi.org/10.1016/j.imu.2022.101029

Goodenough, O., & Burke, C. (2019, June). *dOrg launches first limited liability DAO*. Gravel & Shea. https://www.gravelshea.com/2019/06/dorg-launches-first-limited-liability-dao/?source=post_page

Information Commissioner's Office (ICO). (2024). Immersive virtual worlds. Retrieved February 6, 2024.

Kaal, W. A. (2021). Blockchain-based corporate governance. *Stanford Journal of Blockchain Law & Policy, 4*, 0–11. https://stanford-jblp.pubpub.org/pub/blockchain-corporate-governance/release/1

Kaal, W. A., & Calcaterra, C. (2017–2018). Crypto transaction dispute resolution. *The Business Lawyer, 73*(1), 109–137. https://www.jstor.org/stable/26419193.

Kappe, F., & Steurer, M. (2010). The open Metaverse currency (OMC)—A micropayment framework for open 3D virtual worlds. In *Lecture notes in business information processing: E-commerce and web technologies* (Vol. 61, pp. 97–106). Springer. https://doi.org/10.1007/978-3-642-15208-5_9

Khan, P. (n.d.). Do we need a new governance regulatory regime? *Experience Journal*. Retrieved December 1, 2022.

Kye, B., Han, N., Kim, E., Park, Y., & Jo, S. (2021). Educational applications of Metaverse: Possibilities and limitations. *Journal of Educational Evaluation for Health Professions, 18*, Article 2022. https://doi.org/10.3352/jeehp.2021.18.32

Lee, H. K., Park, S., & Lee, Y. (2022). A proposal of virtual museum Metaverse content for the MZ generation. *Digital Creativity, 33*(2), 79–95. https://doi.org/10.1080/14626268.2022.2063903

LeewayHertz. (2022, March 15). *Interoperability and the future of the Metaverse*. CoinMonks. https://medium.com/coinmonks/interoperability-and-future-of-metaverse-6ff152edc382

Madiega, T., Car, P., Niestadt, M., & Van de Pol, L. (2022, June). *Metaverse: Opportunities, risks, and policy implications*. European Parliamentary Research Service (EPRS).

Marr, B. (2022, March 21). A short history of the Metaverse. *Forbes*. https://www.forbes.com/sites/bernardmarr/2022/03/21/a-short-history-of-the-metaverse/?sh=55bb42759688

McKinsey Digital. (2022, October). *Digital twins: From one twin to the enterprise Metaverse*. McKinsey & Company. https://www.mckinsey.com/capabilities/mckinsey-digital/our-insights/digital-twins-from-one-twin-to-the-enterprise-metaverse

Nakavachara, V., & Saengchote, K. (2022). Does unit of account affect willingness to pay? Evidence from Metaverse LAND transactions. *Finance Research Letters, 49*, Article 103089. https://doi.org/10.1016/j.frl.2022.103089

Ogundare, I. (2023, February 16). Centralized and decentralized Metaverse: A complete guide. *Coinspeaker*.

Petrigna, L., & Musumeci, G. (2022). The Metaverse: A new challenge for the healthcare system: A scoping review. *Journal of Functional Morphology and Kinesiology, 7*(3), 63. https://doi.org/10.3390/jfmk7030063

Rabinovich-Einy, O., & Katsh, E. (2019). Blockchain and the inevitability of disputes: The role for online dispute resolution. *Journal of Dispute Resolution, 2*, 47. https://scholarship.law.missouri.edu/cgi/viewcontent.cgi?article=1837&context=jdr

Riva, S. (2019/2020). Decentralized autonomous organizations (DAOs) in the Swiss legal order. *Yearbook of Private International Law, 21*, 601.

Rolo, A. G. (2019). Challenges in the legal qualification of decentralized autonomous organizations (DAOs): The rise of the crypto-partnership? *Revista de Direito e Tecnologia, 1*(33), 63–72. https://papers.ssrn.com/sol3/papers.cfm?abstract_id=3417900

Salami, I. (2020). Decentralised finance: A holistic approach to regulating the crypto industry. *Journal of International Banking and Financial Law, 35*(7), 429, 496–429, 499. https://papers.ssrn.com/sol3/papers.cfm?abstract_id=3733647

Salami, I. (2021). Challenges and approaches to regulating decentralized finance. In F. Johns & G. A. Sarfaty (Eds.), *The global governance implications of blockchain*. AJIL Unbound.

Shen, B., Tan, W., Guo, J., Zhao, L., & Qin, P. (2021). How to promote user purchase in Metaverse? A systematic literature review on consumer behavior research and virtual commerce application design. *Applied Sciences, 11*(23), 1–29. https://doi.org/10.3390/app112311087

Skalidis, I., Muller, O., & Fournier, S. (2022). CardioVerse: The cardiovascular medicine in the era of Metaverse. *Trends in Cardiovascular Medicine*. https://doi.org/10.1016/j.tcm.2022.05.004

Stephenson, N. (1992). *Snow crash*. Bantam Books.

Strutt, D. (2022). A simple tool for remote real-time dance interaction in virtual spaces, or "dancing in the Metaverse". *Critical Stages, 25*, 1–18. https://www.critical-stages.org/25/a-simple-tool-for-remote-real-time-dance-interaction-in-virtual-spaces-or-dancing-in-the-metaverse/

Suh, W., & Ahn, S. (2022). Utilizing the Metaverse for learner-centered constructivist education in the post-pandemic era: An analysis of elementary school students. *Journal of Intelligence, 10*(1), 17. https://doi.org/10.3390/jintelligence10010017

Svantesson, D. J. B. (2017). *Solving the internet jurisdiction puzzle* (pp. 91–112). Oxford University Press.

Swaminathan, V. (2023, January 30). The role of data in the Metaverse. *Forbes*. https://www.forbes.com/sites/forbestechcouncil/2023/01/30/the-role-of-data-in-the-metaverse/

Team Mudrex. (2023, March 8). *Types of Metaverse explained: A comprehensive overview*. Mudrex. https://mudrex.com/learn/types-of-metaverse-explained/

Templin, S. (2019). Blocked-chain: The application of the unauthorized practice of law to smart contracts. *The Georgetown Journal of Legal Ethics, 32*(957), 961.

The Metaverse Development Company. (n.d.). LeewayHertz. Retrieved May 5, 2024, from https://www.leewayhertz.com/metaverse-development-company/

UNCITRAL. (2006). UNCITRAL Model Law on International Commercial Arbitration (1985), with amendments as adopted in 2006. United Nations Commission on International Trade Law.

Vermont Act No. 205 (S.269). (2018). An act relating to blockchain business development.

Vidal-Tomás, D. (2022). The new crypto niche: NFTs, play-to-earn, and Metaverse tokens. *Finance Research Letters, 47*, Article 102742. https://doi.org/10.1016/j.frl.2022.102742

Wharton Blockchain and Digital Asset Project, & World Economic Forum. (2021, May). DeFi beyond the hype: The emerging world of decentralized finance. Wharton, University of Pennsylvania. https://wifpr.wharton.upenn.edu/wp-content/uploads/2021/05/DeFi-Beyond-the-Hype.pdf

Wyoming Act No. 73 (SF0038), Wyoming Decentralized Autonomous Organization Supplement. (2021). https://legiscan.com/WY/text/SF0038/id/2359146

Wyoming Statutes (W.S.). (2021). Title 17, Chapter 31.

Zeuch, K. (2023, February 17). Metaverses—Decentraland, Sandbox and Axie Infinity. *Medium*.

Chapter 12
Law Enforcement and Policing Against Crime, Misconduct, Discrimination, Harassment, and Fraud in the Metaverse

Markos Rennau

Abstract As the metaverse increasingly integrates into daily life, it poses complex challenges for law enforcement, particularly regarding crimes such as fraud, discrimination, and harassment. The immersive and often anonymous nature of virtual worlds complicates the addressing of these issues compared to the physical realm. Fraud manifests through virtual property theft, identity theft, and financial scams, exploiting system vulnerabilities and the pseudonymous structure of these environments. Concurrently, discrimination based on race, gender, and appearance, reflected through avatars, reinforces real-world biases, while harassment—ranging from verbal abuse to cyberstalking—undermines psychological well-being and fosters toxic online cultures.

Preventing crime and promoting safety in the metaverse requires innovative strategies, including leveraging digital data, machine learning for monitoring, and robust collaboration with platform operators. Effective community moderation, clear guidelines, and user education initiatives are crucial for fostering inclusivity and respect among users. Additionally, the decentralised nature of the metaverse complicates jurisdiction and accountability, emphasising the need for international cooperation.

To combat these challenges, stakeholders must implement comprehensive security measures, enhance regulatory oversight, and promote digital literacy. Collaboration between law enforcement, platform providers, and users is vital for effective crime prevention and response. Training for law enforcement in virtual forensics, cybersecurity, and community engagement can navigate the unique legal and ethical complexities of the metaverse. By fostering a culture of vigilance, empathy, and transparency, stakeholders can safeguard the integrity of virtual environments, creating safer and more inclusive spaces that reflect shared values of accountability and respect for all participants.

Keywords Law enforcement · Metaverse · Policing · Discrimination · Crime · Digital literacy · Security

M. Rennau (✉)
Royal Docks School of Business and Law, University of East London, London, UK
e-mail: M.Rennau@uel.ac.uk

N. Islam, I. Salami (eds.), *Metaverse Innovation*, Applied Innovation and Technology Management, https://doi.org/10.1007/978-3-031-97080-1_12

12.1 Introduction

The metaverse, a term coined by Neal Stephenson in his 1992 novel *Snow Crash*, represents a virtual 3D shared space that blends physical and digital realities. As this immersive digital world becomes increasingly intertwined with daily life, it introduces unique challenges related to crime, misconduct, discrimination, harassment, and fraud. Law enforcement must adapt to these evolving threats to ensure user safety and security.

Traditional crimes such as theft, assault, and fraud manifest in novel ways in the metaverse. For instance, the 2007 case of a Dutch teenager arrested for stealing digital furniture in Habbo Hotel underscores the real-world value of virtual goods (BBC News, 2007). Similarly, a woman in Japan was arrested for virtually 'killing' her ex-husband's avatar in Maple Story, highlighting the significant repercussions of emotional harm in virtual spaces (The Guardian, 2008). Fraud is another major issue, with scams like the Eve Online Ponzi scheme defrauding users of significant assets (Skipper, 2015). Disruptive behaviours such as 'griefing', which involves intentionally ruining others' experiences, also pose challenges.

Discrimination and harassment are prevalent in virtual environments, mirroring real-world biases. Users can face prejudice based on their avatars' appearance, which may reflect real-world identities or chosen representations. Research indicates that avatars of colour often encounter racial slurs and other forms of abuse (Nakamura, 2002). Harassment, ranging from verbal abuse to stalking, is pervasive, with around 30% of users reporting some form of harassment (Yee, 2006). This can lead to social isolation, emotional distress, and reluctance to participate in virtual spaces. Platforms must address these issues through robust policies, advanced moderation tools, and fostering inclusive communities.

Fraud in the metaverse encompasses deceptive practices like digital asset misappropriation, financial scams, and identity theft. Hackers may steal virtual goods or real money by exploiting security vulnerabilities or manipulating user trust (Interpol, 2024). Financial scams, including Ponzi schemes and virtual currency fraud, exploit the pseudonymous nature of virtual transactions, facilitating money laundering and other illicit activities (Laue, 2011). Identity theft and impersonation are also growing concerns. Addressing these threats requires collaboration between platform operators, law enforcement, and policymakers to implement protective measures and preserve the integrity of virtual economies.

Policing in the metaverse presents distinct challenges and opportunities. The transnational and decentralised nature of virtual platforms complicates jurisdictional issues, making it difficult for law enforcement agencies to investigate and prosecute crimes across borders (Cheong, 2022). Additionally, the pseudonymous nature of virtual identities allows criminals to hide behind layers of anonymity. The rapid pace of technological innovation in the metaverse—augmented by advancements in blockchain, virtual reality, and augmented reality—adds further complexity for law enforcement (Interpol, 2024). However, virtual environments generate vast amounts of digital data that can aid in detecting criminal behaviour. Tools like machine learning and data analytics can help identify patterns and allow for proactive intervention (Europol, 2022). Furthermore, virtual communities often self-regulate through community moderation, easing the burden on law enforcement by addressing minor infractions internally. Collaborative efforts between law enforcement, platform operators, and users can help foster a safer, more secure metaverse.

In summary, as the metaverse continues to grow, it brings with it a range of criminal, social, and regulatory challenges. From theft and fraud to discrimination and harassment, virtual environments are not immune to the same societal issues that plague the physical world. Effective policing and enforcement in the metaverse require adapting existing legal frameworks, leveraging technology, fostering community partnerships, and promoting inclusivity. The metaverse offers new opportunities for connection and innovation, but ensuring its safety demands coordinated, proactive efforts from all stakeholders involved.

12.1.1 Types of Crime in the Metaverse

The metaverse, encompassing its immense and diverse virtual landscapes, is susceptible to an array of criminal activities. These illicit acts often bear a resemblance to those occurring in the tangible world but have been modified to suit the distinct attributes of the digital domain. Within this context, hacking, identity theft, and cyberstalking have emerged as some of the significant threats.

Hacking in the metaverse can involve unauthorised access to user accounts, leading to the theft of virtual property or currency. More severe cases may see hackers exploiting platform vulnerabilities, disrupting the virtual economy, or compromising user privacy and security. For instance, in 2006, 'Second Life' experienced hacking incidents where attackers generated in-game currency by exploiting system vulnerabilities (Lazarus, 2006). Such incidents can result in substantial losses of virtual property, undermine platform trust, and cause real-world financial losses for users invested in virtual goods or currency.

Identity theft in the metaverse can be particularly distressing. Malicious users may impersonate others' avatars, causing reputational damage or other harm. For example, an avatar could be used to perform actions the real user would never engage in, leading to reputational damage (Cheong, 2022). In severe cases, personal information could be stolen and misused outside the metaverse.

Cyberstalking involves tracking a user's movements across virtual spaces, leading to feelings of constant surveillance and fear (Harewell et al., 2021). This can be especially distressing in the metaverse, where users feel a strong sense of presence and immersion. Cyberstalkers may track every move, invade private virtual spaces, or harass users across platforms. Harewell et al. (2021) found that over 40% of individuals reported encountering cyberstalking in the virtual realm, highlighting the prevalence and impact of online harassment. The immersive nature of the metaverse intensifies the distress caused by cyberstalking, underscoring the need for effective anti-stalking measures and support for victims.

While the metaverse introduces thrilling opportunities for social interaction and creativity, it also brings forth fresh challenges in the realm of cybercrime. Potential offences such as hacking, identity theft, and cyberstalking await users within this virtual landscape.

12.1.2 Misconduct in the Metaverse

Misconduct in the metaverse refers to behaviours that disrupt the experience for other users or violate the norms and rules of the virtual community (Staniunas, 2023). Two common forms of misconduct are trolling and griefing (Thacker & Griffiths, 2012).

Trolling involves individuals intentionally provoking or upsetting others for amusement. Trolls may use inflammatory or off-topic messages to derail conversations or create conflict. In the metaverse, trolling can take on new dimensions due to the immersive and interactive nature of these environments. For instance, a troll might disrupt a virtual event or harass other users through their avatar, leading to significant distress for victims and creating a hostile environment that deters participation. The impact of trolling can spill over into the real world, causing emotional distress and other psychological harm (Bishop, 2013; Thacker & Griffiths, 2012).

Griefing is specific to online gaming communities, which are a significant part of the metaverse. Griefers derive pleasure from ruining the gaming experience for others by destroying virtual property, obstructing gameplay, or exploiting game mechanics in unintended ways. This can significantly disrupt the user experience and lead to users leaving the game or platform altogether. Persistent grief can cause significant emotional distress for victims (Thacker & Griffiths, 2012).

The anonymity provided by the metaverse can inspire inappropriate behaviour, as individuals may feel immune to real-world repercussions. However, this same anonymity can also foster a sense of liberation and creativity among users. While anonymity allows users to explore different identities and express themselves freely, it can also lead to harmful behaviours like trolling and griefing (Bartle, 2004).

Preventing misconduct in the metaverse is a complex challenge requiring a combination of technological solutions, community moderation, and user education. Technological solutions could include features that allow users to block or report disruptive behaviour. Community moderation involves members of the metaverse community enforcing norms and rules, while user education involves teaching users about appropriate behaviour and how to deal with misconduct. These strategies can help create a more positive and inclusive environment (Chen et al., 2014).

To sum up, misconduct such as trolling and griefing can significantly disrupt the user experience in the metaverse. As the metaverse continues to evolve, it is crucial to develop effective strategies for preventing misconduct and ensuring a positive and inclusive environment for all users.

12.1.3 Anonymity and Crime in the Metaverse

Anonymity in the metaverse is a double-edged sword (Obanoz, 2015). It can foster creativity and freedom of expression, but it can also facilitate crime and misconduct. This dichotomy presents a significant challenge for the governance and regulation of the metaverse. The cloak of anonymity can inspire individuals to engage in unlawful or disruptive actions, believing they are shielded from real-world repercussions. Users can create avatars that bear no resemblance to their real-world identities, providing a sense of impunity and leading to behaviours they would avoid in the physical world (Bartle, 2004). For instance, anonymity can facilitate trolling, where individuals intentionally provoke or upset others for amusement, and more serious crimes like cyberstalking, where a user's movements are tracked across virtual spaces, causing feelings of constant surveillance and fear. The anonymity provided by the metaverse can make it difficult for law enforcement to identify and prosecute offenders, leading to a sense of lawlessness and further encouraging criminal behaviour (Goodison et al., 2015).

Despite its potential drawbacks, anonymity also has significant benefits. It allows users to experiment with different identities and forms of self-expression. For example, a user might choose an avatar representing a different gender, race, or species, exploring aspects of identity that might be constrained in the physical world (Nakamura, 2002). Anonymity can also provide a sense of safety for users exploring sensitive topics or controversial ideas, promoting freedom of speech and diversity of thought (Bartle, 2004). Striking a balance between anonymity and accountability is a key challenge for the metaverse. One approach is to implement systems that allow for pseudonymity, where users maintain persistent identities without revealing their real-world identities, providing accountability while preserving the benefits of anonymity (Bartle, 2004). While anonymity can facilitate crime and misconduct in the metaverse, it also has significant benefits. Striking a balance between anonymity and accountability is crucial for the governance and regulation of the metaverse. Developing strategies that harness the benefits of anonymity while mitigating its potential drawbacks is essential as we continue to explore this new frontier.

12.1.4 Preventing Crime in the Metaverse

Preventing crime and misconduct in the metaverse is a complex challenge that requires a multifaceted approach involving technological solutions, community moderation, and user education.

Technological solutions play a crucial role in safeguarding the metaverse. Robust security measures, such as encryption and two-factor authentication, can protect user accounts and virtual property. Blockchain technology can secure transactions and ownership of virtual assets. Additionally, artificial intelligence (AI) and machine learning algorithms can detect and prevent malicious activities by monitoring user behaviour and identifying patterns indicative of trolling, griefing, or other misconduct (Chen et al., 2014). These algorithms can also detect phishing attempts and fraudulent transactions.

Community moderation is essential for maintaining order in the metaverse. This involves community members enforcing norms and rules and taking action against violators. Tools that allow users to report disruptive conduct and policies outlining consequences for such behaviour facilitate community moderation. Proactive moderation, where moderators actively monitor for signs of misconduct or automated systems flag potentially disruptive behaviour, can also be effective (Seering et al., 2019).

User education is a crucial component of crime prevention. Educating users about potential risks and how to protect themselves is vital. For instance, users should be taught the importance of strong, unique passwords and the dangers of sharing personal information with strangers (Furnell, 2021). Additionally, educating users about the norms and rules of the metaverse and the consequences of violating them can foster a culture of respect and responsibility, helping to prevent misconduct.

Preventing crime and misconduct in the metaverse requires a combination of technological solutions, community moderation, and user education. As the metaverse continues to evolve, these strategies will need to adapt to new challenges and opportunities.

12.1.5 Discrimination and Harassment in the Metaverse

Discrimination and harassment in the metaverse mirror societal issues found in physical spaces but take on new forms with unique impacts. Users may face discrimination based on their avatars, reflecting real-world or chosen identities, leading to an unwelcoming environment for marginalised groups. Harassment, ranging from verbal abuse to stalking, can cause severe psychological distress, deterring participation, limiting social interaction and creativity, and undermining trust in metaverse platforms. Addressing these issues requires clear community guidelines, advanced moderation tools, user education, and fostering a culture of respect and inclusivity.

Discrimination in the metaverse takes various forms, reflecting the complexities of virtual interactions and identities. Users encounter discrimination based on avatar appearance, race, gender, and other personal attributes, mirroring and extending real-world biases (Nakamura, 2002). Avatar appearance often serves as a vector for discrimination, with users facing biases based on physical attributes like body size, skin colour, or facial features (Karandikar, 2022). Racial biases persist in virtual interactions, with users of colour encountering prejudice and microaggressions (Dwivedi et al., 2022). Gender discrimination also permeates virtual spaces, with women facing sexism and harassment, and transgender and non-binary users encountering discrimination and erasure. Additionally, users with disabilities may face accessibility barriers, and ageism, socioeconomic discrimination, and cultural biases further influence experiences and interactions.

Addressing discrimination requires concerted efforts from platform operators, policymakers, and users (Bucher & Helmond, 2018). Implementing inclusive design principles, such as customisable avatars and diverse representation, promotes diversity and empowerment. Community moderation and anti-discrimination policies help deter discriminatory conduct and create safer environments. Fostering awareness, empathy, and allyship can challenge discriminatory norms and advocate for inclusive virtual communities.

Harassment in the metaverse encompasses behaviours that infringe upon users' rights and dignity, creating hostile environments (Brodsky, 2022). Verbal abuse, including derogatory remarks and hate speech, is prevalent (Fox & Tang, 2014). Cyberbullying, characterised by repeated harassment through digital communication, inflicts emotional harm and psychological distress. Sexual harassment, particularly affecting women and marginalised groups, includes unwanted advances and sexualised commentary (IEEE & Council of Europe, 2023). Stalking behaviours, such as persistent surveillance and intrusive communications, violate users' privacy and autonomy (Citron, 2014). Collective forms of harassment, like trolling, griefing, and raiding, disrupt virtual communities and foster toxicity (Massanari, 2017).

Addressing harassment requires proactive measures that promote respect, empathy, and accountability (Nakamura, 2002). Community moderation, supplemented by clear and enforceable platform policies, plays a crucial role in deterring and responding to harassment. Empowering users to report incidents and providing robust mechanisms for accountability can create safer and more inclusive environments (Bucher & Helmond, 2018).

User education initiatives, focused on promoting digital literacy and empathy, are essential for cultivating respectful and responsible online behaviours (Livingstone, 2008). By raising awareness about the impacts of harassment and fostering bystander intervention skills, users can contribute to creating positive and supportive virtual communities. Additionally, partnerships between platform operators, civil society organisations, and law enforcement agencies are vital for coordinating responses and implementing best practices in metaverse governance (Interpol, 2024).

Harassment in the metaverse poses significant challenges that require collaborative efforts from stakeholders across sectors (Wall & Williams, 2013). By understanding the dynamics of online harassment and its impact on users' safety and well-being, policymakers, platform operators, and users can work together to develop effective strategies for preventing and combating harassment in virtual environments. Through ongoing research, innovation, and education, the metaverse can realise its full potential as a vibrant and empowering space for diverse communities.

Discrimination and harassment in the metaverse reflect and perpetuate real-world biases and inequalities. By addressing these issues through inclusive design, community moderation, and user education, stakeholders can create safer and more empowering virtual environments that celebrate the richness of human identity and experience.

12.1.6 *Impact of Discrimination and Harassment in the Metaverse*

Discrimination and harassment in the metaverse have profound psychological and social impacts on users, influencing their well-being and sense of belonging within virtual communities (Brodsky, 2022; IEEE & Council of Europe, 2023). From heightened stress and anxiety to social withdrawal and diminished self-esteem, victims experience a range of negative outcomes that mirror and extend beyond real-world experiences (Citron, 2014; Interpol, 2024). Understanding these impacts is crucial for fostering inclusive and supportive virtual environments.

Discrimination and harassment can have detrimental effects on users' mental health and emotional well-being (Fox & Tang, 2014). Victims may experience heightened levels of stress, anxiety, and depression in response to repeated acts of discrimination or harassment. The cumulative impact of microaggressions and hostile interactions can erode users' self-esteem and confidence, undermining their sense of identity and agency within virtual spaces. Virtual environments may exacerbate the psychological toll through mechanisms such as anonymity and social comparison (Nakamura, 2002). Perpetrators may exploit the perceived anonymity of online interactions to engage in more aggressive and harmful behaviours, intensifying the emotional distress experienced by victims. Additionally, the constant exposure to idealised representations of identity and beauty in virtual spaces may heighten users' feelings of inadequacy and self-doubt, amplifying the impact of discriminatory practices and norms.

Discrimination and harassment also have profound social consequences, affecting users' relationships and interactions within virtual communities. Victims may withdraw from social activities or disengage from virtual platforms altogether to avoid further exposure to harmful behaviours. The fear of judgement or reprisal may inhibit users from expressing their authentic selves and participating fully in virtual spaces, limiting their opportunities for social connection and support.

Furthermore, discrimination and harassment perpetuate exclusionary dynamics and power imbalances within virtual communities, reinforcing social hierarchies and marginalising vulnerable groups (Massanari, 2017). Individuals subjected to discriminatory or harassing behaviours may encounter a sense of estrangement or exclusion from their contemporaries, intensifying feelings of solitude and desolation. The normalisation of discriminatory practices and attitudes within virtual spaces may discourage bystander intervention and collective action, perpetuating a culture of silence and complicity.

Addressing the psychological and social impacts of discrimination and harassment requires multifaceted approaches that prioritise user safety, well-being, and empowerment (Bucher & Helmond, 2018). Providing accessible mental health resources and support services can help victims cope with the emotional toll of discriminatory experiences and seek assistance when needed. Fostering a culture of empathy, respect, and accountability through community moderation and user education initiatives can promote positive social norms and mitigate the prevalence of discriminatory behaviours.

Additionally, promoting diversity and representation within virtual environments can enhance users' sense of belonging and validation (Rueda & Lara, 2020), counteracting the negative effects of discrimination and harassment. By amplifying marginalised voices and perspectives, platforms can create more inclusive and equitable spaces that celebrate the richness of human diversity and promote mutual understanding and solidarity. Discrimination and harassment in the metaverse have significant psychological and social impacts on users, affecting their mental health, relationships, and sense of belonging within virtual communities. By addressing these impacts through proactive measures that prioritise user safety, well-being, and empowerment, stakeholders can create safer, more inclusive, and supportive virtual environments that reflect the values of respect, empathy, and diversity.

12.1.7 Preventing Discrimination and Harassment in the Metaverse

Preventing discrimination and harassment in the metaverse requires a multifaceted approach that encompasses proactive measures to promote respectful and inclusive virtual communities (Massanari, 2017). By addressing systemic vulnerabilities and fostering a culture of empathy, respect, and accountability, stakeholders can create safer and more empowering virtual environments that prioritise user safety and well-being.

Community moderation plays a crucial role in deterring and responding to discriminatory behaviours and harassment in the metaverse (Bucher & Helmond, 2018). Empowering users to report incidents of discrimination or harassment and providing robust mechanisms for enforcement and accountability can help maintain the integrity of virtual spaces. Moreover, fostering a sense of collective responsibility and solidarity within virtual communities encourages bystander intervention and collective action against harmful behaviours. Moderators, equipped with clear guidelines and training on diversity and inclusion, can effectively identify and address discriminatory practices and attitudes within virtual environments (Massanari, 2017). By actively monitoring user interactions and intervening in instances of harassment or abuse, moderators can create safer and more welcoming spaces for all participants. Additionally, establishing transparent and accessible channels for feedback and dispute resolution promotes trust and accountability in community moderation processes.

User education initiatives are essential for promoting digital literacy and empowering users to recognise and address discrimination and harassment in the metaverse. Providing resources and training on respectful online behaviour, diversity awareness, and bystander intervention equips users with the knowledge and skills to navigate virtual spaces responsibly. Moreover, raising awareness about the impacts of discrimination and harassment and promoting empathy and allyship fosters a culture of mutual respect and support within virtual communities (Onu et al., 2023). Educational campaigns, workshops, and interactive tutorials can engage users in meaningful dialogue and reflection on issues of diversity, equity, and inclusion (Bucher & Helmond, 2018). By facilitating open and honest discussions about the complexities of identity and power dynamics in virtual environments, these initiatives promote critical thinking and self-reflection among users. Furthermore, integrating digital citizenship education into school curricula and youth programmes cultivates responsible and ethical online behaviours from an early age, laying the foundation for a more inclusive and equitable digital future.

Platform policies play a pivotal role in setting clear expectations and standards for user conduct and fostering a safe and respectful online environment (Marinett, 2021). Implementing comprehensive anti-discrimination and anti-harassment policies, supplemented by robust enforcement mechanisms and consequences for violations, sends a strong message that discriminatory behaviours will not be tolerated. Besides, transparent and accessible reporting procedures empower users to seek assistance and recourse in cases of discrimination or harassment, promoting accountability and trust in platform governance. Platforms should also prioritise inclusive design principles that mitigate the risk of discrimination and harassment and promote diversity and representation (Massanari, 2017). Providing customisable avatar options, diverse content moderation teams, and inclusive language and imagery guidelines ensures that virtual environments reflect the richness of human diversity and accommodate users from diverse backgrounds and identities. Therefore, conducting regular audits and assessments of platform policies and practices helps identify and address systemic biases and gaps in enforcement. In conclusion, preventing discrimination and harassment in the metaverse requires collaborative efforts from stakeholders across sectors. By implementing proactive strategies such as community moderation, user education, and platform policies, stakeholders can create safer, more inclusive, and empowering virtual environments that reflect the values of respect, empathy, and diversity.

12.2 Fraud in the Metaverse

Fraud in the metaverse involves deceptive practices within virtual environments, exploiting the unique aspects of digital platforms. As virtual worlds grow, so do opportunities for fraud, including virtual property theft and financial scams. Understanding metaverse fraud is crucial for identifying threats and protecting users. Common fraud types include digital asset misappropriation, financial scams, and identity theft. Regulatory challenges arise due to the decentralised nature of virtual environments, making it difficult for traditional legal frameworks to address these issues. Collaborative efforts from various stakeholders are needed to combat fraud and maintain the integrity of virtual economies.

12.2.1 Types of Fraud in the Metaverse

Fraud in the metaverse encompasses a variety of deceptive practices and schemes that exploit the unique features of virtual environments, posing significant risks to users' financial assets and personal information. Understanding the different types of fraud, such as scams, phishing, virtual property theft, and currency exchange fraud, is essential for users and platform operators to recognise emerging threats and implement effective preventive measures.

Scams are a prevalent form of fraud in the metaverse, involving deceptive schemes designed to trick users into providing money, virtual assets, or personal information (Interpol, 2024). Common examples include Ponzi schemes, where perpetrators promise high returns on investments but use funds from new investors to pay returns to earlier investors, creating a cycle of deception and financial losses. Other scams may involve fake giveaways, prize draws, or contests, where users are enticed to participate by false promises of rewards or benefits.

Phishing is a tactic used by fraudsters to trick users into divulging sensitive information, such as login credentials or financial data, by posing as legitimate entities or organisations (Leukfeldt, 2014). In the metaverse, phishing attacks may involve fake login pages or communication channels that mimic trusted platforms or services, luring users into providing their account credentials or personal information. Perpetrators may then use this information to gain unauthorised access to users' accounts, steal virtual assets, or engage in identity theft.

Virtual property theft is a significant threat in the metaverse, where users' digital assets, such as virtual currencies, in-game items, and virtual real estate, are valuable targets for fraudsters. Perpetrators may employ hacking techniques, social engineering, or account takeovers to gain unauthorised access to users' accounts or virtual possessions, subsequently transferring or selling stolen assets for profit. The pseudonymous nature of virtual transactions and the lack of centralised oversight make it challenging to recover stolen assets or hold perpetrators accountable (Interpol, 2024; IEEE & Council of Europe, 2023; Laue, 2011).

Currency exchange frauds involve fraudulent activities related to virtual currency exchanges and trading platforms within the metaverse (Ambolis, 2023). Perpetrators may create fake exchanges or trading platforms that promise favourable exchange rates or trading conditions to attract users' deposits or investments. However, once users deposit their funds or virtual assets, the perpetrators may abscond with the funds or manipulate trading conditions to their advantage, resulting in financial losses for users. In conclusion, the metaverse presents a fertile ground for various types of fraud, ranging from scams and phishing to virtual property theft and identity theft. Users and platform operators must remain vigilant and implement robust security measures to protect against these threats. By raising awareness, enhancing cybersecurity measures, and promoting responsible digital practices, stakeholders can mitigate the risks of fraud in the metaverse and safeguard the integrity of virtual economies.

12.2.2 Impact of Fraud in the Metaverse

The potential impact of fraud in the metaverse extends beyond individual users to affect the integrity of virtual economies and the overall trust and stability of virtual communities. Understanding the consequences, such as financial losses, erosion of trust, damage to reputation, psychological impact, and disruption of virtual economies, is crucial for users, platform operators, and policymakers to develop effective mitigation strategies and safeguard the sustainability of virtual environments.

One of the most immediate and tangible impacts of fraud in the metaverse is financial losses incurred by users who fall victim to fraudulent schemes (Interpol, 2024; IEEE & Council of Europe, 2023). Whether through scams, virtual property theft, or currency exchange frauds, users may suffer significant monetary losses, undermining their trust and confidence in virtual platforms and transactions. Moreover, the anonymous nature of virtual transactions combined with insufficient regulatory oversight makes it difficult to retrieve stolen funds or hold offenders responsible, thereby increasing the financial strain on victims.

Fraud erodes trust and confidence in virtual communities, undermining the integrity of virtual economies and the credibility of platform operators. Users who fall victim to fraud may become disillusioned with virtual platforms and transactions, leading to decreased engagement and participation. Furthermore, the perception of insecurity and vulnerability may deter new users from joining virtual communities or investing in virtual assets, hindering the growth and development of the metaverse ecosystem (Vaz & Brown, 2018; Dilla et al., 2013).

Fraud can also damage the reputation and credibility of virtual platforms and service providers, tarnishing their brand image and market standing. Incidents of fraud may attract negative publicity and media attention, raising concerns among users and stakeholders about the reliability and safety of virtual environments. Platform operators may face legal and regulatory scrutiny for failing to prevent fraudulent activities or protect users from harm, leading to reputational damage and financial liabilities (Norris et al., 2019).

The psychological impact of fraud in the metaverse can be profound, causing emotional distress, anxiety, and distrust among affected users. Victims of fraud may experience feelings of betrayal, shame, and helplessness, leading to stress-related health issues and impaired well-being. Additionally, the sense of insecurity and vulnerability resulting from fraudulent experiences may deter users from engaging in virtual interactions or investing in virtual assets, limiting their opportunities for social and economic participation within virtual communities (Smaili & de Rancourt-Raymond, 2024; Ud Din & Almogren, 2023).

Fraud disrupts the stability and functionality of virtual economies, undermining the efficiency and fairness of transactions within virtual environments. Instances of virtual property theft, currency exchange frauds, or market manipulation can distort supply and demand dynamics, leading to price volatility and market distortions. Likewise, the erosion of trust and confidence among users may reduce liquidity and trading activity in virtual markets, hindering the growth and development of virtual economies (Trozze et al., 2022). In conclusion, the impact of fraud in the metaverse is multifaceted and far-reaching, affecting users, platform operators, and the overall stability of virtual communities and economies. By understanding the potential consequences of fraud and implementing robust security measures, stakeholders can mitigate the risks and safeguard the integrity and sustainability of virtual environments.

12.2.3 Preventing Fraud in the Metaverse

Preventing fraud in the metaverse requires a comprehensive approach that combines robust security measures, user education, regulatory oversight, transaction monitoring and fraud detection, and collaboration and information sharing to mitigate risks and safeguard the integrity of virtual environments. By implementing proactive strategies and fostering a culture of awareness and vigilance among users and stakeholders, virtual communities can reduce the prevalence and impact of fraudulent activities.

Implementing robust security measures is essential for protecting users' financial assets and personal information from fraudulent activities in the metaverse. Platform operators should invest in state-of-the-art encryption technologies, multi-factor authentication, and intrusion detection systems to secure users' accounts and transactions. Furthermore, regular security audits and vulnerability assessments can help identify and address potential weaknesses in platform infrastructure and software, reducing the risk of data breaches and unauthorised access (Sharma & Zamfiroiu, 2023).

User education is crucial in preventing fraud by empowering users to recognise and respond to potential threats and vulnerabilities in the metaverse. Providing resources and training on cybersecurity best practices, such as password hygiene, phishing awareness, and safe browsing habits, equips users with the knowledge and skills to protect themselves from fraudulent activities. Raising awareness about the different types of fraud prevalent in the metaverse and the consequences of falling victim to scams can help users make informed decisions and exercise caution in their online interactions (Onu et al., 2023; Sirvermez & Baltaci, 2023).

Regulatory oversight is essential for creating a regulatory framework that promotes transparency, accountability, and consumer protection in the metaverse. Policymakers should collaborate with industry stakeholders to develop and enforce regulations and standards for virtual transactions, virtual asset exchanges, and platform governance. Besides, implementing robust enforcement mechanisms and penalties for non-compliance can deter fraudulent activities and hold perpetrators accountable for their actions (Gucluturk, 2023; Yin et al., 2023).

Implementing transaction monitoring and fraud detection systems can help identify and mitigate fraudulent activities in real time, reducing the risk of financial losses and reputational damage for users and platform operators. Machine learning algorithms and artificial intelligence technologies can analyse user behaviour and transaction patterns to identify anomalies and suspicious activities, triggering alerts and interventions as necessary. In addition, incorporating blockchain technology into virtual transactions can enhance transparency and traceability, reducing the risk of fraud and manipulation (Smaili & de Rancourt-Raymond, 2024).

Collaboration and information sharing among stakeholders are essential for combating fraud in the metaverse effectively. Platform operators, financial institutions, law enforcement agencies, and regulatory bodies should collaborate to exchange information and best practices, identify emerging threats, and coordinate responses to fraudulent activities. Establishing partnerships with cybersecurity firms and industry associations can provide access to specialised expertise and resources for detecting and preventing fraud (Uzun, 2023). In conclusion, preventing fraud in the metaverse requires a concerted effort from users, platform operators, policymakers, and regulators to implement robust security measures, promote user education, and enhance regulatory oversight. By prioritising transparency, accountability, and consumer protection, stakeholders can create safer and more resilient virtual environments that foster trust, innovation, and economic growth.

12.3 Law Enforcement in the Metaverse

Law enforcement in the metaverse faces unique challenges and opportunities due to the convergence of virtual environments with real-world legal frameworks. Key challenges include jurisdictional issues, the pseudonymous nature of virtual identities, and the rapid pace of technological innovation. Despite these challenges, opportunities exist for leveraging technology and collaboration to enhance crime prevention and investigation. Virtual environments generate vast amounts of data that can be analysed to detect criminal behaviour, and virtual communities often self-regulate, reducing the burden on law enforcement. Effective law enforcement in the metaverse requires addressing jurisdictional issues, staying updated on technological advancements, and collaborating with virtual platforms and community stakeholders.

12.3.1 Digital Forensics Tools in the Metaverse

Digital forensics tools play a critical role in investigating crimes in the metaverse, enabling law enforcement agencies to collect, analyse, and preserve digital evidence from virtual environments. As virtual worlds continue to evolve and expand, digital forensics practitioners must adapt their methodologies and techniques to address the unique challenges posed by virtual platforms and technologies. Digital forensics tools are instrumental in uncovering evidence of criminal activities within virtual environments, ranging from cybercrimes and fraud to harassment and exploitation (Casey, 2011). These tools enable investigators to acquire data from virtual platforms, storage devices, and network communications, reconstruct digital events, and identify perpetrators. Digital forensics techniques, such as data carving, file analysis, and network packet inspection, can reveal hidden artefacts and traces of criminal conduct, providing valuable insights for criminal investigations (Lovanshi & Bansal, 2019).

Investigating crimes in the metaverse poses several challenges for digital forensics practitioners, including jurisdictional issues, data privacy concerns, and the complexity of virtual environments (Simon & Choo, 2014). Virtual platforms operate across multiple jurisdictions, making it difficult to establish legal authority and obtain access to digital evidence stored on servers located in different countries. Likewise, the pseudonymous nature of virtual identities and transactions complicates the process of identifying and attributing criminal activities to specific individuals, who may exploit anonymity to evade detection and accountability.

Another challenge is the dynamic and ephemeral nature of digital evidence within virtual environments, where data can be easily altered, deleted, or obscured (Casey, 2011). Virtual platforms generate vast amounts of data, including user interactions, transactions, and communications, which must be collected and analysed in a timely manner to preserve evidentiary integrity. The rapid pace of technological innovation and adaptation within the metaverse requires digital forensics practitioners to stay abreast of emerging tools and techniques for investigating virtual crimes effectively.

Digital forensics tools employ a variety of techniques and methodologies to overcome the challenges of investigating crimes in the metaverse. These tools enable investigators to acquire data from virtual platforms and devices, such as computers, smartphones, and gaming consoles, using forensic imaging, data recovery, and network forensics techniques. Digital forensics practitioners can leverage specialised software tools, such as virtual machine analysis tools, memory forensics frameworks, and blockchain analysis platforms, to extract and analyse digital evidence from virtual environments (Simon & Choo, 2014). In conclusion, digital forensics tools play a vital role in investigating crimes in the metaverse, enabling law enforcement agencies to uncover evidence of criminal activities and hold perpetrators accountable. By addressing the unique challenges posed by virtual platforms and technologies, digital forensics practitioners can leverage advanced tools and techniques to collect, analyse, and preserve digital evidence, ensuring the integrity and admissibility of evidence in criminal proceedings.

12.3.2 Training for Law Enforcement in the Metaverse

Training law enforcement officers to operate effectively in the metaverse is essential to address the unique challenges posed by virtual environments and emerging technologies. As virtual worlds continue to evolve and expand, law enforcement agencies must equip their personnel with the knowledge, skills, and resources to navigate virtual platforms, investigate virtual crimes, and protect public safety within virtual communities. This includes understanding virtual environments, developing digital forensics skills, enhancing cybersecurity awareness, engaging with virtual communities, and considering legal and ethical implications.

Training programmes for law enforcement officers should provide comprehensive education on virtual environments, including their structure, features, and dynamics. Officers must understand the different types of virtual platforms, such as social media networks, online gaming platforms, and virtual reality environments, and their respective user demographics, cultures, and norms. Officers should be familiar with the legal and regulatory frameworks governing virtual activities, such as intellectual property laws, data privacy regulations, and platform policies (Europol, 2022).

Digital forensics skills are essential for law enforcement officers to investigate crimes in the metaverse and collect admissible evidence for criminal proceedings (Simon & Choo, 2014). Training programmes should provide officers with hands-on experience in digital evidence collection, preservation, and analysis, covering techniques and tools for acquiring data from virtual platforms, storage devices, and network communications. Additionally, officers should be trained to recognise and respond to emerging threats and vulnerabilities in virtual environments, such as cybercrimes, fraud, and exploitation (Qin et al., 2022; Interpol, 2024; Seo et al., 2023).

Cybersecurity awareness is crucial for law enforcement officers to protect themselves and others from cyber threats in the metaverse. Training programmes should include modules on cybersecurity best practices, such as password hygiene, phishing awareness, and safe browsing habits, to mitigate the risk of data breaches, account compromises, and other security incidents. In the case of cybersecurity preparedness, officers should receive training to detect and address incidents ranging from malware infections to denial-of-service attacks and data breaches. This training is crucial to safeguard public safety and maintain operational resilience. By equipping officers with the skills to swiftly respond to cyber threats, we enhance our collective ability to protect critical systems and data (Interpol, 2024; Europol, 2022; Qin et al., 2022).

Community engagement is essential for building trust and cooperation between law enforcement agencies and virtual communities. Training programmes should emphasise the importance of establishing positive relationships with virtual platform operators, community leaders, and users to foster a culture of collaboration and accountability. In the context of community policing, officers should receive training to address community concerns and grievances, including issues like harassment, discrimination, and exploitation. This training should equip them with effective communication skills, conflict-resolution techniques, and strategies for fostering positive relationships with the community (Hennig-Thurau et al., 2023).

Law enforcement officers must navigate complex legal and ethical considerations when operating in the metaverse. Training programmes should provide officers with a solid understanding of relevant laws, regulations, and judicial precedents governing virtual activities, such as jurisdictional issues, data privacy rights, and free speech protections. In the realm of virtual communities, officers should be trained to uphold ethical standards and professional conduct, respecting users' rights and dignity while enforcing the law. In conclusion, training law enforcement officers to operate effectively in the metaverse is crucial to address the unique challenges and opportunities presented by virtual environments. By providing officers with comprehensive education, digital forensics skills, cybersecurity awareness, community engagement strategies, and legal and ethical guidance, law enforcement agencies can enhance their capabilities to protect public safety and uphold the rule of law within virtual communities (Interpol, 2024, Europol, 2022).

12.3.3 Collaboration with Metaverse Platforms

Collaboration between law enforcement agencies and metaverse platform providers is crucial for addressing emerging threats, enhancing public safety, and fostering trust within virtual communities. As virtual environments continue to evolve and expand, law enforcement agencies must establish partnerships with platform operators to share information, coordinate responses, and develop proactive strategies for combating crime and misconduct in the metaverse. This includes data sharing and analysis, platform governance and policy development, incident response and crisis management, user education and awareness, and ensuring regulatory compliance and enforcement.

Partnership with metaverse platform providers enables law enforcement agencies to access valuable data and insights for investigating crimes and protecting public safety. Platform operators collect vast amounts of data on user interactions, transactions, and content moderation activities, which can provide valuable intelligence for identifying emerging threats and trends. By sharing data with law enforcement agencies, platform providers can support criminal investigations, facilitate evidence collection, and enhance situational awareness within virtual environments (Hennig-Thurau et al., 2023).

Engagement with metaverse platform providers enables law enforcement agencies to participate in governance and policy development initiatives. Platform operators frequently establish community standards, content moderation policies, and enforcement mechanisms to regulate user behaviour and uphold platform integrity. By collaborating with law enforcement agencies, platform providers can gain insights into legal and regulatory requirements, integrate law enforcement perspectives into policy decisions, and enhance the efficacy of platform governance mechanisms (Marinett, 2021).

Partnering with metaverse platform providers enables law enforcement agencies to coordinate responses to critical incidents and emergencies within virtual environments. In the event of cybercrimes, terrorist threats, or public safety incidents, platform operators play a crucial role in disseminating information, implementing protective measures, and facilitating communication between users and law enforcement authorities. By establishing communication channels and protocols for incident response and crisis management, law enforcement agencies and platform providers can ensure swift and effective responses to emerging threats (Uzun, 2023; Yang, 2023).

Engaging with metaverse platform providers allows law enforcement agencies to engage with users and raise awareness about online safety, cybersecurity, and legal rights and responsibilities. Platform operators often provide educational resources, training programmes, and awareness campaigns to empower users to protect themselves from cyber threats, harassment, and exploitation. Through strategic collaboration with law enforcement agencies, platform providers can amplify the reach and impact of these initiatives, foster responsible online behaviour, and cultivate trust and confidence within virtual communities. By aligning efforts, sharing resources, and leveraging technology, this partnership can create a safer digital environment for all users (Onu et al., 2023; Sirvermez, & Baltaci, 2023).

Collaboration with metaverse platform providers facilitates regulatory compliance and enforcement efforts by law enforcement agencies. Platform operators are subject to legal and regulatory obligations, such as data privacy laws, content moderation requirements, and law enforcement cooperation mandates. By working closely with law enforcement agencies, platform providers can ensure compliance with regulatory requirements, respond promptly to law enforcement requests for assistance, and support investigations and enforcement actions as needed (Gucluturk, 2023; Yin et al., 2023). In conclusion, collaboration between law enforcement agencies and metaverse platform providers is essential for addressing emerging challenges and opportunities within virtual environments. By sharing data and insights, contributing to platform governance, coordinating incident responses, educating users, and ensuring regulatory compliance, law enforcement agencies and platform operators can enhance public safety, protect user rights, and promote trust and confidence within virtual communities.

12.4 Legal Frameworks in the Metaverse

Clear legal frameworks are essential to define crimes, establish user rights and responsibilities, and ensure accountability within the metaverse. As virtual environments continue to evolve and expand, policymakers and regulators must develop comprehensive legal frameworks that address the unique challenges and opportunities presented by virtual platforms and technologies. This includes defining crimes in the metaverse, protecting user rights and responsibilities, establishing jurisdictional authority, enforcing intellectual property rights, and promoting ethical conduct and corporate responsibility.

Legal frameworks in the metaverse must clearly define criminal offences and establish penalties for violations. Crimes in virtual environments can range from cybercrimes and virtual property theft to harassment and exploitation. By delineating specific criminal behaviours and their consequences, legal frameworks provide guidance for law enforcement agencies, platform operators, and users to identify and address illicit activities within virtual communities (Seo et al., 2023; Qin et al., 2022).

Legal frameworks should protect user rights and establish clear responsibilities for platform operators and users. Users in the metaverse are entitled to fundamental rights, such as freedom of expression, privacy, and property ownership. Platform operators have a duty to ensure the safety, security, and integrity of virtual environments, while users have a responsibility to comply with community standards, respect others' rights, and refrain from engaging in criminal activities.

Legal frameworks must clarify jurisdictional authority and regulatory oversight in the metaverse. Virtual platforms operate across multiple jurisdictions, making it challenging to determine which laws and regulations apply to virtual activities. Policymakers and regulators must establish clear jurisdictional boundaries and mechanisms for resolving conflicts of law, ensuring that law enforcement agencies have the authority to investigate and prosecute crimes that occur within virtual environments (Krishnaa, 2023).

Legal frameworks should enforce intellectual property rights and address issues of copyright infringement and piracy in the metaverse. Virtual platforms often host user-generated content, virtual goods, and digital assets that may be subject to intellectual property laws. Platform operators must implement measures to prevent unauthorised copying, distribution, and use of copyrighted materials, while users must respect the intellectual property rights of others and comply with licensing agreements and terms of use (Kalyvaki, 2023).

Legal frameworks should promote ethical conduct and corporate responsibility among platform operators and users. Platform operators have a duty to implement transparent and accountable governance mechanisms, enforce community standards and content moderation policies, and protect users from harm. In addition, users should be encouraged to uphold ethical standards, exercise digital citizenship, and contribute positively to virtual communities (Rashedul, 2023). In conclusion, clear legal frameworks are essential to define crimes, establish user rights and responsibilities, and ensure accountability within the metaverse. By delineating specific criminal behaviours, protecting user rights, clarifying jurisdictional authority, enforcing intellectual property rights, and promoting ethical conduct, legal frameworks provide the foundation for a safe, secure, and equitable virtual environment.

12.5 Conclusion

In summary, the metaverse represents a transformative evolution of our digital interactions, introducing a complex array of challenges that reflect and intensify existing societal issues, particularly regarding crime, discrimination, harassment, and fraud. As users engage in these immersive environments, they encounter not only opportunities for creativity and connection but also significant threats that mirror those found in the physical world. The unique dynamics of the metaverse necessitate a rethinking of law enforcement and policing strategies, requiring innovative, multi-faceted approaches that involve collaboration among various stakeholders, including platform operators, policymakers, and users.

A critical takeaway is the urgent need for robust legal frameworks tailored to the metaverse's distinct environment. Traditional laws may be insufficient, as the pseudonymous nature of many virtual identities complicates offender identification and prosecution. This potential sense of lawlessness can embolden criminals, highlighting the necessity for international cooperation to establish comprehensive guidelines that govern these virtual spaces effectively. Without such frameworks, the risks of misconduct and fraud will only escalate, threatening the overall integrity of virtual communities.

Technological solutions are essential in combating crime within the metaverse. Advances in artificial intelligence, machine learning, and blockchain technology can enhance security measures, protect user identities, and facilitate the detection of fraudulent activities. For instance, AI algorithms can identify harmful behaviour patterns, allowing for proactive interventions before issues escalate. Implementing secure transaction methods and robust account protection mechanisms is vital for safeguarding users against theft and fraud, fostering a safer virtual environment where creativity and connection can flourish.

Community moderation plays a pivotal role in maintaining respect and inclusivity. By empowering users to report incidents and ensuring moderators are well-equipped with skills and guidelines to address misconduct, platforms can cultivate a sense of collective responsibility. This proactive approach not only deters harmful behaviour but also nurtures solidarity among users, fostering an environment of mutual respect. User education is equally vital; initiatives promoting digital literacy and empathy empower users to recognise and challenge discriminatory practices, ensuring a more responsible and engaged user base.

Discrimination and harassment remain critical issues that must be addressed through clear anti-discrimination and anti-harassment policies. Such policies should be comprehensive and enforced transparently, reinforcing the message that harmful behaviours are unacceptable. Furthermore, platforms should prioritise inclusive design principles, ensuring that virtual environments reflect the rich diversity of human identity. This includes offering customisable avatar options and promoting diverse representation in content and moderation teams.

Finally, addressing fraud in the metaverse requires a collaborative effort from all stakeholders. The varied nature of fraudulent activities, from scams to virtual property theft, poses significant challenges to users and platform operators alike. Understanding these risks is essential for creating a safe digital environment. Effective regulatory oversight should promote transparency and accountability while adapting to the unique challenges posed by decentralisation. Law enforcement agencies must be equipped with digital forensics training to navigate the complexities of virtual environments, enhancing their ability to investigate crimes and protect users.

Ultimately, the path forward in the metaverse will necessitate adaptability, vigilance, and a commitment to user safety and well-being. By embracing technological solutions, fostering community engagement, and prioritising education, stakeholders can work together to create a vibrant, inclusive, and secure metaverse. This concerted effort will ensure that as the metaverse continues to evolve, it remains a space where creativity thrives without compromising the safety and dignity of its users. Through ongoing collaboration and proactive measures, we can build a metaverse that embodies the principles of equality, respect, and shared human dignity, unlocking its full potential as a dynamic and supportive digital frontier.

References

Ambolis, D. (2023) *How to protect yourself from fraud in metaverse: Types of frauds in metaverse.* Accessed February 11, 2024, from How To Protect Yourself From Fraud In Metaverse: Types Of Frauds In Metaverse (blockchainmagazine.net)

Bartle, R. (2004). *Designing virtual worlds.* [PDF]. Accessed February 11, 2024, from DesigningVirtualWorlds.pdf

BBC News. (2007). *Billions stolen in online robbery.* Accessed February 15, 2024, from BBC NEWS | Technology | Billions stolen in online robbery.

Bishop, J. (2013). The effect of de-individuation of the Internet Troller on Criminal Procedure implementation: An interview with a Hater. *International Journal of Cyber Criminology, 7*(1), 28–48.

Brodsky, S. (2022). *Harassment will continue in the metaverse, experts say. Virtual worlds can still mean real problems.* Accessed February 14, 2024, from Harassment Will Continue in the Metaverse, Experts Say (lifewire.com)

Bucher, T., & Helmond, A. (2018). The affordances of social media platforms. In J. Burgess, A. Marwick, & T. Poell (Eds.), *The SAGE handbook of social media* (pp. 233–253). SAGE Publications.

Casey, E. (2011). *Digital evidence and computer crime: Forensic science, computers, and the internet.* Academic Press.

Chen, J., Hsieh, G., Mahmud, J. & Nichols, J. (2014). *Understanding individuals' personal values from social media word use.* In Proceedings of the 2014 ACM Conference on Supporting Groupwork (pp. 1–55). Accessed February 15, 2024, from (99+) Understanding individuals' personal values from social media word use | Gary Hsieh - Academia.edu.pdf

Cheong, B. C. (2022). Avatars in the metaverse: Potential legal issues and remedies. *International Cybersecurity Law Review, 3*, 467–494. https://doi.org/10.1365/s43439-022-00056-9. Accessed February 12, 2024.

Citron, D. K. (2014) *Hate crimes in cyberspace.* Harvard University Press, U of Maryland Legal Studies Research Paper No. 2015-11. Accessed February 12, 2024, from SSRN: https://ssrn.com/abstract=2616790

Dilla, W.N., Harrison, A.J., Mennecke, B.E. & Janvrin, D.J. (2013). The assets are virtual, but the behaviour is real: An analysis of fraud in virtual worlds and its implications for the real world. *Journal of Information Systems*, 27(2), pp.131–158.

Dwivedi, Y. K., Hughes, L., Baabdullah, A. M., et al. (2022). Metaverse beyond the hype: Multidisciplinary perspectives on emerging challenges, opportunities, and agenda for research, practice and policy. *International Journal of Information Management, 66.* https://doi.org/10.1016/j.ijinfomgt.2022.102542. Accessed 11 February 2024.

Europol. (2022). *Policing in the metaverse: What law enforcement needs to know.* Europol.

Fox, J., & Tang, W. Y. (2014). Sexism in online video games: The role of conformity to masculine norms and social dominance orientation. *Computers in Human Behaviour, 33*, 314–320. https://doi.org/10.1016/j.chb.2013.07.014

Furnell, S. (2021). Categorising cybercrime and cybercriminals: The problem and how it has changed. *Journal of Information Warfare, 20*(4), 68–76.

Goodison, E. S, Davis R. C., & Jackson B. A. (2015). *Digital evidence and the U.S. criminal justice system: Identifying technology and other needs to more effectively acquire and utilize digital evidence*. Accessed February 16, 2024, from (99+) Digital Evidence and the U.S. Criminal Justice System | Sean Goodison - Academia.edu

Gucluturk, O. G. (2023). The role of the law in metaverse regulation. In F. S. Esen, H. Tinmaz, & M. Singh (Eds.), *Metaverse. Studies in big data* (Vol. 133). Springer.

Harewell, J. L., Pina, A., & Storey, J. E. (2021). Cyberstalking: Prevalence, characteristics, and impact. In A. Powell, A. Flynn, & L. Sugiura (Eds.), *The Palgrave handbook of gendered violence and technology*. Palgrave Macmillan. https://doi.org/10.1007/978-3-030-83734-1_11

Hennig-Thurau, T., Aliman, D. N., Herting, A. M., et al. (2023). Social interactions in the metaverse: Framework, initial evidence, and research roadmap. *Journal of the Academy of Marketing Science, 51*, 889–913. https://doi.org/10.1007/s11747-022-00908-0

IEEE & Council of Europe. (2023). *The metaverse and its impact on human rights, the rule of law and democracy*. Accessed February 10, 2024, from 1680ae6bce (coe.int)

Interpol. (2024). *Metaverse a law enforcement perspective. Use cases, crime, forensics, investigation, and governance*. Accessed February 9, 2024, from https://www.interpol.int/content/download/20828/file/Metaverse%20-%20a%20law%20enforcement%20perspective.pdf

Kalyvaki, M. (2023). Navigating the metaverse business and legal challenges: Intellectual property, privacy, and jurisdiction. *Journal of Metaverse, 3*(1), 87–92. https://doi.org/10.57019/jmv.1238344. Accessed February 16, 2024.

Karandikar, S. (2022). *The risks of sexual harassment in the metaverse*. Accessed February 16, 2024, from The risks of sexual harassment in the metaverse - News & Views (gqlittler.com)

Krishnaa, R. R. (2023). Challenges in the metaverse jurisdiction and International Treaty Law. *Intergovernmental Research and Policy Journal*. Challenges in the Metaverse Jurisdiction and International Treaty Law - IRPJ = Intergovernmental Research and Policy Journal (euclid.int)

Laue, C. (2011). Crime potential of metaverses. In K. Cornelius & D. Hermann (Eds.), *Virtual worlds and criminality*. Springer. https://doi.org/10.1007/978-3-642-20823-2_2

Lazarus, D. (2006). *Real fear in virtual world*. Accessed February 12, 2024, from Real fear in virtual world (sfgate.com)

Leukfeldt, E. R. (2014). Phishing for suitable targets in the Netherlands: Routine activity theory and phishing victimization. *Cyberpsychology, Behaviour & Social Networking, 17*, 551–555.

Livingstone, S. (2008). Taking risky opportunities in youthful content creation: Teenagers' use of social networking sites for intimacy, privacy and self-expression. *New Media & Society, 10*(3), 393–411.

Lovanshi, M., & Bansal, P. (2019). Comparative study of digital forensic tools. In R. K. Shukla, J. Agrawal, S. Sharma, & G. Singh Tomer (Eds.), *Data, engineering and applications*. Springer.

Marinett, M. (2021). The new frontier of platform policy. *Internet Policy Review, [online] 10*(3). Accessed Febraury 28, 2024, from https://policyreview.info/articles/analysis/new-frontier-platform-policy

Massanari, A. (2017). #Gamergate and the fappening: How Reddit's algorithm, governance, and culture support toxic technocultures. *New Media & Society, 19*(3), 329–346.

Nakamura, L. (2002). *Cybertypes: Race, ethnicity, and identity on the internet*. Routledge.

Norris, G., Brookes, A., & Dowell, D. (2019). The psychology of internet fraud victimisation: A systematic review. *Journal of Police and Criminal Psychology, 34*, 231–245.

Obanoz, M. G. (2015). *Anonymity a double-edged sword: What are the implication of anonymity of the sender in electronic word of mouth*? Accessed February 12, 2024, from Anonymity a Double-Edged Sword: What are the implications of anonymity of the sender in electronic word of mouth? — BrandBa.se

Onu, P., Pradhan, A., & Mbohwa, C. (2023). Potential to use metaverse for future teaching and learning. *Education & Information Technolgies*. https://doi.org/10.1007/s10639-023-12167-9. Accessed February 12, 2024

Qin, H. X., Wang, Y., & Hui, P. (2022). *Identity, crimes, and law enforcement in the metaverse*. Accessed February 14, 2024, from 2210.06134.pdf (arxiv.org)

Rashedul, H. (2023). *Governance and the metaverse: A systematic scoping review*. Accessed February 14, 2024, from https://ssrn.com/abstract=4581731 or https://doi.org/10.2139/ssrn.4581731

Rueda, J., & Lara, F. (2020). Virtual reality and empathy enhancement: Ethical aspects. *Frontiers in Robotics and AI, 7*, 506984. https://doi.org/10.3389/frobt.2020.506984

Seering, J., Wang, T. Y., Yoon, J., & Kaufman, G. (2019). Moderator engagement and community development in the age of algorithms. In *Proceedings of the 2019 CHI Conference on Human Factors in Computing Systems* (pp. 1–13).

Seo, S., Seok, B., & Lee, C. (2023). Digital forensic investigation framework for the metaverse. *Journal of Supercomputing, 79*, 9467–9485.

Sharma, R. C., & Zamfiroiu, A. (2023). Cybersecurity threats and vulnerabilities in the metaverse. In *International Conference on Intelligent Metaverse Technologies & Applications (iMETA)*, Tartu, Estonia, pp. 1–7. https://doi.org/10.1109/iMETA59369.2023.1029495.

Simon, M., and Choo, K-K. R. (2014). Digital forensics: Challenges and future research directions. In K. Il-Su & L. Jianhong (Eds.), *Contemporary trends in asian criminal justice: Paving the way for the future* (pp. 105–146). Korean Institute of Criminology. Accessed February 18, 2024, from SSRN: https://ssrn.com/abstract=2421339

Sirvermez, U., & Baltaci, Ş. (2023). Metaverse applications in education: Systematic literature review and bibliographic analysis of 2010–2022. In F. S. Esen, H. Tinmaz, & M. Singh (Eds.), *Metaverse. Studies in big data* (Vol. 133). Springer.

Skipper, B. (2015). *EVE Online corporate thief steals $13,000 worth of assets in daring heist*. Accessed February 10, 2024, from EVE Online corporate thief steals $13,000 worth of assets in daring heist | IBTimes UK

Smaili, N., & de Rancourt-Raymond, A. (2024). Metaverse: welcome to the new fraud marketplace. *Journal of Financial Crime, 31*(1), 188–200.

Staniunas, S. (2023). *Misconduct and the metaverse: Legal prevention and prosecution of virtual sexual harassment*. Accessed February 13, 2024, from Online Publications – Fordham Undergraduate Law Review

Stephenson, N. (1992). *Snow crash* (p. 14). Bantam Books, Bantam Dell.

Thacker, S. & Griffiths, M.D. (2012). An exploratory study of trolling in online video gaming. International Journal of Cyber Behaviour, *Psychology and Learning, 2*(4), 17–33.

The Guardian. (2008). *Woman jailed in Japan after 'killing' virtual husband*. Accessed February 11, 2024, from https://www.theguardian.com/world/2008/oct/24/japan-virtual-murder

Trozze, A., Kamps, J., Akartuna, E.A., et al. (2022). Cryptocurrencies and future financial crime. *Crime Science, 11*(1). https://doi.org/10.1186/s40163-021-00163-8. Accessed February 13, 2024.

Ud Din, I., & Almogren, A. (2023). Exploring the psychological effects of metaverse on mental health and well-being. *Information Technology and Tourism, 25*, 367–389.

Uzun, M. M. (2023). Metaverse governance. In F. S. Esen, H. Tinmaz, & M. Singh (Eds.), *Metaverse. Studies in big data* (Vol. 133). Springer.

Vaz, J. & Brown, K. (2018). Cryptocurrencies, institutions and trust. Prepared for the Australian Centre for Financial Studies as part of the Funding Australia's Future IV: Fintech series. Melbourne: Monash Business School.

Wall, D. S., & Williams, M. L. (2013). Policing cybercrime: Networked and social media technologies and the challenges for policing. *Policing and Society: An International Journal of Research and Policy, 23*(4), 409–412. https://doi.org/10.1080/10439463.2013.780222

Yang, Y. (2023). Recommendations for metaverse governance based on technical standards. In *Humanities and Social Sciences Communications*. Lanzhou University. https://doi.org/10.1057/s41599-023-01750-7

Yee, N. (2006). The demographics, motivations, and derived experiences of users of massively multi-user online graphical environments. *Presence: Teleoperators and Virtual Environments, 15*(3), 309–329.

Yin, E., Moynihan, M., & Walsh, A. (2023). *Regulating the metaverse. A Publication of the Penn Program on Regulation. The Regulatory Review*. Accessed February 12, 2024, from Regulating the Metaverse | The Regulatory Review (theregreview.org)

Chapter 13
Virtual Property Rights in the Metaverse

Elizabeth Uwaifo

Abstract As digital assets (more narrowly defined as crypto assets) and the Metaverse grow in significance, there is an increasing need for certainty on the property rights relating to crypto assets. To what extent are the rights thereto recognised under English law and beyond? This chapter considers the challenges of ascertaining property rights in crypto assets derived from transactions in a borderless Metaverse. This chapter notes the need for the establishment of robust and universally accepted methods for determining ownership and property rights to ensure trust, security, and fair transactions within the virtual environment.

There is ample support in English case law and statute for the position that crypto assets are neither categorised as things in action nor things in possession, but rather as belonging to a distinct category within the personal property law of England and Wales. Such recognition will help in supporting the continued growth and integration of digital assets into the global financial system.

However, there remains a gap. Legal certainty requires a predictable set of rules across the Metaverse. An international treaty could be a pivotal step in establishing a clear and predictable framework for the recognition, protection, and enforcement of property rights in the Metaverse, providing consistency between English law principles and other systems of law and offering a unified legal framework for these rights.

Keywords Digital assets · Metaverse · Property rights · Ownership · Control · Legal status

E. Uwaifo (✉)
Radix Legal & Consulting Ltd., London, UK
e-mail: euwaifo@radixlc.com

N. Islam, I. Salami (eds.), *Metaverse Innovation*, Applied Innovation and Technology Management, https://doi.org/10.1007/978-3-031-97080-1_13

13.1 Introduction

The emergence of the Metaverse presents a host of complex legal challenges due to its unique nature as a digital, interconnected, and borderless environment. In the Metaverse, participants are operating from different countries around the world, each with their own rules and laws for operating in their local markets. The legal framework for operating in the Metaverse is still evolving and varies from one jurisdiction to another. The current practice for determining ownership and property rights within the Metaverse is based mostly on self-regulation. It is often the case that the Metaverse platforms that create the digital space and assets specify the rules for ownership and dispute resolution. To what extent are the entitlements and privileges generated within a platform in the Metaverse respected and protected by law?

The objective of this chapter is to ascertain the legal status of digital assets (more narrowly defined as crypto assets below) as items of property under English law. To what extent are their rights recognised under English law and beyond? This will require an exploration of the requirements of the English law of property and how they impact digital assets, the recognition of property rights under English law, and the recognition of property rights of digital assets in the borderless Metaverse.

13.1.1 Which Digital Assets?

There has also been an increasing range of products that constitute digital assets. Traditionally, digital assets encompassed data files, intellectual property, and software. Some of these are large records of information. However, in recent times, there has been a growth in new digital asset classes that command significant amounts of notional value such as cryptocurrencies, decentralised finance (DeFi) transactions, non-fungible tokens (NFTs), and other assets powered by distributed ledger technology (DLT) and/or secured by cryptography. Digital assets of the latter type have the semblance of property and will be the focus of this chapter. Such digital assets will be identified in this chapter as *crypto assets*.

13.1.2 The Need for Legal Clarity

Crypto assets have continued to grow in economic significance and have become significant economic commodities. According to recent market reports, the total market capitalisation of cryptocurrencies surpassed $2 trillion in 2021, demonstrating their growing importance in the global financial system (CoinMarketCap, 2021). NFTs, a newer category of digital assets, saw explosive growth in 2021 with their total sales volume reaching over $10 billion in the third quarter alone (NonFungible.com, 2021). The values being traded daily continue to grow.

The rise in the value and volume of digital asset transactions underscores the need for clear legal frameworks to govern their ownership and transfer. Legal certainty regarding property rights in digital assets is crucial for several reasons:

1. *Market confidence*: Clear legal definitions and protections for digital assets enhance investor confidence, promoting greater participation in digital markets.
2. *Dispute resolution*: Well-defined property rights provide a basis for resolving disputes related to the ownership and transfer of digital assets, reducing the risk of fraud and theft.
3. *Regulatory compliance*: Establishing clear property rights helps in aligning digital asset transactions with existing legal and regulatory frameworks, facilitating smoother integration into the broader financial system.
4. *Economic stability*: Legal recognition of digital assets as property ensures that they can be used as collateral in financial transactions, contributing to the stability and liquidity of digital asset markets.
5. *Innovation*: Legal clarity encourages innovation by providing a secure environment for the development of new digital assets and related technologies.

It is, therefore, increasingly important to have a robust legal framework to govern the ownership and dealings in such assets. Ensuring legal certainty in the property rights attached to digital assets is essential for fostering trust, promoting market stability, and encouraging innovation.

This chapter explores the need for legal certainty regarding their property rights. It seeks to ascertain the legal recognition and protection such assets will have under English law of property. Such recognition and protection will be paramount in shaping the future of finance and technology.

The authors wish to acknowledge the sterling work done to advance legal certainty in digital assets by the Law Commission (see Law Commission, Digital Assets: Final Report Law Com No. 412 (2023)) and the UK Jurisdiction Taskforce (UKJT) published a legal statement in which they address the legal status of cryptoassets and smart contracts (see UK Jurisdiction Taskforce (UKJT), 2019).

13.2 Unique Features of Crypto Assets

Key features of crypto assets that are the subject of this chapter are as follows:

1. *Self-defining rules*: The defining parameters of the crypto asset are ultimately determined by the rules of the system that creates the asset. Their only manifestation or feature is a digital record on a distributed ledger (i.e. they do not represent any legal rights or interests); the rules governing dealings in them are

established by the informal consensus of participants rather than by contract or in some other legally binding way; and the consensus rules determine which version of the distributed ledger is definitive (UKJT Legal Statement, 2019, paras 24–34).

2. *Public and private data parameters*: Functionally, crypto assets are typically represented by a pair of data parameters, one public (it is disclosed to all participants in the system or to the world at large) and one private. The public parameter contains, or references, encoded information about the asset such as its ownership, value, and transaction history. The private parameter—*the private key*—permits transfers or other dealings in the crypto asset to be cryptographically authenticated by digital signature. Knowledge of the private key confers practical control over the asset; it should, therefore, be kept secret by the holder. As an example, bitcoin is defined as "an electronic coin as a chain of digital signatures. Each owner transfers the coin to the next by digitally signing a hash of the previous transactions and the public key of the next owner and adding these to the end of the coin. A payee can verify the signatures to verify the chain of ownership" (https://bitcoin.org/bitcoin.pdf). More complex crypto assets may operate with multiple private keys (*multisig*) with control of the asset shared or divided between the holders.
3. *Distributed decentralised ledger*: Dealings in a crypto asset are broadcast to a network of participants and, once confirmed as valid, added to a digital ledger. The main function of the ledger is to keep a reliable history of transactions and so prevent double spending, i.e. inconsistent transfers of the same crypto asset to different recipients. The ledger may be distributed and decentralised, that is, shared over the network with no one person having a responsibility for maintaining it or any right to do so. A common type of distributed ledger uses a blockchain, which comprises blocks of transactions linked together sequentially, but other models are also in use. The geographic location of the distributed ledger is usually not known.
4. *Consensus driven*: For some crypto assets, the rules governing dealings are established by the informal consensus of participants rather than by contract or in some other legally binding way. Consensus rules (employing methods such as *proof-of-work (PoW)* or *proof-of-stake (PoS)*) may also determine which version of the distributed ledger is definitive. A consensus mechanism is a method for validating entries into a distributed database and keeping the database secure. The database may be called a blockchain—so the consensus mechanism secures the blockchain. Under PoS, validators are chosen based on the number of staked coins they have. PoS was created as an alternative to PoW, the original consensus mechanism used to validate transactions and open new blocks. PoW mechanisms require miners to solve cryptographic puzzles for the privilege of earning transaction fees. PoS is seen as less risky regarding the potential for an attack on the network as it structures compensation in a way that makes an attack less advantageous.

The key point to note here is that rules that validate transactions are self-enforcing in practice, even if not enforceable in law, because only transactions made in compliance with them and duly entered in the ledger will be accepted by participants as valid.

13.2.1 Novel Distinguishing Features of Crypto Assets

Based on the above features, the following have been identified (UKJT Legal Statement, 2019, para 31) as the principal novel and characteristic features of digital assets that need to be accommodated in determining their legal and proprietary status:

(a) Intangibility—crypto assets are not tangible in the traditional sense
(b) Cryptographic authentication
(c) Use of a distributed transaction ledger
(d) Decentralisation
(e) Rule by consensus

13.3 Property Under English Law

The tenets of the English law of property will now be explored in advance of ascertaining the position thereunder of crypto assets.

The term property does not describe a thing itself but a legal relationship with a thing. It is a way of describing a power recognised in law as permissibly exercised over the thing (*Yanner v Eaton* [1999] HCA 53). It is a comprehensive term that has been used to describe many kinds of relationships between a person and a thing (*Yanner v Eaton*). The fundamental proprietary relationship is ownership: The owner of a thing is, broadly, entitled to control and enjoy it to the exclusion of anyone else. However, ownership is just one kind of property right. Other examples of property rights include the right to grant a licence providing temporary permission to use land or other property for a specific purpose (*Street v Mountford* [1985] AC 809), the right to grant security over property for the payment of a debt, and the right to create a trust over property for the benefit of another person. This chapter will later consider how these rights align with crypto assets.

13.3.1 What Constitutes Property?

There is no general or comprehensive definition of property in statute or case law. Property has been broadly described by statute. For instance, the Conveyancing Act 1881, s 2(i) states that unless a contrary intention appears, the property includes real and personal property, and any estate or interest in any property, real or personal, and any debt, and anything in action, and any other right or interest (our emphasis).

The test set out by Lord Wilberforce (in *National Provincial Bank v Ainsworth* [1965] 2 All ER 472 at 494, [1965] AC 1175) as to whether something can be admitted into the category of property turns on whether that thing (i) is definable, (ii) is identifiable by third parties; (iii) is capable in its nature of assumption by third parties; and (iv) has some degree of permanence or stability (often described as the *Ainsworth test*). Among other things, these criteria imply that the very existence of the thing itself cannot depend on the will or act of another person and that the holder must be able to control the thing to the exclusion of all other persons. In the words of Lord Wilberforce:

> Before a right or an interest can be admitted into the category of property, or of a right affecting property, it must be definable, identifiable by third parties, capable in its nature of assumption by third parties, and have some degree of permanence or stability.

Certainty, exclusivity, control and assignability have also been identified as characteristics of property rights (*Fairstar Heavy Transport NV v Adkins* [2013] EWCA Civ 886).

Although possession of those characteristics may not always be sufficient, and they are not themselves capable of precise definition, a number of cases have treated them as important indicia of property (see for example, R v Toohey; Ex parte Meneling Station Pty Ltd [1982] HCA 69).

According to the UKJT Legal Statement, crypto assets are able to meet the Ainsworth test on the basis that they are identified as the combination of (1) the public data parameter (containing or referencing encoded information about the asset such as its ownership, value, and transaction history); (2) the private data parameter (the private key); and (3) the system rules which ensure that the data can be spent (i.e. rendered inert) only once (and, therefore, to the exclusion of others). Digital assets that do not meet these defining features of crypto assets would not qualify as property and fall outside the scope of our definition of crypto assets.

13.3.2 Types of Property

Under English law, property is traditionally divided into real property, which includes interests in land, and personal property, which includes interests in other things. English law also traditionally recognised two distinct categories of personal property rights: rights relating to things in possession (tangible things) and rights relating to things in action (legal rights or claims enforceable by action). Given that personal property rights are rights in relation to things, commentators have pointed out that it is more accurate to refer to "rights in things in possession" and to "rights in things in action" as such description captures the divide between the property right and the object of the property right (see, for instance, Bridge et al., 2021, para 4.002).

In the 1885 case of Colonial Bank v Whinney, Lord Justice Fry said that "All personal things are either in possession or in action. The law knows no *tertium quid* between the two" (see *Colonial Bank v Whinney* (1885) 30 Ch D 261 at 285, by Fry LJ).

Later in this chapter, this statement will be analysed deeper and in the context in which it was made which, one can argue, casts doubt on the literal meaning. In any case, the courts of England and Wales have redefined the scope of things that the common law treats as capable of attracting personal property rights even where those things do not fall easily within either of the two traditionally recognised categories.

As crypto assets emerge as a significant category within the broader property spectrum, it becomes crucial to understand how they fit within these established legal categories. This section will examine the traditional distinctions of personal property, explore where crypto assets align within this framework, and consider the implications for their legal treatment. On the basis that crypto assets cannot be real property, the focus will be on the extent to which crypto assets can be treated as personal property.

13.3.3 *Why Does It Matter If a Crypto Asset Is Capable of Being Property?*

It matters because, in principle, proprietary rights are recognised against the whole world, whereas other (personal) rights are recognised only against someone who has assumed a relevant legal duty. Proprietary rights are of particular importance in an insolvency where they generally have priority over claims by creditors and when someone seeks to recover something that has been lost, stolen, or unlawfully taken. They are also relevant to the questions of whether there can be a security interest in a crypto asset and whether a crypto asset can be held in trust. Proprietary rights or otherwise of crypto assets will determine the rights of holders of crypto assets exercisable outside of the system creating the assets.

Traditional Categories of Personal Property

The question is important because it has been said that the law recognises property as only things in action and things in possession and nothing else. The case famously cited in support of this proposition is *Colonial Bank v Whinney* (1885) 30 Ch D 261 (CA), 285 in which L J Fry said: "All personal things are either in possession or in action. The law knows no *tertium quid* [third thing] between the two". It is arguable that this case rules out a third category of property. This calls for a deeper analysis of the Colonial Bank case. The UKJT conducted a helpful analysis, which is largely reflected below (UKLT Legal Statement, 2019, paras 70-51)).

The Colonial Bank case concerned a dispute about shares deposited as security for a loan. The borrower was declared bankrupt, and there was a contest for the shares between the plaintiff bank and the trustee in bankruptcy. The case was not about the scope of property generally; there was no dispute that the shares were property. The relevant question was whether they were things in action within the meaning of the Bankruptcy Act 1883, an issue of statutory interpretation. If so, then they were excluded from the bankrupt estate by section 44 of that Act.

L J Lindley and L J Cotton held that the shares were not things in action. They relied principally on previous case law where the court had come to a similar conclusion in relation to the predecessor statute, the Bankruptcy Act 1869. They also drew some support from sections 50(3) and 50(5) of the 1883 Act which appeared to make a distinction between shares and things in action.

L J Fry reached the opposite conclusion, principally reasoning from what he considered to be the essential nature of a share. A share constituted "the right to receive certain benefits from a corporation and to do certain acts as a member of that corporation" and was, in his view, closely akin to a debt. He supported his conclusion by a comparison of shares to other established things in action such as partnership interests and interests in funds.

In making the statement that personal things are either in possession or in action and that there is no third category, L J Fry did not intend to rule that an intangible thing is not property if it is not a thing in action. The question before him was whether the shares were things in action for the purpose of the Bankruptcy Act, not whether they were property. Accordingly, his statement should not be taken as a basis for limiting the scope of property generally.

Moreover, in making the statement L J Fry attributed a broad meaning to things in action. He approved a passage from Personal Property by Joshua Williams which described things in action as a kind of residual category of property: "In modern times [sc. by the 19th century] … several species of property have sprung up which were unknown to the common law … For want of a better classification, these subjects of personal property are now usually spoken of as ... [things] in action. They are, in fact, personal property of an incorporeal nature…".

On appeal, the House of Lords also framed the question as one about statutory interpretation. They reversed the Court of Appeal's decision, approving the judgement and reasoning of L J Fry. They did not explicitly address the issue of exhaustive classification between things in action and things in possession and said nothing about the definition of property. Lord Blackburn did say, however, that "in modern times lawyers have accurately or inaccurately used the phrase [things] in action as including all personal chattels that are not in possession". Thus, the extent to which the House of Lords agreed with L J Fry on the classification issue seems to have been on the basis that the class of things in action could be extended to all intangible property (i.e. it was a residual class of all things not in possession) rather than on the basis that the class of intangible property should be restricted to rights that could be claimed or enforced by action.

The UKJT in the Legal Statement opines that *Colonial Bank* is not therefore to be treated as limiting the scope of what kinds of things can be property in law and, on the contrary, it shows the ability of the common law to stretch traditional definitions and concepts to adapt to new business practices (in that case the development of shares in companies).

Colonial Bank was referred to in *Allgemeine Versicherungs-Gesellschaft Helvetia v Administrator of German Property* ([1931] 1 KB 672, 704) by L J Slesser as showing "how the two conditions of [thing] in action and [thing] in possession are antithetical and how there is no middle term". However, the case was not about the scope of property generally but about whether something that was undoubtedly property should be classified as a thing in possession or a thing in action. It involved a dispute about the proceeds of the sale of diamonds that had been seized by the British authorities during World War I and later assigned by the German owner to his insurer. If the right in the diamonds that had been assigned was a thing in action within the meaning of section 6(1) of the Trading with the Enemy Act 1914 then under the Act the insurer could not enforce it.

Colonial Bank was also referenced more recently in 2014 in *Your Response v Datateam*. The claimant sought to assert a lien over a database in digital form but faced the obstacle of the previous decision of the House of Lords in *OBG Ltd v Allan* (*OBG Ltd v Allan (n 15)*) that there could be no claim in conversion for wrongful interference with a thing in action because it could not be possessed. In an attempt to distinguish the case from OBG the claimant argued that, even if the database could not be regarded as a physical object, it was a form of intangible property different from a thing in action and so was capable of being possessed.

The Court of Appeal rejected the argument. L J Moore-Bick said that *Colonial Bank* made it "very difficult to accept that the common law recognises the existence of intangible property other than [things] in action (apart from patents which are subject to statutory classification) but, even if it does, the decision in *OBG Ltd v Allan* [2008] AC 1 prevents us from holding that property of that kind is susceptible of possession so that wrongful interference can constitute the tort of conversion". He said that there was "a powerful case for reconsidering the dichotomy between [things] in possession and [things] in action and recognising a third category of intangible property which may also be susceptible of possession and therefore amenable to the tort of conversion" but the Court of Appeal could not do that because it was bound to follow the decision in *OBG*. The other members of the court agreed.

The Court of Appeal did not, and did not need to, go so far as to hold that intangible things other than things in action could never be property at all, only that they could not be the subject of certain remedies. The intangible thing with which they were concerned was a database which (as L J Floyd said) would not be regarded as property anyway because it was pure information. They did not have to consider intangible assets with the special characteristics possessed by crypto assets.

Things in Possession

Under the current law, a thing in possession is any object which the law considers amenable to possession. This includes assets which are "tangible, moveable, and visible and of which possession can be taken" (Bridge et al., 2021, para 1.018). Since things in possession are capable of being physically possessed, rights in them can be asserted by use and enjoyment as well as by the exclusion of others from them (Bridge et al., 2021, para 4.002). Examples include everyday items like furniture, vehicles, and jewellery. These items are "tangible, moveable, and visible" and can be owned and controlled directly through physical means and ownership rights. The legal principle underpinning this category is that physical possession grants enforceable property rights against the world except against those with a superior, possessory right. For example, the finder of a gold watch has a legal right by virtue of their possession of the gold watch. This right is good against the world except against the person who lost the watch (and anyone with a right prior to the person who lost the watch, and so on).

A distinctive feature of things in possession is that they are tangible. They exist regardless of whether anyone lays claim to them and regardless of whether any legal system recognises or is available to enforce such claims.

Things in Action

The second broad category of personal property rights is rights relating to things in action. Things in action encompass intangible rights that can only be claimed or enforced through legal action. These rights do not involve physical possession but rather a legal claim against another party. Common examples include debts, shares in companies, and rights to sue for breach of contract. The defining characteristic of things in action is their enforceability through the legal system rather than physical control, distinguishing them from tangible property.

A distinctive feature of things in possession is that they are things which exist regardless of whether anyone lays claim to them and regardless of whether any legal system recognises, or is available to enforce, such claims. This is the concept of tangibility. In contrast, things in action have no independent form and exist only as far as they are recognised by a legal system. This means that the presence of a thing in action in the world is dependent on there being both a party against whom the thing in action (the right) can be enforced and a legal system willing to recognise and enforce that right.

Some commentators have argued that the category of things in action is much broader. Their argument is that the category of things in action can be treated as a residual category of things that captures any object of personal property rights that is not a thing in possession (see for example, K Low 2023, p 688 (para 20.1)). However, the Law Commission is of the view that to water down the definition of things in action would not be helpful for the development of the law. They noted that such an approach risks diluting or confusing the defining features of things in action (in the narrow sense) which now can (for the most part) be clearly identified and would mean that different things in action would be subject to different treatment (see Law Commission, Digital Assets: Final Report Law Com No. 412 (2023)).

13.4 Crypto Assets and English Law of Property

This chapter will now examine the characteristics of crypto assets and how they align with the established categories of personal property in more detail. The UKJT Legal Statement includes a helpful analysis of the features of crypto assets that may be regarded as genuinely novel or distinctive as compared with conventional assets. The analysis is helpful in identifying features of crypto assets that are relevant in addressing issues of legal and proprietary status and is largely reflected below.

13.4.1 Do Crypto Assets Possess the Characteristics of Property?

As noted earlier, crypto assets are not uniform in their design and they do not all share the same characteristics. Consequently, the authors have had to make assumptions and narrowed the focus to crypto assets that are powered by DLT. As mentioned previously, such assets are typically represented by a pair of data parameters, one public (in that it is disclosed to all participants in the system or to the world at large) and one private. The public parameter contains, or references, encoded information about the asset such as its ownership, value, and transaction history. The private parameter (the private key) permits transfers or other dealings in the asset to be cryptographically authenticated by digital signature. Knowledge of the private key confers practical control over the asset. How do these characteristics align with characteristics of personal property?

- *Definability, certainty, and identifiable by third parties*: The public parameter of a crypto asset, interpreted in accordance with the rules of the relevant system, is sufficient in principle both to define the asset and to identify it to any person with access to the system network.
- *Control and exclusivity*: This is satisfied by the cryptographic authentication process which permits the holder of the private key, and only that holder, to deal in the crypto asset. The holder is therefore able to control it to the exclusion of others (subject to the powers of other keyholders where there are multiple private keys).
- *Capable of assumption by third parties*: The kinds of transfers and other dealings that may be made on crypto assets will depend on the rules of the system that creates the asset and thus must be worked out on a case-by-case basis. However, the assets are, in their nature, capable of assumption by third parties and are, in that sense, assignable even if some of the methods of assumption and assignment may be novel. Even if identifying the legal owner in particular cases may not always be straightforward they are clearly designed with the aim of being transferable between system participants.

- *Permanence*: Crypto assets appear to be permanent as they may exist only until they are, for example, cancelled, redeemed, repaid, or exercised.
- *Stability*: This may raise an issue for two reasons because of the consensus mechanism built into the system creating the asset. The first is that it may take some time for a consensus to form as to the state of the ledger and the validity and sequence of the transactions. In bitcoin, for example, the top six blocks in the blockchain (containing, on average, an hour of transactions) are considered at risk of revision, in that any provisional consensus may change. Even older ledger records are theoretically vulnerable although the probability of change becomes vanishingly small over time. The second is that a change in the consensus rules may be proposed but not unanimously adopted, leading to a fork in the system where different groups of participants follow different rules, often recognising different transactions and keeping different ledgers. In effect, the cryptosystem divides into two systems each with their own, separate crypto assets and respective ledgers.

Notwithstanding the questions regarding stability, it can be safe to say that at least for a commercial crypto asset system with a significant number of participants, an established history of transactions, and a generally stable set of rules, there is sufficient permanence and stability to satisfy the property characteristics. This view is supported by the Court of Appeal which has said that "a crypto asset such as bitcoin is property" under the law of England and Wales (*Tulip Trading v Van Der Laan* [2023] EWCA Civ 83, [2023] 4 WLR 16 at [24]–[25], by Birss LJ).

If crypto assets constitute property under English law, what type of property? As noted above, there are two traditional categories of property—things in possession and things in action.

13.4.2 Crypto Assets as Things in Possession

There is a conceptual difficulty in treating crypto assets as things in possession. The concept of possession typically assumes that there is a continuous thing which is capable of being physically possessed and delivered on transfer. It is challenging to pinpoint exactly what that thing is in the context of crypto assets.

13.4.3 Analogy with Electronic Trade Documents

In assessing whether crypto assets fit in the category of things in possession, it is helpful to consider the position of electronic trade documents which are considered to be things in possession and ascertain whether there are analogies that impact the categorisation of crypto assets as things in possession.

Possession of electronic trade documents like bills of lading and bills of exchange has long been recognised in various domestic law and international trade rules as establishing which party has certain rights and entitlements. However, tangibility is an important characteristic of things in possession: Some physical control over a tangible thing is generally required to engage the factual and legal concepts of possession. If tangibility is a defining feature of things in possession, it is questionable whether electronic trade documents qualify as things in possession.

The concept of possession has a fundamental role in the functionality of paper trade documents such as bills of lading and bills of exchange, both at common law and in domestic statutes (see for example, Bills of Exchange Act 1882, s 2). Possession of a trade document is crucial in establishing which party has certain rights and entitlements, how the documents are held, and how they are used in collateral arrangements. Treating electronic trade documents as possessable things allows them to be plugged into an existing legal framework with respect to a limited category of documents that already enjoy a special status in law.

The status of electronic trade documents under English law has been settled by clause 3 of the Electronic Trade Documents Act 2023 which allows a person to "possess, indorse and part with possession of an electronic trade document" provided that the document satisfies certain criteria. Electronic trade documents are not tangible in the conventional sense but, under the Act as referenced above, the concept of possession is not limited in its application to tangible things.

However, possession is not defined in the legislation and remains a common law concept. The Law Commission noted that although electronic trade documents are treated by the law as being intangible, there were policy and practical considerations that directed that electronic trade documents should be treated as possessable things (see Electronic Trade Documents (2022) Law Com No. 405 from para 2.61).

It is to be noted that electronic trade documents attempt to replicate the legal functionality of paper trade documents. However, this same analysis cannot be applied to crypto assets. Unlike electronic trade documents, crypto assets and others like them were designed to avoid replicating some of the features of paper-based documents. Most obviously, crypto assets were designed to facilitate communication of value on a global and trust-minimised basis without the need for physical exchanges of tangible things (Nakamoto, 2018).

13.4.4 Crypto Assets as Things in Possession?

Crypto assets do not fit neatly into the category of things in possession due to their intangible nature. Traditionally, tangibility is a key requirement for something to be considered a thing in possession. As explained above, the Electronic Trade Documents Act 2023 introduced a significant development by recognising the possession of electronic trade documents provided they meet certain criteria. This legislative change suggests that possession under English law can extend to certain digital items that replicate the legal functionality of their physical counterparts. However, crypto assets were designed to facilitate communication of value on a global and trust-minimised basis without the need for physical exchanges of tangible things. This makes it difficult to fit crypto assets into the things in possession category.

13.4.5 *Crypto Assets as Things in Action*

Crypto assets are composite things: notional quantity units manifested by the combination of the active operation of software by a network of participants and network-instantiated data. Although those notional quantity units themselves can be considered abstract and can have value, that explanation is not complete because the software and data together manifest a thing that is independent of any rights that may be claimed over that thing. For a crypto asset, the thing itself (the crypto) is not co-extensive with the right in relation to it in the way that a thing in action is. Crypto assets would continue to exist even if the law were to fail to recognise them as objects of personal property rights and even if there were to be a law to prohibit their existence. Their features—the ability of people to use, enjoy, and interact with them (and exclude others from them)—would also continue to exist: The functionality of the crypto asset system would remain unaffected. This point is demonstrated in the case of the Mt. Gox crypto exchange in 2014 in Japan (see: Gullifer et al., 2019 for a detailed consideration of this case and a translation of the judgement). In this case, the proprietary status of crypto assets was considered after the bankruptcy of the Mt. Gox crypto exchange in 2014. In August 2015, the Tokyo District Court held that bitcoin was not a thing that was capable of ownership within Article 85 of the Japanese Civil Code. That finding prevented the potential argument that customers of the exchange had a proprietary right or interest in the bitcoin held by the exchange (as opposed to merely a personal claim against the exchange). Regardless of that finding, the bitcoin in question (and its functionality and utility) continued to exist and distributions of the remaining Mt. Gox held bitcoin to creditors of Mt. Gox were scheduled for 2023.

Crypto assets can, therefore, typically be used and enjoyed independently of whether any rights or claims in relation to them are enforceable by action. It may be the case that crypto assets could generate rights of action against the systems, operator, or intermediary operating or holding the asset. However, that could only give rise to things in action as against the system operator or intermediary.

Another argument that has been made by commentators is that the category of things in action can be treated as a wide, residual category of things that captures any object of personal property rights that is not a thing in possession (Low, 2023, p 688 (para 20.1)). This approach is, however, not consistent with the common law (see the below review of a selection of recent case law on the subject).

The Law Commission was not convinced that such an approach was desirable and rejected the argument on the basis that it was not entirely clear how this would be practical or helpful for the development of the law (Law Com No 412 (2023) para. 3.36). They concluded that such an approach risked creating additional legal uncertainty, diluting or confusing the defining features of things in action (in the narrow sense), which presently could largely be clearly identified, and would mean that different things in action would be subject to different treatment. They concluded that, if different things are to be treated differently, it is cleaner to recognise a separate third category rather than multiple sub-categories of a broad residual category.

13.5 A Third Category of Property Rights

The previous analysis within this chapter has highlighted the complexities of categorising crypto assets within the traditional framework of things in possession and things in action. It was noted that crypto assets have unique characteristics that do not fit neatly into either category. They exist as units of data on a blockchain and are independent of any legal system's recognition. Their value and functionality are maintained by the underlying technology rather than legal claims. The crypto assets would continue to exist and function even if the law did not recognise them as objects of personal property rights. This independence from traditional legal frameworks suggests a need for a distinct category that acknowledges their unique properties and the practical considerations of their use and transfer.

The Law Commission launched a consultation to confirm (among other things) the existence of a third category of personal property into which crypto assets will fall. The responses they received from consultees and their conclusions provide a comprehensive analysis (Law Commission Final Report). What is the case for this third category of property that may accommodate crypto assets?

13.5.1 Is There a Case Under English Common Law for a Third Category of Property?

The Case Law

There is case law showing that the English courts have moved towards the recognition of a third category of things to which personal property rights can relate. In several cases, the English courts have concluded that certain things (often digital assets) are capable of being objects of personal property rights even where the thing in question does not neatly fit within either of the traditionally recognised categories of things to which personal property rights can relate.

Such a conclusion has been reached in the context of non-digital as well as digital assets. This has been the case in respect to milk quotas, European Union carbon emission allowances, export quotas, and waste management licences. For example, in *Dairy Swift v Dairywise Farms Ltd* [2000] 1 WLR 1177, the court considered whether a milk quota was property under s 436 Insolvency Act 1986 and decided in the affirmative concluding that a milk quota could be the subject of a trust. In *Armstrong v Winnington* [2012] EWHC 10, [2013] Ch 156, the court considered the proprietary status of carbon emission allowances in the context of claims for restitution and knowing receipt. The court concluded that a carbon emission allowance was "not a [thing] in action in the narrow sense as it cannot be claimed or enforced by action". The court nevertheless held that an EU carbon emissions allowance could be the subject of a tracing claim as a form of other intangible property even though it was neither a thing in possession nor a thing in action. In *Re Celtic Extraction Ltd* [2001] Ch 475, [2000] 2 WLR 991, the court had to decide whether a waste management licence could constitute property for the purposes of the Insolvency Act 1986. Focusing on transferability as a key component of property, the Court of Appeal held that a waste management licence could be property. However, this was either by virtue of being a thing in action or falling within the meaning of "every description of property".

The above cases are, admittedly, in respect of statutory interpretation. The case law goes beyond statutory interpretation.

In *AA v Persons Unknown* [2019] EWHC 3556 (Comm), [2020] 4 WLR 35 at [55]–[61]), Mr Justice Bryan said that it would be fallacious to proceed on the basis that the law of England and Wales recognises no form of property other than things in possession and things in action. He explicitly recognised the difficulty in the classification of cryptoassets (which, on their face, are things which are neither things in action nor things in possession). He held that a crypto token could be an object of personal property rights even if it was not a thing in action in the narrow sense.

In *Tulip Trading v Van Der Laan* [2023] EWCA Civ 83, [2023] 4 WLR 16 at [24]–[25], the Court of Appeal held that "a crypto asset such as bitcoin is property" under the law of England and Wales and Birss LJ cited *AA v Persons Unknown* in support of the proposition that the digital asset in question is a thing which is capable of being an object of personal property rights.

Another case in point, albeit with a divergent conclusion, is *Fetch.ai v Persons Unknown* [2021] EWHC 2254 (Comm) which involved crypto tokens held on the Binance crypto token exchange. The court held that crypto tokens (crypto assets in our definition) were capable of being objects of personal property rights. However, in contrast to the judgement in *AA v Persons Unknown* [2019] EWHC 3556 (Comm), [2020] 4 WLR 35, Judge Pelling QC described the "assets credited to the first applicant's accounts on the Binance Exchange" as [things] in action. This is a divergence from the reasoning endorsed in AA v Persons Unknown. The Law Commission provides a reasonable explanation for that departure. In their view, given that Binance Exchange generally operates as a non-custodial holding intermediary, they considered that the better interpretation of the Fetch.ai judgement is that the court correctly classified the applicant's right against Binance Exchange as a thing in action (broadly, a personal contractual claim to the return of assets equivalent to those held). This interpretation maintains the case as supportive of the proposition that English law recognises crypto assets as property.

Statutory Recognition

Several important twentieth-century statutes define property in terms that assume that intangible property is not limited to things in action.

- The Theft Act 1968
- The Proceeds of Crime Act 2002
- The Fraud Act 2006

All define property as including things in action and other intangible property. It might be said that those statutes are extending the definition of property for their own, special purposes but they at least demonstrate that there is no conceptual difficulty in treating intangible things as property even if they may not be things in action.

Moreover, the Patents Act 1977 goes further in providing, at s30, that a patent or application for a patent "is personal property (without being a thing in action)". This recognises that personal property can include things other than things in possession (which a patent clearly is not) and things in action.

Academic Commentary

The idea that crypto assets are capable of being objects or things in themselves has been widely affirmed in legal and academic commentary, including G Virgo (2023, para 4.3.1), Gullifer (2022, para 1.58), Bridge et al. (2021, para 8-049).

13.5.2 What Are the Defining Characteristics of the Third Category of Property?

The case law demonstrates that the courts of England and Wales now recognise crypto assets as distinct things which are capable of being objects of personal property rights and are neither things in possession nor things in action. The Law Commission has recommended the formal recognition of a third category of personal property to accommodate crypto assets. This concurs with the findings of the UKJT which, in 2019, concluded that the common law recognised crypto assets.

The Law Commission proposed that legislation is needed to confirm "that a thing will not be deprived of legal status as an object of property rights merely by reason of the fact that it is neither a thing in action nor a thing in possession".

The question that then arises as to the parameters that define such third category of property is: Do established legal and equitable principles apply to arrangements involving third-category personal property in the same way as they apply to arrangements involving other personal property? The Law Commission recommended that such areas of further development are best left to the common law, noting that the common law is sufficiently flexible, dynamic, and resilient to continue evolving to accommodate crypto assets.

The development of a clear legal framework for crypto assets is crucial for ensuring market stability, fostering innovation, and providing legal certainty in the rapidly evolving digital economy. Recognising digital assets as a distinct category within the personal property law of England and Wales will help in addressing the challenges and support the continued growth and integration of digital assets into the global financial system. However, there remains a gap. Crypto assets are traded and used in a borderless Metaverse often without thought to a governing law. Legal certainty will require a predictable set of rules across the Metaverse. This calls for collaboration among countries in setting a framework of rules and regulations that would be incorporated into the laws.

13.6 The Global Dimension

Addressing the legal status of crypto assets under English law will provide guidance where English law is the applicable law. What of situations where it is not applicable? The emergence of the Metaverse presents a host of complex legal challenges due to its unique nature as a digital, interconnected, and borderless environment. In the Metaverse, when people are online, participants are operating from different countries around the world, each with their own rules and laws for operating in their local markets. Transactions in crypto assets occurring in such self-defining systems may not expressly adopt English law as the governing law and the transaction participants may not be within English jurisdiction. How does one promote the establishment of robust and universally accepted methods for determining ownership and property rights to ensure trust, security, and fair transactions within the virtual environment? This raises a host of policy, legal, and regulatory issues that are outside the scope of this chapter.

The authors wish to highlight the role and work of the World Intellectual Property Organisation (WIPO) in this respect. This is instructive in the attempt to address a global challenge. There may be lessons to be learnt in addressing the challenges faced in the quest for clarity in property rights for crypto assets in the Metaverse.

13.6.1 The WIPO

The World Intellectual Property Organisation (WIPO) is the global forum for intellectual property (IP) services, policy, information, and cooperation. It is an agency of the United Nations with 193 member states. Its mission is to lead the development of a balanced and effective international IP system that enables innovation and creativity for the benefit of all.

Under the WIPO Copyright Treaty, adopted in 1996 by member states of the WIPO under the Berne Convention for the Protection of Literary and Artistic Works 1886, provisions were made for additional copyright protections to account for advancements in information technology.

Among other things, the treaty:

- Expanded copyright protection to computer programs (Article 4)
- Expanded protection to the expressive selection and arrangement of database data and material (Article 5)
  - Subject to certain limitations and exceptions, provided authors with specific exclusive rights concerning their literary and artistic works

The treaty also required that signatories:

- Protect against the:
  - Circumvention of technological copy-prevention systems for copyrighted works (Article 11)
  - Unauthorised modification of electronic rights management information (Article 12)
- Adopt measures to ensure that the treaty is applied and that enforcement procedures and remedies are available for any acts of copyright infringement covered by the treaty

The treaty relies on national legislation to be implemented into local law.

13.6.2 The WIPO's Engagement with the Metaverse

The WIPO recognised the Metaverse as a transformative technology with significant implications for IP rights. The organisation has tackled the Metaverse from various perspectives including the protection of digital assets, the enforcement of IP rights in virtual environments like AI, and the importance of international collaboration to address these issues through ongoing discussions (WIPO, 2021, 2022).

The WIPO observed that the seamless integration of digital and physical realities posed unprecedented challenges for IP enforcement and the protection of the rights of holders in a borderless digital landscape (WIPO, 2023). It has made efforts to address these challenges.

13.6.3 Legal Issues and Concerns

In the ninth WIPO conversation (IP and Frontier Technologies). The WIPO emphasises key challenges related to Metaverse and IP protection. The issues highlighted by the WIPO are similar to issues affecting property rights generally and include:

Legal Uncertainty The virtual nature of assets and content in the Metaverse introduces profound legal uncertainties, particularly concerning copyright. Traditional concepts of territorial jurisdiction and the application of copyright laws are challenged when virtual environments transcend physical boundaries. They noted that questions arise about which jurisdiction's laws apply to virtual creations, how international treaties like the Berne Convention are interpreted in virtual contexts, and how effectively IP rights can be enforced across decentralised digital platforms.

Ownership and Control Ownership and control in the Metaverse raised significant concerns about monopolistic practices as companies consolidate power over data flows, user interactions, and digital economies. This concentration of influence could potentially suppress competition, hinder innovation, and limit diversity within virtual environments. The WIPO noted that major tech companies were aggressively expanding their presence in the Metaverse through mergers and acquisitions (M&A), reflecting a global trend observed across markets in the United States of America, The United Kingdom, Europe, and Asia-Pacific. The WIPO noted that this surge in M&A activity was particularly pronounced in the gaming sector, driven by synergies between technologies and markets. Microsoft's $75 billion acquisition of Activision Blizzard in January 2022 and Sony's subsequent $3.2 billion purchase of Bungie underscore this trend. Alongside these developments, questions arose about ownership rights concerning virtual assets, avatars, and digital items as well as the implications for creators' rights and equitable compensation within virtual economies.

Interoperability and Standards The Metaverse's potential relies on interoperability, allowing seamless interaction between different virtual, augmented, and physical worlds. Establishing interoperability standards that enable fluid interaction and data continuity between platforms was crucial for realising the Metaverse's full potential. However, achieving those standards posed significant technical, logistical, and regulatory challenges, including defining common protocols, data portability frameworks, and ensuring compatibility across diverse technological ecosystems.

Inclusivity and Fairness Inclusivity and fairness were critical concerns raised by the Metaverse, encompassing issues of inclusivity, security, privacy, and data protection. As data in the Metaverse grows exponentially in value and technologies become more integrated into users' daily lives, ensuring equal access and opportunities for all individuals while safeguarding their rights and personal information presents for them a significant challenge.

Protection of Traditional Knowledge and Cultural Heritage The replication and appropriation of cultural artefacts, traditional crafts, languages, and landscapes in the Metaverse raised profound concerns about the protection of Indigenous peoples' traditional knowledge and cultural expressions. Safeguarding these cultural assets in the virtual realm requires robust mechanisms to ensure that Indigenous peoples have control over how their cultural heritage is represented, used, and monetised in virtual environments. This would involve respecting Indigenous sovereignty, implementing informed consent frameworks, and developing protocols for ethical engagement with traditional knowledge holders.

Enforcement Challenges Enforcing intellectual property rights in the Metaverse presented intricate challenges due to the digital and decentralised nature of virtual assets and transactions. The WIPO noted that determining applicable laws, jurisdiction, and resolving disputes had become increasingly complex in a borderless and digitally immersive environment. They further noted that online platforms were beginning to establish dispute resolution frameworks but there was a critical need for clarity, consistency, and harmonisation of enforcement mechanisms to effectively protect creators' rights, combat piracy, and ensure fair competition in virtual economies.

The WIPO was of the view that addressing these issues required careful consideration, collaboration among stakeholders, and the development of appropriate policies and guidelines to ensure a fair, inclusive, and innovative Metaverse while protecting IP rights.

13.6.4 The WIPO's Recommendations

The WIPO advocated the following steps in tackling the challenges identified:

- Foster dialogue and collaboration
- Promote international cooperation
- Support capacity building and education
- Develop guidelines and best practices
- Monitoring technological advancements

By taking these steps, the WIPO noted that it could strike a balance between protecting IP rights and fostering innovation in the Metaverse, ensuring that creators and innovators are incentivised to contribute while also addressing the legal and ethical concerns associated with the virtual world.

13.6.5 Key Lessons from the WIPO's Approach to IP Rights

As the legal challenges of establishing property rights in digital assets within the Metaverse are confronted, significant lessons can be drawn from the WIPO's approach to addressing IP rights in the Metaverse. This analysis examines the WIPO's strategies and suggests the potential of an international treaty as a way forward for clarifying and enforcing property rights in the Metaverse.

The WIPO's initiatives and strategies provide a robust framework for addressing the complex issues associated with property rights in the digital realm. Below are some crucial lessons that can be learnt from the WIPO's efforts.

1. Adapting Legal Frameworks to Technological Advances
The WIPO has emphasised the need to adapt existing IP laws to address new technological developments. This adaptability ensures that legal protections remain relevant and effective. The WIPO Copyright Treaty (WCT) and the WIPO Performances and Phonograms Treaty (WPPT) are prime examples of how the WIPO has updated legal frameworks to encompass digital and internet-related rights.

Lesson: Legal frameworks for property rights in the Metaverse must be flexible and capable of evolving with technological advancements. Existing property laws may need to be updated or new regulations introduced to cater specifically to digital assets.

2. International Cooperation and Harmonisation
In furtherance of its mandate to improve IP protection, the WIPO has made efforts to foster international cooperation and harmonise laws across different jurisdictions. The Berne Convention for the Protection of Literary and Artistic Works ensures a consistent level of copyright protection across its member countries, facilitating international cooperation in IP enforcement.

Lesson: Property rights in the Metaverse would benefit from international cooperation to ensure consistent legal treatment of digital assets across borders. An international treaty could help harmonise property rights laws and provide a unified framework for dealing with disputes and enforcement.

3. Emphasis on Enforcement Mechanisms
The WIPO has highlighted the importance of robust enforcement mechanisms to protect IP rights. Effective enforcement ensures that rights holders can assert and defend their rights in a digital context. For example, the Agreement on Trade-Related Aspects of Intellectual Property Rights (TRIPS) includes provisions for the

enforcement of IP rights, obligating member countries to provide legal means for rights holders to protect their IP.

Lesson: Developing effective enforcement mechanisms is crucial for property rights in the Metaverse. This could involve international collaboration on enforcement strategies and the development of technology-based solutions to monitor and protect digital assets.

4. Promotion of Public Awareness and Education

The WIPO places significant emphasis on raising public awareness and educating stakeholders about IP rights. This helps in reducing infringement and increasing respect for IP laws. The WIPO rolled out various educational programmes and resources with the aim to aim to inform the public about IP rights and the importance of protecting them.

Lesson: Educating stakeholders about property rights in the Metaverse is essential. Awareness campaigns and educational programmes can help users understand their rights and responsibilities regarding crypto assets, reducing potential conflicts and infringements.

13.6.6 Potential of an International Treaty for Metaverse Property Rights

Given the borderless nature of the Metaverse and the complexity of crypto asset ownership, an international treaty could provide a viable path forward. Below is how an international treaty could address the challenges and ensure a coherent approach to property rights in the Metaverse.

1. Standardisation of Property Rights

An international treaty could establish a standardised set of property rights for digital assets, ensuring that these rights are recognised and enforceable across different jurisdictions.

- *Benefit*: It would provide a clear and consistent framework for property rights, reducing legal uncertainties and facilitating international trade and investment in digital assets.

2. Cross-Border Enforcement Mechanisms

The treaty could include provisions for cross-border enforcement of property rights, allowing for effective action against infringements no matter where they occur.

- *Benefit*: This would help protect rights holders from international digital piracy and unauthorised use of their digital assets, ensuring that their rights are respected globally.

3. Dispute Resolution Framework
An international treaty could establish mechanisms for resolving disputes related to digital assets, such as arbitration or mediation, which could provide quicker and more efficient resolution than traditional court systems.

- *Benefit*: This would offer a reliable and efficient way to handle conflicts over digital property, thereby reducing litigation costs and encouraging fair outcomes.

4. Support for Technological Innovation
By providing a clear legal framework and robust protections for digital assets, an international treaty could encourage innovation and investment in the Metaverse and related technologies.

- *Benefit*: It would create a stable legal environment that supports the growth of new business models and technological advancements in the digital economy.

5. Promotion of International Collaboration
The treaty could facilitate collaboration among countries to address common challenges related to the Metaverse such as cybersecurity, digital identity, and the regulation of virtual economies.

- *Benefit*: It would foster international cooperation and coordination, ensuring that the global community works together to tackle the complex issues arising from the Metaverse.

An international treaty could be a pivotal step in establishing a clear and predictable framework for the recognition, protection, and enforcement of property rights in the Metaverse, providing consistency between English law principles and other systems of law and offering a unified legal framework for these rights. Such a treaty would not only support technological innovation and economic growth but also ensure that the Metaverse remains a fair and secure environment for all users.

The WIPO's approach to IP rights in the digital age offers valuable guidance on a holistic approach to addressing the challenges of property rights in the Metaverse. Key strategies to consider are adapting legal frameworks, promoting international cooperation, emphasising enforcement mechanisms, and raising public awareness. A robust system can be created for protecting digital assets in virtual environments.

By leveraging these strategies, one can better navigate the complexities of property rights in the digital frontier of the Metaverse.

13.7 Conclusion

Transactions in the Metaverse in respect of crypto assets are presently regulated by self-regulating systems where the platform generating the transaction prescribes the rules and regulations governing ownership and other rights among users and the users voluntarily submit to the rules. This appears to work satisfactorily when regulating the relationship among the users of a platform or the members of a given community of adoptees of the relevant rules. However, the individual or community-prescribed rules will not likely cover legal issues that involve claims from third parties who are not on the platform such as a trustee in bankruptcy or issues relating to the consequences of a right of ownership such as entitlement on the inheritance of crypto assets or a right to grant security over crypto assets.

Such issues need to be addressed under English law assuming there is a basis for the application of English law. However, a resolution under English law is an incomplete solution given the borderless nature of the Metaverse. The concepts of country, jurisdiction, and national legal order do not exist in the Metaverse.

Given that the Metaverse is not confined by geographical borders, international collaboration is crucial. There is a need for a harmonisation of laws dealing with transactions and other activities in the Metaverse. Governments, regulatory bodies, and industry stakeholders from various countries need to align on common standards and guidelines. Establishing robust and universally accepted methods for determining ownership and property rights will be essential to ensure trust, security, and fair transactions within the growing virtual world of the Metaverse.

References

Bridge, M., Gullifer, L., Low, K., & McMeel, G. (2021). *The law of personal property* (3rd ed.). Sweet & Maxwell.

Coin Market Cap. (2021, December 31). Historical snapshot. https://coinmarketcap.com/historical/20211231/

Gullifer, L. (2022). *Goode and Gullifer on legal problems in credit and security* (7th ed.). Sweet & Maxwell.

Gullifer, L., Hara, M., & Mooney, C. (2019). *English translation of the Mt. Gox judgment on the legal status of bitcoin prepared by the Digital Assets Project*. Oxford Business Law Blog, University of Oxford.

Law Commission, Digital Assets: Final Report Law Com No. 412 (2023)

Low, K. (2023). Cryptoassets and the renaissance of the tertium quid? In C. Bevan (Ed.), *Handbook on property law and theory*. Edward Elgar.

Nakamoto, S. (2018). Bitcoin: A peer-to-peer electronic cash system. https://www.bitcoin.org

NonFungible.com. (2021). Yearly NFT market report 2021. https://nonfungible.com/reports/2021/en/yearly-nft-market-report

UK Jurisdiction Taskforce. (2019, May). Legal statement on cryptoassets and smart contracts. https://lawtechuk.io/ourreports/

Virgo, G. (2023). *The principles of equity & trusts* (5th ed.). Oxford University Press.

WIPO. (2021). Blockchain and digital assets: A new frontier for intellectual property rights.

WIPO. (2022). Blockchain technologies and IP ecosystems: A WIPO white paper. https://www.wipo.int

WIPO conversation seventh session. (2023). Intellectual property in the digital age: Addressing the challenges of the metaverse. https://www.wipo.int/en/web/frontier-technologies/metaverse-and-ip

World Intellectual Property Organization Copyright Treaty. (1996). https://www.wipo.int/wipolex/en/text/295166

World Intellectual Property Organization Performances and Phonograms Treaty. (1996). https://www.wipo.int/wipolex/en/text/295578

Index

N. Islam, I. Salami (eds.), *Metaverse Innovation*, Applied Innovation and Technology Management, https://doi.org/10.1007/978-3-031-97080-1

MIX
Papier aus verantwortungsvollen Quellen
Paper from responsible sources
FSC® C105338

If you have any concerns about our products,
you can contact us on
ProductSafety@springernature.com

In case Publisher is established outside the EU,
the EU authorized representative is:
Springer Nature Customer Service Center GmbH
Europaplatz 3, 69115 Heidelberg, Germany

Printed by Libri Plureos GmbH
in Hamburg, Germany